1 SAMUEL

Brazos Theological Commentary on the Bible

Series Editors

R. R. Reno, General Editor
Creighton University
Omaha, Nebraska

Robert W. Jenson
Center of Theological Inquiry
Princeton, New Jersey

Robert Louis Wilken
University of Virginia
Charlottesville, Virginia

Ephraim Radner
Wycliffe College
Toronto, Ontario

Michael Root
Lutheran Theological Southern Seminary
Columbia, South Carolina

George Sumner
Wycliffe College
Toronto, Ontario

1 SAMUEL

FRANCESCA ARAN MURPHY

Brazos Press

a division of Baker Publishing Group
Grand Rapids, Michigan

© 2010 by Francesca Aran Murphy

Published by Brazos Press
a division of Baker Publishing Group
P.O. Box 6287, Grand Rapids, MI 49516-6287
www.brazospress.com

Printed in the United States of America

Library of Congress Cataloging-in-Publication Data
Murphy, Francesca Aran.
    1 Samuel / Francesca Aran Murphy.
        p.   cm. — (Brazos theological commentary on the Bible)
    Includes bibliographical references and indexes.
    ISBN 978-1-58743-172-2 (cloth)
    1. Bible. O.T. Samuel, 1st—Commentaries. I. Title. II. Title: First Samuel. III. Title.
BS1325.53.M87 2010
222′.4307—dc22   2010021037

10   11   12   13   14   15   16   7   6   5   4   3   2   1

To Derek Evan Cross and Paolo Guietti

CONTENTS

SERIES PREFACE

Near the beginning of his treatise against Gnostic interpretations of the Bible, *Against the Heresies*, Irenaeus observes that Scripture is like a great mosaic depicting a handsome king. It is as if we were owners of a villa in Gaul who had ordered a mosaic from Rome. It arrives, and the beautifully colored tiles need to be taken out of their packaging and put into proper order according to the plan of the artist. The difficulty, of course, is that Scripture provides us with the individual pieces, but the order and sequence of various elements are not obvious. The Bible does not come with instructions that would allow interpreters to simply place verses, episodes, images, and parables in order as a worker might follow a schematic drawing in assembling the pieces to depict the handsome king. The mosaic must be puzzled out. This is precisely the work of scriptural interpretation.

Origen has his own image to express the difficulty of working out the proper approach to reading the Bible. When preparing to offer a commentary on the Psalms he tells of a tradition handed down to him by his Hebrew teacher:

> The Hebrew said that the whole divinely inspired Scripture may be likened, because of its obscurity, to many locked rooms in our house. By each room is placed a key, but not the one that corresponds to it, so that the keys are scattered about beside the rooms, none of them matching the room by which it is placed. It is a difficult task to find the keys and match them to the rooms that they can open. We therefore know the Scriptures that are obscure only by taking the points of departure for understanding them from another place because they have their interpretive principle scattered among them.[1]

1. Fragment from the preface to *Commentary on Psalms 1–25*, preserved in the *Philokalia* (trans. Joseph W. Trigg; London: Routledge, 1998), 70–71.

As is the case for Irenaeus, scriptural interpretation is not purely local. The key in Genesis may best fit the door of Isaiah, which in turn opens up the meaning of Matthew. The mosaic must be put together with an eye toward the overall plan.

Irenaeus, Origen, and the great cloud of premodern biblical interpreters assumed that puzzling out the mosaic of Scripture must be a communal project. The Bible is vast, heterogeneous, full of confusing passages and obscure words, and difficult to understand. Only a fool would imagine that he or she could work out solutions alone. The way forward must rely upon a tradition of reading that Irenaeus reports has been passed on as the rule or canon of truth that functions as a confession of faith. "Anyone," he says, "who keeps unchangeable in himself the rule of truth received through baptism will recognize the names and sayings and parables of the scriptures."[2] Modern scholars debate the content of the rule on which Irenaeus relies and commends, not the least because the terms and formulations Irenaeus himself uses shift and slide. Nonetheless, Irenaeus assumes that there is a body of apostolic doctrine sustained by a tradition of teaching in the church. This doctrine provides the clarifying principles that guide exegetical judgment toward a coherent overall reading of Scripture as a unified witness. Doctrine, then, is the schematic drawing that will allow the reader to organize the vast heterogeneity of the words, images, and stories of the Bible into a readable, coherent whole. It is the rule that guides us toward the proper matching of keys to doors.

If self-consciousness about the role of history in shaping human consciousness makes modern historical-critical study critical, then what makes modern study of the Bible modern is the consensus that classical Christian doctrine distorts interpretive understanding. Benjamin Jowett, the influential nineteenth-century English classical scholar, is representative. In his programmatic essay "On the Interpretation of Scripture," he exhorts the biblical reader to disengage from doctrine and break its hold over the interpretive imagination. "The simple words of that book," writes Jowett of the modern reader, "he tries to preserve absolutely pure from the refinements or distinctions of later times." The modern interpreter wishes to "clear away the remains of dogmas, systems, controversies, which are encrusted upon" the words of Scripture. The disciplines of close philological analysis "would enable us to separate the elements of doctrine and tradition with which the meaning of Scripture is encumbered in our own day."[3] The lens of understanding must be wiped clear of the hazy and distorting film of doctrine.

Postmodernity, in turn, has encouraged us to criticize the critics. Jowett imagined that when he wiped away doctrine he would encounter the biblical text in its purity and uncover what he called "the original spirit and intention of the authors."[4] We are not now so sanguine, and the postmodern mind thinks

2. *Against the Heretics* 9.4.
3. Benjamin Jowett, "On the Interpretation of Scripture," in *Essays and Reviews* (London: Parker, 1860), 338–39.
4. Ibid., 340.

interpretive frameworks inevitable. Nonetheless, we tend to remain modern in at least one sense. We read Athanasius and think him stage-managing the diversity of Scripture to support his positions against the Arians. We read Bernard of Clairvaux and assume that his monastic ideals structure his reading of the Song of Songs. In the wake of the Reformation, we can see how the doctrinal divisions of the time shaped biblical interpretation. Luther famously described the Epistle of James as a "strawy letter," for, as he said, "it has nothing of the nature of the Gospel about it."[5] In these and many other instances, often written in the heat of ecclesiastical controversy or out of the passion of ascetic commitment, we tend to think Jowett correct: doctrine is a distorting film on the lens of understanding.

However, is what we commonly think actually the case? Are readers naturally perceptive? Do we have an unblemished, reliable aptitude for the divine? Have we no need for disciplines of vision? Do our attention and judgment need to be trained, especially as we seek to read Scripture as the living word of God? According to Augustine, we all struggle to journey toward God, who is our rest and peace. Yet our vision is darkened and the fetters of worldly habit corrupt our judgment. We need training and instruction in order to cleanse our minds so that we might find our way toward God.[6] To this end, "the whole temporal dispensation was made by divine Providence for our salvation."[7] The covenant with Israel, the coming of Christ, the gathering of the nations into the church—all these things are gathered up into the rule of faith, and they guide the vision and form of the soul toward the end of fellowship with God. In Augustine's view, the reading of Scripture both contributes to and benefits from this divine pedagogy. With countless variations in both exegetical conclusions and theological frameworks, the same pedagogy of a doctrinally ruled reading of Scripture characterizes the broad sweep of the Christian tradition from Gregory the Great through Bernard and Bonaventure, continuing across Reformation differences in both John Calvin and Cornelius Lapide, Patrick Henry and Bishop Bossuet, and on to more recent figures such as Karl Barth and Hans Urs von Balthasar.

Is doctrine, then, not a moldering scrim of antique prejudice obscuring the Bible, but instead a clarifying agent, an enduring tradition of theological judgments that amplifies the living voice of Scripture? And what of the scholarly dispassion advocated by Jowett? Is a noncommitted reading, an interpretation unprejudiced, the way toward objectivity, or does it simply invite the languid intellectual apathy that stands aside to make room for the false truism and easy answers of the age?

This series of biblical commentaries was born out of the conviction that dogma clarifies rather than obscures. The Brazos Theological Commentary on the Bible advances upon the assumption that the Nicene tradition, in all its diversity and

5. *Luther's Works*, vol. 35 (ed. E. Theodore Bachmann; Philadelphia: Fortress, 1959), 362.

6. *On Christian Doctrine* 1.10.

7. *On Christian Doctrine* 1.35.

controversy, provides the proper basis for the interpretation of the Bible as Christian Scripture. God the Father Almighty, who sends his only begotten Son to die for us and for our salvation and who raises the crucified Son in the power of the Holy Spirit so that the baptized may be joined in one body—faith in *this* God with *this* vocation of love for the world is the lens through which to view the heterogeneity and particularity of the biblical texts. Doctrine, then, is not a moldering scrim of antique prejudice obscuring the meaning of the Bible. It is a crucial aspect of the divine pedagogy, a clarifying agent for our minds fogged by self-deceptions, a challenge to our languid intellectual apathy that will too often rest in false truisms and the easy spiritual nostrums of the present age rather than search more deeply and widely for the dispersed keys to the many doors of Scripture.

For this reason, the commentators in this series have not been chosen because of their historical or philological expertise. In the main, they are not biblical scholars in the conventional, modern sense of the term. Instead, the commentators were chosen because of their knowledge of and expertise in using the Christian doctrinal tradition. They are qualified by virtue of the doctrinal formation of their mental habits, for it is the conceit of this series of biblical commentaries that theological training in the Nicene tradition prepares one for biblical interpretation, and thus it is to theologians and not biblical scholars that we have turned. "War is too important," it has been said, "to leave to the generals."

We do hope, however, that readers do not draw the wrong impression. The Nicene tradition does not provide a set formula for the solution of exegetical problems. The great tradition of Christian doctrine was not transcribed, bound in folio, and issued in an official, critical edition. We have the Niceno-Constantinopolitan Creed, used for centuries in many traditions of Christian worship. We have ancient baptismal affirmations of faith. The Chalcedonian definition and the creeds and canons of other church councils have their places in official church documents. Yet the rule of faith cannot be limited to a specific set of words, sentences, and creeds. It is instead a pervasive habit of thought, the animating culture of the church in its intellectual aspect. As Augustine observed, commenting on Jeremiah 31:33, "The creed is learned by listening; it is written, not on stone tablets nor on any material, but on the heart."[8] This is why Irenaeus is able to appeal to the rule of faith more than a century before the first ecumenical council, and this is why we need not itemize the contents of the Nicene tradition in order to appeal to its potency and role in the work of interpretation.

Because doctrine is intrinsically fluid on the margins and most powerful as a habit of mind rather than a list of propositions, this commentary series cannot settle difficult questions of method and content at the outset. The editors of the series impose no particular method of doctrinal interpretation. We cannot say in advance how doctrine helps the Christian reader assemble the mosaic of Scripture. We have no clear answer to the question of whether exegesis guided by

---

8. *Sermon* 212.2.

doctrine is antithetical to or compatible with the now-old modern methods of historical-critical inquiry. Truth—historical, mathematical, or doctrinal—knows no contradiction. But method is a discipline of vision and judgment, and we cannot know in advance what aspects of historical-critical inquiry are functions of modernism that shape the soul to be at odds with Christian discipline. Still further, the editors do not hold the commentators to any particular hermeneutical theory that specifies how to define the plain sense of Scripture—or the role this plain sense should play in interpretation. Here the commentary series is tentative and exploratory.

Can we proceed in any other way? European and North American intellectual culture has been de-Christianized. The effect has not been a cessation of Christian activity. Theological work continues. Sermons are preached. Biblical scholars turn out monographs. Church leaders have meetings. But each dimension of a formerly unified Christian practice now tends to function independently. It is as if a weakened army had been fragmented, and various corps had retreated to isolated fortresses in order to survive. Theology has lost its competence in exegesis. Scripture scholars function with minimal theological training. Each decade finds new theories of preaching to cover the nakedness of seminary training that provides theology without exegesis and exegesis without theology.

Not the least of the causes of the fragmentation of Christian intellectual practice has been the divisions of the church. Since the Reformation, the role of the rule of faith in interpretation has been obscured by polemics and counterpolemics about *sola scriptura* and the necessity of a magisterial teaching authority. The Brazos Theological Commentary on the Bible series is deliberately ecumenical in scope, because the editors are convinced that early church fathers were correct: church doctrine does not compete with Scripture in a limited economy of epistemic authority. We wish to encourage unashamedly dogmatic interpretation of Scripture, confident that the concrete consequences of such a reading will cast far more light on the great divisive questions of the Reformation than either reengaging in old theological polemics or chasing the fantasy of a pure exegesis that will somehow adjudicate between competing theological positions. You shall know the truth of doctrine by its interpretive fruits, and therefore in hopes of contributing to the unity of the church, we have deliberately chosen a wide range of theologians whose commitment to doctrine will allow readers to see real interpretive consequences rather than the shadow boxing of theological concepts.

Brazos Theological Commentary on the Bible has no dog in the current translation fights, and we endorse a textual ecumenism that parallels our diversity of ecclesial backgrounds. We do not impose the thankfully modest inclusive-language agenda of the New Revised Standard Version, nor do we insist upon the glories of the Authorized Version, nor do we require our commentators to create a new translation. In our communal worship, in our private devotions, in our theological scholarship, we use a range of scriptural translations. Precisely as Scripture—a living, functioning text in the present life of faith—the Bible is not semantically fixed. Only a modernist, literalist hermeneutic could imagine that this modest fluidity is a liability. Philological precision and stability is a consequence of, not a basis for, exegesis. Judgments about the meaning of a text fix its literal sense, not the other way around. As a result, readers should expect an eclectic use of biblical translations, both across the different volumes of the series and within individual commentaries.

We cannot speak for contemporary biblical scholars, but as theologians we know that we have long been trained to defend our fortresses of theological concepts and formulations. And we have forgotten the skills of interpretation. Like stroke victims, we must rehabilitate our exegetical imaginations, and there are likely to be different strategies of recovery. Readers should expect this reconstructive—not reactionary—series to provide them with experiments in postcritical doctrinal interpretation, not commentaries written according to the settled principles of a well-functioning tradition. Some commentators will follow classical typological and allegorical readings from the premodern tradition; others will draw on contemporary historical study. Some will comment verse by verse; others will highlight passages, even single words that trigger theological analysis of Scripture. No reading strategies are proscribed, no interpretive methods foresworn. The central premise in this commentary series is that doctrine provides structure and cogency to scriptural interpretation. We trust in this premise with the hope that the Nicene tradition can guide us, however imperfectly, diversely, and haltingly, toward a reading of Scripture in which the right keys open the right doors.

R. R. Reno

ABBREVIATIONS

Bible Versions

ESV   English Standard Version
KJV   King James Version
NIV   New International Version
NKJV New King James Version
NRSV New Revised Standard Version

Biblical Books

Acts	Acts	Gal.	Galatians
Amos	Amos	Gen.	Genesis
1 Chr.	1 Chronicles	Hab.	Habakkuk
2 Chr.	2 Chronicles	Hag.	Haggai
Col.	Colossians	Heb.	Hebrews
1 Cor.	1 Corinthians	Hos.	Hosea
2 Cor.	2 Corinthians	Isa.	Isaiah
Dan.	Daniel	Jas.	James
Deut.	Deuteronomy	Jer.	Jeremiah
Eccl.	Ecclesiastes	Job	Job
Eph.	Ephesians	Joel	Joel
Esth.	Esther	John	John
Exod.	Exodus	1 John	1 John
Ezek.	Ezekiel	2 John	2 John
Ezra	Ezra	3 John	3 John

Jonah	Jonah	2 Pet.	2 Peter
Josh.	Joshua	Phil.	Philippians
Jude	Jude	Phlm.	Philemon
Judg.	Judges	Prov.	Proverbs
1 Kgs.	1 Kings	Ps.	Psalms
2 Kgs.	2 Kings	Rev.	Revelation
Lam.	Lamentations	Rom.	Romans
Lev.	Leviticus	Ruth	Ruth
Luke	Luke	1 Sam.	1 Samuel
Mal.	Malachi	2 Sam.	2 Samuel
Mark	Mark	Song	Song of Songs
Matt.	Matthew	1 Thess.	1 Thessalonians
Mic.	Micah	2 Thess.	2 Thessalonians
Nah.	Nahum	1 Tim.	1 Timothy
Neh.	Nehemiah	2 Tim.	2 Timothy
Num.	Numbers	Titus	Titus
Obad.	Obadiah	Zech.	Zechariah
1 Pet.	1 Peter	Zeph.	Zephaniah

INTRODUCTION

First and Second Samuel were originally a single book. It was cut in twain by the exigencies of scroll length when it was translated into Greek, for the Septuagint. Chronicles, written perhaps around 400 BC, calls 1–2 Samuel and 1–2 Kings "the book of the kings of Israel and Judah" (2 Chr. 35:27) (Toorn 2007: 33). In the Septuagint, 1–2 Samuel and 1–2 Kings are treated as a single four-part treatise called *Biblia Basileion* ("The Books of Kingdoms"). Samuel is the first half of the "Book of Reigns," and Kings the second.[1] Since Samuel and Kings were each divided in half, the group was termed 1–4 Regnorum ("Kingdoms" or "Reigns"). The historical writings, or "Former Prophets"—Judges, Ruth, Samuel, and Kings—are arranged in Greek Bibles as a long continuum. Septuagintal differences from the Hebrew text of the Old Testament are especially prominent in Judges, Samuel, and Kings.[2] Pre-Vulgate, Old Latin translations of this writing call it *Regnorum* ("Kingdoms") and preserve the four-part division. The church fathers down to Augustine often depend on one of the Greek versions of 1 Samuel or on an Old Latin translation from these Greek texts, containing phrases that are otherwise unknown to us. Those who rendered the treatise into Latin often selected the Greek renditions over the Hebrew, in what becomes the normal text of scripture of the Middle Ages. When Jerome created the Latin Vulgate Bible, he retained the Greek division of 1 Samuel–2 Kings into four books, but changed the title to Regum. Hence, the medievals call 1 Samuel by the name 1 Regum, which creates confusion when this book is referred to as 1 Kings. The Hebrew text of 1 Samuel–2 Kings was first divided in four in the 1516–17 Bomberg edition of the Masoretic Text. This edition named the books 1–2 Samuel and 1–2 Kings. Protestant exegetes adopted this nomenclature, followed eventually by Roman

1. Jennifer M. Dines, *The Septuagint* (London: Clark, 2004), 12.
2. Ibid., 2–3.

Catholics. Even before that, some Vulgate copies had 1–2 Samuelis: since the Hebrew edition was definitive for them, Protestants selected this title.

We are only beginning to realize now how much the historical and textual exegesis of the Bible that began in the seventeenth century is dependent on the material circumstances of book production in that era and the images of "editors," "correct editions," and "authors" upon which it focused scholarly attention. Van Seters argues that "the early modern practice of publishing ancient texts and the development of the book trade and of printing changed the way in which 'editing' was understood. It is in the critical reproduction of the classics and sacred texts that the one responsible for producing a text for public reading, an *edition*, became an *editor* distinct from the author himself." Since in antiquity, Van Seters says, "editing" meant "putting on a public performance," "the specialization of the verb 'to edit,' its product, 'edition,' and the one producing an edition, the 'editor' . . . should not be anachronistically read back into antiquity" (2006: 18, 14, emphasis original). That means that the idea of 1 Samuel as a compilation issuing from the scholarly editing of earlier archival documents is anachronistic. Rather than thinking of 1 Samuel as the effect of the kind of editorial oversight of which the Bomberg edition of the Hebrew Bible is an example, we should, Van Seters argues, conceive it as the deliberate product of an author. Toorn goes further in his quest to excise "anachronism" from our perception of the Old Testament. Claiming that thinking of the scriptures as books written by single authors does not make sense, he worries that "generations of Bible students have been raised on the notion that the books of the Bible should be read and interpreted *e mente auctoris*. The *e mente auctoris* maxim was first formulated in the seventeenth century." But "the notion of the author that it implies" is, he says, "an invention of the early modern era." Rather, Toorn believes, we should imagine the Bible as the work of collections of scribes. The author would then be, not so much a "romantic," individual artist, but "a craftsman" and "the individuality of the author . . . is . . . reflected in . . . the skill to perfect conventional forms." None of the Regum texts name its author: "If the author is a representative of the scribal craft, anonymity is a fitting phenomenon. To us, . . . only those who write for a firm or an advertising agency, as a clerk or copy writer, write anonymously. This modern practice . . . matches the process of producing texts in antiquity" (2007: 29, 27, 47). When one of the scriptwriters on *Kings*, a television series dramatizing the story of 1–2 Regum in modern dress, read Toorn's book, he thought his idea of the "scribal studio" matched the collective craftsmanship involved in producing film scripts. It helped us to recognize once again the material culture behind the composition of the Bible when it reappeared among us once more.

We recognized it again, and this time articulately, for the medievals realized that its oral tradition mattered to the Bible. Toorn claims that a theological paradigm shift occurred when the Bible was first written down by the scribes. Before the Bible was written down, the source of religious authority was the human expert who passed on the oral tradition, whereas once it became a written text "revelation denotes a product rather than an interaction." In the oral tradition, the individual human act of communing with the deity was the anchor of theological authority. With the coming of the Bible as a book, those individuals, who had taken "their legitimacy from the revelation they possessed in person," had to refer and defer to "the sum of knowledge laid down in a body of texts" (2007: 206–7). Both Orthodox Judaism and Orthodox and Catholic Christianity have sought to preserve the event or act quality of revelation, and its anchorage in persons as well as in texts, by their commitment to revelation in oral as well as in written tradition.

Medieval cathedrals, built by teams of craftsmen, were overseen by master builders, and some, like Saint Denis in Paris, owe their integrated esthetic conception to a single individual, like Abbot Suger. The best television series have as their executive director a mastermind, like David Simon. The director gives the series an overall moral vision. Commitment to a traditional, theological reading of 1 Samuel has the advantage that the Judeo-Christian imagination senses the significance of the moral personality, as the creative author of great historical events and artifacts. This is because the figure of the prophet looms large within it. Augustine gave a cue to this way of imagining when he conceived Regum not only as a history of the Israelite monarchy, but also as a prophecy of the kingdom of God. We will term the anonymous script writer of 1 Samuel its "author" because the term retains the shadow of the prophet and his mantle.

A prophetic interpretation of 1 Samuel is in line with the traditional understanding of its authorship, for it's not quite true that the romantics first found the idea of its individual authorship significant. The Talmud assigns the whole of 1 Regum to the prophet Samuel. This takes something of a leap of faith, since Samuel dies in 25:1, but Gregory the Great is said to have taken wing, claiming that 1 Sam. 25–31 is literally prophetic. Others keep their feet on the ground and note that the parallel history in Chronicles has something to say on the matter: "As for the events of King David's reign, from beginning to end, they are written in the records of Samuel the seer, the records of Nathan the prophet and the records of Gad the seer, together with the details of his reign and power, and the circumstances that surrounded him and Israel and the kingdoms of all the other lands" (1 Chr. 29:29–30 NIV). Until the early nineteenth century, most readers assumed that Samuel wrote 1 Sam. 1–24 and that Nathan and Gad wrote 1 Sam. 25–31 and 2 Samuel. So they recognized 1–2 Regum as both prophetic and the integrated work that only a mastermind can produce.

One scholar complains that the Vulgate created by Jerome "was primarily a liturgic and literary work and not meant to be a literal or scientific translation" of the biblical Hebrew.[3] The Christian Bible is not a Bible of autonomous scholars, but of the deposit of scholarship and worship that is the tradition of the church. Because the Christian's original means of encountering the Old Testament is public worship, the Vulgate and its vernacular successors are primarily liturgical

---

3. Avrom Saltman, ed., *Pseudo-Jerome: Questions on the Book of Samuel* (Leiden: Brill, 1975), 8.

documents. The author of 1 Samuel was not only an independent historian, but also a writer who put his historical gifts at the service of the church. Independent but not autonomous, he wrote as one responsible for a religious community. His task was more like that of a bishop writing a pastoral letter or like that of a prophet, than that of a scholarly historian. For an individual scholar, history is a piece of the past about which he writes, perhaps imposing a philosophy of history upon it. For a people, on the other hand, "history is the remembered past," the past as it belongs to us.[4] One overdramatizes the contrast if one says that the author of 1 Regum was a liturgist not a historian: and yet, there is something in it, since our "prophet" was sowing the seeds of a communal memory.

4. John Lukacs, *Historical Consciousness; or, The Remembered Past*, new ed. (New York: Schocken, 1985), 152.

SERIES ONE

GRACE AND NATURE

1 Samuel 1–3

Israel first enters history not as a place but as a people. It is pictured alongside Ashkelon, Gezer, and Yanoam on a late-thirteenth-century BC Egyptian stele as one of four entities defeated in battle by Pharaoh Merneptah. While the other three are depicted as hilltop cities, the image for Israel is "open country." The Merneptah Stele indicates that in the Late Bronze Age Israel signified a people, not a specific territory with a capital city. Capital cities are the seats of kings. Israel had none (Hackett 1998: 196).

"Jacob and Sons," from *Joseph and the Amazing Technicolor Dreamcoat*, presents the biblical idea of Israel as a collection of tribes, each named after one of Joseph's sons (Gen. 29–30). Historians draw on anthropological models from other tribal societies to interpret the cultural and political implications of Israel's tribalism. A tribal society differs from a centralized political system in that each tribe is politically independent. The tribes of Israel were perceived by observers like Egypt's Pharaoh Merneptah as a unitary entity, perhaps even a confederacy,[1] without having a unitary political center of authority. Sahlins's classical anthropological study shows that a tribal society differs from a political culture by having no "sovereign governing authority": a tribal society is not equivalent to a territory. This is what we see in the Merneptah Stele. Just as the development from a tribal

---

1. The question of whether a confederacy or a tribal league existed in premonarchic Israel is an old chestnut that has yet to be cracked. For sane observations on the matter, see Halpern 1981: 177–82.

1

to a political society in France can be epitomized as "from the Merovingian 'king of the Franks' to the Capetian 'king of France,'" so Israel evolves from Samuel as leader of the Israelites to David as king of Israel (1968: vii–viii, 6). This is what happens in 1–2 Samuel.

Although one can speak metaphorically of "tribal politics" in the same way that one refers to "office politics," tribes are literally prepolitical, because their mechanisms for providing social order are nonpolitical institutions like the moral authority of heads of families. First Samuel is the historical and spiritual drama of a transition from a prepolitical to a political world. Because its focus is families that are as yet nested in a tribal culture, the patriarchal world of the premonarchic Old Testament still feels of "immediate relevance" to "new Christian societies, above all in Africa." According to sociologist Philip Jenkins, because the "first books of the Bible show us a world based on patriarchal clans that practice polygamy," they make such good sense in the global south that African Christianity has developed "beliefs and practices that look Jewish rather than Christian" to modern Western Christians.[2] First Samuel is about the development, under God's providence, of a tribal brotherhood into a state. It is a work of political theology. A Christian political theology is not a compromise between the tribal and the political. "Behold, I make all things new," says Christ in Rev. 21:15: the tribes of humanity come into their own in the city of God, because they are made new by Christ.

The culture depicted in Judges and 1 Samuel was what anthropologists call a "segmentary tribal society." In such a society, ties of political and social allegiance are to close kinship groups. In a segmentary, as opposed to a unilinear, tribal society, kinship lineages include horizontal networks of brothers, as well as vertical lines of descent from father to son. The cultural foci of Israel's segmentary tribal society were domestic groups. Most legal and moral arbitration took place within the family: "the nuclear family, the extended family (Hebrew *bet ab*), the clan (Hebrew *mishpaha*), and the tribe (Hebrew *shebet* or *matteh*)." When they come under threat, "segmentary societies tend to rely on charismatic leaders" like the "nonpermanent, ad hoc leaders" in the book of Judges (Hackett 1998: 191, 195–97). Within a segmentary tribal society, the clan is the elemental group and understood as a "descent unit," welded together by ties of "patrilineal or matrilineal descent." Because the society's ethical and legal governance was kin based, authority was transmitted from father to son. The economics, politics, and religion of segmentary tribal culture "are not conducted by different institutions specially designed for the purpose, but coincidentally by the same kinship and local groups: the lineage and clan segments of the tribe, the households and villages" (Sahlins 1968: 23, viii). This is the world of Judges and 1 Samuel.

The Israelite leaders we see in the book of Judges are people who took charge during military emergencies. The charisma of some earned them an enduring,

2. Philip Jenkins, *The Next Christendom: The Coming of Global Christianity* (Oxford: Oxford University Press, 2002), 131.

though local, role, as arbitrators of the law. But this was sporadic: the judges were military heroes first and foremost, and only secondarily were they "administrative or governing leaders as well" (Hackett 1998: 178). Othniel, Gideon, Deborah, Samson, and Jephthah were fighting judge-prophets. They were given the Spirit of the Lord to defend the people's place in the land. In Judg. 11 Jephthah is offered military chieftainship by the Gileadite elders on the pragmatic condition of defeating the Ammonites: "The exercise of civil authority depended upon success in the field." In peacetime, a few of Israel's judges arbitrated justice at a local level. The judge operated in tandem with the village elders. In Ruth 4:4 Boaz requires "the presence of the elders of my people" (NIV) to initiate the legal procedure by which he buys Ruth's lands and marries her. The author of Ruth follows the legal etiquette set out in Deut. 25:5–10 and probably captures "the actual functioning of the assembly in local jurisprudence." Such local gatherings of "the people" consisted of representative elders, the fathers at the head of each family (Halpern 1981: 113, 199). As was natural in a household-based culture, many expected that the office of judge could be passed from father to son. So too, the various branches of the Levite priesthood, as with Eli's family at Shiloh, passed the "clerical collar" from father to son.

The first four chapters of 1 Samuel are set in Shiloh. The twelfth and eleventh centuries BC were a time of "vastly increased settlement in the northern hill country (around Shechem and Shiloh), with an increase also in the southern hills," around Hebron. The household-based colonies in which these tribal peoples lived were "small, usually unfortified agricultural-pastoral villages. The regions of intensive settlement expanded throughout the premonarchic era" (Hackett 1998: 193). Population growth led Israel beyond a segmentary tribal society to a centralized state.

First Samuel takes up the story from Judges and Ruth. Israel is on the threshold, between semihereditary, semicharismatic acephalous leadership and a centralized state with a hereditary monarchy. As in Judges, a central question is who will represent Israel in its military struggle, who will maintain the law, who will judge Israel? The political interest is focused not on the construction of the centralized state itself, but on the persons who bring it about: Samuel, a judge-prophet; Saul, the first designated to judge or rule Israel as "king"; and David. Saul never achieves what we would recognize as the political level of kingship. As described in 1 Samuel, Saul represents a first step toward political government, the "big man." The big man is still an essentially tribal figure, and thus Saul's social, affective, and religious world is prepolitical. Government by big men is often a prelude to chieftainship. David is what social anthropologists call a chieftain. He crosses the threshold into politics proper. The historical and cultural differences between Saul and David set the context for the varied theological judgments made upon them.

The book begins with a childless woman in a tribal society, in which contempt is heaped on women who do not deliver population growth. The first role that it addresses is motherhood. In Israel's polygamous society, Hannah is one of Elkanah's two wives, the barren one. Because nature has not taken its course in her marriage to Elkanah, Hannah asks God for a son. Antiochene theologian Saint John Chrysostom contrasts her tiny request with more worldly demands: politically ambitious men who are "suing and grasping for a kingdom" should be "ashamed" to remember Hannah, "praying and weeping for a little child" (*Homilies on Ephesians* 24, in Franke 2005: 196). Literary critics of the Hebrew Bible have taught us to see the barren woman's request for fertility as a "type scene," a model story that is repeated across scripture, so that when we meet a barren woman, we can expect that pretty soon she will be mother to a hero-child (Alter 1981: 51). Ancient Christian commentators found theological types in scripture. Here the type of the barren-woman-turned-mother represents the theological truth that God assigns spiritual gifts. Hannah's pregnancy is not strictly miraculous, since she is not evidently incapable of childbearing, not too old like Sarah, for instance. Hannah's fertility is not miraculous but providential, the hand of God working unseen within nature and history. For Chrysostom, the moral of the story is patience and providence: "Let us not take this" story "with a grain of salt," he says, but "even" when some "disaster" seems "insupportable to us, let us . . . wait on God's providence" (2003: 74–75). This typical episode sets the history that 1 Samuel recounts rolling because the book is about God's providential dealing out of roles.

On the family's annual pilgrimage to Shiloh, Hannah makes a bargain: if the Lord gives her a son, she will give him back, dedicating him to God. Hannah meets the terms of her prayer: as soon as he is "weaned," Samuel is handed over to Eli, priest of the temple at Shiloh. First Sam. 2 shows the failure of the hereditary priesthood: the adopted son, Samuel, is a worthier successor to Eli than his own sons. An oracle of doom is delivered against Eli's dynasty. In 1 Sam. 3, in a classic "prophetic call narrative," Samuel is given the word of the Lord for Eli's house. Samuel will not be one more Shiloh priest. His role in the emergence of Israel's monarchy is to be the word bearer of the Lord, Israel's true judge.

In this period, Israelite religiosity was not monotheistic. Israel's empirical religion was syncretistic, offering worship to both Yahweh and Asherah (Dever 2002: 186). Sometimes pictured as Yahweh's consort, Asherah was a fertility goddess. In 1 Sam. 1 Elkanah's earth-mother/wife Peninnah taunts Hannah for her childlessness. The popular religion with which the author was familiar, the "religion of hearth and home" that "fell mainly to women in Israel" (Dever 2002: 193–94), dealt with conception, childbirth, and lactation: the key elements of this female popular religion included rituals for childbirth, sacred *marzeah* feasts, pilgrimages, saints days, baking cakes for Asherah the "Queen of Heaven" to ensure fertility.

The scene of Hannah's annual humiliation is a pilgrimage to Shiloh in which—here the text becomes unclear—Hannah seems to be given a smaller portion of the sacrificial offering because "the LORD had shut up her womb." Diggings at Israelite settlements have turned up several thousand pottery female figures, little Peninnahs, with classic "Elizabeth Taylor" mammaries and childbearing hips. These were offerings or "invocations to Asherah," which archeologist Ziony Zevit calls "prayers in clay." Hannah's silent faith, in turning not to Asherah but to the LORD for the gift of a child, was isolated. The author intends this sketch of worship at Shiloh and Hannah's prayer of thanksgiving, in which fertility is stripped from the earth-mothers and bursts from the barren, to show that childbearing, popularly conceived as the gift of "Asherah, the Great Lady herself" (cited in Dever 2002: 196, 193), is dealt out by Yahweh alone. Set in the context of a cult presided over by a priestly family that has outlived its fruitfulness, the birth of a prophet-son to the barren Hannah represents Yahwistic as against Asheristic fertility.

That the postexilic copyists of the Hebrew Bible and the Septuagint translators don't seem to know what to make of the rituals in these chapters may indicate that the author is describing folk practices that had died out within Diaspora Judaism, after 586 BC. One translation of the Hebrew of 1:5 says Elkanah "gave to Hannah a double portion, because he loved her, though the Lord had closed her womb"—whereas the Septuagint reads: "And, although he loved Hannah, he would give Hannah only one portion, because the Lord had closed her womb." Did custom dictate that an infertile woman was given more of the sacrificial meats or less of them? We do not know.

The earliest Christian commentary on 1 Samuel had no standard text on which to draw. The church of the first four centuries preferred Greek Septuagint texts of the Old Testament to the Hebrew Bible. Christian commentators drew from more than one Septuagint version, and sometimes they created their own translation. When Origen the Great preached on 1 Samuel in Jerusalem in the early 240s, the congregation heard one text read from the lectionary, while the Alexandrian scholar preached on a somewhat different text, adjusted against his own translation of the Hebrew text and the Septuagint. The text that Origen's audience heard was the "common and familiar [version] that was regarded [as] the sacred text" by ordinary Christians, because that was the one they heard in church (Van Seters 2006: 85). Origen was the author of the Hexapla, a multicolumn compilation of two Hebrew and three Greek versions of the Old Testament. This scholar both regarded it as a necessity to get at the right reading of the original and appreciated that he had no authority to impose his academic findings on a familiar lectionary. Bishop Alexander had invited Origen to preach in Jerusalem. And yet, preaching on 1 Sam. 1–2, in front of the bishop of Jerusalem, Origen clearly "commented on a slightly different text" from the Septuagintal or *koine* version than the congregation had just heard, "corrected after the Hebrew or after other Greek translations of the Bible made by Aquila, Symmachus, and Theodotus," and "Bishop Alexander had no . . . objections" (Origen 1986: 68). No single rendition of the sacred text was sacred.

In his sermon the Alexandrian biblical scholar seems to allegorize the figures of Elkanah, Hannah, Peninnah, and Eli. Origen makes Hannah stand for grace, and Peninnah for conversion. Many still retain the impression that Origen inherited this allegorical reading of the Old Testament from the Jewish Platonist Philo.

Philo sought to make the Hebrew stories palatable to his Greek contemporaries by treating the historical figures, stories, and rituals of the Pentateuch as allegories for Platonic archetypes. For Philo, the scriptures are accidentally historically and essentially philosophical. The antiliteralist Philo was no philologist. But Origen, author of the Hexapla, was a text critic. If we picture Origen's exegesis as an inheritance from Philo's Platonizing, then his exhaustive, literal-minded work as a philologist and translator of the Hebrew Bible becomes inexplicable: why would someone whose exegetical principles replaced the letter with allegories go to such lengths to discern the precise meaning of the letter? For those who envisage Origen as a Christian epigone of Philo, his combination of text criticism and allegorical exegesis remains a circle that cannot be squared (Van Seters 2006: 93–94). In fact, it gives a false impression to describe Origen as a Platonizing or allegorizing exegete.

For Origen, "canon" in reference to the Old Testament did not mean a list of books but a way of interpreting scripture, that is, through Christ. "Canonical" meant a criterion by which to unlock scripture before it meant a criterion for inclusion in scripture—because reference to Christ was the criterion for inclusion. When Origen uses the "canon of faith" in relation to the Old Testament, it "does not function to decide which book is or is not suitable for inclusion, because the Hebrew Scriptures were long since inherited from Judaism as sacred. Instead, *canon* here functions as the mode or norm of interpretation" (Van Seters 2006: 359). Origen's preaching on 1 Samuel exhibits the canon of faith by being christological. Origen's rationale for including Hebrew texts within the Christian scripture and for interpreting them is not a rule of allegory, but the rule of Christ. The "one who is God the Word," said Origen, " 'has the key of David' (Rev. 3:7)": "When the Word became flesh, he opened up with this key the scriptures which were closed before his coming."[3] For Origen, Hannah represents grace. What is Platonist about grace?

Episode One: Two Wives (1 Sam. 1:1–10)

When he preached on 1 Sam. 1–2 in 241, Origen evidently thought that the first question that would strike his audience was how come the "righteous Elkanah" was a polygamist (1986: 104). Someone who wished to take that literally and follow suit could use Elkanah as an example of an Old Testament saint who practices polygamy. Polygamy is still a live issue in some non-Western cultures. Living at a greater distance from the original situation of the text, the immediate object of modern Western readers' attention will be, not Elkanah's marital status, but the psychology of the situation. The situation evokes our emotional sympathy. We

---

3. Origen, *Scholia in Apocalypsen* 20, cited in Origen, *Spirit and Fire: A Thematic Anthology of His Writings*, ed. Hans Urs von Balthasar, trans. Robert J. Daly (Edinburgh: Clark, 1984), §130.

hear the voices of the different characters (Polzin 1989: 19). The modern reader hears Peninnah cruelly teasing Hannah for her childlessness, and Elkanah, stuck in the middle, treating Hannah as a childlike, daughter figure. In this vein, Peninnah is the stereotype of the catty woman, and Elkanah the stereotype of the father-husband. Far from spontaneously assuming, with Origen, that because Elkanah is in scripture, he must be a "righteous man," we may wonder whether his question, "Am I not more to you than ten sons?" (1:8 NRSV), is not unimaginative and selfish. Elkanah becomes the stereotypical smug husband who believes that he is all the world to his wife.[4]

One problem with reading the story as a conflict of psychological stereotypes is that Westerners can easily slide into making their own psychology the criterion for understanding the story, substituting their affective reaction to Hannah's humiliation and initiative for the scriptural text. In our identification with the heroine Hannah, we picture ourselves as the heroines of the story, initially crushed, but triumphing over our detractors by the end. In fact, though, the story does not use its voices to convey a drama of subjective psychology. The drama is about the role of motherhood, awarded as a consequence of single-minded dedication to God. Origen brings this out, when, following a Septuagint version, he comments that "whereas Peninnah is said to have many sons and to have received many 'portions,'" Hannah, "because she is just one person, received 'one single portion,' and she weeps over her barrenness" (1986: 104). Origen supposes, that is, that each wife was given a portion of the sacrifice proportionate to the quantity needed to share with her offspring, and Hannah has none: her single portion marks her isolation. As we mentioned, 1:5 is difficult to translate: one Greek version, like the one Origen selected, renders this as a "single portion," whereas the Masoretic Text (the Hebrew version from the sixteenth century) gives us an untranslatable phrase, which McCarter renders by the conjectural "a single portion equal to theirs"—on the basis that the equality of Hannah's portion to Peninnah's gives the second wife a psychological motive for taunting the first wife (jealousy).[5] The question is whether to interpret and translate the text on the basis of the presumed psychology of the characters. In the polygamous societies of precolonial Africa, honor was not a psychological matter, but a socially objective value. Women granted honored status to those who produced children, because they "prided themselves most on fertility—the body of a childless Igbo woman might be mutilated before burial" (Iliffe 2005: 116).

Hannah was isolated because she was a nongenerative member of a tribal society, whose basic social and political unit was the family. The Elkanahs are going up to Shiloh "to sacrifice" (1:3): Israel's main sanctuary had shifted from Shechem to Bethel and thence to Shiloh as a result of the internecine tribal warfare described

4. Gabriel Josipovici, *The Book of God: A Response to the Bible* (New Haven: Yale University Press, 1988), 155; cf. Polzin 1989: 22–23.

5. P. Kyle McCarter Jr., *I Samuel: A New Translation with Introduction, Notes, and Commentary,* Anchor Bible 8 (New York: Doubleday, 1980), 51–52.

in Judges (Boling 1975: 184). Archeologists infer that premonarchic Israel was governed locally by dominant families from the biblical place names, such as Ramathaim-zophim (1:1), named after Ephraim and literally meaning "high Ephraim, hill of Ephraim." Human religiosity is often political at heart: a tribal political situation favors worship of the goddess of human fertility. Where the dominance of families is at stake, one worships the deities of child production, the deities believed to enlarge the tribe.

And yet, it is not Asherah, but "the LORD," we are twice told (1:5–6), who has "shut up her womb," and it is only the LORD who can open it. What Hannah wants and achieves is not psychological closure but open converse with the one God. The heart of the drama in this episode is interior, within the heart that Hannah opens to God the life-giver. It is a secret meeting between Hannah and the LORD that the "omniscient narrator" (Polzin 1989: 19) of 1 Samuel is making public. In this encounter, Hannah is given the social role for which she asks from God.

The lector at Jerusalem read a story that began, "There was a man of Ramathaim-zophim, of Mount Ephraim." Origen's sermon sets aside this translation, preferring Aquila's more literal Greek translation of the Hebrew: "It does not escape me," Origen said, "that some copies have 'There was a man,' but other copies which seem to be more correct have 'There was one man'—on which the Jews themselves, with whom we otherwise disagree, agree with us." Origen picks this out because he wishes to expand on this apparent polygamist's singleness. Very few people, he says, are really "one alone": rather, each of us is a multiple personality. We shift from one mood and role to another, adopting different personas and scripts as the situation dictates: "Look at how the face of this man is sometimes irritated, sometimes struck down, but just a little later, joyous, then newly troubled and then softened, at one moment preoccupied with divine things and acts which lead to eternal life, and a second later throwing itself into projects of concupiscence or of worldly vanity: you see how this man . . . is not 'one' but appears to have in him as many personalities as he does behaviors, for, according to the scriptures . . . , 'a fool is changed as the moon' [Sir. 27:11]. . . . We who are still 'foolish' and imperfect cannot be called 'one,' since we always change in our opinions and in our desires as in our thoughts." Because most of us have not traveled far on the narrow path to sanctity, our personal identity reduces to a shifting series of public faces and voices. Our sense of what our role should be is created by and for other people, who too have fluctuating personas. On the other hand,

> when it comes to the righteous, not only can one say of each of them that he is "one," but even that it is suitable to say of all of them together that they are "one." . . . Scripture depicts them as having "a single heart and a single mind" [Acts 4:32]. . . . They have the "same feelings, the same thoughts" [1 Cor. 1:10], they venerate "one single God, confessing one single Lord Jesus Christ" [1 Cor. 8:6]. . . . The righteous is one who truly imitates "one single God" for . . . that is also what the prophet says, "Hear O Israel, the Lord your God is one God" [Deut. 6:4]. . . . God is proclaimed "one" . . . because he can never be other than himself, that is to say because he never

changes himself, he never changes to another thing, as David attests in saying of him, "But thou art always the selfsame, and thy years shall not fail" [Ps. 101:28]. This phrase has the same meaning: "I am the Lord your God and I do not change" [Mal. 3:6]. Likewise the righteous, the "imitator of God" [Eph. 5:1], made "to his image" [Gen. 1:27], is called "one" when he arrives at perfection, because he too . . . does not change but remains always one; for as long as someone remains in vice, he is shared out between multiple things, dispersed between diverse things, and from the fact that he is taken with many types of vices, he cannot be called one. (Origen 1986: 106–9)

The single-mindedness and isolation of Hannah expresses the oneness of the God she worships. Origen's concern about Elkanah's polygamy takes him to the nub of the matter: the text is about polytheism versus monotheism, that is, in effect, about whether God exists. Without God, there is no single identity or role for the human person. The most elemental issue for the evolution of a tribal society into a political culture is the ascription of uniquely valuable and independent personhood to the members of the society. It is not possible for a society to fully achieve and sustain this transition without faith in the unity of God. That is, it is not possible without the conception of God put forward in the Old and New Testaments. Politics and social anthropology are far from Origen's mind in his exegesis of 1 Sam. 1, but he sees what is going on here.

We may still want to ask whether Elkanah's authentic oneness or Hannah's singleness of purpose knots 1:1–20 together. Why does the sermon give us an encomium of the male in the story, not of Hannah herself? Origen honors the husband rather than the wife with this virtue because, otherwise, Elkanah would be righteous merely because he is a heroically ascetic contemplator of the One. His sermon is marking what made Elkanah different from those philosophers who trained in the celibate disciplines of self-formation in which the Greek schools of Origen's time excelled. For Alexandrian Stoics, Epicureans, and Neoplatonists philosophy was a matter of practicing spiritual exercises. Plotinus's "writings are full of passages describing such spiritual exercises, the goal of which was not merely to *know* the good, but *to become identical with it*, in a complete annihilation of individuality." For Porphyry, diligent rehearsal of such techniques carried the expert to the grand finale of the soul's "conversion toward the Intellect and the One." Such spiritual exercises intend to achieve "a return to the self, in which the self is liberated from the state of alienation into which it has been plunged by worries, passions, and desires. The 'self' liberated in this way is no longer merely our egoistic, passionate individuality: it is our *moral* person, open to universality and objectivity, and participating in universal nature or thought."[6] The Alexandrian seeker strove to create a role or identity for himself.

6. Pierre Hadot, *Philosophy as a Way of Life: Spiritual Exercises from Socrates to Foucault*, ed. Arnold I. Davidson, trans. Michael Chase (Oxford: Blackwell, 1995), 60, 100–101, 103.

If Origen had made Hannah represent oneness-with-the-One, he would have assimilated her spiritual ascent to Greek meditation practice. In modern terms, we might think of the analogy to moralistic therapeutic theism, the religion of many of the empirical members of the Christian church. Like the Greek meditator, the therapeutic theist exercises mental muscles to improve his or her individual spiritual performance. Breaking with pagan individualism by staying close to the biblical story about a family, Origen represents Elkanah as being not only one or righteous, that is, one of the saints, on the ground that he is reliant on another, his wife, who is grace. Elkanah is righteous because he is wedded to grace.

Peninnah represents the first step, conversion. Grace and conversion are supposed to be the root meanings of the Hebrew names Hannah and Peninnah. Although they are "not without value nor completely alien to God," "the sons of 'conversion' are not such that they can be near to God or fixed on him." The fruits of conversion are merely good works: "The children engendered through the one who is grace . . . are brought near to God," like Samuel. As Christians, Origen says, "we seek first to please through good works and then we procreate a son through 'grace' and through the 'gift of the Spirit'" (1986: 113–15). Origen thus specifies the meaning of the role of motherhood for those who believe in a God who is both one and gracious. He does not disparage conversion, though he sets grace higher.

Origen conferred with scholars in the large Jewish community in his hometown of Caesarea and gathered his etymologies of Peninnah and Hannah "from a Jewish dictionary called *Translation of Hebrew Names* to which he often alludes" (1986: 73). In his day, catechumens who had been formally enrolled for entrance into the church were converts, awaiting the baptism of grace at Easter. Converts had been proven in the eyes of the faithful, by their knowledge of the creeds and by good living. In his Jerusalem congregation, converts and baptized would be mingled. Speaking of the practice of baptism in "the 'golden age' of Christian liturgy," Alexander Schmemann writes that "there is a difference . . . between the faith which *converts* an unbeliever . . . to Christ and the faith which constitutes the very life of the Church and of her members and which St. Paul defines as having in us Christ's mind, i.e., his faith, his love, his desire. Both are gifts of God. But the former is a *response* to the call which the latter is the very *reality* of that to which the call summons. . . . It is his personal faith in Christ which brings the catechumen to the Church; it is the Church that will instruct him in and bestow upon him Christ's faith by which she lives."[7] Both converts and the baptized had a designated role in the society of the church, and the merely converted were not walled off from the baptized. Converts too have been given a role, in the gift of the call to baptism: their vocation is to prove themselves in learning the faith and obeying its precepts. Origen's faith enables him to see indirectly that the original

---

7. Alexander Schmemann, *Of Water and the Spirit: A Liturgical Study of Baptism* (London: SPCK, 1976), 7, 67–68.

text does not characterize the two women in terms of contrasting psychological stereotypes, but situates them in terms of the roles a tribal society would give a fertile and a barren wife. By imaginatively assimilating Peninnah to the converts, moreover, he does not place this representative of empirical Israel beyond the pale, but rather includes her as a support player in the full drama.

Episode Two: The Political and the Personal (1 Sam. 1:11–20)

When Hannah silently offers to return the gift of a son to God, she says, "No razor shall touch his head" (1:11 NRSV). She is offering her son in advance as a Nazirite. The Nazirites were an Israelite order that, since the time of the judges, dedicated themselves to God by setting themselves apart from their culture. They indicated their self-separation from average practicing Yahwists by never cutting their hair or shaving their beard. A Nazirite "cut himself off from the normal ways of life by abstention." Under the monarchy, this self-separation from Israel's empirical religion(s) intensified, as a sign of "opposition to the Canaanisation of the cult of Jahweh" (von Rad 1962: 62–63). Just as, for instance, the early modern reforming Carmelites belonged to a medieval order, so the reforming Nazirite movement of monarchic times had its roots and exemplars in the older, tribal culture of the judges, in which the charismatic Samson was a legendary Nazirite. For anyone who read this during monarchic times, Samuel would appear to link the old times and his own, where Nazirism had come to represent a "no!" to the Israelite monarch's diplomatic evenhandedness between Yahwism and the gods of their powerful neighbors. Nazirites foreswore alcohol: so it is striking that, while Hannah is silently offering a Nazirite vocation for her would-be son, Eli is inferring that this female mumbler must be under the influence.

To modern readers, Eli is reminiscent of those officious ecclesial functionaries who haunt the doorways of churches to police lay deportment within the house of God: "How long will you go on being drunk? Put your wine away from you" (ESV). Hannah's response to this cutting rebuke is to tell Eli that, far from being a pitcher full of wine, "I have been pouring out my soul before the Lord" (1:15 ESV). So single-minded is Hannah about laying her plight before the Lord that she forgets her surroundings, forgets the public face of prayer, forgets what she looks like, and speaks her heart and her whole soul to the one God. She doesn't worry that she is no one and God is, assuredly, someone. Her need is so pressing that it overwhelms public concerns, and under the impulse of desire, she addresses "the Lord of hosts" without ceremony, ignoring the Lord's doorkeeper, Eli the priest. Picturing the scene as if it were set in the Constantinople of Theodosius and Eudoxia, John Chrysostom imagines the situation by analogy with the direct approach of a desperate widow to the emperor, bypassing his entourage and the mediation of a powerful patron: "Just as a widow who is destitute and all alone . . . will often not be alarmed at the imminent triumphal procession of emperor, bodyguards, shield bearers, horses . . . but without the need of a patron will brush past them all and with great confidence accost the emperor . . . under pressure of her sense of need, so too this woman was not embarrassed, was not ashamed, though the priest was sitting there, to make her request in person and with great confidence approach the king" (2003: 76–77). If we surround the scene with the panoply of kingship and hierarchical priesthood, as existed in Chrysostom's times, we may imagine that Eli speaks sharply to Hannah because, in her urgency, Hannah had importunately shunted aside his role of ensuring that communication between God and people transverses the official channels. Chrysostom's image of the scene connects to what the author is doing with this piece of premonarchic history. Eli does have an official role.

The full story of Regum runs from the reign of Saul in ca. 1010 BC to 586 BC, when Judah was subjugated by the Babylonians and the royal family was taken into exile (2 Kgs. 25:30). For anyone who oversaw it all, the priestly house of Eli stands for the story of the rise and fall of the kingdoms of Israel and Judah. Eli looks rather regal: "Eli the priest was sitting on the seat beside the doorpost of the temple of the LORD" (1:9 NRSV). The Hebrew for "sitting" shifts to the imperfect to emphasize that he is "beseated." Anyone who has seen photos of Egyptian or Babylonian statues can picture him, knees straight, like a monarch. The priest sits on "the throne" (*al-hakkisse*). Eli isn't just sitting around outside his temple: he is "beseated," as one in the judgment seat (Polzin 1989: 23). Without being a capital city, the shrine at Shiloh, which housed the ark, had become a political focus, recognized by most of the Israelite tribes. Eli was at the apex of the network of local judges and assemblies, a "superjudge" (Ishida 1977: 32–33). Though it is not the only historical category, continuity is a basic element of public historical life. It is unlikely that Israel made a sudden leap from sporadic local rule by charismatic judges to installing Saul as leader of all Israel. It is more likely that initial steps were taken toward a political center, which all or many of the Israelite tribes acknowledged, even while their juridical structure continued to function locally. This text seems to be backhanded evidence that such a development had taken place and that weighty Eli combined political with clerical authority. Because of the continuous, small steps between Eli, Saul, David, and the later monarchs of Israel and Judah, and the absence of an absolute cultural or legal break between premonarchic and monarchic times, there is a similarity even between Eli and the last king of Israel. The reader of the whole sweep of 1 Samuel–2 Kings can look back, through this "remembered past"[8] and say, "In my end is my beginning; in my beginning is my end."

The Hebrew *heykal* can mean either a king's "palace" or "temple." The author is a realist, not a Manichean. His history is never crudely antimonarchic. He knows on the one hand that both temple and palace were magnets for syncretistic

---

8. John Lukacs, *Historical Consciousness; or, The Remembered Past*, new ed. (New York: Schocken, 1985), 9.

compromise, for worldly cynicism. Temple evokes palace in the flat-footed figure of Eli. He knows on the other hand that the grace that Hannah requests and represents is not only for herself, but a gift for all Israel. Eli and Hannah are the outer and the inner sides of the one Israel. The son for whom she bargains will have the role of anointer of kings.

On any literal reading of the scene between petitioner and priest, Eli initially misinterprets Hannah's act of private prayer as a drunkard's talking to herself; for the literal reader of this portion of scripture, Eli steps into the role of so many biblical characters who look at the externals, not at the heart. Cyprian of Carthage makes the literal-minded comment that Hannah "prays to God . . . silently and modestly within the very recesses of her heart. She spoke with a hidden prayer but with manifest faith. She did not speak with the voice but with the heart, because she knew that so the Lord hears, and she effectually obtained what she sought, because she asked with faith" (*The Lord's Prayer* 5, in Franke 2005: 199). Alexandrian theologian Clement observes that, as Hannah's example shows, "prayer is . . . a conversation with God . . . not opening the lips, we speak in silence, yet we cry inwardly. For God hears . . . the whole inward conversation" (*Stromateis* 7.7, in Franke 2005: 199). John Chrysostom adversely contrasts public, written works with Hannah's invisible prayer: "This is what prayers arising from the soul's pangs are like: her mind took the place of paper, her tongue a pen, and her tears ink; hence her appeal has lasted to this very day. Such letters, in fact, prove indelible, dipped as they are in that ink" (2003: 78).

Some modern scholars are almost as much taken aback by such literal readings of this scene as, according to Chrysostom, Eli was by Hannah's bypassing the network in which she should function as client and he as the patronal contact to the divine king. For many contemporary writers, what counts as real is public prayer, not silent inward cries and petitions. This is because they believe all human language, and thus all human religion, is public and not private. So, for instance, Josipovici notes that, though Hannah may have prayed silently, she still had to use words, the public language of her time: "Her lips move and she forms words. She speaks from the heart . . . but she speaks the language of men and women. . . . Prayer finds its forms in the forms of ordinary language and in the linguistic and social usages of the community to which the one who prays belongs. . . . Hannah moving her lips is crucial testimony to the fact that prayer . . . is an utterance, an *outering*."[9] This is true insofar as it goes: Hannah's petition to God does not fly above ordinary thoughts and words. Rather, she is pictured "making a deal with God" and offering "the price from what is coming to her," since she has nothing else to bargain with (Chrysostom 2003: 78): "O LORD of hosts, if you will indeed look on the affliction of your servant and remember me and not forget your servant, but will give to your servant a son, then I will give him to the LORD all the days of his life" (1:11 ESV). Josipovici's description of Hannah's petitionary

9. Josipovici, *Book of God*, 160–62.

vow as an "outering" captures something of the down-to-earth quality of the peasant woman's bargain.

But perhaps it does not capture all of it, for the inward character of Hannah's prayer, its spirituality, mirrors that she is praying for something to happen inside her body—the conception of a child. Hannah's silent tears and God's response created an analogy between private intimacy with God and physical fertility that lasted in Christian spirituality down so far as the metaphysical poet George Herbert, who prayed, "Send water to my dry roots." Herbert was likely recalling the psalmist, who affirmed that the believer is "like a tree planted by streams of water, which yields its fruit in season" (Ps. 1:3 NIV). Since its God is living (Exod. 3), scripture doesn't cleanly separate life in the physical and spiritual senses: God is present in places where rivers flow (Eden, Zion, new Jerusalem), and Canaan is "a land . . . which drinks water by the rain from heaven" because it is "a land that the LORD your God cares for" (Deut. 11:11–12 ESV) (Martin-Achard 1960: 10–12). Chrysostom grasps the force of this metaphor of "going to ground interiorly," asking God to act on us within and being rewarded with renewing rains: "Instead of saying anything at first, she began with wailing and shed warm floods of tears. And just as, when rain storms fall, even the harder ground is moistened . . . and easily bestirs itself to produce crops, so too did this happen in the case of this woman: as though softened by the flood of tears and warmed with the pangs, the womb began to stir in that wonderful fertility." For Chrysostom, tracking the metaphorical link between silent inwardness and physical fruitfulness, the private prayer is the model of the true prayer: "I seek," he says, "those tears which are shed not for display but in compunction; those which trickle down secretly and in closets and in sight of no person, softly and noiselessly; those which arise from a certain depth of mind, those shed in anguish and in sorrow, those which are for God alone. Such were Hannah's, for 'her lips moved,' it is said, 'but her voice was not heard.' Her tears alone uttered a cry more clear than any trumpet. And because of this, God also opened her womb and made the hard rock a fruitful field" (*Homilies on Hannah* 1 and *Homilies on the Gospel of Matthew* 6.8, in Franke 2005: 197–99).

When Hannah struck her bargain, there was no extant ceremonial or liturgical form of public language that we know of for making a Levite vow on behalf of a son as yet unborn: the terms of Hannah's petitionary bargain were invented by her. She was not keeping to the known forms of prayer, but inventing her own and so provoking a clerical misapprehension. Hannah's prayer was private because she was acting outside the rubrics. The offer that she makes to God is creative, going beyond even Abraham's acquiescence in Isaac's being taken from him, because she herself invents the terms, rather than having them imposed upon her. When Hannah vows, "I will give him to the LORD all the days of his life" (1:11 ESV), she speaks as an authentic daughter of Abraham, Chrysostom believes, because Abraham "gave when it was demanded of him" whereas Hannah "offers even before it is demanded" (*Homilies on Ephesians* 24, in Franke 2005: 197). In this episode,

14

which introduces the overall theme of Regum, the author goes to lengths to show the priority of the personal over the political, by contrasting Hannah's interior cries for help and Eli's narrow-sighted public gaze. The insistence of church fathers like Clement, Origen, and Chrysostom on inward faith is rooted as much in the Old Covenant as in the New. Literally and physically, as well as spiritually, this inward root was the womb of Samuel.

The separation that Hannah offers for her wished-for son by dedicating him as a Nazirite reflects her own isolation. It's partly for this reason that the efforts by public-language enthusiasts to avoid making the scene into a conflict between silent inward prayer and looking at the externals falls short of understanding it. If we consider the historical context, we can see that the privacy of Hannah's prayer is not just superimposed on it by the "platonizing" Clement and Origen. It is a feature of the period the author is describing, albeit such a novel one that Eli cannot compute it. Like our modern prayer-as-public-language advocates, Eli identifies prayer with a collective, publicly observable activity, exactly what it would be in a tribal culture. For the tribal religious sensibility, the feeling of group solidarity was deep and intense, and an "individual's life was enclosed in that of larger units superior to it—kindred and tribe. . . . There was no tension between inward and outward, between the 'I' and the world, since outside in every department of natural life the sacred regulations held sway which the cult exalted and into which man had to fit" (von Rad 1962: 37). This is how a tribesman such as Eli would have lived and thought. For such a one, seeing Hannah's lips moving but no coherent words emerging was cognitively dissonant. Eli's encounter with Hannah's silent prayer is reminiscent of Augustine's surprise at encountering Bishop Ambrose reading silently, something Augustine had never witnessed, in a culture in which reading was normally a public activity (*Confessions* 6.3). Since Eli lives in a culture in which individuals have a dense collective existence but no private life, he imagines that the outer invariably displays the inner world of persons. Hence, the silent movement of Hannah's lips must exhibit some publicly recognizable sign, and drunkenness is the only explanation that occurs to the fallible tribal priest.

Hannah is a pioneer, leading the religious spirit of her times into new territory. In the new political culture that has begun to appear by the end of the book, not only prayer but the action of God occurs silently and in a hidden manner. Apart from an outbreak of boisterously external miracles in 1 Sam. 6–7, there are few miracles in 1 Samuel. A novel conception of the divine guidance of history appears, and one that fits a political theology. From henceforth, God's action in history is largely, though not solely, presented as providential, working in cooperation with nature and human freedom, rather than in the overt supernatural interruptions of nature that we call the miraculous. The mistaken equation of the outer and the inner, the failure to appreciate that the outer and the inner can diverge, and that what really is and what seems to be can part company, becomes a signature of the book as a whole. It returns repeatedly, for instance when seven sons of Jesse are paraded before Samuel, and he thinks each is suitable to be anointed king, until the Lord tells him to anoint the forgotten, youngest son, David. "Do not look at his appearance or at his physical stature" (NKJV), Samuel is told, because "the LORD does not see as man sees; for man looks at the outward appearance, but the LORD looks at the heart" (16:7). The Spirit is staking his ground in the privacy of the hearts of men and women. In a political society, God's ethical imperatives are discerned more by reflection on divine providence than by the outward display of miracles. In most of 1 Samuel, "the causal chain of events is closed without a break" because such is the terrain on which God's political providence operates (von Rad 1962: 315–16). The story of Eli's incomprehension of Hannah's private prayer contains a recollection of a transition from a tribal to a political culture. Our author's accuracy as a social anthropologist is largely inadvertent and backhanded, and all the more telling for that. In one sense, 1 Sam. 1–7 is a continuation of Judges and Ruth, presenting the same social world and religious sensibility as its predecessors. Samuel himself will become a judge, and one who wishes to uphold the tribal, familial order against incipient monarchism (1 Sam. 8). But in another way the rift between the tribal and the monarchic epochs begins with Samuel's conception. Continuity and discontinuity, or analogy and anomaly, are the two elements of which history is made.

Philologists tell us that Samuel's name is an echo of an earlier period in Israel's development of doctrine, harking back to the times before El, the God of the fathers, had been identified with Yahweh the Lord. We read at the end of the story that, when "Hannah conceived and bore a son . . . she called his name Samuel, for she said, 'I have asked for him from the LORD'" (1:20 ESV). Biblical philologists contend that the real meaning of Samuel is "his name is El," that is, "he calls on El" in worship or "El is his God."[10] Nothing in Israel's history is lost or remaindered. Every stage of the way from the patriarchs to the tribal culture of the conquest, to the monarchy and the prophets, is gathered up and made new in Christ.

Episode Three: Samuel Handed Over (1 Sam. 1:21–28)

On the Feast of the Holy Family, in the octave of Christmas, the lectionary lays this story about Hannah's taking baby Samuel to the temple alongside Luke 2:41–52, in which Mary and Joseph lose the boy Jesus during their annual pilgrimage to Jerusalem and find him in the temple: "And his mother said to him, 'Son, why have you treated us so? Behold, your father and I have been searching for you in great distress'" (Luke 2:48 ESV). Both Hannah and Mary freely abandon their God-given son to God. Christian readers have always traced a thread from Samuel to Christ, seeing Samuel as a type of Christ. Both Samuel and Jesus find where they really belong in the temple. Their vocation and identity is wider than their original

10. McCarter, *1 Samuel*, 62.

families, in God: "And he said to them, 'Why were you looking for me? Did you not know that I must be in my Father's house?'... And his mother treasured up all these things in her heart" (Luke 2:49, 51 ESV). Hannah's sacrifice of her only son Samuel to the Lord is the sacrifice of the heart. This gives her sacrifice authentic freedom. Her gesture creates a space of freedom in which Samuel can become himself. Just as "Jesus... had to choose between his Father and his family: 'Son, why have you treated us so?,' so the Christian will make the weighty decisions of his life from the perspective of Christ, that is, of faith."[11]

It is more helpful to consider lectionary pairings like Hannah/Samuel and Mary/Christ pictorially than to think about them chronologically. If one sets two pictures of the two mother/son narratives alongside one another, one can easily grasp the analogy. In medieval times, when most Christians were illiterate, they got their sense of scripture from the images on the walls of churches. In the seventh century Gregory the Great advised a bishop who looked askance on painting the scriptures, "What scripture presents to its readers, a picture presents to the gaze of the unlearned. For in it even the ignorant see what they ought to follow, in it the illiterate read" (Epistle to Bishop Serenus of Marseilles, *Registrum Epostolarum*, Epistle 13). We tend to think of this way of appreciating scripture as *faute de mieux* and that we know it much better now that we *read* scripture rather than *looking* at it. Samuel is being apprenticed to the priesthood at Shiloh. His training by Eli may have included mastery of the scribal craft, since he will write up a "law of kingship" and deposit it in the Shiloh temple (1 Sam. 10:25). Toorn claims that in Babylon and Israel "the native verbs for 'reading' literally mean 'to cry, to speak out loud.'... These verbs reflect the way texts were used. Written documents were read aloud, either to an audience or to oneself. Silent reading was highly unusual. Even the student who read in solitude 'muttered' his text (Ps. 1:2; compare Acts 8:30). So when someone was urged to read something assiduously, the phrase was that he should not allow the text 'to depart from his mouth' (Josh. 1:8)." When, before the codex and the printed book, "texts were for the ears rather than the eyes,"[12] an audience had to be made to *see*, and thus remember, the narrative: the storybooks written with this intention indwelt the imagination before they were conceptualized. Hence, 1 Sam. 1:21–28 is perfectly visual: it doesn't talk about the depth of Hannah's sacrifice, it makes us see Hannah, weaning Samuel and taking him to the temple. It could have been written for preliterate people who will see it in their mental imagination rather than hearing it in their mind's ear, as literate congregations may tend to do. Two pictures, Hannah and Mary, make congenial sense alongside one another; take away the image and conceptually audit the text as a time sequence, and Samuel and Christ are distanced. The medieval, largely

11. Hans Urs von Balthasar, "Nine Propositions on Christian Ethics," in *Principles of Christian Morality*, by Hans Urs von Balthasar, Joseph Ratzinger, and Heinz Schurmann; trans. Graham Harrison (San Francisco: Ignatius, 1986), 77.

12. Toorn 2007: 87, 12. Toorn thinks that both 1 Sam. 1 and 10:25 are "retrojection[s] of later practice, Shiloh being a forerunner and cipher of the Jerusalem temple."

illiterate, audience of the twin episodes and the largely preliterate audience of the first story had something in common that is theologically important: visual linkages mattered more to them than temporal ones.

The story pictures the "child" that Hannah is giving up as "young" (1:24), that is, that a hard maternal sacrifice is being offered. John Chrysostom calls Hannah "a priestess in her very being, imitating the patriarch Abraham and rivalling him for preeminence: whereas he took his son and descended, she let hers stay permanently in the temple" (2003: 102). The Shilonite priesthood seems to have acquired political authority. After the fall of Eli's house, Samuel replaces him as Israel's central judge, a premonarchic "king." But Samuel is also a prophet, one who speaks directly with God: unlike Israel's kings, who hear the word second-hand through the prophet, Samuel is addressed by God himself. Samuel is a living analogy to the prophet, priest, and king that Christ will be in the fullest sense. Of none of Israel's kings can it be said with historical plausibility that he was prophet, priest, and king. It can credibly be said of only Samuel.

Episode Four: Hannah's Song of Thanksgiving (1 Sam. 2:1–11)

From Heinrich Ewald in the nineteenth century to W. F. Albright and Frank Cross in the twentieth century, the theory has persistently resurfaced that a lost epic lies behind the Pentateuch and some portions of the Deuteronomistic History. Others discount this hypothesis (Van Seters 1983: 18–20, 225–27; Halpern 1996: 18–19). Since there can, in principle, be no evidence for a lost epic of ancient Israel, the theory does not stand up as evidence of the antiquity and thus the veracity of the Old Testament. One reason the notion of an epical origin of the Old Testament nonetheless holds some intuitive appeal is that epic poetry is a more fitting language in which to address the divine than prose. In the course of showing that early Greek historical writings are not "prose versions of the *Iliad* or the *Odyssey* or of the works of Hesiod," Van Seters notes that the early historians gave reductive explanations of many of the Homeric stories. Herodotus, for instance, claims to have asked the Egyptians about Paris and Helen and to have been told that they fled to Egypt, not to Troy, implying that the glorious heroes of Homer fought the Trojan War for nothing (1983: 22). It is the relatively reductive tendency of prose that makes it a less apt medium for speaking of divine things than epic poetry. Homer's epics, not Herodotus's *History*, became the bible of Greece. Van Seters notes that, though the historical prose of the ancient Near East is "never simply a 'translation' from poetry to prose," "interaction between epic and prose historiography often occurs": for instance, the epic of Nebuchadnezzar I commences with a poetic lament over the absence of the god Marduk (1983: 95–96). That was to begin in the exalted key in which the Mesopotamian author meant to go on, that is, relating human affairs to divine sponsorship and its withdrawal. When the biblical writers break into poetry, they condense the atmosphere of the Old Testament into its own exemplary register and key. Biblical historians would like to characterize God as one who "lifts the beggar from the ash heap, to set them among princes" (2:8 NKJV) on every page they write, but, chained to their historical intentions, only the primordial medium of poetry enables them to do so.

For some commentators, the "hymn of praise to Yahweh" in the Song of Hannah is "inappropriate in its present context." The reference to Yahweh's "king" in 2:10 seems to place the composition of the poem in monarchic or later times (Wevers 1971: 157). This poem fits its context in several ways. Both Hannah's infertility and her prayer to God for deliverance are representative: cry for shelter stands for the plight of Israel at the end of the era described in the book of Judges. Flinders Petrie considered that the time "of the judges was a terribly barbaric age; its fragmentary records speak of savage retaliations, and fierce struggles of disorganized tribes. Judge after judge rises out of a mist of warfare, only to disappear and leave a confusion as black as before. Ehud, Baraq, Gideon, Gaal, Abimelech, Jephthah, Samson . . . lead up to the hideous tragedy of the slaughter of Benjamin" (quoted in Boling 1975: 9). Whereas the wealthy can purchase refuge from social disruption, the poor are exposed to the consequences of lawlessness, the unseen collateral victims of tribal warfare. Hannah's thanksgiving to God does not happen when she becomes pregnant or when Samuel is born, as if what she wanted was a child to rival Peninnah's brood. The author has her praise God when she hands Samuel over to the temple, because what Hannah wants from God is a deliverer for Israel. Hence Hannah's claim that, with the birth of her son, "the bows of the mighty men are broken" (1:4) and "the poor [are lifted from] the dust" (1:8). In her childless isolation and her appeal to God, Hannah is a real symbol of Israel's need for renewal. Prestate societies lack the political and legal means of restraining retaliation against slights to honor. "Stateless peoples found violent defence of honor difficult to restrain" (Iliffe 2005: 108–9) because violence is not inhibited by political authority. Hence, the instinctive response to homicide from outside the small community was often "the revenge killing of the murderer or a close kinsman. . . . A single revenge killing normally ended the matter. If not, the result might be endemic small-scale warfare between communities lacking desire or machinery for reconciliation." This cycle has turned throughout Judges, which concludes as the "Israelites avenge a fearful wrong and nearly eliminate a tribe"—the Benjamites (Judg. 19–21). The "relationship with God is at a low ebb," and the persistent chorus of Judges is, "There was no king in Israel" (Campbell and O'Brien 2000: 220–21). The gift of Samuel to the Lord signals the beginning of the end of the judges epoch and so points forward to the Lord's "giv[ing] strength to His king" (1 Sam. 2:10 NKJV), for Samuel will be a prophet, a charismatic kingpin, and an anointer of kings. Hannah's song is a forward glimpse to the lighter side of the monarchic era, what was best about it, in David's faithful establishment of the united kingdom of Israel and Judah and, with that, an end to intertribal war.[13] A reversal of Israel's

13. Brian E. Kelly, "Samuel, Books of," in *Dictionary for Theological Interpretation of the Bible*, ed. Kevin Vanhoozer (Grand Rapids: Baker Academic, 2005), 718.

fortunes is celebrated here: "Israel will triumph over its foes; . . . God will empower the king. Samuel the prophet will replace Eli the priest; Israel will triumph over the Philistines; Samuel will anoint kings" (Campbell and O'Brien 2000: 222).

Where the figure of Eli foreshadows Jehoiachin and the dark ending of the Jewish kingdoms (2 Kgs. 25:30), Hannah's psalm points us to the highest expression of David's faith, in the king's psalm of 2 Sam. 22. There too, the singer celebrates God's life-giving power. David's praise song is very like Hannah's:

> The LORD is my rock and my fortress and my deliverer;
> The God of my strength, in whom I will trust;
> My shield and the horn of my salvation,
> My stronghold and my refuge;
> My Savior, You save me from violence.
> I will call upon the LORD, who is worthy to be praised;
> So shall I be saved from my enemies.
> When the waves of death surrounded me,
> The floods of ungodliness made me afraid.
> The sorrows of Sheol surrounded me;
> The snares of death confronted me.
> In my distress I called upon the LORD,
> And cried out to my God;
> He heard my voice from his temple,
> And my cry entered his ears. . . .
> You will save the humble people;
> But Your eyes are on the haughty, that You may bring them down. . . .
> He is the tower of salvation to His king,
> And shows mercy to His anointed,
> To David and his descendants forevermore. (2 Sam. 22:2–7, 28, 51 NKJV)

Hannah's song is almost as military in its imagery as David's, and so it may be considered "not particularly apt . . . for a mother who has just given up a child to God" (Campbell and O'Brien 2000: 222). But what Hannah wants is a deliverer, a savior. She is of the race of Deborah, the bulldog breed. The song recalls the peculiarly feminine plight from which the LORD rescued her: "The barren has borne seven, but she who has many children is forlorn" (2:5 ESV). Using Hebrew poetic antithesis, the song elaborates the thread that puts the power of fertility in Yahweh's hands alone. As in Moses's song in Exod. 32, Hannah's psalm witnesses to God's power over life and death (Martin-Achard 1960: 52). "The LORD kills and makes alive; He brings down to the grave and brings up" (1 Sam. 2:6 NKJV): "resurrection" from the spiritual death of the years of the judges can be only by an event that transforms the circumstance of the whole people. The same theme will be reproduced by Luke in Mary's Magnificat (Luke 1:46–55).

Christians link Hannah's song to the Magnificat because of the analogous situation: a thanksgiving to God for sending a hero to rescue Israel in its helplessness and need for grace. The Magnificat celebrates the birth of a son to a virgin. Reading Hannah's song as the literary seed for the Song of Mary, we see that the original issue of Asheristic versus Yahwistic power over childbirth makes fertility the expression of divine energy and creativeness, God's power to create anew, out of nothing, in grace. It was by this energy of grace that the church was propagated.

The story of 1 Sam. 1–2 shows that Hannah is an isolated figure in a dark world, the milieu characteristic of noir movies, in which little is as it seems and in which it is difficult to see or tell the reality of things. Out of the human tendency to avoid unpleasantness, we tend to reconfigure the story in a moralistic way and imagine Hannah as though she were typical of Israelite culture, whereas in fact she is presented as atypical, an isolated oddity. We make the light that shines on Hannah alone shine on everyone around her, imposing our moralism on the story because its own realism is too grim for us to endure. We need to take off the moralistic lenses, which brighten the picture and make us blur over the way scripture points up the discrepancy between Hannah and her community. The archeological discovery of deep-seated religious syncretism in empirical Israelite religion is a reminder of the disparity between what we fondly imagine as Israelite monotheism and the empirical or sociological reality. Hannah was a maverick in a culture that mixed soliciting the gods of sexual reproduction with pilgrimages to the shrine of Yahweh. What was outward and public in Israelite religious was not true to Israel's God; only what was inward and secret, in Hannah, was genuinely committed to the God of Israel. The "noirish" "gap between appearance and reality" naturally gives rise to the search for characters who provide the thread through the labyrinth.[14] These characters, with their secret lives, lead us to the real Israel. That is what writers like Cyprian of Carthage meant when they said that Hannah is depicted as "a type of the church" (*The Lord's Prayer* 5, in Franke 2005: 199). Augustine read the text for the bare story it presents and found the thread in Hannah. For him, this lone woman stands for the presence of the "city of God," the community that loves God, within empirical Israel. With him, we can recognize that "through this woman (whose very name, Hannah, means 'God's grace'), there speaks, by the spirit of prophecy, the Christian religion itself, the City of God itself, whose king and founder is Christ; there speaks, in fact, the grace of God itself, from which the proud are estranged so that they fall, with which the humble are filled so that they rise up. . . . Therefore, let the church of Christ speak, the 'City of the great king,' the church that is 'full of grace,' fruitful in Children; let her speak the words that she recognizes as spoken prophetically about herself, so long ago, by the lips of this devout mother." As a precursor of Mary, Hannah speaks for the church: "Her heart is truly strengthened and her horn truly exalted, because it is 'in the Lord her God' not in herself that she finds strength and exaltation" (*City of God* 17.4).

14. Thomas S. Hibbs, *Arts of Darkness: American Noir and the Quest for Redemption* (Dallas: Spence, 2008), 16.

The song uses poetic antithesis to insist that Yahweh is the only God: it is very much rooted in 1 Sam. 1. Hannah praises God: "There is none holy like the LORD; there is none besides you; there is no rock like our God" (2:2 ESV). The creative energy that makes anew, out of nothing, is unique to God: this life-giving power belongs to God alone because God draws life from no one, but exists and is life itself. Origen notes that it is odd for Hannah to say, "There is none beside you." Not satisfied with monotheist affirmations like "there is no God except you" or "there is no Creator except you," the song goes further and asserts that "there is none—nothing—beside you," as if only God exists. That seems counterintuitive, since we know that other things do exist. Drawing out the motif of God's unique fertility, Origen told his congregation that Hannah's expression means that

> nothing among the beings that exist has being by nature. You are the only one who is not given being by anyone. All of us, in effect, that is to say the whole of creation, do not exist before being created and it is only through the will of the Creator that we exist. And since there was a time when we were not, it is not quite accurate to say of us that we are. . . . God is the only one who always has being and who has no beginning in being. . . . When Moses wanted to learn from God what his name was, God taught it to him in these terms, "I am Being, that is my name." If there were among creatures any other thing that could receive this designation, the Lord would never have said that this is his own name. He knows that he alone is, while creatures have received being from him. In comparison to the solid body, the shadow is not, and by comparison to fire, smoke is not; . . . in relation to the nature of God, "that which is in the heavens and on the earth, things visible and invisible" are not, but in relation to his will they are that which he has willed them to be, he who made them. (Origen 1986: 140–42)

"The bows of the mighty are broken," says Hannah, "but the feeble bind on strength" (2:4 ESV). The Christian affirmation that God is his own being emerges from believing that God's power is sufficient to make himself humble and to turn the divine humiliation of the incarnation into a triumph. If you grasp how "God has chosen the one who is stupid in the world to confound the wise, and the one who is feeble in the world to confound the one who is strong" (1 Cor. 1:27, author's translation), Origen says, "you will understand how 'the stumbling have girded on strength.' The 'feeble' were the Gentile peoples, since they were 'alien to the covenant' of God [Eph. 2:12]. . . . The 'strength' is thus Christ the 'Lord,' by whom we have been 'girded,' we who were 'strangers to the testament and without God in this world' [2:12]" (1986: 149).

Origin asks whether Hannah's "song" is a prayer. Taken literally, as Origen rightly reads it, it is not actually a prayer: much of it is not addressed to God, but is full of statements about God, addressed to other human beings. Much of the song seems not to be literally a prayer to God, but a directive of how to live before the Almighty. That it is not literally a prayer shows that it is something deeper, an expression of the conversation of Hannah's heart and soul with God, as when, in mute and solitary communion she "poured out [her] soul before the LORD" (1 Sam. 1:15). Hannah's song need not be literally a prayer, Origen says, because Hannah's whole personality and every gesture is a prayer. Paul enjoins us to "pray without ceasing" (1 Thess. 5:17): "You thus see whether all the acts of the one who habitually lives in the service of God, all the gestures and all the words which he does or says before God, do not come back to prayer. If one understands by prayer only that which the world knows by this name, Hannah does not appear to pray in this discourse . . . but if every act of a righteous person who acts according to God and according to the divine commandment is considered as a prayer" then this gesture of Hannah's, too, is a prayer. This is "the lesson that the Psalms give us in the words, 'The lifting up of my hands [is] the evening sacrifice' [Ps. 141:2]" (1986: 129). Hannah herself is a walking epic song.

Episode Five: Worthless Men (1 Sam. 2:12–36)

In 1 Sam. 4 a Philistine army will overrun Shiloh. The prophecy of the anonymous "man of God" (2:27) announces more than the military reversal of the next chapter: the sins of these sons will be paid out in the slow evisceration of Eli's dynasty (Campbell and O'Brien 2000: 224). Shiloh is not the holy pilgrimage shrine it looks like. "The sons of Eli were worthless men" (2:12 ESV). As priests, they were the curators of sacrifices in the temple. They exploited their proximity to the cooked meats, cynically seizing the best of the offering before it had been burned for Yahweh, grabbing the food by force if the "customer" proved obstinate. They were taking "the offering of the LORD with contempt" (2:17 ESV). They were exploiting their position as Aaronide priests to pick up women outside the temple. They also exploited a fact made clear in a subsequent episode: by now, in the time it took for Samuel to grow from babe to "boy" (2:18), Eli is partially sighted or blind. He cannot see what his sons are doing before his eyes, in the temple, but has heard the tale from others: Elkanah tells them, "I hear of your evil dealings from all the people. No, my sons; it is no good report that I hear the people of the LORD spreading abroad" (2:23–24 ESV).

Eli is both judge and priest, as are his sons. The "tribal structure is generalized; in this lies its primitiveness. It lacks an independent economic sector or a separate religious organization, let alone a special political mechanism. In a tribe, these are . . . different *functions* of the same institutions: different things a lineage . . . may do" (Sahlins 1968: 15, emphasis original). Lineage functionalism has, by the end of the Bronze Age, run dry as a transmitter of Yahwistic faith and cult. The revelation received at Sinai must be given a new *modus operandi*. One might think a belief that the future lies with Samuel and the prophets has been grafted into our text (Campbell and O'Brien 2000: 222, 224). But prophet is not set in contrast to priest in this chapter: Samuel looks wholly clerical, the "boy clothed with a linen ephod" (2:18 ESV), and the "man of God" proclaims, not the replacement of sacrificing priests by prophets, but "a faithful priest" (2:35).

The author slips in anachronisms, such as having the sons rendezvous with women "at the tent of meeting" (2:22 ESV). This priestly term updates the scenario to the original audience's frame of reference and makes it easy for a later audience to grasp spontaneously the extent of the misdemeanor. Some propose that not only a "prophetic reform" ideology, but also two further separate documents, anti-Elide material and a Samuel story, were spliced together here. The idea that two distinct documents are interspersed here is based on the narrative about Eli's sons (2:12–17, 22–25, 27–36) being interwoven with the narrative of Samuel and family (2:18–21, 26; 3:1; 3:19–4:1a). This conjecture helps us to notice the simultaneous interplay of different story arcs: first a scene in the temple, with the sons abusing the sacrifice (2:12–17); then the altar boy ministering in his miniature liturgical dress, developing into a domestic scene, with Hannah arriving with Samuel's "robe" and being blessed for further childbearing by Eli (2:18–20); to Ephraim seeing the produce of this blessing (2:21); cutting back to Eli's remonstrating with his sons (2:22–25); and concluding with Samuel maturing "in stature and in favor with the Lord and also with men" (2:26 NIV). Modern media, both radio and television, regularly intersperse developing story arcs. Whether in *The Archers* or *The Wire*, the audience effect of this technique is of a dramatic hyperrealism. Radio and film can do this far more prodigiously than the novel can, just because they are cruder media. Outside scripture, ancient historians like Herodotus eschew it. Their customary preference is for the sustained narrative. It is one of the esthetic features that, by contrast, makes the immediate feel of the Old Testament more simple and primitive, because the narration feels to be moving with the events themselves, rather than making its task to give the audience a masterly overview. The impact is hyperrealistic because, rather than feeling as if they were standing back from and contemplating a finished picture, audiences feel projected into the events of the scenes. The objective realities of the temple misdoings and Samuel's family displace their own act of perceiving them. The author's use of this technique is naturally a hostage to fortune, so far as analysts of the text are concerned, since every scene shift can be ascribed to a different documentary source. The author has laid out these pictures in small progressive pieces in order to achieve documentary realism. What he means to do is contrast the priesthood of Samuel with that of Eli's sons, and as vividly as possible.

Having inverted their proper roles, Eli's sons are antipriests. First Sam. 2:12–36 means to show that the coming Philistine raid and the accompanying slaughter of these local officials is not a random catastrophe in a frontier temple town, but the hand of the Lord's vengeance at work. It is providential. The author's theodicy is clear and straightforward: in his history, "worthless men" like Hophni and Phineas get their deserts. Obedience is also rewarded, here when Elkanah and Hannah visited their son at Shiloh, "Eli would bless Elkanah and his wife, and say, 'May the

LORD give you children by this woman for the petition she asked of the LORD.' So then they would return to their home. Indeed the LORD visited Hannah, and she conceived and bore three sons and two daughters" (2:20–21 ESV). Hannah is requited for her genuine sacrificial offering of Samuel.

The author has a Teiresias figure, a man of God, come forward to deliver the prophetic word of judgment to Eli: "I promised that your house and the house of your father should go in and out before me forever," but now the LORD declares: "Far be it from me, for those who honor me I will honor, and those who despise me shall be lightly esteemed. Behold, the days are coming when I will cut off your strength and the strength of your father's house, so that there will not be an old man in your house" (2:30–32 ESV). The shield of the LORD has been withdrawn and replaced with a sword, turned against them: he will guard "the feet of his faithful ones, but the wicked shall be cut off in darkness, for not by might shall a man prevail. The adversaries of the LORD shall be broken to pieces; against them he will thunder in heaven" (2:9–10 ESV). The prophecy foretells the Philistine assault but also strips this family of its legacy, the Aaronide priesthood. The deaths of Hophni and Phineas will be a prophetic sign of the death sentence on the priesthood of their house: "And this that shall come upon your two sons, Hophni and Phinehas, shall be the sign to you: both of them shall die on the same day" (2:34 ESV). Deuteronomy states that a prophet who really has a message from the Lord is to be recognized by whether what the prophet proclaims comes true (Deut. 18:21–22): the anonymous messenger offers the deaths of Hophni and Phineas as the sign of the truth of his claim that Eli's dynasty is no longer under the divine mercy. Though Deuteronomy had yet to be written down, the culture under scrutiny makes Deuteronomic assumptions as if, for instance, the law existed in oral tradition.

The judgment of dynastic annihilation that the anonymous prophet lays on Eli and his sacrilegious sons expresses the LORD's sovereign refusal to permit blasphemers to defile his holy place. He will not harbor faithless retainers in his temple. The promise is broken. God declares his power to revoke the legacy of priesthood to this branch of the Aaronide priesthood: the promise "that your house and the house of your father should go in and out before me forever" no longer stands.

The severity of the revocation of the legacy reflects the purity of holiness required of God's priests and the distance that this holiness makes between itself and sin. The oracle goes beyond the present case. This is not because the punishment is too extreme to fit the crimes of Hophni and Phineas. No one who saw this story reach its climax on film would think other than that these "worthless men," who turned the nature of a temple on its head and made it serve their own greed and lusts, deserved other than what they get. If they had been stealing and cheating in a workaday enterprise, they would have committed larceny against fellow humans. Precisely because they are priests, their crimes are turned against God. And so Eli tells them that he can't mediate for them, with God: "If someone sins against a man, God will mediate for him, but if someone sins against the LORD, who will mediate for him?" (2:25 ESV). As a local judge, perhaps, a Shilonite "superjudge," Eli can use his discretion in mediating between humans: he can set the divine will for clemency above the human desire for revenge against a fellow human, appealing above man to God. But if the crime is not against a fellow human but against God, not even the superjudge to all Israel can help him, for he cannot appeal "above God to God."

Like the "sin against the Holy Spirit," the crimes of Hophni and Phineas are irreversibly damnable. The oracle seems to speak for more than the cutting off of this one branch of the Aaronide priesthood because the apocalyptic tone of God's judgment fits the extremity of God himself. We see that this is an intolerant God and that this is how he can judge any misdemeanor: "The only one of you whom I shall not cut off from my altar shall be spared to weep his eyes out to grieve his heart, and all the descendants of your house shall die by the sword of men. . . . And I will raise up for myself a faithful priest, who shall do according to what is in my heart and in my mind. And I will build him a sure house, and he shall go in and out before my anointed forever. And everyone who is left in your house shall come to implore him for a piece of silver or a loaf of bread and shall say, 'Please put me in one of the priests' places, that I may eat a morsel of bread'" (2:33, 35–36 ESV). The oracle speaks for more than this local branch of the Aaronide priesthood because it is a reminder of the character of Yahweh, his refusal to cohabit with sin.

First Sam. 2:12–36 contrasts Hophni and Phineas with the virtuous priest, Samuel. The "robe" that he wears will reappear several times in the story, for instance, in the context of the tearing of the kingdom from Saul (15:27–28). In antithesis and parallel to Eli, Samuel also points us toward the monarchy: his role in the story to come will be as the radar for the legitimacy of Israel's kings. The priest of the Lord will elect and deselect Yahweh's kings. As the mouthpiece and delegator of Yahweh's will, obedience is the virtue that is most important in him. Elkanah, Samuel's father, is of the tribe of Aaron, and Samuel is a little ephod-wearing priest. The replacement of the house of Eli with that of Samuel is thus not the end of the Aaronide priesthood as such, but just of Eli's branch. The shift from one branch of Aaron's tribe to another, indicated by the words "I will raise up for myself a faithful priest, who shall do according to what is in my heart and in my mind," was according to Augustine "in a degree fulfilled" in the elevation of Samuel's line and "finally fulfilled" in the eternal priesthood of Christ, "the true priest of the new covenant" (*City of God* 17.5). Because the Old Testament is not just any history but a providential history, what is on one level a self-enclosed narrative about the cultural evolution of Israel is at the same time on the way to a universal narrative about the spiritual transformation of humanity as a whole by Christ. Every step that every part of humanity takes, from the tribal to universal humanism, is summed up in this one story.

Episode Six: The Calling of Samuel (1 Sam. 3)

This story is about vocation or calling. "Vocation" comes from the Latin *voceo* ("to call"): a vocation is not a project I make for myself, but a call to me, from someone else, to which I hear and respond. Vocation results from calling. The lectionary for Second Sunday in Ordinary Time, Year B, unlocks the meaning of Samuel's invocation by pairing it with John 1:35–42, in which Jesus calls Andrew and Peter to be his disciples. Samuel begins to be the person God intends by being called and responding, "Speak, for thy servant heareth" (1 Sam. 3:10). But why is a classic prophetic call narrative used to characterize Samuel, who was hardly a classic prophet, like Isaiah, and what is it doing here, at the outset of Regum, when Samuel was not a king?

For several centuries, the books of Samuel and Kings have been so consistently mined for information about Israel's monarchy that we have learned to identify this section of the Bible as scripture's slice of political history. The early church fathers tend rather to notice ethical points, like Eli's failure to discipline his sons. That focus may be governed by esthetic or textually literal criteria. In fact, 1 Samuel sets the rise of the monarchy in Israel in the context of theological ethics.

Carol Meyers tells us that "it is important that we think of ancient Israel as a monarchy apart from the individuals who first occupied the throne. Particularistic history writing, of which the Bible is a prime example, often ascribes social change to the talent, luck, or whim of a few highly visible leaders. Although the role of individuals in bringing about a royal state and in heading its organizational structures is significant, that role is not necessarily primary. We must set aside the 'great man' notion of the emergence of the Israelite monarchy, as resulting from the charisma of a person and/or the supernatural direction of a deity, in order to examine the social dynamics and environmental features of state formation and organization."[15] This historian is claiming that the originating causes of the monarchy were not primarily individuals, like Samuel, Saul, and David, but rather the general social dynamics of ancient Middle Eastern culture. This is a natural way for a secular historian to consider the matter: the Christian scriptures are not just a prime example of "particularistic history writing," that is, historiography that sees individual persons as the prime agents in history, but rather a main source of this way of understanding human affairs. We find the Old Testament realistic, perhaps truer to life than social science, because it fits our implicit sense that this is the way the world works.

Much in our own history "gives the lie to the determinist and social-scientific . . . philosophy of the modern world, according to which history is 'made' by material conditions and institutions, and is no longer formed by the thoughts, words

---

15. Carol Meyers, "Kinship and Kingship: The Early Monarchy," in *The Oxford History of the Biblical World*, ed. Michael D. Coogan (Oxford: Oxford University Press, 1998), 221–71 at 224–25.

and acts (in sum, by the character: in itself an old-fashioned word, eschewed by political scientists and sociologists) of outstanding men."[16] It's not Christians alone who can see the point of these words, though they were written by a Christian historian. Even where the gospel has not yet been preached, some cultures have glimpsed the significance of the role of individuals in making history. Even after the preaching of the gospel has, as it were, come and gone, in the West, people have a residual feeling for the vocation of persons as the prime movers of history: this is indicated by historical biography remaining a more popular and wider read genre than scientific archeology. A feeling for the significance of personal character in history is why each culture has its heroes and heroines, though some of them have extensive mythical attributes. What such ancient cultures and even our postmodern culture are reaching for, in their intuitive sense that characters are the makers of history, finds its anchor in the biblical teaching that the one God guides history by calling out unique actors to stage a providential history. By dint of his call, Samuel is not just an individual hero, but a prophet, a peculiarly "individual individual." He is an individual's individual, God's prophet.

A culture that is not educated by the literal sense of narratives like 3:4–9 has no means of making sense of the fleeting intuition that it is characters, not conditions and contexts, that make history. Because the yearning for a person-making vocative is thwarted in secular, post-Christian cultures, such societies oscillate between atomism and collectivism in their ethical imperatives, finding it "impossible to achieve a synthesis between the fulfillment of the individual and that of the community."[17] Today, it is usually only those scholars who advertently take up the role of Christian historians, who can intellectually appropriate the perception that historical events are expressions of the agencies and moral characters of particular personas. Most ancient Near Eastern cultures created national records and lists of their kings with their purported achievements. Israel surpassed them in history writing and created, in Regum, the first real long-range historical work because it grasped more deeply than these collectivist cultures the principle that "men are free and responsible moral agents is the fundamental principle of historical thinking: no free will, no history—no history in *our* sense of history."[18]

In the culture out of which ancient Israel sprang the collective had the upper hand, in the shape of the family and tribe. Eli's crime is to have let the domestic collective get the upper hand, putting his sons before God. Eli lacked "the zeal to demand from" his sons "the Lord's vindication" because "he loved them more than the statutes of the Lord," says Isaac of Nineveh (*Ascetical Homilies* 10, in Franke 2005: 211): someone quite different will have to lead Israel to the next stage of its historical evolution. Even before hereditary monarchy, priesthood has become a hereditary office for "Eli's house" (Hackett 1998: 182). In his time, the

16. John Lukacs, *The Duel: The Eighty-Day Struggle between Churchill and Hitler* (New Haven: Yale University Press, 2001), 9.
17. Von Balthasar, "Nine Propositions on Christian Ethics," 103.
18. Lukacs, *Historical Consciousness*, 252, emphasis original.

tribes of Israel were "autonomous entities governed by their lineage heads" but, simultaneously, Eli, "priest of the ark at Shiloh," had come to "exercise sway over a united confederacy." Eli has transmitted his priestly office to his sons, and, for the adopted Samuel, the highest persona in his register is the "big daddy" of the clan, Eli. It is possible that "Eli, as priest and judge, may have designated Samuel his successor in both capacities. . . . In the most chronologically proximate reports, the league labored under a sacral authority" (Halpern 1981: 182–83).

When he is "called" in the night, this adoptive son assumes that the authoritative voice must be that of "father Eli": "And he ran unto Eli, and said, 'Here am I, for thou calledst me.' . . . And the LORD called yet again, 'Samuel.' And Samuel arose and went to Eli, and said, 'Here am I, for thou didst call me.' And he answered, 'I called not, my son; lie down again.' . . . And the LORD called Samuel again the third time. And he arose and went to Eli, and said, 'Here am I, for thou didst call me'" (3:5–8). In order to become a moral individual, a person, Samuel must be called out of the familial collective and enter a direct relationship to God. God does not, here, just call an individual to effect a change in Israel's culture: he creates an individual so to do. Samuel fails to recognize the voice of his God: what he hears, when the Lord Yahweh calls Samuel is, according to philologists, *simuhuil*, that is, "his name is El." El was the God of the fathers, the God, we might say with some African theologians, "of the ancestors," with the proviso that El was the ancestors' *God*, the *God* of Abraham, Isaac, and Jacob, not an ancestral God, a God equivalent to the "ancestral spirits."[19] The biblical Elohim is not altogether different from the tribal "high god" God who is imagined as the human father of the tribe writ spiritual. Small wonder that when the Lord calls "his-name-is-El," Samuel thinks it is father Eli calling. In this call story, "the person Samu-el, a pre-Yahwist shrine [Shiloh], and allegiances that cluster around earlier rituals are all taken over by Yahweh. . . . El and Yahweh are united. A single voice for Yahwism is confirmed" (Flanagan 1988: 256). Only when the Lord calls with a single voice and reveals his unity, and only when the recipients of this revelation absorb this communication of "Who he is," can they become unified individuals, persons who act on history and cocreate it.

The initiation that began when Elkanah and Hannah deposited Samuel in the temple is brought to fruition by God. Rather than being a temple servant, he must say in response to his divine vocation or calling, "Speak, LORD, for thy servant heareth" (3:9). For scripture, the moral subject, like Abraham, the Jewish paradigm of vocation, "is constituted by the call of God and by obedience to his call (Heb. 11:8)."[20] In stories like that of Abraham and Samuel, the scriptures give us this idea of what a moral subject is, and by so doing, they give us a certain understanding of history. Because "biblical ethics is based on the call of the personal God and

19. Temba L. J. Mafico, "The Biblical God of the Fathers and the African Ancestors," in *The Bible in Africa: Transactions, Trajectories, and Trends*, ed. Gerald O. West and Musa W. Dube (Leiden: Brill, 2000), 483.

20. Von Balthasar, "Nine Propositions on Christian Ethics," 89.

man's believing response," biblical history writing created what Carol Meyers terms the "particularistic principle." The idea here, which enabled Israel to begin to rise above the tribal or collectivist principle, is that God's call separates a person from his or her culture, and this break with the internal social dynamic of a culture gives them the spiritual wherewithal to found a genuine community, spreading from and embedded in the work or task that is named in the divine call.

Such characters are made individuals in order to give their lives to their community. This episode opens the way for social rebirth: "The emergence of Samuel, a prophet, a new figure untainted by the old order, dispels the cloud of instability and evil" that Judges has left behind (Campbell and O'Brien 2000: 215). Before it could have kings, Israel must have a prophet to anoint them. As the first prophet to Israel's kings, Samuel's thankless task, inaugurated here, is to repeat God's judgment to priests and kings. He will have to say unwanted words, such as that God "will judge his house for ever for the iniquity which he knoweth: because his sons made themselves vile, and he restrained them not" (3:13). Samuel's vocation is not the expression of his own genius personality: the last of the judges personifies what judging really means by taking an absolute standard, the word of God, as the measure of the justice he metes to human persons. This absolute standard is not a concept of justice, but "the LORD reveal[ing] himself to Samuel in Shiloh by the word of the LORD" (3:21). Absolute justice is not a standard or measure of justice, but its measurer, the Creator of justice. By mediating God's justice to the people, Samuel becomes the measuring rod of integrity in Israel: "All Israel from Dan even to Beer-sheba knew that Samuel was established to be a prophet of the LORD" (3:20).

Since his role is to be a prophet, there is no place in this for Samuel's subjective perceptions. He has objectively to hear God's judging word and objectively to recount it. It seems it would take an extraordinarily harsh personality to tell Eli, his master, that Eli's dynasty is tarnished with unforgivable sin: "I have sworn unto the house of Eli, that the iniquity of Eli's house shall not be purged with sacrifice nor offering for ever" (3:14). But it actually requires a complete absence of self-interest, something greater than simple generosity: "Generosity is a virtue: yet it often means no more than the willingness to give of one's possessions. Magnanimity is both rarer and greater: the capacity of giving of oneself. Magnanimity, too, is often the true source of loyalty."[21] Given away at weaning by Hannah, Samuel is called to a life of self-dispossession. This self-giving or magnanimity not only identifies Samuel as an individual character, but is passed on by him to the people so that Israel became, in its real character, a Samuel-esque people. Social scientists may look in vain in empirical Israel for statistical evidence of the predominance of this trait. Even though scientific historians can easily tabulate that the British Isles were not populated by the cast of *In Which We Serve* in 1942, numbering in fact only 19% allotment diggers, 10% ration-card sellers, 51% black marketers,

---

21. Lukacs, *Duel*, 26.

---

and 20% out-and-out spivs, Britain really became Churchillian, and, analogously, Israel took its real identity from the character given to Samuel at his call. Its real identity is its vocation before God, which it has therefore given to the rest of the world and made it memorable, as a nation that placed politics under divine judgment. The address from God that forms every human's unique personality creates the true, historically creative community: "The call isolates the subject in preparation for this encounter (Abraham must leave clan and homeland), and in facing the call ("Here am I," Gen. 22:1) he is given his mission, which becomes a norm for his conduct henceforth. In the solitary dialogue encounter with God, Abraham, in virtue of his mission, becomes the founder of a community whose laws governing the horizontal relationships all depend, in the biblical testimony, on the founder's or mediator's vertical relationship with God or on God's founding act."[22] The prophet has an isolated role and outline, because he must stand alone, above the community. "As prophet, Samuel is God's medium of communication to Israel (1 Sam 3:20), with an immediacy given to no other since Moses" (Campbell and O'Brien 2000: 215). The Abrahamic model of person formation by divine calling is heightened in the role of the prophet.

The twilight scene in which the call story begins could grace a pre-Raphaelite painting: the lights slowly fading from temple and its environs. First we are shown Eli laying up for the night, sleep gathering in his rheumy eyes: "Eli was laid down in his place, and his eyes began to wax dim, that he could not see" (3:2). The temple is shutting down for the night, and "the lamp of God" is about to be put out "in the temple of the LORD, where the ark of God was, and Samuel was laid down to sleep" (3:3). "The temple of the LORD" makes us think of Solomon's Temple, as yet unbuilt, of course, not of a backwoods temple-shrine in Shiloh. The empirically minded fifth-century Antiochene theologian Theodore of Mopsuestia rightly asks why the psalmist can refer to what is really a tabernacle as a temple and answers that "the tabernacle may be called the temple, the testimony of Kings [i.e., Regum] clearly instructs, since the construction of the temple had not begun at the time": the Shiloh shrine is temple because the ark of the covenant there domiciled in its tabernacle (*Exposition on Psalms* 10, in Franke 2005: 210). Living in the house of the LORD was evidently taken literally: because it characterizes their sleep positions by reference to the temple lamps, we can see that Eli is sleeping in an antechamber to the temple, and Samuel perhaps before the ark. The pre-Raphaelites would enjoy illustrating this because it is lucidly allegorical, representing by the state of visionless sleep that the people are not awake to the presence of God, that "the word of the LORD was precious [or sparse]; there was no open vision" (3:1). The divine call comes when, at a real and spiritual moment of twilight, "the word of the LORD" is sparse and the light of "open vision" has almost been quenched in the land. The priest himself, the obvious recipient of the call, has become spiritually sluggish (Eli's "eyes began to wax dim, that he could not see"; 3:2). The temple

22. Von Balthasar, "Nine Propositions on Christian Ethics," 90.

light is about to be dimmed: "And ere the lamp of God went out in the temple of the LORD" (3:3); then, as the unwitting prophet-to-be is "laid down to sleep" (3:4), God's word strikes. God's word is so much an unknown word, a new sign, that neither the boy nor the priest his "father" spontaneously recognize it.

Samuel's first task, of telling Eli the divine punishment for failing to check his sons, typifies his role throughout 1 Samuel. Over and again, Samuel will be compelled to deliver unwelcome oracles. Today, he is derided by many for his apparent cruelty to Saul, the king whose legitimacy Samuel is ordered by God to withdraw. Those scholars determined on taking Saul as a tragic figure set up Samuel as his tormentor. Even sympathetic readers will find it difficult to resonate with the older Samuel, who coldly hacks a living Amalekite king to pieces (15:33). When Samuel "told [Eli] every whit, and hid nothing from him" (3:18), we get a taste of the mettle of this prophet. Like a child, he repeats the Lord's words, word for word, because they are the Lord's words: "And Samuel grew, and the LORD was with him, and did let none of his words fall to the ground" (3:19). Samuel does not act like this because like some creative genius or great man he has an inbuilt, insuperable integrity that enables him so to behave. In fact, "Samuel feared to show Eli the vision" (3:15). If we read those later deliveries of harsh oracles in this light, we know that Samuel may not have been temperamentally cut out for this role. Eli, the surrogate father, has to encourage the boy to enter his harsh mission: "I pray thee hide it not from me: God do so to thee, and more also, if thou hide anything from me of all the things that he said unto thee" (3:17). Eli helps Samuel to become the kingmaker and king-unmaker he will later be. Like Peninnah, he is necessary to the full drama. Eli selflessly prompts Samuel to take up the mission he will give to others. Unlike some of the kings he foreshadows, Eli is not a hostile and unwilling recipient of the prophetic judgment, but insists on its accurate delivery.

Without its prophetic kingmakers and king-unmakers, its inspired denouncers of the deeds of kings, Israel's monarchy would have been indistinguishable from dozens of other ancient Near Eastern kingships, great and small. It was the theological and ethical imperative that—by its resounding negatives, prohibitions, and condemnations—made Israel's history creative. It is characters in the role typified by Samuel who made Israel's history more stimulating than the monarchies of the Tiglath-pilesers and Merneptahs of the ancient world. The first two books of Regum are named for Samuel because he was called and named by God for the task of telling God's truth to kings.

SERIES TWO

THE CARNIVAL OF THE ARK

1 Samuel 4–7

The end of the Late Bronze Age and beginning of the Iron Age (ca. 1200–1000 BC), in which 1 Samuel is set, was an era of the razing of cities by fire-bearing armies and of reurbanization. When in around 700 BC Hesiod drew up the classical declinist survey of human civilization, from Gold to Silver to Bronze to his own Iron Age, he interposed the Heroic Age between Bronze and Iron. After the men of Gold, Silver, and Bronze, "Zeus son of Cronos created yet another" race, Hesiod claims, "a fourth . . . juster and better, a divine race of heroes, who are called demi-gods, the earlier race upon the boundless earth. They were killed by evil war and terrible battle, some at seven-gated Thebes, . . . others were brought in ships over the great gulf of the sea to Troy for the sake of Helen of the beautiful hair."[1] Hesiod placed the Heroic Age at the height of Mycenaean culture, between 1400 and 1200 BC, where Homer set the Trojan War, in the *Iliad*. Hesiod had to break his esthetic sequence for the sake of known historical fact, since Greek culture had reached the first of its great heights in the thirteenth-century Heroic culture of Mycenae. Homer's tragic epic has its foundation in facts. The culture the *Iliad* describes was destroyed by raiding maritime warriors, the Sea Peoples. The Hittite capital Hattusas was also toppled, as were great cities in Ugarit, Canaan, and Cyprus: the raiding immigrants were drawn to the eastern Mediterranean by its wealth. The migration avalanche unsettled older civilizations: "Contemporary

1. Hesiod, *Works and Days*, cited in C. M. Bowra, *Homer* (London: Duckworth, 1972), 79.

Egyptian records speak of a dangerous threat by the 'Sea-peoples,' to whom they also ascribe the destruction of Hattusas." The Sea Peoples mounted a concerted attack across the eastern Mediterranean seaboard and made inroads into Asia Minor.[2] From a Homeric perspective, the Sea Peoples were bastard Mycenaeans: these denizens of the outlying Mycenaean culture of Anatolia cut the high culture of Mycenaean Greece down to islands of aristocratic homesteaders, described in the *Odyssey* as seagirt and surrounded by barbarism.

The archeological record tells of the demise of Bronze Age cultures—Mycenae, the Egyptian New Kingdom, and Hittite Anatolia—and the dispersal of peoples that had lost their territories. Tribes were on the move: the Sea Peoples emigrated from Greece, transposed their Mycenaean culture to southern Canaan, and transmuted into the biblical Philistines (McNutt 1990: 145). Hesiod used Iron to designate the lowest stage in cultural decline, because its use was last discovered and because wrought iron "lacked the warm, lustrous beauty of bronze."[3] It was useful, but not beautiful like the men of the Bronze Age: Homer clads his heroes in bronze.[4]

The use of iron may have passed at this era from the Hittites in Anatolia to the Philistines, now domiciled in southern Canaan.[5] Reurbanization followed upon mass destruction and mass emigration, preparing the ground for the rise of states, like that of Israel. The appropriation of iron as the commonplace weapon in Palestine coincides with Israel's political transition from the tribal leadership to monarchy (McNutt 1990: 209).

A symbol of divine approbation that emerges from this history is victory in battle. The premonarchic era as a whole is not a Heroic Age for our author, but the books of Joshua, Judges, and 1 Samuel are peopled with heroes, men and women who illuminate dark times. "Hero" in Greek originally meant "warrior," and the values of a heroic culture are prowess in war and honor.[6] The author is describing a heroic culture, with its own objective social values.

The oracle of doom of 1 Sam. 2–3 is carried out with an unexpected twist. A background character takes center stage: the protagonist is the ark alongside which Samuel slept. This bonsai temple had been constructed on the Lord's specifications (Exod. 25–27); it had been carried through the wilderness (Num. 10:35–36); it was sacred to Israel because it contained the tables of stone on which the finger of God had written the law (Exod. 31:18; 32:16, 19; 34:1). As the commandment bearer, the ark is the presence of the Lord. To go into battle without it

---

2. Joachim Latacz, *Homer: His Art and His World*, trans. James P. Holoka (Ann Arbor, MI: University of Michigan Press, 1998), 38–39.

3. J. D. Muhly, R. Maddin, T. Stech, and E. Özgen, "Iron in Anatolia and the Nature of the Hittite Iron Industry," *Anatolian Studies* 35 (1985): 67–84 at 68.

4. Bowra, *Homer*, 47.

5. Mendenhall 1973: 146–47 makes a claim for the importance of iron to the Philistine advance. McNutt 1990: 133–34, 138–40, 152–53 disputes this.

6. M. I. Finley, *The World of Odysseus* (London: Chatto & Windus, 1956), 125.

was to advance into defeat (Num. 14:44) (Hackett 1998: 209). In 1 Sam. 4 the Israelites carry this "hand" of God into battle against the Philistines. The author dryly indicates why the stratagem is a nonstarter: "Hophni and Phinehas were there with the ark of the covenant of God" (4:4).

When, as foretold (2:30–31; 3:12–15), Israel's armies are overmastered, the Philistines seized the ark. Kidnapping the cult objects of a conquered enemy was commonplace in the ancient Near East. Taking these trophies meant gaining the power of their gods. The Philistines think they have commandeered Israel's deity for themselves: "like divine images in Mesopotamia," the ark could become "one of the spoils of war" because "such losses can be interpreted as the defeat of one's own god by the enemy's god." The image was abducted to the victor's temple. When it involves interplay between God and pagan peoples and their deities, biblical comedy takes the form of satire. Such comic scenes contrast the sovereignty of the biblical God with the limping impotence of the fertility gods of Israel's neighbors. By satirizing them from on high, the drama makes its villains the object of laughter. Philistia in possession of the ark becomes a comic figure. Set against "the ark of the covenant of the LORD of hosts" (4:4), Philistia's fertility gods look ridiculous. The captured ark is no trophy wife; it proves a positive menace to its captors. Because the ark is the monstrance of the Lord and the cult images of the pagans represent their deities, the ark's "capture and deportation set the stage for a 'battle' between Yahweh and the Philistine god Dagon" (Hackett 1998: 209–11).

Why did a dozen tribes think they had a shared identity? That it answers this question is a strong argument for the existence of a premonarchic tribal league. The league had a religious character, since what united the Israelite tribes "was their coalescence as 'the people of YHWH' (Num. 11:29; 17:6; Judg. 5:11, 13 [cf. 20:2]; Zeph. 2:1) . . . not to mention all those passages where YHWH refers to Israel as 'my people.'" One can infer from 1 Samuel that, above its lineage heads, Israel had a sacral, supratribal leadership: the house of Eli had some kind of headship (Halpern 1981: 181–82). It took the lead in war time, when the tribes had to act in concert.

Our author's preferred designation for Israel as a whole is "the people of God." He likes to describe the relationship between God and people as a "covenant." He conceives of the affiliation between God and people as a legal, covenantal bond: "This is shown by his . . . use of the term 'ark of the covenant of Yahweh' to describe the ark." The ark is "the repository of the autograph" of the Decalogue, the "original form of God's law."[7] The covenant is a deal: "Yahweh will protect them . . . and they in return will not worship other gods" (Hackett 1998: 211).

Twenty years after the end of the "carnival of the ark," we observe that the original "owners" of the ark are no less pagan than the defeated Philistine raiders:

7. Martin Noth, *The Deuteronomistic History*, trans. Jane Doull and John Barton (Sheffield: JSOT Press, 1981), 90, 92.

"And Samuel said to all the house of Israel, 'If you are returning to the LORD with all your heart, then put away the foreign gods and the Ashtaroth from among you and direct your heart to the LORD and serve him only, and he will deliver you out of the hand of the Philistines'" (7:3 ESV). Ashtaroth were figurines of the goddess known in Canaan as "Asherah" and in Egypt as "Qudshu." The headpiece of both queens is a hathor wig, worn by aristocratic Egyptian and Canaanite womenfolk. Down to the seventh century BC, stylish Judean ladies in Jerusalem were buried resting with their heads against stone copies of the "bouffant wig" of "the queen of heaven" (Jer. 7:18) (Dever 2002: 180). If the first audience of 1 Sam. 4–7 laughed at the ark's escapades, they knew they were telling jokes against themselves. The author was not satirizing a cult of which the Israelites could throw up their hands and feign ignorance.

Episode One: Lost Inheritance (1 Sam. 4:1–11)

First Sam. 4:1–11 is set at Ebenezer, where the Israelite army is "encamped" (4:1 ESV): launching their attack from Aphek, the Philistines spring into Ebenezer with devastating effect. This victory at Ebenezer, thought to have taken place around 1050 BC, brought the Philistines within a day's march of Shiloh. Recent archeological excavations by Israel Finkelstein at Shiloh have borne out the work done there by W. F. Albright earlier in the century: like Troy, Shiloh was razed about 1050 BC. As we saw in the story of Hannah and Elkanah, Shiloh had been a great eleventh-century pilgrimage center: its destruction echoes centuries later in the Psalms (e.g., Ps. 78:60–64), Prophets (e.g., Jer. 7:12), and here. Between 1050 BC and 1000 BC, the Philistines were at the height of their dominance in Palestine (Stager 1998: 170).

Within scripture, this episode follows the campaign history of Judges, in which the Philistine threat to the Israelite settlers was never neutralized. The story reverts to the cyclic process seen throughout Judges: apostasy followed by subjugation to a Canaanite tribe. In each of the six apostasy/oppression cycles of Judges, a charismatic figure emerged to defeat the oppressor: Othniel, Ehud, Deborah, Gideon, and Jephthah each repel a Canaanite tribe. Samson, sixth in the series, targets the Philistines. They take setbacks from him, but are not put out of action. First Sam. 4–7 presents Samuel as the new judge:[8] "And the word of Samuel came to all Israel" (4:1) indicates his call to arms. Samuel disappears after 4:1, giving place to the ark story, reappearing only in 1 Sam. 7, as a military savior figure.

With its initial military rout, comeback, and downfall, the episode is a tightly rhymed drama. The first Philistine assault issues in the death of "four thousand" Israelite soldiers "on the field of battle" (4:2 ESV). The preliminary reversal has

8. David Jobling, *The Sense of Biblical Narrative: Structural Analyses in the Hebrew Bible* (Sheffield: JSOT Press, 1986), 47–49.

an obvious solution: "Let us bring the ark of the covenant of the LORD here from Shiloh, that it may come among us and save us from the power of our enemies. So the people sent to Shiloh and brought from there the ark of the covenant" (4:3–4 ESV). The ark is given its full title—"the ark of the covenant of the LORD of hosts, who is enthroned on the cherubim" (4:4 ESV)—out of respect for the seat of the Decalogue, but also to create the dramatic anticipation that the hand of providence now rides with the Israelites. The "elders," that is, the lineage heads, "call for YHWH's presence": "Let us bring the ark of the covenant of the LORD here" (4:3 ESV). God's presence "is provided, in the form of the ark, by Eli's sons (4:5–11)" (Halpern 1981: 181). The elders think that once the ark is "come among us" Israel will be "save[d] . . . from the power of our enemies" (4:3 ESV). In our unsacramental culture, we naturally read their hope in the ark's prowess moralistically and sarcastically. We imagine that, with this pragmatic call for backup, the elders must have osmotically absorbed from Canaanite culture a magical idea of the relationship of their deity to his domicile. But in fact, the elders had every reason to think that the ark is literally the presence of the Lord, and the subsequent chapters bear out their faith in its power. The author is not satirizing the elders' reckoning. He doesn't intend his readers to shake their heads in disapproval of their superstition. In Judges, the conquest of the land is initiated by priests carrying the ark across the Jordan; in Josh. 6 Jericho falls when the people march around it carrying the ark. The elders' decision to "bring the ark of the covenant of the LORD here from Shiloh" (4:3 ESV) is a strategy of good faith, not magical superstition.

The next sentence dampens our hopes: "And the two sons of Eli, Hophni and Phinehas, were there with the ark of the covenant of God" (4:4 ESV). The battle at Ebenezer is lost, not because of the elders' supposing that the ark would automatically save them, but because of the impious behavior of Eli's sons (Van Seters 1983: 348). For the reader, it is human to hope that the presence of the ark will override that of Hophni and Phinehas. This raises the tension. The Israelites give an earth-shaking shout of triumph, and the Philistines squeal in terror: "Nothing like this has happened before!" (4:7). As the sons of Eli, the priest-*sophet* (Ishida 1977: 33), Hophni and Phinehas were the ark's elite guard, cultically qualified to close in around the great wooden shrine. Hophni and Phinehas died defending "their" ark.

This neat story indicates that the ark is the physical manifestation of a conditional covenant between God and "the people of God." God is absolutely faithful to them insofar as they, in turn, are faithful to God. He does not withdraw his presence from the ark, but he can withhold the allegiance to Israel that the covenant entails. As Theodoret of Cyr says, when "God gave the ark to the Philistines . . . it was sinful men they had conquered and not God" (*On Divine Providence* 10.49–50, in Franke 2005: 212). The people are God's people only when they turn in covenant obedience to him: "God is nobody's property." For the author and for the Old Testament as a whole, "the term 'people of God' does not simply mean Israel in the sense in which it is open to empirical observation and discovery. Purely empirically no people is the people of God. . . . Israel is described by the term people of God to the extent that it is turned toward the Lord, . . . in the act of . . . transcending itself which alone turns it into what it is not of itself."[9] As in Hannah's prayer, Yahweh is demonstrating that "I will be who I will be" is his name: neither God nor the ark of the covenant belong to Israel; Israel is God's people only insofar as it keeps its side of the covenant.

Episode Two: The Glory Has Departed (1 Sam. 4:12–22)

Hebrew poetry often uses doublets, in which the second line repeats and exaggerates the content of the first line. Such parallelism turns up in Songs, Psalms, and prophetic oracles.[10] First Sam. 4 does something analogous in a narrative form. Where its first half gave an overview of the drama of the ark, the second half zooms in on one person's reaction to the loss. This episodic parallelism intensifies the significance of the loss. Whether or not the history in Joshua–2 Kings was written to be read aloud, the paradigm of ancient religious literature was the heard rather than the written word, and the live audience rather than the silent reader: "Religious readers, paradoxically, need not know how to read."[11] Because they have a listening rather than a reading audience in view, ancient religious literatures are repetitive. Recasting narratives or teachings in varied forms ensures that the penny drops into the memory: "The traditional texts from Israel and Mesopotamia are full of the stylistic devices of oral performance such as rhythm, repetition, stock epithets, standard phrases, and plots consisting of interrelated but relatively independent episodes." The "oral delivery of the texts determined their style," since "texts were," historically, "an extension . . . of the oral performers" (Toorn 2007: 14). Nineteenth-century novelist Émile Zola claimed that he used repetition because it "strengthens its unity. The device is somewhat akin to the motifs in Wagner" (quoted in Eslinger 1983: 61–76). Making scenes and episodes partially mirror each other gives the narrative its memorable rhythmic coherence.

The narrator has told the same story twice, in 4:1–11 and 4:12–22, once showing the big picture of the battle and then showing its effects in Shiloh. A basic principle of the religious mind is analogy, a sense that the world has a God-given order. The premodern mind is religious in that broad sense, whether or not its artifacts are deliberate religious writing. The word "analogy" is abstract: what the religious mind experiences is a sense of architectural order in the physical

---

9. Joseph Ratzinger, *Church, Ecumenism, and Politics: New Essays in Ecclesiology*, trans. Robert Nowell and Frideswide Sandeman (New York: Crossroad, 1988), 18–19.

10. Robert Alter, *The Art of Biblical Poetry* (New York: Basic Books, 1983).

11. Paul J. Griffiths, *Religious Reading: The Place of Reading in the Practice of Religion* (Oxford: Oxford University Press, 1999), 40.

world and in human events. Thus, for Herodotus, "there is a balance between the continents of Asia and Europe," and the "Persian Wars may . . . be understood as a violation of this balance, which is then set right by the gods." A simple means of expressing a sense of balance and symmetry is repetition. So "Herodotus repeats similar events and episodes; these are associated with one another by analogy rather than arranged in logical or temporal sequence." Likewise, "the biblical authors prefer to place similar episodes in a series" (Van Seters 1983: 34, 39). Any reader hearing 1 Samuel in a religious setting or reading it privately out of curiosity can pick up implicit as well as explicit cues that nature and history have an architectural order: our author expresses his faith in analogy by his repetitions, just as an ancient architect would.

One cue that the original listeners would have picked up was the Benjamite, one of Israel's crack troops. As left-handed wielders of the sling, the Benjamites were Israelite "military specialists"; deployed as infantry in the hill country, "such warriors . . . enjoyed tremendous prestige among the armies of the tribes" (Halpern 1996: 43). The symbolic value of a Benjamite fugitive is, as in a movie of the dying days of World War II, having a garrison light upon a fleeing S.S. man, "with his clothes torn and with dirt on his head" (4:12 ESV). The bedraggled Benjamite indicates that the army is a write-off.

We wait to hear the news in Eli's ears. The narrative keeps its auditors in suspense, identifying with Eli's tense expectation. The messenger, dirtied by battle and flight, runs straight past the blind Eli, waiting at the gate, and on into the city. The townsfolk in Shiloh hear of the disaster before "blind Eli keeping watch" (Polzin 1989: 57). The dramatic potential of scenes in which a fearfully anticipated messenger slowly unravels an unwanted truth has been exploited from *Oedipus Rex* to the Vietnam movie *We Were Soldiers* (2002). Eli has been "enthroned" "on his seat" (4:13 ESV) in judgment at the gate for forty years. He is the personage to whom the news should have been unfolded first. The wait for the messenger to deliver the report diminishes him from *sophet*-priest to elderly man. Its import is filtered to the unseeing man, through the "uproar" (4:14). When the messenger finally notices him, the delivery is drawn out, with the messenger's self-identification: "I am he who has come from the battle; I fled from the battle today." Eli cannot see his parlous condition, so the messenger identifies himself as a runaway. The unseeing Eli asks the fugitive, "How did it go, my son?" (4:16).

Modern literary and theological exegetes are increasingly disinclined to read the Old Testament history cycle as a straightforward moral parable, with good guys and bad guys, and increasingly inclined to compare the Old Testament figures and scenes to counterparts in Greek tragedy. This helps us to appreciate more of the subtlety and beauty of the text than the moralizations of a simple homily or some kinds of conservative biblical exegesis might do. There is a kinship to the "messenger bringing news of disaster" scenes in Greek tragedy in this episode. Eli's character deepens as the gulf between status and reality widens, with his increasing blindness: first misinterpreting Hannah's prayer, then having to learn from gossip what his sons are doing under his nose, and now literally sightless in Shiloh. We have watched him become the impotent, aged man he now is. It is important, though, not to estheticize Eli's authentic pathos. Like the protagonists of Greek tragedy and like all fallen human beings, he has a flaw. The Old Testament doesn't just give wooden moral lessons, but that should not make us forget that its deep esthetic wealth is largely directed to exhibiting an ethical providence in history. Eli has come to this pass because he lacked insight and failed as a father. As Caesarius of Arles sternly attests, Eli's manner of death expressed God's judgment: "He fell backwards from his stool and died of a broken neck, and his name was blotted out of the book of life, because he did not punish his sons with great severity" (Sermon 5, in Franke 2005: 213).

The point of this tale is not esoteric but universally human, and that belongs to its theology. Hannah, Elkanah, and Peninnah went on pilgrimage to Shiloh because it was the central shrine in Israel. In order "to cope with the most serious" military "crisis that they had ever experienced," Israel's tribes had formed a league, centered on Shiloh, the ark-temple. Though the "elders of the tribes collectively conducted the military operations, while Eli remained at Shiloh (4:3)," Eli had risen to a great status: "It is very likely that he was appointed as leader by the confederation, and at the same time, his office of *sophet* was recognized, presumably, to be as hereditary as the priesthood. . . . This was an attempt to establish a stable leadership and replace the spontaneous charismatic leader by a hereditary priestly one" (Ishida 1977: 33). In their rise, Eli and his house had been guilty of overreach, or what the ancient Greeks called hubris: by failing to discipline his sons, Eli has acted as if the familial claim to ark guardianship was a given. The "man of God" who prophesied the end of the Elide dynasty specifically accused Eli of hubris, of setting himself in his sons above God: "Why then do you scorn my sacrifices and my offerings that I commanded, and honor your sons above me by fattening yourselves on the choicest parts of every offering of my people Israel?" (2:29 ESV). In the context of his responsibility to the ark, to "punish his sons with great severity" (using Caesarius of Arles's phrase) would have been an act of humility. Knowing a bit about the historical backstory helps us to recognize that the fall of the house of Eli is a sufficiently serious matter to call for a theodicy, an explanation of God's justice. In its little way, it's like the fall of the house of Agamemnon, as Aeschylus depicts it, occasioned by the father's hubris. Hubris is a lack of balance, because the proud man overestimates his place in the scheme of things. Balance in the moral order is restored by retribution: "Like Herodotus, the Old Testament exhibits a dominant concern with the issue of divine retribution for unlawful acts as a fundamental principle of historical causality. Human responsibility and divine justice are frequently stated themes. . . . For both, history is theodicy" (Van Seters 1983: 39–40). Aeschylus and Herodotus have a similar touch to our author, a kindred esthetic of divine justice, which reminds us of the basic humanity of his history, its moral simplicity and universality.

For the ancient Egyptians, the word *akh* means both "beneficial" and "glorious," with a spectrum of meaning, "reaching from earth to heaven, with functional value at one end and supernal brightness at the other."[12] *Kabod* in the Old Testament is similarly polysemic in meaning and analogous in its referents. It can mean "plump," "prosperous," or "commanding." If Judg. 3 is to be believed, Moabite kings were both fat and commanding. As a Polynesian tribesman told an importunate anthropologist, "Can't you see he's a chief. See how big he is!" (Sahlins 1968: 26–27). Hebrew *kabod* ("glory") can refer to both human and divine glory. *Kabod* is a name for God; lower down the scale of analogous meanings, it can mean a "weighty" person, like a king; still lower, it can simply mean "heavy" (the English word "heavy" has a similar connotation in colloquial speech). *Kabod* takes a human quality we can appreciate on a visible, sensible level and applies it to God. In our analogical religious language, wise Christians never cease to be tribesmen. Because its earthly connotation is a quality the human eye can appreciate, when *kabod* is applied to God, we cannot "separate the concept of 'glory' from an idea of the visibility—visible, indeed, to the senses—of the divinity of God" (von Balthasar 1983–91: 7.357). The *kabod* of the Lord is materially recognizable in the ark. Because the author uses it in positive and negative senses (Polzin 1989: 46), the word *kabod* can be freighted with irony. When Eli tips "backward" off his judgment throne "by the side of the gate," his obesity kills him: "His neck was broken and he died, for the man was old and heavy [*kabod*]" (4:18 ESV).

This half of the story is told from the perspective of its impact on Eli. The breathless Benjamite tells him the worst of it last, after the Philistine victory and the death of his sons: "Israel has fled before the Philistines, and there has also been a great defeat among the people. Your two sons also, Hophni and Phinehas, are dead, and the ark of God has been captured" (4:17 ESV). His family line is explicitly described as surviving the death of the two sons: Eli was waiting for news of the ark. The reason given for the blind judge's vigil is that "his heart trembled for the ark of God" (4:13 ESV). The ark is the great responsibility of Eli's house, and it has come to harm. The theological meaning of *kabod* is spelled out in the final verses: When she hears of the catastrophe, Eli's daughter-in-law goes in labor and names her son Ichabod (*i-kabod*), meaning "the glory has departed from Israel" (4:22 ESV). The "man of God" prophesied, not that the death of Eli's sons would be the end of his dynasty, but that their passing "on the same day" would be a "sign" of its coming termination (2:34 ESV) (Campbell and O'Brien 2000: 224). His daughter-in-law does not greet the news that "you have borne a son" to carry on the line as a recompense for the loss of the father: "She did not answer or pay attention" (4:20 ESV). Ichabod is nothing to her. He no more stands for new life than a leaf on a dying tree. Ichabod is born into the loss of inheritance, a survivor in a dead dynasty.

12. John A. Wilson, *The Culture of Ancient Egypt* (Chicago: University of Chicago Press, 1951), 68.

Episode Three: Warts and All (1 Sam. 5)

In the 1180s BC some of the Sea Peoples emigrated from Mycenaean Anatolia and resettled en masse on the southeast coast of Canaan. As ship after ship deposited its "Philistine" immigrants, the incomers drove out the original Canaanite seafront dwellers. The invaders came overland as well as by sea (Mendenhall 1973: 146). The spoor of their conquest is found in the destruction layers of numerous Late Bronze Age Canaanite cities. Having occupied a territory of 380 square miles in southeast Canaan, they created five major strongholds: Ashdod, Ashkelon (their seaport), Gezer, Gath, and Ekron. These five cities, all of which appear in 1 Samuel, were the Philistine Pentapolis, ruled by five Philistine lords (Hebrew *seren*). Philistine territory is recognizable today by its distinctive pottery, of the Mycenaean type. The Philistines may reasonably be conceived as the artists of ancient Canaan. They were never stronger than in 1050–1000 BC (Stager 1998: 152–62). The makers of pottery and of goddess statues that we would regard as charming, if they turned up in Anatolian Mycenae, became the quintessential bad guys of the Old Testament history. Here the Mycenaean esthetes degenerate into "terrorists raiding Israelite settlements."[13] Three of the Pentapolis are mentioned in 1 Sam. 5: Ashdod, near the northern coast of their seafronted dominion (5:1, 3, 5, 6 [referring to the city's coasts], 7), Gath (5:8), and Ekron (5:10), a smaller city twelve miles inland from Ashdod.

The demonstration of the Lord's power over these invincibles is comedic. Comedy can gravitate heavenward, but also downward. The Bible has human heroes and heroines, and their successes generate an atmosphere of comedy: the inspired flight of these comic heroes takes them *upward* against all the odds and the obstacles. But because "there is none besides" this God (2:2), when God is the sole actor, the progress meets no real obstacles. Because God is "enthroned above the cherubim" (2 Kgs. 19:15 NRSV), his movement is a descent upon the earth: "He bowed the heavens also, and came down" (2 Sam. 22:10) from on high. When the comedy is driven by God, then, a satirical bite is taken out of a pagan figure of fun. As Theodoret of Cyr says, "Dagon who was adored as God by them . . . was made to fall before the ark, and God prepared to stage a spectacle for the spectators, so that the Philistines might perceive the difference between false god and true God" (*On Divine Providence* 10.50–51, in Franke 2005: 215). An infernal comedy ensues, in which the cult image of Dagon and so the Philistines themselves are demolished by the unabductable ark.

First Sam. 1–3 used the literary technique of interspersed story arcs. First Sam. 4–6 shifts to epical, sustained narrative. So commentators suppose that the ark stories in 1 Sam. 4–6 must comprise a distinct block of materials (Campbell and O'Brien 2000: 226). First Sam. 1–3 has an inward, up-close focus. Since 1 Sam.

13. Carol Meyers, "Kinship and Kingship: The Early Monarchy," in *The Oxford History of the Biblical World*, ed. Michael D. Coogan (Oxford: Oxford University Press, 1998), 238.

4–7 as a whole turns to the outside realm, the Philistines, it is not surprising that the viewer moves from the short-range to wide-angled, long-range, and sustained shots. Surveying its foes from a geographical and religious distance, 1 Sam. 4–6 offers light relief. The judges were sometimes tricksters, masking their military weakness behind deceptive displays, and the ark is the trickster itself, unmasking the actual weakness of the Philistines. Whereas the human judges threw wool over their foes' eyes, with left-handed Ehud's hidden dagger, Gideon's trumpets, and Samson's riddles (Judg. 3; 7; 14), what makes fools of the Philistines here is their own blindness. Only an epical stance, with the satirist standing outside the events, can convey the comedy of uncovered delusion.

Stories don't always make overt cognitive moral judgments, like "this is a bad person" or "this is a good person doing something wrong." Equally important in storytelling is inclining the audience spontaneously to side against a person or their actions by making us laugh at them. Making an action or a character risible is an affective way of guiding an audience to an implicit, precognitive moral judgment against them. It's as well to keep the precognitive sense in mind, when stressing the moral point of the story, because, when one's mind wanders back to what is literally happening here, it is inescapably ridiculous. Black or satirical comedy makes an opponent comical by showing how empty their self-constructions are, from the outside. The false assumption here is that the ark is a tame cult image to go on the temple shelf alongside the fertility god Dagon. The ark is named differently from the previous episode. Among the Israelites, the ark is "the ark of the covenant of the LORD of hosts, who is enthroned on the cherubim" (4:5 ESV), the manifestation of the covenant. Among the Philistines, though, it is "the ark of the God of Israel" (5:7, 8, 11), "revealing the author's sensitivity for the appropriateness of the terminology he employs" (Van Seters 1983: 350). The Israelites and the Philistines have opposite connections to the ark, and the lessons they learn from it are diametrically opposite, though not in contradiction. The Israelites should know that the ark does not represent their property rights in the Lord of the covenant, and the message they get is losing it. Conversely, the Philistine ark-nappers get their "come-downance" in a media neatly accommodated to their spiritual horizons: if they thought the ark was a magical trophy, let them see some magic! The ark does not alter its identity: it comes among the Philistines as a majestic charismatic warrior.

First Sam. 5–6 is a story of magical powers got out of hand. Having left the ark for its first night in the temple of Dagon, in Ashdod, the Philistines scuttle back, "early on the morrow," and to their consternation—"behold"—"Dagon was fallen upon his face to the earth before the ark of the LORD." What a coincidence! So "they took Dagon, and set him in his place again" (5:3). By first light the next morn, the magic has been reiterated, with embellishments: "Behold, Dagon was fallen upon his face to the ground before the ark of the LORD." This time, the symbolism of Dagon's obsequy to the ark cannot be discounted as an accident, for the image is not just bowed flat before the Lord, but reduced to a "stump," like a doll with its arms and legs torn off: "The head of Dagon and both the palms of his hands were cut off upon the threshold; only the stump of Dagon was left to him" (5:4). In a mocking etiological epigram, the narrator comments that the ground on which the broken limbs had sprawled was henceforth sacred and therefore taboo: "Therefore neither the priests of Dagon, nor any that come into Dagon's house, tread on the threshold of Dagon in Ashdod unto this day" (5:5).

False self-constructions cannot hold up against itchy hemorrhoids in one's private parts. The smiting and destruction of "the hand of the LORD" (5:6) results in bum-warts. Dispatching the curse-working ark from Ashdod to another Philistine city does not lift the strong magic. Rather, this Philistine nimbyism off-loads the mockery onto the men of Gath. The people of Gath are rewarded for their openhandedness with genital warts. News of the disastrous consequences of harboring the magic trophy has spread: when the Philistines try to haul the ark into Ekron, the inhabitants refuse it permission to land, crying out in fear: "They have brought about the ark of the God of Israel to us, to slay us and our people." The narrator describes a plague of genital warts, but the voices of the victims put it more expressively as slaughter. No one escapes: "The men that died not were smitten with the haemerrhoids" (5:12). An infernal comedy often delivers one-to-one comeuppance to its figure of fun. That is what happens with the punishments meted out in Dante's *Inferno*.

We find the stories in 1 Sam. 5–6 puzzling. Once we get our heads around the esthetics of the story and place it in the genre of satirical comedy, we are still far from assent to the truth or even the goodness of the outbreak of the miraculous that occurs in 1 Sam. 5–6. In defending the reality of the miracles of scripture, John Henry Newman agrees with David Hume in this much, that an authentic miracle would be one that tallies with what we know by reason of the God who creates nature and human morality. Within the "system of Providence as a whole," he argues, a miracle is not so much an anomalous "disruption" of the system as a whole as it is a "deviation . . . for the sake of the superior system"; Newman is picturing God's intentions in nature, as subsidiary parts within the higher system of God's intentions in morality, which in turn subserve the divine intentions in revealing himself to and saving the human race. In the Old Testament, the purpose of God's extraordinary intervention in nature is "to confirm the natural evidence of one God, the Creator of all things, to display His attributes and will . . . and to enforce the obligation of religious observances, and the sinfulness of idolatrous worship."[14] These ark miracles exhibit the nullity of Dagon alongside the power of Yahweh.

Our bafflement could be exacerbated by Newman's explanation. He wants to show the rational credibility of the scriptural miracles by indicating that, in comparison with other alleged miracles, these alone fit the character of God, as

14. John Henry Newman, *Two Essays: Biblical and Ecclesiastical Miracles*, 9th ed. (London: Longmans, Green, 1890), 17–18.

known by reason from nature and morality. On this account, the scripture miracles are rationally defensible because miracles like the plagues of Egypt were "directed against the prevalent superstitions of that country" and exhibit "originality, beauty, and immediate utility."[15] But it takes more Christian esthetic education than most of us possess to find beauty in a story of a punitive infliction of bum-warts on the Philistines. Even if we use euphemisms like "hemorrhoids," we find much that is original in this divine punishment but little that is beautiful in the Philistines of Ashdod, Gath, and Ekron enduring this affliction "in their secret parts" (5:9).

Like the succeeding story, the equally puzzling narrative in 1 Sam. 5 about the bizarre devices by which the Philistines rid themselves of their uncovetable and uncovenanted ark seems to belong more in the world of modern, postscriptural miracles, among the snake handlers of the Appalachians and the bleeding Madonnas of the southern Mediterranean, than in the stern world of the Bible. Newman defends the reality of postbiblical or ecclesiastical miracles, the exotic exorcisms and miraculous relics to which the church fathers unanimously gave some credence. He notes their differing affective qualities: whereas scriptural miracles are "on the whole, grave simple and majestic," those of later times "often" have "a romantic character and . . . that wildness . . . which enters into the notion of romance." There is little that is serious or "majestic" in the means by which the trickster punishes the Philistines' caper, and much that is wild. The great English theologian could see that too. Newman observes that "a sort of analogy exists" between biblical and postbiblical miracles. Some of the biblical miracles, like the exotic exploits of Elisha and the "mysterious wildness and eccentricity" of Samson, he says, are as "romantic" as those attributed to Christian heroes like St. Anthony.[16]

Today, Archbishop Rowan Williams of Canterbury quite naturally visits Lourdes, a French village renowned for its miraculous healings—and no less miraculous absence of epidemics, according to Flannery O'Connor.[17] But in Newman's time Anglican divines stood foursquare against the credibility of extraordinary divine interventions in postbiblical times. One reason the Anglican apologists gave for the incredibility of ecclesiastical miracles was that we lack a regulative device for discerning them. They are wayward: since the church has no standing power to exercise miracles, they may happen at any time. To answer this objection, Newman fixes upon the august, but unruly and irregulable figure of the ark of the covenant of the Lord. Church history teaches us, he writes,

> the doctrines of an abiding presence of Divinity such as dwelt upon the Ark, showing itself as it would and when it would, and without fixed rules . . . which for a while was latent, and then became manifest again; which to some persons, places

15. Ibid., 25.
16. Ibid., 116, 119, 166–68.
17. Flannery O'Connor, Letter to "A," 5 May 1958: "The miracle is that the place don't bring on epidemics"; in *Letters of Flannery O'Connor: The Habit of Being*, ed. Sally Fitzgerald (New York: Farrar, Straus & Giroux, 1979), 280.

or generations was an evidence, and to other was not. The ideas of "regular succession," conscious "exercise" of power ... are ... foreign to a theory of miraculous agency of this kind; yet ... such an appointment may rightly be called a "standing power," and ... the Ark was a standing instrument of miraculous operation, yet it did not send forth its virtue at all times, nor at the will of man. What was the nature of its mysterious powers we learn from the beginning of the First Book of Samuel; where we read of it first as stationed in the tabernacle, and of the Almighty speaking from it to the child Samuel; next it is captured in battle by the Philistines; but next, when it is set up in the house of Dagon, the idol, without visible cause, falls down before it, and its worshippers are smitten. Next, the cattle which are yoked to it are constrained against their natural instinct to carry it back to Israel. And then the men of Bethshemeth are smitten for looking into it. Was there, or was there not, then a standing power of miracles in the Jewish Church? There was ... no "regular succession" of "individuals" who exercised supernatural gifts with a divinely enlightened discretion; even the Prophets were not such a body; yet the Divine Presence consisted in much more than an occasional ... intervention in the course of events. ... The supernatural glory might abide, and yet be manifold, variable, uncertain, inscrutable, uncontrollable, like the natural atmosphere; dispensing gleams, shadows, traces of Almighty Power, but giving no such clear and perfect vision of it as one might gaze upon and record distinctly in its details for controversial purposes. Thus we are told, "The wind bloweth where it listeth."[18]

Like modern charismatic healings and sacred apparitions, the miracle of 1 Sam. 5 teaches us that the hand of God can appear at will and in the unlikeliest "Elishas" because it is not subject but sovereign.

To enable his readers to imagine what powers postbiblical charismatics might enjoy, Newman points us to the ark of the covenant. He brings out the imaginative connection between the ark and prophecy. Samuel's absence from the ark stories of 1 Sam. 4–6 is held by some to show that these stories are a discrete addition to 1 Samuel (Campbell and O'Brien 2000: 226–27). It is not surprising that Samuel is discreetly absent from the tale. The ark stories of 1 Sam. 4–6 form a composite unity with the tale of the prophet Samuel, because in them the ark acts like a prophet, performing the prophetic gesture of miracle and signaling divine displeasure in the way of a living prophet.

Episode Four: Restitution (1 Sam. 6:1–7:1)

These chapters are reminiscent of the stories in which the power of Moses's rod is contrasted with that of Pharaoh's magicians (Exod. 7:9–12) and in which the Egyptian magicians' efforts to lift the divine inflictions exacerbate the plagues (7:22; 8:7, 18–19). We may tend to regard the opposition the Old Testament sets up between heathen "priests and ... diviners" (1 Sam. 6:2) and Yahwistic

18. Newman, *Two Essays*, 214–17.

prophets and judges as reflecting a contrast between the superstitious attitudes of the former toward their cult objects and the higher minded and ethical worship of the Yahwists. This causes us some intellectual embarrassment in the face of the decidedly magical behavior of the ark in stories such as this, where God kills "fifty thousand and threescore and ten men" in "Beth-shemesh, because they had looked into the ark of the LORD" (6:19). It may be that the biblical contrast between heathen Philistine or Egyptian and Yahwist is more a matter of esthetics than ethics. In the broad sense, the Egyptian or Philistine esthetic was its attitude toward material culture. Scripture, from Genesis onward, is in two minds about the value of the civilizing processes by which humans conquered their environment. Cain is the ancestor of Jubal, the first musician, and of "Tubalcain, who was a hammerer and artificer in every work of brass and iron" (Gen. 4:21–22 Douay-Rheims). It may have been the esthetic and functional art of firing pots that led to the discovery of the processes necessary to molding bronze. The discovery of how to carburize iron came several millennia later, around 1200 BC: even in Homer's day the transformation of iron under high temperatures was regarded as a quasimagical process. For the biblical writers, such early scientific-esthetic artisanry as metallurgy is numbered in "the same category of paradox and ambivalence as technology and civilization in general." As a technology, a work of human culture, skill in metallurgy is not simply bad, but it is questionable. Science can become bad magic if the direction of the human will is evil. The biblical Tubal-cain, descendant of the first murderer, contrasts with Egypt's artisan god Ptah, the Mesopotamian god of potters and metalworkers Enki, and the Canaanite artisan deity Kothar; all of the latter are unalloyed benefactors of the human race (McNutt 1990: 103, 150, 216, 44, 229, 233). In 1 Samuel and in other Old Testament books, the Philistines are depicted as having the upper hand in iron technology. They are mocked here in their role as metallurgists, being commanded to make "images of your haemerrhoids" and "images of your mice" (6:5), that is, to engineer not beautiful things or devastating weapons, but bum-warts and ineffectual, tiny animals. We should be cautious about our use of words like "superstitious" or "magical" in relation to the Philistine or Egyptian culture: to a modern scientific naturalist, it would be the Philistines who exercised high-minded practicality in their use of the latest technologies, and the Israelites with their spooky ark who are the superstitious ones.

The ark makes its way from Ebenezer to Ashdod and to Ekron, striking mayhem to the rear and panic in its advance. The chaotic and yet majestic progress of the ark has something of the carnivalesque, especially in its details (Polzin 1989: 65), which consistently add the comic touch. On the advice of their priests and diviners, the five Philistine chieftains decide to return the ark bearing gifts that are gold replicas of the plagues it has brought among them: "Five golden haemerrhoids, and five golden mice, according to the number of the lords of the Philistines" (6:4). Although the priests and diviners speak with the voice of Moses ("wherefore then do ye harden your hearts, as the Egyptians and Pharaoh hardened their hearts?"

6:6), their counsel is the counsel of magicians and shamans in every ancient culture: sympathetic magic. By offering the ark images of their twin afflictions, they hope to send the hemorrhoids packing with it. The ark makes its stately progress out of the Philistine domains laden with gold mice and golden warts.

No exegete fully understands the disasters in 1 Sam. 5–6 or the cure for them. "Hemorrhoids" is a translator's guess in 5:6, 9, since the Hebrew word is not sufficiently common to generate analogous cases. And if it is the right translation, why hemorrhoids? In 1 Sam. 6, on the advice of their magicians, the Philistines compensate the ark with a "trespass offering" of "five golden haemerrhoids, and five golden mice" (6:4; cf. 6:5, 11). Why mice? Is it just something a magician would say: "offer gold mice"? Twelfth-century monastic commentator Pierre de Cava combines the two and proposes that the Philistines contracted hemorrhoids by being bitten in the backside by mice.[19] The idea is that the mice transmit the disease, whether by contagion, as we would say today, or as miasmic pollutants, as the late medievals thought. The point is symbolically to return the carriers. No one really knows how the mice scurried into the frame.

The Philistine lords are still "hardening their hearts," fooling themselves down to the bitter end. Like the Olympian pantheon, the gods of the ancient Near East fight equals and near-equals to create the world and to maintain control over it. Even Zeus has a stronger number, in Moira (Fate) (Homer, *Iliad* 16). But in scripture, there is no real contest between Yahweh himself and his adversaries. That doesn't mean there is no drama, and thus no tragedy or comedy. God fights real battles to rescue humanity from its adversary. The drama of God's transcendence is that he chooses when and where to exercise his power. Just because "there is none besides" him (2:2), Yahweh is all powerful: "It is the LORD: let him do what seemeth him good," as Eli says, when Samuel reports Yahweh's decree of doom upon his priestly house (3:18). The dark comedy of 1 Sam. 5–6 lies in the contrast between God's power and the Philistines' attempts to evade or negotiate with Yahweh's majestic providence. On the one hand, the ark, in which the invisible deity was beseated "under the outstretched wings" of the cherubim; on the other, the nervous Philistine kings (Van Seters 1983: 350). Perhaps it's all just a stroke of chance or a run of bad luck, they are still saying in 6:9: "If it goeth up by the way of his own coast to Beth-shemesh, then he hath done us this great

19. Gregory the Great, *Six Books on 1 Kings* 3.78, in Franke 2005: 216. In the introduction to the first volume of the Sources chrétiennes edition of the commentary by "Gregory the Great" on Regum, the editors argue that Gregory himself was in fact the author of this commentary. By the fifth volume, they recognize that the bulk of the evidence (especially because no other commentator apparently knows of this text before the thirteenth century) indicates that the commentary was produced by a twelfth-century Benedictine abbot named Pierre de Cava. Franke's anthology appeared too soon to take note of this, and selections from the commentary appear under the name of the sixth-century pope. I cite Franke's selections from this text wherever they are available, since it is more accessible than the magnificent six-volume Sources chrétiennes edition.

evil: but if not, then we shall know that it is not his hand that smote us; it was a chance that happened to us."[20]

The Philistines here take over from the Egyptians as the representatives of the superior, controlling material culture. Their Pentapolis is mentioned twice: the "trespass offering" that corresponds to the arkan curse is "five golden haemerrhoids, and five golden mice, according to the number of the lords of the Philistines: for one plague was on you all, and on your lords" (6:4), and the entire monarchic cohort comes out to witness the offerings made to the ark, "when the five lords of the Philistine had seen it, they returned to Ekron" (6:16).

The ark, locus of the glory of the Lord, is a *mysterium tremendum et fascinans*, a terrifying and attractive mystery. Painters of Buddha statues paint in the eyes through a mirror, so as not to incur its terrible gaze: the holy is taboo—"high voltage."[21] It is not possible to understand this carnival of the glory of the Lord in his ark without appreciating sacramental power. In Josh. 3 the Levite clergy carrying the ark instruct the people to "keep a distance of about a thousand yards between you and the ark; do not go near it" (3:4 NIV): the waters of the Jordan halt as the "throne" advances, and the people cross on dry land. When the Philistines return to Israelite territory with the ark, "they of Beth-shemesh were reaping their wheat harvest in the valley: and they lifted up their eyes, and saw the ark, and rejoiced to see it" (6:13). They hand the dangerous and sacred object over to the Levites, the priests, and make sacrifices before it. Nonetheless, the Lord "smote the men of Beth-shemesh, because they had looked into the ark of the Lord, even he smote of the people fifty thousand and threescore and ten men: and the people lamented" (6:19). The magical potency of the ark is a visible symbol of the glory it bears. When the analogous term is used "in the strongest sense," God's *kabod* ("glory") is "the free turning of his personal divinity to the creature" (von Balthasar 1983–91: 7.269).

The instinctive reaction most readers have to the slaughter of the men of Beth-shemesh is that it is not right for God to kill "fifty thousand and threescore and ten men" "because they had looked into the ark of the Lord": like the people we see more in this story to lament than to laugh at (6:19). Just as we can gaze with pleasure at the sunbathed moon but cannot look directly at the sun, so, in this life, human beings cannot endure looking upon God. We know that the Israelites were forbidden to make images of God (Exod. 20:3), and we know they have been detected by archeologists in breaking the second commandment. But we understand much less well that it would be death for a human being in this world to encounter God directly. We understand it less well than we should because we set stories like this aside as an importunate reminder that God in the Old Testament was really primitive. In another enigmatic and primitive story, God on Mount

---

20. Meir Sternberg, *The Poetics of Biblical Narrative: Ideological Literature and the Drama of Reading* (Bloomington, IN: Indiana University Press, 1985), 105.

21. Gerardus van der Leeuw, *Religion in Essence and Manifestation: A Study in Phenomenology*, trans. J. E. Turner (London: Allen & Unwin, 1938), 44.

Sinai tells Moses: "Thou canst not see my face: for there shall no man see me, and live. . . . Behold . . . stand upon a rock: And it shall come to pass, while my glory passeth by, that I will put thee in a cleft of the rock, and will cover thee with my hand while I pass by. And I will take away my hand, and thou shalt see my back parts: but my face shall not be seen" (Exod. 33:20–23). It is only with Christ in his human form that we see the face of God (John 12:45).

It is here that the New Testament and the Old change places in terms of style and content. The New Testament, a less esthetically pleasing and less visual book, shows us the face of God in Christ; the Old Testament teaches us that we cannot look direct at the essence of God, and it does so in stories that are thoroughly visual. Modern Christians do not take pleasure in the ark stories of 1 Sam. 5–6 because we don't picture the ark. For that one would need to have the imagination of a draftsman hired to turn these chapters into a comic book. Anyone raised on the Greek and Roman classics found the Old Testament vulgar by comparison. Augustine could not swallow it until he heard Ambrose's figurative explanation of this graphic novel (*Confessions* 5.14). This didn't seem to occur to the nineteenth-century classicists who undertook to analyze this scripture, perhaps because, unlike Augustine, they did not seriously ask themselves whether 1 Samuel could be the object of religious belief. Once we see the ark as colorfully formidable and vulgarly awesome as it would look in a graphic novel, it may be as blindingly obvious to us as it was to the stories' original audience that the men of Beth-shemesh have wittingly blundered into contact with a force that is attractive but also terrifying.

John Henry Newman observes that some epochs of biblical history are replete with miracles and others relatively dry. His explanation of this dispensation of providence was that the capacity to perform miracles was primarily given to human beings in scripture to authenticate their revelation as coming from God. Whereas the prophets and judges and some patriarchs needed miraculous signs of the divine hand, the kings did not, for their lineage was authenticated by God. As Newman puts it, "The power of working them, instead of being assumed by any classes of men indiscriminately, is described as a prerogative of the occasional Prophets, to the exclusion of Priests and Kings. . . . For the . . . claims of the Kings and Priests were already ascertained, when once the sacred office was limited to the family of Aaron, and the regal power to David and his descendants; whereas extraordinary messengers, as Moses, Samuel, and Elijah needed some supernatural display of power to authenticate their pretensions."[22] After 1 Sam. 6, the divine hand will largely work behind the scene, without extravagant miracles. The curtain is falling on the era of the charismatic judges, and its hero goes out with a bang.

The ark contained the "throne" of the Lord and so symbolized that Yahweh is "Israel's ruler" (Eichrodt 1961–67: 1.230): the king sits on the throne. Heralding a crisis in Israel's military defense that leads to the demand for a human king to coordinate Israel's tribes, these stories about the loss and restitution of the

22. Newman, *Two Essays*, 24.

Lord's throne look forward to the establishment of the centralized monarchy in Jerusalem. In 2 Sam. 6, with David's capture of Jerusalem, a "cart," like the cart of 1 Sam. 6, hauls the ark to Jerusalem via the Philistine villages. The panic, death, and destruction that the ark produces in 1 Sam. 4–6 is paralleled by the joy that it generates in David's triumphal march of 2 Sam. 6 (Polzin 1989: 68–69). But in the short term, in 1 Sam. 4:4–6, the ark is carted to Abinadab's hilltop villa. The ark ends washed up at Kirjath-jearim (6:21–7:1), scarcely a prominent Israelite village sanctuary. With its self-possession, ability to wreck damage, and dynamism, the ark represents the kingship of the Lord, his majesty. It has first been stolen and now returns to a tangential position, which is one chapter before the people of Israel will challenge God's kingship by demanding a human king. The adventure, exile, and downstaging of the ark in 1 Sam. 4–6 represents that God's kingship remains marginal to Israel, until 2 Sam. 6: the Lord "has not signaled acceptance of a particular shape to a changed Israel. . . . Correlatively, in 2 Samuel, the narrative about the ark may communicate the conviction that God has endorsed Israel's shape under David; the ark has come to Jerusalem" (Campbell and O'Brien 2000: 219; cf. 227). The outlandish ark carries forward the threads of prophecy and kingship with which 1 Samuel opened. The ark is a sacred object, a priestly thing, and one that enthrones the Lord of hosts, the heavenly king; it is no tame clerical oracle, but a wild, leonine prophet. It would not make theologically esthetic sense to have Samuel alongside the ark in full flow. It would be unpoetical, that is, to set the human priest-prophet-king alongside the divine priest-prophet-king. The human holder of the threefold office cannot be downstage of the divine reality.

Episode Five: The Last of the Judges (1 Sam. 7:2–17)

"Twenty years" pass (7:2): this episode is not a directly temporal successor to the previous ones. The story begins by making clear what the Israelites did wrong in taking the ark into battle against the Philistines (1 Sam. 4): they did so without turning to the Lord. They tried to deploy the ark against the Philistines while still hanging on to their "Baals and the Ashtaroth." Now, at the command of Samuel, they put them away and, reciprocally, turn to Yahweh and "served the LORD only" (7:4 ESV). As a gesture of contrition, the people "drew water, and poured it out before the LORD" (7:6). Making a libation offering is a religious expression held in common by the ancient Israelites and some modern African peoples such as the Ewe-Dome of southeast Ghana.[23] The Ewe-Dome make libations at festivals to *Mawu* (the high god), but also to *togbuiwo* (ancestor spirits) and *trowo* (spirit

---

23. Libations were a widespread feature of the Bronze Age Mediterranean world, appearing often in Homer's epics; Walter Burkert, *Greek Religion*, trans. John Raffan (Cambridge, MA: Harvard University Press, 1985), 70–71.

powers or minor gods).[24] It is a topic of debate among the Christians of the Ewe-
Dome whether such libation offerings have a biblical warrant by dint of their
occurring in the Old Testament.[25] What does it mean "to serve the Lord alone"?
The fifth-century Cappadocian father Basil the Great remarks that "God alone
is substantially and essentially God. . . . In Scripture 'one' and 'only' are . . . predicated of God . . . to exclude the unreal gods falsely so called. As for instance, 'The
Lord alone did lead them and there was no strange god with them,' and 'then the
children of Israel did put away Baalim and Ashtaroth and served the Lord only"
(Letter 8.3, in Franke 2005: 222). Scripture recounts these stories about Israel's
oscillations between "Baals and . . . Ashtaroth" and Yahweh because, for human
beings, monotheism is never just a theory, but a decision—for the one God and
against the easier substitutes. The author tells this story in the appreciation that
foreign gods were never alien to the empirical Israelite cult and culture. They
were to be part and parcel of the monarchy that the people will demand in the
next episode.

Following the gesture of "return," and because of it, Samuel, acting as a prophet-
judge, leads the people to victory against the Philistines. He boxes the Philistines
out of Israelite territory, bringing the story of the conquest of the land toward its
close. The Shilonite confederate, that is, the placement of Eli's house at the head
of the Israelite tribes, had bitten the dust with the defeat at Ebenezer. Samuel replaces Eli, becoming the high *sophet* ("judge"; 7:15–17) over all the tribes, "as Eli's
legitimate successor by way of the reorganization of the collapsed confederation."
Like Eli, Samuel exercises leadership of the tribes and serves as a focal point for
their collective muster in times of war without himself entering the field of battle.
Like Eli, he is a seer-*sophet* or prophet-*sophet*. Samuel's reconstruction of the tribal
"league is to be regarded as a kind of continuation of the Shilonite confederation,
since both organizations had the same structure" (Ishida 1977: 34).

First Sam. 7 aims to show that Samuel himself, as prophet-judge, brought
peace and safety from external threat: "The hand of the Lord was against the
Philistines all the days of Samuel" (7:13). Not all the charismatic judges were
warriors: minor judges like Tola and Jair (Judg. 10:1–5; cf. 12:8–13 for a list
of others) "were the successful administrators in the period, whose nonviolent
administrations generated no blood-and-thunder tradition" (Boling 1975: 189).
Samuel too functioned as an administrator: "He went on a circuit year by year
to Beth-el, Gilgal, and Mizpah. And he judged Israel in all these places. Then he
would return to Ramah, for his home was there, and there also he judged Israel"
(1 Sam. 7:16–17). In one sense, 1 Sam. 7 downplays the need to replace judging
with kingship. In this chapter, Samuel may seem to function as a prophet-general,

---

24. Rebecca Yawa Ganusah, "Pouring Libation to Spirit Powers among the Ewe-Dome: An
Indigenous Religious and Biblical Perspective," in *The Bible in Africa: Transactions, Trajectories,
and Trends,* ed. Gerald O. West and Musa W. Dube (Leiden: Brill, 2000), 278.

25. Philip Jenkins, *The Next Christendom: The Coming of Global Christianity* (Oxford: Oxford
University Press, 2002), 131–32.

like Moses (Exod. 17:8–16) or Elijah (1 Kgs. 18:36–40) (Campbell and O'Brien 2000: 232). But Samuel wields power in an unsoldierly way. He does not even gaze on the battle, as Moses did. Rather, as the Philistines advance on Mizpah, he offers a "nursing lamb" in sacrifice "to the LORD" and "cried out to the LORD for Israel" (7:9 ESV). His role is as an intercessor and mediator, a conductor between the people and God. We are given a battle scene that consists, in what is explicitly said, solely in the total retreat of the foe: "The LORD thundered with a mighty sound that day against the Philistines and threw them into confusion, and they were routed before Israel. And the men of Israel went out from Mizpah and pursued the Philistines and struck them, as far as below Beth-car" (7:10–11 ESV). Samuel looms over the scene like a wonder-working magician.

Historians find it odd that the Bible makes a hero of Samuel, since we can see from 1 Samuel itself that it was during his leadership that the Philistine aggrandizement became so threatening that the people called for a king to replace him (Stager 1998: 170). Though this episode portrays the magnetic repulsion that Samuel's intercession exercises upon Israel's foes, the clearest image one may take from it is Samuel's spiritual height, the force of his personality. Samuel unites the tribes in war against the Philistines by dint of his intrepid reliance upon the one God. What happens in the story theologically is that "the LORD thunder[s]" against the Philistines and throws them into terrified flight; what happens humanly is that all the tribes act as one; and these two, the human and the theological, occur simultaneously. In a secular history, this would be the story of how Samuel's leadership qualities rallied the tribes to coordinate their forces. Once one has increased tribal cooperation, there will be demands for a centralized kingship, just as revolutions happen in periods of reform, not of retrenchment.

Samuel operates as judge to more than one locality, so that the range of villages and tribes under a single ruler is perhaps extended. Historical critics may have questions about the miraculous nature of Samuel's military leadership: "As Samuel was offering up the burnt offering, the Philistines drew near to attack Israel. But the LORD thundered with a mighty sound that day against the Philistines and threw them into confusion, and they were routed before Israel" (7:10 ESV). But the actual sequence of kinds of leadership portrayed by Judges and the books of Samuel makes sense as an anthropological development: (1) military charismatics and a sprinkling of administrator-judges in Judges, followed in 1 Samuel by (2) a priest-superjudge, Eli, succeeded by (3) Samuel, a prophet-judge who combines the charismatic gift of the military leaders with juridical responsibilities and who by dint of respect for his personality gathers several districts under a single legal administration, followed by (4) Saul, a charismatic king, and concluding in 2 Regum with (5) David's centralized political authority in Jerusalem. Backhandedly and in small nearly continuous steps, the tribes become a tribal confederacy, become dissatisfied that their prophet-judge is not also a war leader, install Saul as their "big man," and then become a united kingdom and nation under David. To regard this as purely legendary, as minimalist historians do, is to ascribe to the

author an oversight of the stepwise evolution of human societies that it is historically unlikely that he possessed. Christians believe in the veracity of our author's
record of Israel's development not on the basis of such probabilities, but on the
strength of revelation and tradition, and this scriptural or ecclesial faith can give
a rational account of itself.

Samuel does one thing that, as he saw it, was as good as raising a standing army
to match the Philistines': Samuel took a stone and set it up between Mizpah and
Shen and called its name Ebenezer; for, he said, "Till now the LORD has helped
us" (7:12 ESV). Augustine interprets Samuel's comment in relation to etymology:
he thinks Ebenezer meant "stone of the helper." For Augustine, the stone, set up
on the new border between the Philistine and the Israelite settlement, represents
the choice of direction the Israelites had to make: a "material kingdom" and authentic happiness "in the kingdom of heaven." The stone "points" toward Israel:
"And since there is nothing better than this, God helps us 'so far'" (*City of God*
17.7). In the emblem of the stone, God helps to orient us toward the choice for
God over a merely human kingdom.

SERIES THREE

CHARISMATIC KINGSHIP

1 Samuel 8–12

First Sam. 8–15 looks fairly straightforward. In 1 Sam. 8 we learn that Samuel has made his sons judges and that, like Hophni and Phinehas, they are wrong-uns. To Samuel's dismay, the people demand a king. The Lord tells Samuel to give the Israelites their way. This Samuel does, after warning them of the dangers of kingship. In 1 Sam. 9 a muscular Benjamite gets lost looking for his father's asses, and we grasp, as the handsome youth inadvertently makes his way to Samuel's house, that Saul is the one selected by God. Saul is anointed in private by Samuel. First Sam. 10 sees Saul displayed as king before the people after being chosen by lot from the assembled tribes. In 1 Sam. 11 Saul leads the people in battle against the Ammonites, and in 11:14–12:25 Samuel delivers a public coronation to the victorious Saul. Samuel takes his leave from public life in a speech that speaks severely about the trials and apostasies attendant upon kingship. In 13:1–14 Saul disregards an order to wait until Samuel arrives before making the prebattle sacrifice. Samuel tells him his kingship will not continue. In 13:15–14:52, at the battle of Michmash Pass, Saul and his son Jonathan set the Philistines into flight. But in 1 Sam. 15 in a military encounter against the Amalekites, Saul fails to obey the divine order to annihilate the pagan forces in toto. He keeps the booty, including the Amalekite king, as his own trophies of war. God orders Samuel to strip the kingship from Saul.

This apparently simple narrative has occasioned much exegetical puzzlement: "Historical critics have suggested that the way to understand such ill-framed writing" as they find in 1 Sam. 8–15 "is to determine how it got into such a confused state" (Eslinger 1983: 62). Ever since Eichhorn's *Einleitung ins Alte Testament* (1780–83), scholars have proposed that 1 Sam. 8–15 conflates opposing political opinions. The reason they give for the supposed lack of fit between the episodes is that these chapters juxtapose a governmental preference for monarchy and one against it: "The attitude of a given text toward the monarchy has been, perhaps, the single most important criterion in the subsequent analysis of 1 Sam. 8–12 (or 7–15)" (Halpern 1981: 150). If the original impetus behind the books of Samuel is to write political history, then the texts must take a stand for or against monarchic rule, like Tacitus did in his *Annals*. Eichhorn pioneered the detection in 1 Sam. 8–15 of older promonarchic texts with later, postexilic hindsight about the monarchy, but it was Julius Wellhausen who laid out the precise divisions of pro- and antimonarchic chapter and verse in 1878.

Wellhausen's *Prolegomena zur Geschichte Israels* (1878, 1883) established the Documentary Hypothesis, which assigns different strands in the Pentateuch to a Yahwistic, an Elohistic, a Priestly, and a Deuteronomistic writer. Wellhausen didn't invent the Documentary Hypothesis: he gave it historical cogency by setting J, E, P, and D in a time frame based on the relative religious sophistication of the authors. One can detect the hand of German romantic thinking behind Wellhausen's belief that the Yahwist must be early, because the God he calls "Jahweh" is depicted anthropomorphically; the Elohist, who calls God "El," has a higher theology; and the Priestly writers would have taken many more centuries to arrive at their clerical interest in liturgy and transcendent idea of God. Though it has had its critics, the Documentary Hypothesis has retained a consensual assent among biblical scholars. The hypothesis has remained stable because the analysis of the Pentateuch into J, E, P, and D is anchored in objective philological criteria, that is, the names the texts use for God. In addition to the idealist philosophers, Wellhausen was influenced by the German historians who plotted the cultural development of particular civilizations by imagining the setting for their texts and artifacts. Theodor Mommsen's *Römische Geschichte* (1856) had used the Republican constitution of Rome as a model through which to map the history of the Roman Republic.

Jacob Burckhardt periodizes the Greek cultural epochs to show how the texts and art forms of the Greek artists and writers flow from a specific cultural form. For example, an agonal spirit characterized classical Greece and both explains and is expressed by its artifacts, including the Olympic games, the drama competitions, and the "dialogue form in philosophical discourse."[1] The sequential model of a culture's development enables one to date its artifacts, and, conversely, the artifacts help to build the sequence. Although this method relies on intuition and is currently unfashionable, in the hands of historians like Burckhardt it had as much

1. Jacob Burckhardt, *The Greeks and Greek Civilization*, trans. Sheila Stern, ed. Oswyn Murray (London: HarperCollins, 1998), 182.

objectivity as it had beauty. Applying this method to biblical history, Wellhausen proposed that court historians were responsible for the earliest strands in Joshua-Samuel-Kings. He situated them in the epoch when, as he imagined, Israelite culture attained enlightenment and secularity, at the court of King Solomon. In addition, Wellhausen selected the dates for the composition of the strands in 1 Samuel on the basis of the attitudes to monarchic government that he ascertained within them. Before Israel and Jerusalem were overrun by Babylon in 586 BC and before the exile, a favorable view of monarchy would have been natural, Wellhausen felt. He therefore ascribed his promonarchic sources, like 9:1–10:16 and 1 Sam. 11, to a preexilic writer. After the conquest and destruction of Israel's monarchy, thinkers would have been antagonistic to their erstwhile kings, since they would have blamed the government for getting them into this fine mess. So Wellhausen regarded negative texts like 1 Sam. 7; 8; 10:17–27; and 12 as postexilic. Since he viewed the texts in 1 Sam. 7–15 to which he imputed antimonarchic sentiments as late, Wellhausen claimed they were "totally unhistorical" (Ishida 1977: 28). These suppositions had the least objective basis of Wellhausen's enterprises. The ascription and dating of the sources in 1 Samuel have been subject to persistent contestation and to reformulations that seem merely to add new epicycles, not to furnish objectivity. The governmental hypothesis is unstable, because it comes down to ascribing a slant on monarchy to a text and to guessing when such an opinion would have arisen.

In the 1940s Martin Noth concurred with Wellhausen that 1 Sam. 9 and 1 Sam. 11 are older and with the reasoning behind his view that 8:22; 10:17–27a; and 1 Sam. 12 exhibit the Deuteronomist's antimonarchic agenda. Noth thought that, in 1 Sam. 8, "Dtr. simply traces the institution of the monarchy, of which he disapproves, back to the wicked self-will of the people who want to be like the other nations and no longer be forced to implore God in times of emergency to raise up a 'judge' but rather to have someone in office continuously at their disposal." There is, he believes, no reason for Saul to be selected by lot in 10:17–27a since Samuel has already anointed Saul in 10:1: the Deuteronomist's "main purpose in 10:17–27a is to find a place for a traditional story of Saul's accession." It is a genuine historical problem that Saul appears to be made king three times, privately by Samuel in 1 Sam. 9, after being called out by lot in 1 Sam. 10, and yet again in 1 Sam. 12. Noth thinks therefore that "Dtr." must have both "used an old tradition about Saul's accession" and created his own, and all without noticing the incongruities in his own manuscript.[2]

The later development of the judgeship in Israel prepared the way for the kingship. Eli and Samuel probably both functioned as superjudges, at the apex of the local judge system, giving unified leadership to the tribes. Eli was a priest-*sophet* and Samuel a prophet-*sophet*. These men were not "fighter-judges," like the military

---

2. Martin Noth, *The Deuteronomistic History*, trans. Jane Doull and John Barton (Sheffield: JSOT Press, 1981), 49–52.

leaders of Judges. But as cleric and prophet, Samuel, especially, was a charismatic leader. It seems likely that, in continuity with this development, kingship in Israel was originally a charismatic office. The king would be elected by God and demonstrate his divine charism by success in the field. It is argued, consequently, that Saul's first, private, anointing by Samuel is not a coronation to kingship but simply his designation as the one chosen by God. Philology bears this out, since Samuel anoints Saul as *nagid* in 9:16, not as *melek* ("king"). At this juncture, Saul holds a status loosely equivalent to the American president-elect, where God replaces the ballot as the electing power. *Nagid* meant, not king in full, but "designated heir." Saul's subsequent acclamation as *melek* in 1 Sam. 12, after his defeat of the Ammonites in 1 Sam. 11, is his actual coronation. His acting the part of the charismatic leader in 1 Sam. 11 leads to the ratification of his kingship in 1 Sam. 12. Once one notices the meaning of the different words used for "king" in 1 Sam. 9 and 1 Sam. 12, one need not see these sources as duplicating one another. Even so, that leaves us with 1 Sam. 10, in which Saul is called out by lot and installed as king. It is difficult to explain why Saul could be publicly installed as king twice, in 1 Sam. 10 and 1 Sam. 12. If these are two separate, duplicate documents, nonetheless, "in each account Saul is designated and in some way acclaimed (9:22–24; 10:24); he wins a victory" in both texts, "and he settles down thereafter to rule as king" (Halpern 1981: 9, 173).

Even if our primary interest lies in the final form of the text that we read in our Bibles and breviaries and hear from the lectionary and are disinclined to think of scripture as a puzzle pieced together of differently dated sources, yet, we commonly share the exegetes' wider assumptions. Even those of us who encounter 1 Samuel only in its final forms tend to think it is common sense that "the establishment of the monarchy was a political matter" and that, once we get beyond the theological bias of the text, we can judge the events in 1 Samuel by the "common principle of secular politics" (Ishida 1977: 29–30). But setting aside the religious character of these texts is in fact an obstacle to understanding what happens on a historical and political level in 1 Samuel. Israel's kingship was originally charismatic. This actually helps us to understand the character of Saul's monarchy. The charism of kingship is a gift of God that can be given, withdrawn, extended, and renewed. Charismatic kingship is in the power and gift of God. After being designated as *nagid* in 1 Sam. 9, publicly acclaimed as *melek* by the people's assembly in 1 Sam. 10, and having demonstrated his military charism in 1 Sam. 11, Saul is publicly crowned only in 11:14–12:25. A religious reading that appreciates that Saul was, uniquely among Israel's kings, "charismatic all the way down" may be best placed to understand this history.

Episode One: From Family to State and Back (1 Sam. 8)

With Samuel's swinging denunciation of the practices of monarchy, the older source critics from Wellhausen to Noth ascribe 1 Sam. 8 squarely to the antimonarchic source (Wevers 1971: 159). On this hypothesis, Samuel's speech in 8:11–18 expresses postexilic disillusion with the worldly monarchs. More latterly, source criticism has unearthed both anti- *and* promonarchic orientations in 1 Sam. 8 and regards it as "a largely positive base layer that has been expanded to express strongly negative concerns." The positive concern is the desire for social justice, that is, not being ruled by Samuel's wicked sons. This optimistic source is taken to come from several hands, since different rationales are offered for the petition: the problem the elders raise is Samuel's unscrupulous sons (8:5), whereas the people speak of the need for leadership against foreign invaders (8:19–20) (Campbell and O'Brien 2000: 233, 218, 246).

All authors of nonfiction quote from divergent sources. Any historian worth his salt uses oral and written sources. Practiced writers shape their disparate materials to serve the ends of their own work. Weaker writers lose control of their material. When we narrow our sights to the literally political or governmental, we picture 1 Samuel as if it were a debate among Whigs and Tories in seventeenth-century England. And, clearly, a single text in which Whig and Tory sentiments are left in conflict is unlikely to flow from a single hand, if that text is literally about what type of government one's country should have, and no more.

In 8:6, "the thing displeased Samuel" is more literally rendered as "the thing was evil in the eyes of Samuel." In Judges, Israel does "evil" before God when it worships other gods; for instance, "The children of Israel did evil in the sight of the LORD and served the Baals" (2:11 ESV; cf. 6:1). One modern commentator claims that "'to do evil' was to commit a sociopolitical offense," to break God's law, because "God was previously acknowledged as the chief executive of the state" (Boling 1975: 76). The ark stories were a textual reminder of the divine kingship, since "the royal throne of the Ark" is one of "the symbols of this rule" (Eichrodt 1961–67: 1.230). We cannot grasp why the elders' request is evil to God and to Samuel unless we appreciate that establishing a human king would be in some sense a displacement of the kingship of God over Israel. But in what sense was divine kingship understood? There is much literal symbolism of kingship here. A covenant was a treaty "cut" either between sovereigns or between a sovereign and an inferior, weaker people. The Sinai revelation is a covenant making. God proclaims, "You shall be for me a priestly kingdom and a holy nation" (Exod. 19:6 NRSV); then, like a king, God gives Israel its law (Exod. 20) and describes how the ark, with its throne, and the tabernacle are to be constructed (Exod. 25–27). A basic question about 1 Sam. 8–12 is the meaning of God's kingship. How literally are we to take this kingship? To take it literally is to take it "governmentally." In the seventeenth century, the materialist philosopher Thomas Hobbes takes God's kingship absolutely *au pied du le lettre*: "I find," he writes in *Leviathan*,

> the KINGDOME OF GOD, to signifie in most places of Scripture, a Kingdome *properly so named*, constituted by the Votes of the People of Israel in peculiar manner; wherein they chose God as their King by Covenant made with him, upon Gods

promising them the land of Canaan; and but seldome metaphorically. . . . This Covenant, at the foot of Mount Sinai, was renewed by Moses (Exod. 19:5), where the Lord commanded Moses to speak to the people in this manner, *If you will obey my voice indeed, and keep my Covenant, then yee shall be a peculiar people to me. . . . And yee shall be unto me a Sacerdotall Kingdome, and a holy Nation.*

As a materialist, Hobbes naturally interprets the events of the Deuteronomistic History literally: "The Books of *Joshua, Judges, Ruth,* and *Samuel,* down to the time of *Saul,* describe the acts of God's people, till the time they cast off God's yoke, and called for a King, after the manner of their neighbor nations."[3] The seventeenth-century political scientist was one of the fathers of modern source criticism. He interprets the kingship of God in a literal, governmental sense. Modern exegetes are following in his footsteps in holding that, when Israel made a covenant with the Lord at Sinai, that covenant "casts Yahweh in the role of Suzerain, Great King, King of kings, so that every man confessing faith in Yahweh becomes thereby a citizen of Israel. . . . Israel is the nucleus of the earthly half of the kingdom of Yahweh" (Boling 1975: 24).

If we take 1 Sam. 8 on a literal political level, there is every pragmatic political reason to sympathize with the people rather than with Samuel or the Lord. Once we take Samuel as the spokesman for an antimonarchic party, his grounds for objecting to the petition look both self-contradictory and ungrounded in the realities of the situation. It can be argued that Samuel himself has made his sons judges, obeying the logic of rule by inheritance rather than the logic of rule by charisma, as seen in the heroes of Judges, and his heirs are unworthy of the role. Therefore, the elders seem to say, if we are to have hereditary rulers rather than charismatic ones, why not follow the logic out, as other nations do, and have kings: "Behold, thou art old, and thy sons walk not in thy ways: now make us a king to judge us like all the nations" (8:5). By making sons who "walked not in his ways, but turned aside after lucre, and took bribes, and perverted judgement" (8:3) into judges to succeed himself, Jobling contends, Samuel himself was the first to subvert the idea of rule by God through God's elected charismatic leaders. Moreover, the reasons that the elders give for their request seem soundly pragmatic: as Jobling notes, waiting for judges spontaneously to emerge did not work as a governmental mechanism because it could not generate a smoothly automatic transition from one judge to the next, as a hereditary office would do. There was no leadership during the gap times between lone individuals selected by Yahweh as judges.[4] On a narrowly political exegesis of 1 Sam. 8 as an antimonarchic text, the elders and the people look to be in the right. As it entered the Iron Age, "an ethos encouraging a high birth rate . . . emerged" in Israel's highland villages; the

3. Thomas Hobbes, *Leviathan,* ed. C. B. MacPherson (London: Penguin, 1985 [orig. 1651]), 442, 444, 424, emphasis original.
4. David Jobling, *The Sense of Biblical Narrative: Structural Analyses in the Hebrew Bible* (Sheffield: JSOT Press, 1986), 54, 52.

"self-sufficient family"[5] had proven too explosively successful to sustain a tribal culture: enjoying a population of about 75,000 by the eleventh century BC, Israel's size alone made the centralization of the tribes around a monarchy a natural step (Dever 2002: 111, 126–28). Samuel seems to be standing out against the tides of reproductive history.

Jobling's points are useful because they make us ask seriously, without just glossing the question, whether there is any reason to interpret the supposedly political judgments of 1 Sam. 8 in a benign way, once we read them governmentally. Given that Samuel's designated heirs are described as judges who "took bribes and perverted judgement" (8:3), is it not rational to prefer a different prospective ruler? Given that the tribes of the ancient Near East were competing for agricultural space, it seems defensible to desire "that our king may judge us, and go out before us, and fight our battles" (8:20). Jobling argues that the request that Yahweh choose a king through Samuel is morally legitimate. If we really are looking at an episode in Israel's government, then Samuel looks like a stubborn old man, willfully disregarding his age and the unsuitability of his sons as successors in the obstinate pursuit of his own high standing (Polzin 1989: 87). Yahweh comes out even worse, since he acquiesces in the request (8:9, 22) and yet seems to harbor a grudge against the one he anoints, making Saul the scapegoat for an exercise that he himself condoned (Exum 1992: 38). Indeed, the "more righteous weight given to Samuel's 'displeasure' at the demand, the more difficult it becomes to excuse God's order to comply with it" (Campbell and O'Brien 2000: 235).

Jobling is wrong to conceive of Samuel as making a break with the tradition and a partial step toward monarchic government when he passes the office of judge to his sons. The crucial difference between the government of a segmentary tribal society and monarchic politics is not that the one is hereditary and the other is not. Most cultural authority is hereditary in a tribal culture (Sahlins 1968: 17, 10). Historically, Samuel is a conservative denizen of the heroic culture of the judges, in which "the family . . . was charged with preserving standards of conduct and with punishing any breach."[6] The privileges of hereditary priority are taken seriously in such a society; that is why we are told that Joel was the "firstborn" and that Abiah was Samuel's "second" (8:2), and why "elders" (8:4) come to speak with Samuel about their request. Ancestors are important in African societies because they are part of the "traditional protocol of approaching elders and superiors": "Africans . . . sat by age in a circle, which . . . began and ended at the head of the circle. . . . With regard to the worship of God, Africans regarded the circle to comprise their ancestors who are stratified by age in a relationship with each other. The circle extended far back, and linked with God, who was the head of the entire family

5. Carol Meyers, "Kinship and Kingship: The Early Monarchy," in *The Oxford History of the Biblical World*, ed. Michael D. Coogan (Oxford: Oxford University Press, 1998), 239.
6. M. I. Finley, *The World of Odysseus* (London: Chatto & Windus, 1956), 83.

circle of the living and the dead."[7] Such was the society whose demise Samuel mourns and foretells in 1 Sam. 8.

Deuteronomy depicts the Israelite elders as exercising important judicial functions: it is they who cast judgment on rebellious sons and errant brides (Deut. 21:18–21; 22:13–21). They negotiate and are party to treaties with foreign tribes (Num. 22:4; Judg. 11:8). Their assemblies carried weight and were an indispensable, local thread in the network of legal connections that held each tribe and the confederacy of Israelite tribes together. It is not possible realistically to imagine premonarchic Israel functioning without them. It makes historical sense for the elders to have the authority to petition Samuel for a king (Halpern 1981: 199–202, 215–17).

In this prestate, segmentary tribal culture, the household is the transmitter of Israel's moral norms. In tribal societies, the extended family largely rules itself, "by the niceties of respect and authority embodied in family relations" (Sahlins 1968: 17). The people in 1 Sam. 8 do not criticize Samuel for making his sons judges, since that was natural in this prestate society; they criticize the kind of judges that Joel and Abiah are (Hackett 1998: 200). What distinguishes tribal segmentary society from monarchy is not the hereditary principle, which is common to both, but that in a monarchy authority is imposed on kinship groups from without. What Samuel foresees is not just the emergence of monarchy but Israel's coming to be a state. He pictures the state as substituting its powers for those of the family. Unlike the tribe, a "state has a true government, public and sovereign, structurally separated from the underlying population and set above them. The mass of people in the state domain become subjects, and the government sovereign, by virtue of the force invested in the latter." Premonarchic Israel was a segmentary tribal society, a culture in which brothers were all equals, as brothers. Samuel responds in just the way any stalwart tribesman might react to the imposition of a state upon a "brotherhood" culture, if he had the gift of prophecy. He says the unity and autonomy of the family will be sacrificed if Israel's tribalism gives way to statehood. Just as, in tribal cultures generally, the household is a "little chiefdom within the chiefdom" (Sahlins 1968: 6, 17), so for Samuel the family is a little Israel within Israel. Samuel speaks for a heroic culture, in which the autonomous "house of the father," the *bet ab*, is the carrier of morality. And, just as the elders do not object to Joel and Abiah on the grounds of nepotism, to Samuel's having made his sons judges, but to the kind of judges they are, so Samuel does not object to monarchy, but lays bare the kind of state they will have. Israelite families had a moral basis in the oral traditions of the law: what ethos will underpin the state?

When Samuel says that their king "will take your sons, and appoint them for himself, for his chariots, and to be his horsemen; and some shall run before his

---

7. Temba L. J. Mafico, "The Biblical God of the Fathers and the African Ancestors," in *The Bible in Africa: Transactions, Trajectories, and Trends*, ed. Gerald O. West and Musa W. Dube (Leiden: Brill, 2000), 485–86.

chariots.... And he will take your daughters to be confectionaries, and to be cooks, and to be bakers" (8:11, 13), he is depicting the replacement of a brotherhood ethos with the authority of the state. Monarchies look impressive; the people want a king "like all the nations" (8:20) because the kings they could observe, like the Philistine lords, can tap immense collective resources. Samuel tries to impress upon the gullible people that it is they who will pay to make their state competitive. As in premodern Tahiti and Hawaii, so in the primitive state that emerged in Early Iron Age Israel, "masses of people may be called out for the building of an extensive irrigation complex, a great temple, or the stylish home of the paramount. On a ruling chief's command, goods and services are levied against the people for these enterprises, or for support of the chief and his retinue of ceremonial and executive officials, noble relatives, and idle hangers-on." Samuel warns that states are dependent for their superior security on one who can set himself above the law: "A paramount chief can do with impunity unto others what others would be foolish to do unto him—like carrying off someone's daughter, or his crops" (Sahlins 1968: 25–26, 92). Moreover, because "a state system involves the formal concentration of power on a basis other than kinship," in a nation-state "kinship ceases to be the only determinative factor in organizing community life."[8] Centralized political authority loosens kinship ties because economic control no longer rests in the household, but in the state.

Israel's moral law had been applied by kinship groups. Its moral coherence was articulated as a sense of brotherhood. The people know they have a right to justice in their rulers: that is a source of their objection to Samuel's sons having "perverted justice" (8:3 ESV). Their belief that equality under the law is due to all and that they have a right to a just ruler follows from God's giving the charism of leadership to a few "on behalf of his people in their entirety." The belief in "Israel's election as the chosen people of Yahweh set the nation apart from other peoples. It was a special feature of its identity. All other callings and elections, whether to kingship, priesthood, or prophecy, were viewed in association with the choice of the people as a whole."[9] Monarchy potentially endangered this belief in the election of the people as a whole.

Political steps that break with past practice are normally debated at the point leading up to their occurrence. Heated controversy and civil war preceded England's shift toward parliamentary democracy under a constitutional monarch, as did America's Declaration of Independence. These developments are no longer seriously contested: only recondite academic coteries question their validity. The Deuteronomist never criticizes Solomon for raising taxes to pay for an expensive entourage. This cannot be due to enhanced respect for the person of the Davidic king, since "the Deuteronomist has no qualms ... about attacking Solomon for apostasy (1 Kgs. 11:1ff.), a perhaps somewhat more serious violation" (Halpern

8. Meyers, "Kinship and Kingship," 222–24, 239.
9. Ibid., 360.

1981: 218). It is true that Israelite kings will take the lands of others to build up their own palatial estates. Judean kings did tax the people to pay for the upkeep of the court (1 Kgs. 4:7; 20:15) (von Rad 1962: 58–59). Given that the later prophets and editors of the histories only abuse their kings as idolaters, not as centralizing bureaucrats, it seems "the credit for 1 Sam. 8:11–18 cannot be laid on Dtr's already overburdened shoulders" (Halpern 1981: 218). All historical probability places Samuel's warning early, rather than late. That is, the most likely historical context for the negative contrast of the fraternal ethos and that of the state is the one symbolically given by the text: at the outset of the monarchy, not after its demise in 586 BC.

Within the wisdom tradition that produced the Proverbs, like follows like. Samuel's reply to the people's request is that, if your hearts cannot rise above raison d'état, then government is precisely what you will get: having created a centralized administration, your king will "take your fields, and your vineyards, and your olive-yards, even the best of them, and give them to his servants" (1 Sam. 8:14). Because the "foresight" behind the appeal is instrumental, what was yours will become his: "your sons" (8:11), "your daughters" (8:13), "your fields, and your vineyards, and your olive-yards" (8:14), "your seed" (8:15), "your menservants, and your maidservants, and your goodliest young men, and your asses" (8:16), and not least in an agricultural economy "your sheep" (8:17)—all will be instrumentalized as coachmen for "his chariots" and as "his horsemen" and as runners before "his chariots" (8:11), as food for "his officers" and "his servants" (8:15), as laborers for "his work" (8:16), making you collectively "his servants" (8:17).

The ancient Egyptians conceived of the king as the *ka*, the "vital force" or soul of the whole people. In art and drama, the archaic notion of the king as the "herdsman" of his people is imaginatively gratifying.[10] In reality, this meant the confiscation of lands: the regal practices that Samuel refers to were common among the Canaanites and in Bronze Age Ugarit and Alalakh (Halpern 1981: 219). The realistic assessment of power relations for which the elders ask entails a rigorous collectivism, in which what is mine or yours is absolutely his, just because he, the king, is us: "Redistribution is chieftainship said in economics" (Sahlins 1968: 95).

Once Samuel had delivered this top-to-bottom condemnation of kingship, the elders could not weakly repeat their original complaint about the sons (8:5). In reaction, and to get what they want, they must raise the stakes above a local and immediate issue to a threat equaling that described by the prophet and, in fact, flowing on from his words: yes, the people say, we do want a man to symbolize and represent us, "that we also may be like all the nations, and that our king may judge us, and go out before us, and fight our battles" (8:20). What they want

10. John A. Wilson, "Egypt," in *Before Philosophy: The Intellectual Adventure of Ancient Man*, by H. Frankfort, H. A. Frankfort, John A. Wilson, Thorkild Jacobsen, and William A. Irwin (London: Penguin, 1949), 95, 88–89.

from the outset is "a king to judge us like all the nations" (8:5, 20): the text would look artificial and stilted, not like a real debate unless the partners developed the rationales, matching argument to argument and often inadvertently mirroring their opponents.

Many scholars think that Samuel's ire is exacerbated because the elders slyly slide their appeal under a verbal cover. In 8:5–6 the verb they use for the power their desired "king" will deploy is "judge." The Hebrew for "to judge," *spt*, doesn't necessarily mean wielding the charisma of the legendary judges. To *spt* simply means "to discern, to decide between." For Samuel, a *sophet* was a "judge": when the people ask for "a king to judge us like all the nations" (8:5), Samuel, it is thought, is "displeased" to hear their perpetration of a diplomatic sleight of hand. The people seem to be playing on the wider use of *spt* as meaning "to administer" to mitigate the extent of the reversal they want: a king can *spt* just as much as a judge can *spt*. Repeated, the old man hears "a king to judge us" (8:6) to mean that judging is slyly being slipped into kingship, and that annoys him.

But it could be that the elders are not just being sly. Rather, they really may envisage their putative king as a man with judging (judicial and military) functions. In fact, their first king is something more than a judge and less than a fully fledged political figure, like David in Jerusalem. Samuel feels rejected by their expedition to him, as is clear from God's consoling word, it is "not . . . you" they reject (8:7). Samuel has by force of his personality united the tribes; what is lacking to him is the authority that the kings of other nations have, to unify the sacral and military powers in one single figure. Samuel had been a "kingpin charismatic judge"; Saul will be a judging king. We want to be *spt* by a king, a military leader, the elders are saying, not *spt* by a mere prophet-judge: with the accent on the word *melek*, there is no sleight of hand about the meaning of the request.

But why would that make God say to Samuel of this request, "They have rejected me, that I should not reign over them" (8:7)? The Hebrew verb *m's* means "to reject." This is a keyword of the chapter (Gunn 1980: 60). Yahweh tells Samuel: "They have not rejected thee, but they have rejected me, that I should not reign over them" (8:7). The word *m's* recurs when Samuel calls Saul out by lot, to be appointed king: "But today you have rejected your God, who saves you from all your calamities and your distresses, and you have said to him, 'Set a king over us'" (10:19 ESV); and at the final dismissal of Saul from his appointment, at Gilgal, when Samuel tells Saul, "I will not return with you. For you have rejected the word of the LORD, and the LORD has rejected you from being king over Israel" (15:26 ESV).

The reason why the Lord says that in asking for a king the people "have rejected me" is filled out in 8:8: "According to all the works which they have done since the day I brought them up out of Egypt even unto this day, wherewith they have forsaken me, and served other gods." Asking for a king is a species of idolatry. The precise species of idolatry depends, however, on how we conceive God's kingship over Israel. The petition for a human king would be literally idolatry and the rejection of God absolute, if God's kingship is conceived of as literally governmental. Hobbes seems to equate kingship with government when he states that "the Books of *Joshua*, *Judges*, *Ruth*, and *Samuel*, down to the time of *Saul*, describe the acts of God's people, till the time they cast off God's yoke, and called for a King, after the manner of their neighbor nations."[11] Is it right to assume with Hobbes that human kingship is predominantly a political or governmental matter? Christopher Dawson thinks not. The British monarchy has flourished, despite its loss of political power: "The experience of the last centuries," Dawson observes, "shows that the importance of monarchy does not depend on its political power. In fact it is not strictly a political institution since it represents those elements in the national life which transcend the political plane, but without which a purely political system cannot function satisfactorily." Rather than being a material power by which one dynasty controls the fate of the nation, monarchy is, first, Dawson believes, "an organ of social unity, the focus of a common loyalty." Second, and most centrally, its "function is moral: to be a living embodiment of the principle of justice and the earthly representative of divine authority and power." Dawson does not think such a conception of monarchy was uniquely English or even uniquely Christian: "The characteristic monarchical principles of impartial authority, personal loyalty, and the duty of the king to protect the weak against the strong are common to East and West. . . . They have been accepted without question for ages as the foundation of the state; and it is only when a government fails in its fulfillment of them that it forfeits the allegiance of its subjects, because it has already lost what the Chinese used to term *The Mandate of Heaven*."[12] It is important to get this straight, because a materialist conception of monarchy as a specific form of power relation, the rule of one over many, has misguided the interpretation of 1 Sam. 8–15. Even in its human form, monarchy is not about government, but about justice.

God's kingship over Israel was not a political but an ethical matter. God's political kingship of Israel is a metaphor for the sovereignty of God, whose revealed law is present in the ark of the covenant. If our author believed that God had been literally and not metaphorically Israel's king, then, a human king would be absolutely prohibited, like breaking the moral law. If we picture the Sinai covenant as making God a literal sovereign of a literal human kingdom, then we shall be compelled to fragment 1 Sam. 8 into sources articulating contrasting theologies: more importantly, it becomes impossible to rationalize God's compliance with the request (Campbell and O'Brien 2000: 236–37). If we take our lead from Augustine, rather than from Hobbes, the axiom that God's covenant kingdom with Israel symbolizes the city of God helps us to make literal sense of 1 Samuel. This church father's symbolical understanding of the Old Testament kingdom helps

11. Hobbes, *Leviathan*, 424.
12. Christopher Dawson, "The Tradition of Christian Monarchy," *The Month* 9 (1953): 261–66 at 265–66.

us not to get so close to the words that we miss the wood for the trees. Reading the story of the earthly kingdom of God in the light of the story of the heavenly kingdom reminds us of an element of the Old Testament story that is too easily mislaid: "The Ark, which—through the divine throne—remains unoccupied ... bear[s] witness to the *invisibility* of the divine Lord, whose presence ... is only assured to the eye of faith" (Eichrodt 1961–67: 1.103, emphasis added). The city of God is not an earthly kingdom: antimaterialism is a basic dynamic of the *City of God*, because it is partly designed to dampen millennialist or literal understandings of the kingdom, rife in the fifth century as they were later to be in the seventeenth century. Having the city of God at the back of our minds inclines us to recall that the authors of Exodus and Samuel were not so primitive as to imagine God as a mythological sovereign seated on a sky throne, who would be literally rejected and replaced if the people were, in Hobbes's words, to "cast off his yoke" and demand to be given a human king.

For Christians, but not for Jews, the ritual law was carnal/literal in its time and place, but allegorical; for Christians and for Jews, the moral law in Exod. 20 is literally true and binding for all times; and for Christians and for Jews, God's kingship was always somewhat metaphorical. It is easy to get confused about this because the land that God has promised is a literal fact in the Old Testament. When that guides us toward locutions like Boling's "earthly half of the kingdom of Yahweh" (1975: 24), we are well on the way toward making Yahweh an earthling. Millennialism—whether truncated, hopeless, and worldly, as Hobbes's seems to be, or elaborately eschatological—is another source of confusion. Here again, in a more subtle, theological way, the idea of the earthly kingdom displaces that of its supernatural king. God's kingship is not of this world.

The distinction between ethics as absolute and politics as relative entails that there is room to maneuver in politics in a way that there is not in ethics. There is scope for Israel's being "a priestly kingdom and a holy nation" (Exod. 19:6 NRSV) in more than one way. We cannot downplay the evil of the desire for a human king; it is idolatrous, but it is a metaphorical and not a literal idolatry. Samuel prophesies that the people's desire will lead them into ever greater subjection. They will lose out, he says, and as such losses accumulate, they will "cry out" against their king "and the LORD will not hear you in that day" (8:18), because they have chosen government instead of covenant, a king instead of God. God grants them their freedom because, since it is metaphorical and not material, the kingdom is a matter for human license.

License, rather than real freedom in cooperation with God, is the aim of the request, and the covenant is not at the forefront of the people's minds when they make it. It's a bit of a stretch to see the elders in 8:5 as motivated by an abstract desire for social justice (Campbell and O'Brien 2000: 218): they object to being exploited by the sons' malpractices; but are they profoundly concerned that, by taking bribes, the sons are breaking the covenant? The voices of Samuel and Yahweh never express literal antimonarchism: "Rather, what Yahweh and Samuel are critical of is the anti-covenantal sentiment they hear in Israel's request" (Eslinger 1983: 66). It is not literally a debate about monarchy, like the controversies between Roundheads and Cavaliers in Stuart England with which Hobbes was familiar. It is, rather, about the morality of kingship, whether it can be rooted in the covenantal ethic and its fraternal ethos.

Human will interacts with divine will in the making of God's providence in history. The people have sent up a prayer petition. To their misfortune, it is answered: "And when they asked, he gave them a king . . . according to their heart, but not according to his heart." Augustine believed that "these things are written that no one may think well of himself if his prayer is heard, when he has asked impatiently for what it would be better for him not to receive, and that no one may be cast down and may despair of the divine mercy toward him if his prayer has not been heard, when he has, perhaps, asked for something that would bring him more bitter suffering if he received it or would cause his downfall if he were ruined by prosperity. In such circumstances, then, we know not what we should pray for as we ought" (Letter 130, in Franke 2005: 224).

Faith and hope in Yahweh are not included within the elders' shortsighted, worldly political pragmatism. The people collectively reject Israel's identity as God's people: they want "a king to judge us like all the nations" (8:5), "that we also may be like all the nations" (8:20): this is foreseen in Deut. 17:14, where the people are made to say, "I will set a king over me, like as all the nations that are about me." They are turning aside from what is theirs and wanting what is his, giving up the unique individuality that is their vocation as God's people. God tells Samuel, the elders want that "I should not reign over them" (1 Sam. 8:7), so the people insist that a man typifying the collective should be the source of their identity, their king.

Samuel's speech looks back to the heroic age of the judges, when there were no kings to despoil the family, and it also looks forward. It does not present the familial ethos as an end in itself. The ethos of brotherhood could survive the demise of segmentary tribalism. Even though the people's request is a rejection of covenant in favor of self-government, "the original covenantal community" is not the only true Israel. Mendenhall rightly sees that primitive, premonarchic Israel, in the afterglow of the Sinaitic covenant, is the most likely time and place in which to set hostility to monarchy: once kingship was established, it was no longer fervently debated. Others would agree that "monarchy, . . . with its accompanying revival of laws, wars, social stratification, taxation, conscription, and general monopolizing of force, constitutes a return to the paganism of the Late Bronze Age when . . . the kings claimed divine prerogatives and sought control over aspects of life that were rightfully within the deity's domain" (Flanagan 1988: 67). But Mendenhall goes further and claims that, in making the transition to statehood and centralized monarchy, Israel sacrificed its "religious and ethical concerns in favor of a political power structure in the time of Solomon" (1973: 157). Where Jobling gave us a negative assessment of the antimonarchic theme in 1 Sam. 8, Mendenhall makes a positive assessment of antimonarchism: both exaggerate its material political features at the expense of its authentically eschatological elements.

The providence of God is larger than any one of its material vehicles: that is another way of saying that the kingship of God is not physical or mythological. Though anthropologists may laud tribal means of production as a model of unalienated labor, in which "work is an expression of preexisting kin and community relations" (Sahlins 1968: 80–81), God is not an epiphenomenon of economic systems. Both in the Lord's description of the people's request as a rejection of himself and in Samuel's denunciation of state power, scripture teaches that the familial culture was idyllic in relation to the states that succeed it. First Sam. 8 describes statehood as a falling away from the more perfect. It is one further step in the ongoing fall of humanity away from walking with the Lord in perfect trust. But to see this step into monarchism as an absolute descent into paganism, a complete loss of faith in the God of Sinai, as Mendenhall would have it, is to narrow the scope of God's action into the binary spectrum supplied, for instance, by Marxist materialism: primitive communism good, later capitalist oppression evil. The overriding reason for thinking that binary opposition too limited is that God does in fact accede to the people's request. Requesting a king is not original sin, and statehood is not fallenness. But, historically, statehood occurs within the context of human fallenness. This is why, in 1 Sam. 8–15, our author advertently recalls voices that speak for and against monarchy. To neglect the presence of both kinds of evidence will be to obtain a flat rather than a rounded meaning in this story of Israel's first human king.

First Sam. 8 helps us appreciate that the city of God is not the sort of polity in which extremes of wealth and poverty would coexist. Some believe that monarchic government aggrandizes such material disparities.[13] This depends on the moral framework of the monarch, that is, on whether an individual king makes it his vocation to promote justice: this is why Thomas Aquinas said that monarchy is the most ethically stringent of all forms of government, demanding "outstanding virtue" of its rulers (*De Regimine Principe* 9).

As the church's tradition reads it, what must be taken literally in the Old Testament is its ethics, not its politics. As a matter of ethics, monarchy can be put in the service of the city of God to the extent that the monarch puts himself at the service of God. The author of Deuteronomy was aware of this ambiguity, recognizing both that monarchy lays great temptation in the paths of the governing class and that, if its rulers dedicate their kingdom to God, monarchy can work. Deuteronomy does not rule out the legality of this form of government, because it does not take the divine kingship over Israel literally. But it hedges its permission of kingship with moral prescriptions:

> When you come to the land which the LORD your God is giving you, and possess it and dwell in it, and say, "I will set a king over me like all the nations that are around

13. Meyers, "Kinship and Kingship," 222.

me," you shall surely set a king over you whom the LORD your God chooses; one from among your brethren you shall set as king over you; you may not set a foreigner over you, who is not your brother. But he shall not multiply horses for himself. . . . Neither shall he multiply wives for himself, lest his heart turn away; nor shall he greatly multiply silver and gold for himself. Also it shall be, when he sits on the throne of his kingdom, that he shall write for himself a copy of this law in a book, from the one before the priests, the Levites. And it shall be with him, and he shall read it all the days of his life, that he may learn to fear the LORD his God and be careful to observe all the words of this law and these statutes, that his heart may not be lifted above his brethren, that he may not turn aside from the commandment to the right hand or to the left, and that he may prolong his days in his kingdom, he and his children in the midst of Israel." (Deut. 17:14–20 NKJV)

When Deuteronomy rules that the king must be "one from among your brethren you shall set as king over you; you may not set a foreigner over you, who is not your brother," it speaks for the segmentary tribal society and so for the ethic of brotherhood. Nonetheless, Deuteronomy prescribes not *whether* the people will have a king, but *how* that king should behave *when* they do: it assumes monarchic government as a consequence of settlement.

Since the nineteenth century, interpreters of the Deuteronomistic History have followed de Wette in thinking of Deuteronomy as a product of the reforms of King Josiah in 622 BC, before the conquest of 586. Since legal systems are not invented out of thin air but emerge through practice and precedent, if Deuteronomy itself is in fact a late document, it must emerge from centuries of practice of Israelite law. Deuteronomy 17 has numerous marks of referring to Israel's original kings. One is that it does not presuppose a setting in which Israel had become inured to dynastic kingship and prophetic investiture of kings was underappreciated, but rather insists on the charismatic character of the king. The phrase "a king . . . whom the LORD your God chooses" "adumbrates an early date: of all Israel's kings, only Saul, David, and, in Chronicles, Solomon, are 'chosen' by the god" (Halpern 1981: 228).[14]

The question that Mendenhall raises—whether the loss was greater than the gain when Israel passed from a culture in which the ethics and faith of Israel was carried by the family to one in which they were patchily sustained by statecraft—deserves an answer. A realist can argue both that God himself persistently lowers the bar from the fall of Adam onward, patiently contriving decreasingly demanding means by which the people can hold their evil impulses in check and that, historically, population growth and external threat necessitated the construction of a centralized political apparatus. It is true in one way to say that "kingship is in this material in the somewhat subtly delineated position of a relative evil

14. For a recent defense of the idea of Deuteronomy as a seventh-century product, a written law that, from its invention in 622 BC, overrules rather than incorporates earlier oral tradition, see Toorn 2007: 87, 222–25, 248–50.

embraced by the god" (Halpern 1981: 154). This answer is realistic, but it is not sufficient. It is not sufficient to appreciating what God is: it pictures the Lord as acting within political constraints, checks and balances of power, compromising like a human king.

The question that Samuel's speech raises—whether a tribal culture can pass into statehood without undermining the family as locus of culture—is still a live one, particularly in those cultures in which the transition is in living memory. As Philip Jenkins notes, "Western Churches might teach the doctrine of the communion of saints, and imagine the supernatural church as a union of living believers with . . . past souls. . . . For the African churches, the notion of continuity with the world of the ancestors is . . . a fundamental component of the belief system. . . . Closeness to native traditions gives a powerful relevance to . . . communal visions of the church, the *ecclesia*."[15] The way in which to answer Samuel's question is neither to picture God in a political way nor to picture politics in a familial way. If the family is an ineliminable part of God's plan for society, this rests in what God himself is. Samuel's warning against statehood is that Israel will cease to be structurally united by fraternal relations of love and instead will be fettered by power relations. It thus rejects God, because God is love. Pope Benedict XVI claims that, because the family is a "community of love and life where differences . . . contribute to forming a 'parable of communion,'" the family is one of the "analogies of the ineffable mystery of the Trinity" (Angelus, 12 February 2006 [Feast of the Most Holy Trinity]). In its eschatological pilgrimage, humanity journeys from families and tribes to states to its final destination in the family of the triune God of love.

Episode Two: The Traveling Question Mark (1 Sam. 9)

"A Benjamite, a mighty man of power" (9:1) was axiomatic for the original audience of 1 Samuel. The tribe of Benjamin were renowned as slingshotters: their elite attack force was "left-handed; every one could sling a stone at a hair and not miss" (Judg. 20:16 ESV). Perhaps, like the Maoris, the Benjamites trained their children for warfare by binding up their right arm, compelling them to become skillful in the use of the left. Iron Age city fortifications, such as the Philistines had, compelled an attacker to expose his right side: if he used his right hand to wield the sword, a shield held up on the left side would afford him little protection. Training a left-hander to use the sling doubled his effectiveness as a warrior: "The southpaw and the slinger were Israelite military specialists" because the "sling's long range and high trajectory . . . made it invaluable in siege. Assyrian reliefs . . . depicting the conquest of Lachish in 701 BC, consistently place slingers to the

15. Philip Jenkins, *The Next Christendom: The Coming of Global Christianity* (Oxford: Oxford University Press, 2002), 133.

rear of attacking columns" (Halpern 1996: 42–43). So from the first sentence of
1 Sam. 9, "There was a man of Benjamin, whose name was Kish, . . . a Benjamite,
a mighty man of power" (9:1 NKJV), the audience is led to expect the answer to
the people's prayer for a "king [to] . . . go out before us, and fight our battles" (8:20
NKJV). As Saul hooves into the reader's view, he looks perfect for the position:
Kish "had a choice and handsome son whose name was Saul. There was not a more
handsome person than he among the children of Israel. From his shoulders upward
he was taller than any of the people" (9:2 NKJV). Samuel has sent the people
back to their cities, their request unrefused (8:22). So, as Saul and his servant
search for Kish's asses, the audience is looking to see how the expedition will lead
to Saul's promotion. The viewer knows that what is needed is to get putative king
and kingmaker together. A graphic piece of storytelling holds the anticipation:
"He passed through the mountains of Ephraim and through the land of Shalisha,
but they did not find them. Then they passed through the land of Shaalim, and
they were not there. Then he passed through the land of the Benjamites, but they
did not find them" (9:4 NKJV). Finally, Saul's servant has the ruse that will take
them to the kingmaker. There is "a man of God," he says, "in this city"—both
seer and city remain anonymous, creating a sort of make-believe suspense, like
in a fairy tale with an inevitable outcome: perhaps "he can show us the way that
we should go" (9:6 NKJV). Divining the whereabouts of a wealthy farmer's lost
asses is an oddly literal interpretation of the skills of the seer or prophet (9:9),
but perhaps Hosea, Ezekiel, and Isaiah were hardened to such distractions. As to
the gift that accompanied the visit, the servant has the present literally in hand:
"Behold," he tells his master, "I have here at hand the fourth part of a shekel of
silver: that will I give to the man of God, to tell us our way" (9:8). Still resisting
the matchmaking, the narrator sends Saul and his servant to Samuel via directions
from "young maidens going out to draw water" (9:11). Biblical heroes who meet
women on the way into a city often go on to marry them. It's as if Saul is being led
to meet the groom in a marriage arranged by others. When the young maidens
tell of his chance appearance in the village, for a sacrifice, the seer preserves his
anonymity. If you *read* the book or attend to it verbally, that is, you don't get the
name of the seer. But if you *saw* the story, graphically, like a sequence of plates
in a comic strip or graphic novel, you are not looking out for a name, but for a
visible rendition of Samuel's face. Saul and the servant don't yet see Samuel, just
a generalized image of a prophet. The preliterate esthetic experience of the event
is of not seeing the face.

It is thus only at the midpoint of the story, when the two come head to head,
that we are told that Saul has come to the one we know from 1 Sam. 8 as the
kingmaker: "As they were coming into the city, there was Samuel, coming out
toward them on his way up to the high place" (9:14 NKJV). Because his identity
has been playfully withheld for so long, the seer's being given his face is a little
revelation. It's as if the story moved from shade to light. The epiphany is elaborated
in the next verses, where we hear that "the LORD" told Samuel the day before that

a Benjamite will come to visit him and that he is the chosen one. Yahweh confirms Samuel's obvious guess in his ear: when the prophet spots Saul, "the LORD said unto him, 'Behold the man whom I spoke to thee of: this same shall reign over my people'" (9:17).

Identifying himself to Saul not as "Samuel" but as "the seer," Samuel breaks the news to Saul with a slowness appropriate to the pace of the story: he tells him, not that he is to be king, but that "all the desire of Israel" "is . . . on thee" (9:20). Samuel takes Saul into his house, makes him sit down for a banquet in "the chiefest place among" the thirty guests (9:22), perhaps an excruciatingly embarrassing experience for one who has minimized his own, his family's, and his tribe's value (9:21), in response to Samuel's remarks. Then the pair go off and commune in secret on "the top of the house," the only spot in an Early Iron Age dwelling where a pair of conspirators could get a bit of privacy.

First Sam. 9 is supposed to derive from an ancient promonarchic source, since the handsome Benjamite is an ideal selection (Wevers 1971: 159). One way of defending the unity of 1 Sam. 8–15 is to bypass the notion of conflicting sources by arguing that it is anti-Saul from start to finish. Some of those who are critical of the consensus that 1 Sam. 8–15 is made up of pro-Saul and anti-Saul sources claim that the depiction of Saul is loaded with negative warning signals. Although we are twice told how tall and "handsome" Saul was (9:2), we are not told that he is a man of God. Throughout the she-ass recovery mission, it is, moreover, the servant who takes the lead, suggesting the trip to the seer and producing the money to give him as a present: it seems to some scholars who think 1 Sam. 8–15 is integrally opposed to Saul that Saul comes across as lacking in initiative when his servant tells him, "Look, *I* find in *my* hand a quarter shekel of silver, and *I* will give it to the man of God" (9:8, trans. Long). Elaborating on Alter's observation (1981: 60) that Saul's encounter with the maidens at the well is an aborted betrothal type scene, it is claimed that this botched type scene is an ominous portent of Saul's character deficiency. Plus, that his servant knows about the seer and that Saul does not and fails to recognize him when they meet could be a metaphorical way of showing that Saul is shortsighted, a bad listener who does not pick up on the cues (Long 1989: 200–203).

It may not be necessary to integrate 1 Sam. 8–15 by finding in it a thoroughgoing assassination of Saul's character. There is more to God's plans than we can know, before the eschaton. One tiny "might have been" is what God intended to do with Saul's chieftainship, had Saul not fallen away. As von Rad wisely observes, "The shadows of the whole succeeding history fall so darkly on his portrait, and the 'No'" is ultimately "so intense and . . . so strongly underpinned theologically, that they well-nigh smother Jahweh's word, 'he shall save my people, for I have looked upon my people' (I Sam. ix.16)" (1962: 327). To reduce God's plan to the "no" alone is to take the political development of Israel as a foregone conclusion. But we do not know what God intended to do with Saul's prepolitical chieftainship, because matters fell out otherwise. From God both having Samuel anoint Saul as king and imposing theocratic demands on him, we can, without attempting to go behind the only script we are given for knowing God's plan, at least understand that God intended to use Saul as an instrument for creating a polity that was neither acephalous tribalism nor secular statism. If 1 Sam. 8–15 is not about government, there is no need to unify it around either a putative antimonarchic theme or an anti-Saulide theme. Perhaps the author preserved the yes and the no for a reason.

Rather than finding hints of negativity in the portrayal of Saul in 1 Sam. 9, one may say that the drama of the episode turns on determinedly presenting Saul in a passive light. Saul is given a modest, quasiridiculous mission, looking for lost she-asses, because that was the story, no doubt. But the story was remembered because being anointed king on the way to find some lost donkeys is a memorably abrupt transition, the fairy-tale way of showing ineluctable necessity. The story is saying in the most emphatic way that Saul did not put himself forward, but was chosen by Yahweh. If he does anything to advance his sleepwalking progress toward Samuel the kingmaker, then the fairy-tale quality of the shepherd who becomes king is undermined; if Saul shows any advertency or volition in the progress toward high honor, then the magical effect of his being guided by remote control is lost. Saul has, we are told, been elected by Yahweh to rule. His passivity indicates that it is the Lord, not Saul, who is pulling the strings. The author wants to show that providence slipped Saul into position. On the stage it could be played for humor: the laugh would be one of recognition, grasping that power is behind this. The man's having exactly the right change spotlights, not Saul's dependence on his servant, but the dependence of all these events on God's providence. Likewise, Saul's ignorance of the prophet's identity is not necessarily a sign of ineptitude. After the events of 1 Sam. 8, a young man who deliberately beat his path to Samuel's door would be self-selected. But here we have a handsome young man, son of a Benjamite, a mighty man of war, and no slouch himself, since height counts on the battlefield, who is not so ambitious and knowing as to figure out who Samuel is or why he wants to put him at the head of his banquet table. The choice is God's alone.

Church fathers like John Chrysostom take at face value the effect of 1 Sam. 9 in making Saul appear "not . . . at all ambitious of becoming a king" (*On the Priesthood* 4.1, in Franke 2005: 229). This seems to fit the author's theological esthetic. Imagine what the tale from the request for a king in 1 Sam. 8 to Saul's rejection in 1 Sam. 15 would have been like as literature if Saul had made his entrée in 1 Sam. 9 as an evident villain. The drama of ascent and descent would evaporate. Biblical bad guys invariably finish last. In their losing, they are the objects of divine satire. The punitive tale of their comeuppance can be dramatic when they are awesome figures like the pharaoh of Egypt. It's hard to see what could have given an embattled Israelite king sufficient splendor to play the bad guy dramatically for twenty chapters, while Yahweh's blows rained down upon him. As it is, Samuel himself evidently takes Saul to his bosom: when Yahweh orders him to dismiss

Saul as king in 1 Sam. 15, "Samuel was angry, and he cried to the LORD all night" (15:11 ESV); after pronouncing his rejection, "Samuel grieved over Saul" (15:35 ESV); he has to be ordered to shake off his sadness: "The LORD said to Samuel, 'How long will you grieve over Saul?'" (16:1 ESV). After 1 Sam. 15, even some of the literary theorists who take him as a tragic figure concede that Saul loses our sympathy, with his mad attempts on the lives of David and Jonathan and his murder of the priest who sheltered David.[16] That we have had some sympathy for this tall, handsome greenhorn gives these stories a pathos they would lack if 1 Samuel had simply constructed a binary opposition between Saul the bad chief and David the good prince-in-waiting. Perhaps a youthful, appealing modesty, shyness, and lack of ambition were engrained in the old legendary portraits of Saul. This historical evidence makes 1 Sam. 9–31 better as literature than it would have been if it had conveyed a melodramatic confrontation of villain versus hero. We come to share what von Rad calls the storyteller's "deep sympathy" for Saul, in his "collapse . . . darkness and despair" (1962: 327). If Saul and Samuel had never been truly matched, Saul's visit to the witch of Endor to ask counsel of Samuel's ghost would not make sense (1 Sam. 28).

In 1 Sam. 9, Samuel is initially faceless, but it is Saul who is really anonymous. The later Saul is pathetic because he once was "a traveling question mark": he once had free will. By giving him this designation, Polzin means to suggest that Saul's "character zone is filled with doubt and uncertainty" (1989: 103). In his empty-handed neutrality, the Saul of 1 Sam. 9 is open "to going to good or to bad." He is an unpainted canvas. What will he make of his beauty and strength, when he becomes king? Though he is a Benjamite and the handsomest guy in Israel, Saul is not a formed character. By presenting him as neither overtly wicked nor some pious Nazirite type, the author creates in Saul a figure who can make of the role of first king in Israel whatever he freely wills. The author can exhibit that use of free will in action, dramatizing Saul's exercise of freedom through the choices he makes.

There are three ways of reading Saul's character in 1 Sam. 9 in the context of Saul's life as a whole. One can say he is passively innocent here and innocent later, falling victim to an arbitrary God. That option subverts the biblical text, since fatalistic determinism is foreign to the Old Testament. An apparently less unbiblical interpretation is to see Saul as already on the slippery slope to the faults for which he will eventually be punished. This is easy to swallow as a moral lesson, since we prefer our bad guys to be rotten all the way down, that is, as we imagine, quite unlike ourselves. This exegesis, which takes Saul in 1 Sam. 9 at less than face value, doesn't let him exercise free will. The third possibility is that the story is pointing home a more stringent moral than we find to our tastes. It acknowledges that human freedom is imperfect, in the sense of not being exercised ex nihilo,

---

16. Bernard P. Robinson, *Israel's Mysterious God: An Analysis of Some Old Testament Narratives* (Newcastle upon Tyne: Grevatt & Grevatt, 1986), 48.

but always in the context of what is given to us. On this reading, Saul has been given a role without asking for it and has to achieve, or fail to achieve, what that role demands. The story is about someone who, as Chrysostom says, did not "run greedily after" kingship, rose nonetheless, "made a bad use of the honor which had been given him by God" and who could not use "I never asked for this" as a legitimate defense (*On the Priesthood* 4.1, in Franke 2005: 229). The question is what use he makes of his freedom. Our human freedom is intertwined in its choices with God's free gifts of opportunities to act. A twelfth-century reader interpreted the story in this uncomfortable sense: "If the story of the sacred history presents to us King Saul, who begins well but does not persevere in the good whence he had begun," Pierre de Cava writes, "this is so that we can see in him that which we ought to imitate and that which we ought to guard against" (2004: 32 §1.1).

The author is saying something theological with Saul's passivity. The wider meaning of Saul's blank or neutral character portrayal is that anyone can become king or that a king could be any man, an anonymous blank: it's what he does with kingship that matters, how the king's will turns, to good or to evil. First Sam. 9 is portraying kingship, like any human artifact, as morally neutral in itself, as expressed by the moral neutrality of Israel's debutant monarch: like kingship, Saul is a blank canvas on which he can choose to inscribe life or death.

Finding divergent sources in 1 Sam. 8–15 seems to have no logical stopping point. This is because it is circular: "If text Y is anti-monarchic, it belongs by definition to the anti-monarchic source; since the source contains such anti-monarchic texts as Y, the source itself is anti-monarchic" (Halpern 1981: 150–51). Some scholars not only think that 1 Sam. 9 is an early, promonarchic source, but also split this chapter into a section that knows about Samuel and a section that does not. Because the seer and his village are unnamed until 9:14, it is argued that this section conflates a source in which Saul is merely promised the kingdom by a nameless seer with one in which Samuel himself anoints him. It is claimed that an "older story [that] told of a chance encounter with an anonymous prophet" has been altered to include Samuel (Campbell and O'Brien 2000: 237–39). This seems to neglect the graphic quality of this story. The withholding of Samuel's "face" is a pictorial device, allowing the story to reach a climax in the unmasking of Samuel's identity at the meeting of the two men. Against the idea that Samuel was later parachuted into a story that was originally just about a seer, Long argues that the slow revelation of the true personas of the seer tracks Saul's slow "process of discovery": it makes the audience observe the opening of Saul's eyes, in his recognition of Samuel (1989: 196–99). This is where the anticipation leads.

On the one hand, everything in the story of Saul's mission is foreordained: Saul is delivered into Samuel's environs by God's design. This man, with his soldierly biceps—"from his shoulders upward he was taller than any of the people" (ESV)—and unique beauty—"there was not a more handsome person than he among the children of Israel" (9:2 NKJV)—is indeed Yahweh's own choice. Yahweh's statement to Samuel is reminiscent of the beginning of Exodus, when the people cry to him for help, and he remembers them and sends a savior: "Tomorrow about this time I will send you a man from the land of Benjamin, and you shall anoint him commander over My people Israel, that he may save My people from the hand of the Philistines; for I have looked upon My people, because their cry has come to Me" (9:16 NKJV). That does not sound ironic. Unless it is a piece of legend that an editorial "blockhead" neglected to omit (Halpern 1996: 114), it signifies that Saul's election was providential and that Yahweh had no initial intention of selecting a figure of fun to signal his disapproval of the people's rejection of his divine kingship. God freely elects Saul with his people's well-being at heart. Saul's ignorance and lack of initiative in the selection signals Yahweh's omnipotence at work. On the other hand, the blank and open portrayal of Saul's character indicates that he himself is a free man, as yet indifferent with respect to the determination of his will. He has yet to make his choice between good and evil. When Saul the "traveling question mark" meets Samuel, the spokesman for Yahweh's free decisions, human free will, such as it is, and divine will meet: "So when Samuel saw Saul, the LORD said to him, 'There he is, the man of whom I spoke to you. This one shall reign over My people.' Then Saul drew near to Samuel in the gate, and said, 'Please tell me, where is the seer's house?' Samuel answered Saul and said, 'I am the seer'" (9:17–19a NKJV). From here on, Saul has entered the arena where he will have to make free choices, and these choices will count.

Perhaps it matters theologically to say that Samuel was in this story from the time of its composition and not parachuted in later on either as the result of the conflation of two texts or of a propagandistic determination to give the prophet a starring role in Saul's emergence. It is not only a matter of the literary unity of 1 Sam. 9, its unity as a book, but also of its pictorial sequentialism, its enabling the visual imagination of a preliterate audience to recapture Saul's experience of discovery (Long 1989: 196–99). The source-critical fidget to detect cut-and-paste signals in 1 Samuel is often sparked by the lack of clear verbal, cognitive information at the outset of a story and the depositing of new data when the story is in full swing. Source critics often resist the claim that what they see as clear indications that older and newer stories have been sewn together are really literary devices, an author's deliberately withholding his hand so as to create esthetic effects, like anticipation. One cogent objection that source critics make to literary readings of biblical texts is that they assume an esthetic sophistication expected in Henry James or Balzac and their readers that it doesn't make historical sense to ascribe to the composers or audience of 1 Samuel. This is a fair criticism. But by the same token one might ask whether the intellectual sophistication of the original intended audience of this text is also exaggerated by source critics. An author writing for an audience that he expects to take in the story imaginatively, like a series of Hebrew hieroglyphics, would "write" the story by laying a trail of pictures, producing something like a comic strip. This way of writing precludes setting all of the cognitive presuppositions of the story up front at the outset. It's part of the esthetic appeal of graphic art that the self-containment of each picture makes each new frame an abrupt transition and a revelation. The self-containment of each frame means that plot developments are often unannounced and dramatic, like the mutation of "the seer" into Samuel, and that characters can change, with their moral decisions, but they rarely develop, in the way they do in a novel, so that Saul can be a good man in 1 Sam. 9–12 and drop suddenly into wickedness in 1 Sam. 13. The jerky, stop-and-go style of 1 Samuel, its lack of cognitive fluency, which produces the fissures and jumps that source critics see as signals of multiple editorship, could be a stylistic feature consequent on the writing's being adapted to the picture thinking of a preliterate culture. Herodotus, by contrast, seems to presuppose an audience who can hold in their mind's eye a wide-ranging conceptual vision containing many particulars. The difference is that Herodotus writes for hearers who think literately, creating cognitive compounds out of what they hear, whereas our author writes for auditors who think graphically. If that were the case, then it is only a dogmatic assumption, based on encountering scripture as a post-Renaissance, edited, printed Bible, that the way in which the traditions of the church have received and communicated it are in discontinuity with its original intentions. One of these traditions, of great longevity, is to communicate its message by painting them. The evidence for this practice goes back at least to the third century AD, where a Christian baptistery and a synagogue in Dura-Europos have frescoes on their walls. Another tradition, one that seems to moderns to be disconcertingly out of tune with the text, is to dwell on individual sentences: when preachers like Augustine or Origen make a meal out of a single phrase in scripture, they may in fact be responding to a picture that is intended to be viewed as it stands, as well as in connection with what follows and precedes it. The tradition simultaneously assumes the integrity of whole episodes and can absorb Samuel's abrupt appearance into a backstory that implies him precognitively rather than explicitly. As sacred scripture, 1 Samuel belongs to a book intended to be the spiritual mainstay, not of an elite, but of anyone, of any intellectual attainment whatever. Thinking of the Bible as a book intended for all humanity may help us to understand its original intentions and means of composition.

Episode Three: The Spirit Blows Where He Wills (1 Sam. 10:1–16)

Biblical exegetes have reached little consensus about the many puzzles posed by 1 Sam. 10. First, there are Saul's three apparent installations: 10:1; 10:2–25 (where Saul is called out by lot); and 1 Sam. 12. Second, there is the mysterious incident among the prophets, giving rise to the saying "Is Saul also among the prophets?" (10:10–12). Third, there is the strange fact, regarded as inexplicable by some, that when Saul returns home, after the anointing and prophesying, he doesn't recount any of these events to his uncle. Instead, with that childish literalism that makes the larger disappear into the smaller, he remarks that Samuel had told them "the donkeys had been found" (10:16 ESV).

Samuel seems both to give the anointed Saul permission to act as he sees fit and simultaneously to claw back the authorization. Samuel tells Saul that on the way home he will encounter a series of "signs" (10:7): women with news of the discovery of the donkeys, three men offering "two loaves of bread" (10:4), and, just past a Philistine garrison, a group of musical "prophets" (10:5), among whom Saul will receive the charisma of "the Spirit of the Lord" (10:6). Once the *ruah*, the Spirit, has rushed over him, Saul must regally seize the initiative: "When these signs meet you, do what your hand finds to do, for God is with you" (10:7 ESV). But in the next verse, Samuel seems to put Saul back under his own authority: "Then go down before me to Gilgal. And behold, I am coming to you to offer burnt offerings and to sacrifice peace offerings. Seven days you shall wait, until I come to you and show you what you shall do" (10:8 ESV). Why is Saul to be turned into a charismatic hero just after having been anointed king, and why is he still under Samuel's authority? Why should the anointed *nagid* or king be subjugated to some random seer? One solution is to posit that 10:7 and 10:8 were composed by different hands, 10:8 being a later theological interpolation to ensure that prophets still held the reins (Long 1989: 58–59). Another way into 10:7–8, which perhaps opens up the meaning of 1 Sam. 10 as a whole, is to think that history seldom produces absolute fissures between an earlier period and its successor. As Israel's earliest king, Saul exhibits the characteristics of a late judge: he will be both a prophetic fighter like Othniel, Samson, Gideon, and Deborah and a charismatic king. This chapter defines in theological terms the kind of kingship Saul will hold. Saul will be neither judge in the sense of Joshua and Judges, an adventitious charismatic leader, nor king as David will be king in Jerusalem, but a "charismatic king." This chapter is crucial to understanding the conditions of Saul's kingship.

Since they followed on the heels of a kinship-based polity, it is sociologically likely that Israel's very first kings were more like chiefs than absolute monarchs: "Traditional societies . . . often do not move directly from a segmentary tribal organization to a hereditary, permanent, centralized monarchy. Many pass through an intermediate stage known as 'chiefdom,' and it is possible to designate Saul's reign and much of David's as more like a chiefdom, with Saul and David as the chiefs, than a full-fledged monarchy." Because there is as yet "no real legal system . . . to enforce the decisions of the chief . . . he is still a type of charismatic leader" (Hackett 1998: 200–201). One could refine this further and demarcate Saul and David. Saul is one step prior to a chief in the echelons of barely-past-tribal society: his first anointing has made him a "big man." Whereas David enters the realm of politics proper and can be called a "chief," the social and religious exigencies that Saul inhabits remain personal and prepolitical. In Melanesian tribal cultures, the big man preceded the chief: the big man depends on personal loyalties and exhibitions of *mana* ("charisma"), rather than holding a permanent official position (Sahlins 1968: 89–91). As the designated big man of the Israelite tribes rather than a consecrated king, Saul has not devolved the display of the divine charisma to a separate caste of prophets. No big man could afford to do so, for his status depends on earning respect as a charismatic figure, not on legal protocol.

We even have to be restrained about calling Saul a "big man" in 10:1–16. Hebrew *nagid* means "anointed king" or "monarch-designate," whereas *melek* is reserved for the active "king." *Nagid* means something like president-elect. Thus far, Saul has been anointed only as *nagid*: he is chief-designate, not yet chief (Eslinger 1983: 65). The vernacular gets at this distinction by having Samuel tell Saul, "Has not the LORD anointed you to be prince over his people Israel?" (10:1). In the ancient Near East, girls were anointed at their formal betrothal (engagement). Saul's anointing "betroths" him to the kingship: it is no public coronation, not a "marriage." The anointing stage of the process to kingship in scripture is nonsecular. Three types of persons anoint in scripture: Samuel, prophets (1 Kgs. 1:45), and priests (1:39). This is the sacral entrance to kingship (Halpern 1981: 13–15).

So why should a military maneuver against the Philistine garrison such as Samuel envisages in 10:8 have to wait on the seer? In the early monarchy, prophets were on hand to ensure that soldiers and battle were duly consecrated. Elijah and Elisha are designated "the chariots of Israel and its horsemen" (2 Kgs. 2:12; 13:14 ESV); kings consult prophets (1 Kgs. 20:13–15, 22, 35–43; 2 Kgs. 3:11–19; 13:14–19) (Long 1989: 63). In this book, the vocation of the prophet Samuel is the model and exemplar of all vocation: the vocation to kingship is a lesser version of the vocation to prophecy. Samuel is like a human, walking ark, combining in himself prophecy, priesthood, and rulership. Saul, the king-designate, prince, or *nagid*, is to be merely one branch of office, and not in independence from the human archetype of vocation to office. Samuel was a child when he was called at Shiloh (1 Sam. 3), and, in emulation of this, Saul had demeaned himself, making himself "little" (15:17), telling Samuel, "Am I not a Benjamite, of the smallest of the tribes of Israel? and my family the least of all the families of the tribe of Benjamin?" (9:21). The designee, the *nagid*, is presented as unworthy, inept, or weak at the moment of appointment, because, going from the model of the role of the prophet, the calling is a symbolic "creation from birth." Jeremiah says he was "set apart" for prophecy in the womb and regarded himself as a "child" in the face of his divine commissioning (Jer. 1:5–6). Later, this metaphor of the king's anointing as being his "birth" is linked to the notion of the adoption of the king as God's son (2 Sam. 7; 1 Chr. 17; 22:10; 28:6; Ps. 89:26–27) (Halpern 1981: 127). Kingship develops its aura of divine adoption under the mantle of prophetic vocation.

In the moment of transition between charismatic judges and kings, Saul the *nagid*/big man is still a charismatic king-designate, and Samuel the seer retains the ancient privilege of the judge to take a lead in warfare. In an archaic culture, the king, who discussed strategies with his lieutenants, was nominally subject to the prophet, who heard and recounted the word of God. In an archaic religious culture, everything is sacralized to some extent: the only living analogy to this is the world of monastic culture. In the documentary *Into Great Silence*, Trappist monks learn to sit, kneel, stand, and read in postures conducive to meditative prayer. That's the kind of discipline and charisma being imposed on Saul. In *The Cup*, a film about football-crazed Tibetan Buddhist monks, the abbot tells a young novice that he will make a good monk because, having sold all he has to watch France beat Brazil, he is evidently unworldly: by comparison to Israel's later kings, including David, the sacral monarchy into which Saul is betrothed in 1 Sam. 10 is an unworldly and prepolitical one.

Some think that the phrase "is Saul also among the prophets?" (10:12) expresses "a somewhat derogatory view of the *nᵉbi'im*" (Van Seters 1983: 254). And yet, one reason why neither Christian nor Jewish readers spontaneously take Saul's moment of overpowerment by the *ruah* of the Lord lightly or derisively is that the phrase "God gave him another heart" (10:9) speaks to them. It doesn't come instinctively to readers in Jewish or Christian tradition to take the report that "the Spirit of God rushed upon" (ESV) Saul and that "he prophesied among" the prophets as intending to disparage Saul, because we take the idea of prophecy and prophetic inspiration seriously. Christian tradition does not specify how we should read this chapter: tradition, in the form of the fathers or the lectionary, does not guide our reading of the story in any clear direction. The one clear principle that we inherit from the church fathers about 1 Samuel as a whole is the assumption of the inspiration of the text, and therefore the historicity of the events it describes. However we understand biblical inspiration and the authors' possession of a new heart, we see that it implies that they see and describe reality well: this gives us an assumption of general realism. An assumption of realism must direct our interpretation of the episode, if we want to read it within Christian tradition. The presupposition that the text is describing something that really happened is a tremendous gift to the historical biblical critic. It hinders the formulation of circular hypotheses about source documents and stimulates us to use our historical imagination to try to figure out what is really going on here. The fixation of exegetical interest on a concern that is ultimately a priori (since anything that doesn't fit the themes of a hypothetical source must necessarily issue from a different hypothetical source) is counterproductive, since it loses sight of the evidence about primitive Israel provided by this text. Faith in the general historicity of 1 Samuel guides reason away from circularity and toward reality.

Both Saul's prophesying and the proverb "is Saul also among the prophets?" (10:12) have been evaluated positively and negatively by critics. The meaning of the proverb itself is unclear, since how one translates the phrase requires an elucidation of a context that is as impenetrable as the saying to which it gave rise. On a negative reading, Samuel instructed Saul, once all the signs are given, to "do what your hand finds to do, for God is with you" (10:7 ESV), that is, to act with all the initiative of a judge/big man and use his brains and free will, for example, against the "garrison of the Philistines" (10:5). Instead, Saul seems to do nothing but prophesy, and prophesy some more: "When they came to Gibeah [the hill], behold, a group of prophets met him, and the Spirit of God rushed upon him, and he prophesied among them. And when all who knew him previously saw how he prophesied with the prophets, the people said to one another, 'What has come over the son of Kish? Is Saul also among the prophets?' And a man of the place answered, 'And who is their father?' Therefore it became a proverb, 'Is Saul also among the prophets?'" (10:10–12 ESV). Instead of turning the charism of the Spirit to military use, as the judges did, Saul gets so caught up in the flow of prophecy that he makes an exhibition of himself. Saul prophesied with the prophets in complete abandonment of his persona, as the son of Kish, "a Benjamite, a mighty man of war" (9:1, author's translation), becoming a son of a prophet instead of the son of a warrior. First Sam. 10:10–12 is not easy to interpret, but the six repetitions of "prophesy" and "prophet" could be mocking, especially if 1 Sam. 8–15 is uniformly hostile to Saul.

If this negative reading is correct, Saul's describing the irrelevant detail and not mentioning the significant facts to his uncle comes to look like an effort at concealment. When we give a not altogether forthright account of our activities, we often highlight the innocuous part as if it were of sole importance. We might therefore imagine what Saul isn't telling in 10:14–16 and that, coming directly before it, 10:10–12 is exposing the lie, and wildly so: everyone knows that what Saul did was prophesy. The information has to be slowly extracted from Saul. In answer to the question "where did you go?" Saul just replies, "To seek the donkeys. And when . . . they were not . . . found, we went to Samuel" (10:14 ESV). Is that it? Uncle Abner has to continue the interrogation: "Please tell me what Samuel said to you." Thinking fast, Saul turns to the donkeys: "He told us plainly that the donkeys had been found." So why "of the matter of the kingdom, of which Samuel had spoken, he did not tell him anything" (10:16 ESV): is it purely a matter of concealing his behavior on Gibeah? Or is the one verse between the prophesying and the meeting with his commanding Uncle Abner rather loaded: "And when he finished prophesying, he came to the high place" (10:13 ESV). Perhaps this is pointed understatement: is *that* it? Perhaps, as Long suggests, Saul keeps silent about "the matter of the kingdom" because that would bring him back to Samuel's instruction to him: "Do what your hand finds to do, for God is with you" (10:7 ESV). Perhaps Saul doesn't want Abner, who will later be captain of his army and likes to get wind of a God-sent military opportunity, to know that he has either just bilked his first assignment by receiving the *ruah elohim* ("the Spirit of the Lord") and doing nothing with it, or that he figures he may not be up to it when the time comes. Long believes that "Saul's silence appears . . . as that of a man who has failed, or is about to fail, in his first assignment and would just as soon keep quiet about it" (1989: 211). Saul has been handed as much rein for initiative as a religious culture gave, and he has done nothing. Rather than using his ingenuity in a spontaneous gesture against the Philistine garrison, forcing them to move against Israel, and then going to Gilgal to await Samuel's arrival (10:8) before counterattack, it looks as if Saul has "prophesied among the [prophets]" and gone home.

But it may be that this exegesis has assumed in advance that everything Saul does in 1 Samuel is to be interpreted negatively. Saul's abortive reign should teach us that God's will is a mystery. We cannot know what Israel's history would have been, if its first, and only sacral, charismatic king had remained in obedience to God. Since the Lord gives him the "manna" of prophecy, we know that God intended Saul to practice a form of charismatic leadership. A positive reading makes better sense than reading the prophesying episode in a pejorative light. Sternberg finds in "the gift of prophecy . . . God's bestowing on man 'another heart' (1 Sam. 10:9) . . . another figure for Plato's inspiration-as-transformation doctrine."[17] For we are explicitly and unironically told that "the Spirit of God rushed upon" Saul (10:10 ESV). The expression "is Saul also among the prophets?" designates the precise character that Saul's kingship was intended to have: a charismatic kingship. After anointing Saul as king-elect, Samuel tells him that "you shall reign over the people of the LORD and you will save them from the hand of their surrounding enemies. And this shall be the sign to you that the LORD has anointed you to be prince over his heritage" (10:1). The sign or proof that this secret unction at Samuel's hands has really turned Saul into the king-elect of Israel will be that he meets prophets and prophesies with them. And the sign of Saul's kingship is like the sacrament of it: it is a real symbol of the type of monarchy he was intended to wield. And yet, having first been a charismatic king, Saul will become the reverse, a demonically haunted despot.

Augustine was asked by Simplician how 1 Samuel could say first "the Spirit of God came upon [Saul]" (10:12) but then later report that "an evil spirit from God came upon Saul" (16:15; 18:10; 19:9). Augustine thought there was no use contrasting the episodes or reading the earlier story with hindsight from the later ones: "It is written, '. . . God gave Saul another heart, and all the signs came to pass on that day. Then he came to the hill and, behold, a chorus of prophets met him . . . and the Spirit of God came upon him and he prophesied among them.' But Samuel had already predicted this when he anointed him. About that, I don't think there is any question. For 'the Spirit blows where he wills' " (*On Various Questions to Simplician* 2.1.1, in Franke 2005: 233). The reiteration of "prophesy" and "prophet" are most likely intended to accentuate—against 20/20 hindsight—that it was indeed God who acted here. The "Spirit blows where he wills" (John 3:8)—even on Saul. Like Augustine, Newman reads 1 Sam. 10:1–16 as an instance in which God miraculously presented "vouchers for the truth of a message" that a prophet delivers: that Samuel tells Saul he will prophesy, and this is what happens, vouches for the authenticity of the word of Samuel as sent from God.[18] The text can't be fully understood on a military-political level. That "God gave him another heart" (10:9) is told us so that we know that all the grace and

---

17. Meir Sternberg, *The Poetics of Biblical Narrative: Ideological Literature and the Drama of Reading* (Bloomington, IN: Indiana University Press, 1985), 78.

18. John Henry Newman, *Two Essays: Biblical and Ecclesiastical Miracles*, 9th ed. (London: Longmans, Green, 1890), 19.

charism needed to exercise his mission as ruler in Israel has been given to Saul. Having acceded to the request and lowered the bar to accommodate human nature as he had been doing since Gen. 3, God puts his free will behind the new ruler. The text is positive about Yahweh's intention to promote the optimal choice. Saul is intended by God to be a charismatic king—that is the meaning of the proverb "is Saul also among the prophets?" (1 Sam. 10:11–12).

Perhaps, in fact, Samuel doesn't expect Saul to take an immediate preemptive strike against the Philistines; perhaps he intends him to use his being filled with the divine Spirit for nonmilitary purposes. The reference to "Gibeath-elohim [the hill of God], where there is a garrison of the Philistines" (10:5 ESV) could be not an injunction to launch an attack on it, but simply precise directions to where Saul will meet up with the musical prophets: Saul got lost on the way out, so Samuel directs him back by reference to an outstanding landmark. Samuel does say to act, but he does not specify when or how: "Do what your hand finds to do, for God is with you" (10:7 ESV) leaves Saul free to act when the moment is right. The story of Saul's prophesying may simply prolong the tale of the dog days of Saul's innocence.

This idyll is cut short by Abner's interrogation. The secret anointing of the king-to-be is a recurrent theme: Saul, David (1 Sam. 16), and Jehu (2 Kgs. 9) are anointed secretly by prophets (Campbell and O'Brien 2000: 241–42). Samuel anointed Saul not only privately, but secretly: that is the most obvious reason why Saul doesn't tell Abner what happened! David's anointing by Samuel in 1 Sam. 16 is veiled with secrecy because he would otherwise be in danger from Saul. The reason for the secrecy of Saul's anointing is likewise to protect him until he has the protection offered by actual kingship. In the kinship society, members of the same lineage were equals in authority, whereas, in the nascent chiefdom or submonarchic era, a single member of the same household or kinship group was elevated in status above the others. He was no longer a brother among brothers. What would Abner have made of a nephew turned chief-designate? The question may have entered Saul's mind, and in that case he is no fool to keep mum. As a close relative, Abner might expect a rise in prestige proportionate to that of his nephew: a "chief redistributes goods," especially to his family members, but Saul had, as yet, nothing to show (Hackett 1998: 201). The requirement to distribute largesse is greater in the case of a big man than it is of the chief, since the former's official standing depends wholly on what he does, not on who he is (that is, it rests on person rather than on office). Because the big man's authority is private rather than public in the legal sense, he has to keep folks on his side by assistance, by "calculated generosity" (Sahlins 1968: 88). Saul's taciturnity is a tribute to his intelligence, since he literally cannot afford to be a big man even in name. The big man's social dependence on personal trust among his affiliates is the correlate of his religious dependence on God: he has nothing to fall back on, no publicly accepted legal or official safety net to shore up his position, and is therefore reliant on God's generosity. The juxtaposition of Saul's prophesying with his dialogue with Abner shows the chief-designate in the two sides of the world he has to inhabit, as a Yahwistic charismatic chieftain. Thus far, he has not flubbed it either as charismatic or as prospective chief. There is no need to prompt this story to give us anti-Saulide cues. Saul's silence before Abner is a mark that he recognizes obedience to the prophet's command as his best shield. Our author shows that God's providence was at work here and that the charisma needed to become a wise and powerful charismatic chieftain was generously given to Israel's first ruler.

Episode Four: The Lottery (1 Sam. 10:17–27)

The hypothesis that 10:1–16 comes from an old, promonarchic source whereas 10:17–27 belongs to the antimonarchic witness of later writers has become a standard criteria for interpreting this chapter. This is partly because of the apparent duplication of coronations, one in 10:1 ("Samuel took a flask of oil and poured it on his head" [ESV]) and the second in the public acclamation of 10:24 ("Long live the king!" [ESV]).

There is no need to multiply coronations here. In 10:1 Saul has been privately anointed by Samuel. He is *nagid*, or chief-designate, since he has yet to be proclaimed in public. First Sam. 10:17–27 presents Saul's public proclamation as king. There need be no textual or historical objections to a private anointing being followed by a public proclamation of the selection, if elevation to kingship or chieftainship commonly included several stages in the ancient Near East. In fact, what happens here is that Samuel displays the winning candidate. It's like when the woman who has already won a beauty contest comes up onto the podium to be seen and acknowledged by the audience with applause. The moment of seeing the writer whose novel has been selected by the jury for a prize being presented as the winner is enjoyable because recognition is a basic social phenomenon: social role or status comes back to acknowledgement by others. Saul has already been "chosen" by "the LORD," and the assembly accept him by acclamation, "Shout[ing], 'Long live the king!' " (10:24 ESV). We in the modern West don't have a formal three-stage ritual of prize winning, but we don't let people know they have won an Oscar by post. There is no repetition of coronations in 1 Sam. 10: the first (10:1) was the jury (God) pronouncing the decision, and the second (10:24) was the public witnessing of the fact, a dramatization of the moment of arrival, something that human nature seems to demand or enjoy. Saul needs this secular epiphany more than a Nobel winner needs to go to Sweden to receive an already awarded prize, because the role of kingship exists only between God, Samuel, and Saul until the people have been enabled socially to construct him as king. Having been brought to see Saul as king, the people's acceptance of him is their cooperation in the divine choice.

But why should the public proclamation entail the casting of lots? The lots work by a process of elimination: "Then Samuel brought all the tribes of Israel near, and the tribe of Benjamin was taken by lot. He brought the tribe of Benjamin near by its clans, and the clan of the Matrites was taken by lot; and Saul the son of Kish was taken by lot" (10:20–21 ESV). By inference from the "Arabian arrow oracle," Eichrodt proposes that the "lot or arrow oracle" permitted "only two possible answers to the question put to it. . . . According to which little stick jumped out when the container of the lots was shaken the answer of the deity was taken to be 'Yes' or 'No'" (1961–67: 1.393, 113). Many commentators who suppose the text is antimonarchic think that the use of lots to mark Saul as the chosen king is in some way "punitive" (Long 1989: 240); those who think 1 Samuel is not just antimonarchic but unfairly antimonarchic (biased against Saul throughout) consider that the use of lots "follows the pattern of 'seizing the culprit'" (Polzin 1989: 104). Is Saul's being taken by lot intended to reflect badly on him or on kingship?

This is one of three biblical episodes in which the lots are used to discover who did something (Polzin 1989: 103). In Josh. 7 lots are used to expose the culprit who stole some booty from Jericho. And in 1 Sam. 14 the lots expose Jonathan as the man who has inadvertently broken Saul's ban on eating during the battle of Michmash Pass—an ambiguous episode that might reflect badly on Saul rather than on the culprit, the innocent Jonathan. So Josh. 7:20 is the only Old Testament example where the casting of lots is a clear metaphor for casting the spotlight on a sinner. That is not enough to go on to presume that the designated king is being exposed by the lottery, representing the exposure of Israel's crime in requesting a king. In Acts 1:26, the eleven Apostles use lots to select a twelfth member to make up for Judas's defection, apparently seeing nothing sinister in the process. Reflection on this example would have oiled some papal conclaves. In ancient times, it was not uncommon for political leaders and juries to be selected by lot, for instance in Greece. It was a rational way of avoiding bribes being passed and of excluding the hereditary principle, where this was seen as potentially tyrannical. From 487/486 BC onward, in Athens, rule passed to three *archontes* (the *basileus* who ran festivals, the chief-general, and the civilian head of state), all of whom were selected by lot from an elected short list; likewise, the magistrates, the *boule*, and juries were all chosen by sortition or lottery. Selection of higher ranking officials by lot ensured that every citizen had an equal shot at rulership, not only those who could afford expensive political campaigns.[19] The Athenian use of sortition is postmonarchic, intended to hinder a return to tyranny; Israel's use of a lottery here is premonarchic and perhaps intended to preserve tribal equality of brothers under the new regime. Israel is making its first faltering steps from a tribal society, which is egalitarian within the framework of kinship hierarchies—that is, a "ranked" but not a "class society" (Sahlins 1968: 76)—toward concentration of power in a king. Selection of a chief by sortition followed by public acclamation keeps the best of both worlds.

19. See the articles "Sortition" and "Archontes" in *The Oxford Classical Dictionary*, 3rd ed., ed. Simon Hornblower and Antony Spawforth (Oxford: Oxford University Press, 1996), 1426, 150.

The reason a follow-up public proclamation, with "discovery" by lot, occurs is that the private anointing of 10:1 was just a designation, not a public calling in. Once we appreciate that ancient Near Eastern kingly installation was built in stages, a lottery is a natural second stage in the elevation. Nor does it seem cogent to claim that this episode jars with Saul's charismatic adventure in the previous chapter, on the grounds that, if Saul's anointing had already occurred, "an element of charade would be unavoidable" (Campbell and O'Brien 2000: 242). It *is* a charade, in the sense that the jury has already pronounced the winner, but it is socially necessary for a king to be designated as such in the open, because he is not just a prize winner but a public office holder. The best way of making the divine designation absolutely visible to all the people—so no one could grumble that the anointee was just Samuel's personal preference, so no one could complain that his own talents went unconsidered, so everyone was compelled to see that the selection occurred ritually, in public, and that the outcome unequivocally designated the Lord's choice—was the casting of lots. This is an objective mechanism, like drawing straws, tossing a coin, or throwing a die: it's a lottery, but its sacral context invokes the religious assumption that the lot will not fall haphazardly, but will finger Yahweh's chosen. A lottery makes the private calling public and sets the stage for collective visual witness of the identity of the designate. By means of the lottery, God and people concur on Saul.

Of course God had the idea first: he's God. The lots don't work mechanically by themselves; the Lord has to come on stage and execute their function: "So they inquired again of the LORD, 'Is there a man still to come?' and the LORD said, 'Behold, he has hidden himself among the baggage'" (10:22 ESV). There were two lots, called "the dark and the light," "Urim and Thummim." They could say yes or no, but they could not say: "He's under the luggage!" It could be that "the LORD said" is a periphrastic (roundabout) way of saying that the lots pointed that way. But if the Urim and Thummim themselves said, "Behold, he has hidden himself among the baggage," that took some interpreting on the part of the seer. The use of "look" or "behold" seems to indicate a personal speaker, like Yahweh's own voice, as heard by someone. What happens when Saul is selected for public proclamation is a repetition by public means of what happened on the hillside outside Gibeath-elohim (10:5): that is, an oracular, charismatic choice.

While we have been meditating on the connotations of the lottery, its winner has been ignominiously attempting to conceal himself behind the no-doubt-capacious luggage that the assembled Israelite tribes brought with them to Mizpah. If we interpret Saul's silence before his uncle to reflect a refusal in Saul to come out in the open, then hiding is metaphorically right for Saul's character: "The climactic moment has come, but the man of the hour is 'hidden among the baggage' (v. 22). ... The incident suggests ... that Saul does not want to be king and must ... be dragged out of hiding for it" (Good 1965: 63–64). But there is another possibility, and we may shirk it, in considering Saul's story, because it is almost too painful to bear. It may be that Saul's hiding is a mark of his humility, of his goodness.

Many modern Old Testament scholars take Saul as a tragic figure and imagine "tragic" to mean a spotless victim of God's capricious preference for David. They think that taking the king by lot "follows the pattern of 'seizing the culprit'" (Polzin 1989: 104). It's not too painful to think of Saul as an innocent pawn in a malicious Fate's game, because somewhere at the back of our minds we know that such a melodramatic picture is fantasy, not reality. This is to hold evil at bay by pretending it isn't there. Holding out with Saul against the evil side of Yahweh may make us feel rather heroic. But suppose Saul is a human enigma, and one without much grandeur, since most of us lack that too: suppose he is a good, humble man who on taking the office of chieftain began to do evil and was therefore rejected by God. That is enigmatic and affecting. Many people yearn for the communitarian culture that they see reflected in sacral kingship; they would prefer human politics to have the hue of a monastery instead of what it actually has, bargains between interest groups and trade-offs between lesser evils. That the communitarian project inevitably fails, as politics, is an enigma, and a tragic one. Saul's failed charismatic kingship is one step further away from the garden. Perhaps this episode, which exposes Saul's premonition that ruling is a burden from which he must hide, can best be read if we consider it in the light of the endless human failure to make the city of God a reality on earth. Human beings remain human and many sided, however great the charisma they receive, and it is not cowardly but realistic to appreciate the diminutive status of a would-be human king alongside the kingship of God. If Saul is hiding among the baggage because he has the virtue of humility, we must draw from 1 Samuel's depiction of his journey a picture of Saul as a good man who went to the bad: that leaves us, not with any explanations, but the deep mystery of human character. This paradox requires a rather simple perception of good and evil. Many commentators today prefer complex definitions of good and bad that solve that enigma. The tragedies of Sophocles and Shakespeare are not complex and shallow, but deep and simple.

Naturally, not everyone's pleasure in taking offense is going to be satisfied or everyone's hurt pride redressed by the use of any public or private mechanism whatever: whereas some "men of valor whose hearts God had touched" (10:26 ESV) accepted the verdict, others, "worthless fellows" were kvetching into God's accession to the people's request, saying, "'How can this man save us?' And they despised him and brought him no present" (10:27 ESV). The narrator calls these men *bene beliyaal*, which was the legalese for breakers of agreements, laws, and covenants (Eslinger 1983: 65). Once the Lord has publicly nominated Saul as his king, any human who is not a "king's man," any antimonarchist, is breaking with the covenant between the Lord and the people. But Saul "held his peace" (10:27). He might be mulishly obstinate, but we don't yet know. Patience may have been imposed by the novelty of the situation, or he may be a taciturn man. His role and character are both still in the balance.

Once extracted from behind the baggage, when Saul "stood among the people, he was taller than any of the people from his shoulders upward. And Samuel said to all the people, 'Do you see him whom the LORD has chosen? There is none like him among all the people.' And all the people shouted, 'Long live the king!' " Once Saul has stepped forth onto the pedestal and has been socially construed as king, "Samuel told the people the rights and duties of the kingship, and he wrote them in a book and laid it up before the LORD" (10:23–25 ESV). A slightly more literal translation of "Samuel told the people the rights and duties of the kingship" is, Samuel "spoke to the people the manner [*mishpat*, literally 'law'] of the kingship [*meluka*] and wrote it in a scroll and laid it up before YHWH." Scholars naturally debate what precisely "the law of the king" was. I follow Halpern in thinking that Deut. 17:14–20 fits the bill. As cited in episode one, Deut. 17:14–20 reflects Samuel's own reservations about kingship and so restricts the rights of the king and enhances the rights of his brothers in just the areas about which the prophet expressed disapprobation in 1 Sam. 8. Although some think Deut. 17 is a product of the Josianic reform, Hos. 8:4; Isa. 30:2; 31:1; and Ezek. 17:15 all attest to the existence of "the law of the king" in the eighth century. In 2 Samuel, King David captures a thousand "chariots" from the "king of Zobah" and "hamstrung all but a hundred of the chariot horses" (8:4 NIV), perhaps a precautionary measure with respect to Deut. 17:16's proscription of the king's accumulation of horsepower ("the king, moreover, must not acquire great numbers of horses for himself" [NIV]) (Halpern 1981: 229–31). It is true that historical critics do not agree on the relationship between Samuel's reference to "the manner of the king" (1 Sam. 8:9, 11–17), this *mishpat* of the *meluka* (10:25), and Deut. 17's "law of the king." But it is wrong to say that, whatever chronological linkage these texts have, "it is not easy to find in them any rejection of the dynastic principle" (Ishida 1977: 41). The phrase in Deut. 17 that most closely links it to the kingship of Saul is "thou shalt in any wise set him king over thee, whom the LORD thy God shall choose" (17:15). This does not categorically prohibit the succession of a son of the royal line to the kingship, but it effectively rules out the dynastic principle as such, because the principle of selection it prescribes is divine choice. For medieval Christians, Samuel was one of us, a distant but real "saint" of the church. If modern Christians tune out when the Old Testament readings about him come round in the lectionary, it's because they think of Samuel as a legend from before the mists of time. It's important to imagine him in the flesh, as a real person who used legal means to hedge Israel's first king with prescriptions that made Saul a sacral king, that is, a king under God and the prophet.

The conclusion to the lottery episode is upbeat, not because the author was under an otherwise inexplicable compulsion to refer at this junction to a promonarchic source, but because the Lord is not a miser. As in the garden of Eden, he has created the perfect conditions: this time, for the step out of the epoch of the judges, he has provided a uniquely well-built leader, "taller than any of the people from his shoulders upward" (10:23 ESV); and, since humanity has taken a step downhill since the garden, he has supplied the anointed chief with a new heart (10:9). Yahweh, the "king of love," has put his free will behind the chief-designate.

The question is whether the human partner will use his own free will, or whether he will hide his talents. Saul could hold fast to the new identity God has given him. Samuel does not hold Saul's shyness against him. It could be a portent of obedience to God that would make him an authentically free man. But Saul could also follow a different path, laid out by the same lack of self-esteem. He could refuse to grasp his own free will and thus reject the divine free grace. He has been elected at the behest of the people and may be absorbed into their idea of government; but he has also been chosen by God. There's a genuine dramatic tension at this point of the story, which is both theological and literary: it is still an open question which way Saul will go.

Episode Five: Saul Regnans (1 Sam. 11)

First Sam. 11 is regarded as deriving from early promonarchic legends (Wevers 1971: 161), and not only because the narrative of Saul's successful reprisal against the Ammonites makes for a uniformly positive presentation of the new king. It seems to horn in straight from the anointing of Saul by Samuel in 10:1, with no public proclamation of Saul as king of Israel in between. As if 10:1–27 had never happened, Saul is back on the farm in Gibeah when the news reaches him of Nahash the Ammonite's threat to the Israelite town of Jabesh. Ever since Wellhausen, critics have argued that, if 1 Sam. 11 had been composed in full awareness of the private anointing and public acclamation in 1 Sam. 10, Saul would have had an army around him, instead of coming in "after the herd out of the field" (11:5) to hear the evil tidings. Saul's kingly regalia and status have evaporated, and he seems to act on the spur of the moment under charismatic inspiration, like a judge (Polzin 1989: 113). He seems to get the reports by chance. "And the Spirit of God came upon Saul when he heard those tidings, and his anger was kindled greatly" (11:6): Saul seems to become "a charismatic leader like Samson" (Wevers 1971: 161).

Against this, Halpern argues that Saul does have a cadre with him, who are taken as a unified body of men: "Then came the messengers to Gibeah of Saul, and told the tidings in the ears of the people: and all the people lifted up their voices, and wept. . . . And Saul said, 'What aileth the people that they weep?'" (11:4–5). "The people" are not specified as the folk of Gibeah, the unguarded assumption of those who spontaneously identify them with these farming civilians. Three times in 11:4–5 they are just called "the people": they might well be the *hayil* mentioned in 10:26: "Saul also went to his home at Gibeah, and with him went men of valor whose hearts God had touched" (ESV). Saul in fact does have some sort of bodyguard or a small volunteer corps with him: he "summons the muster" in 11:7, by chopping up the oxen and sending them to the tribes, because this elite corps is numerically insufficient to deploy in reply to Nahash's threat (Halpern 1996: 184). First Sam. 11:1–3 is not forthcoming about whether the messengers know that the buck now stops with Saul: it doesn't tell whether the news from Jabesh-gilead had gone round the houses before it reached Gibeah or if the messengers made a beeline for Saul. Perhaps the use of the definite article matters: "*the* messengers" come to Gibeah, implying that, rather than reports of the impending Ammonite assault randomly spreading across the countryside and happening to pass through Saul's village, the only messengers ran straight to the chief-designate (Long 1989: 222).

Saul looks like a subsistence farmer, not a king, in 1 Sam. 11 because political, historical, and (lotteries notwithstanding) even economic transformations don't happen overnight. In this ancient culture, the basic metaphor for a group of people, used from bottom to top of Israel's society, is the household. The shape of the smallest household can be seen in the commandment against coveting one's neighbor's oxen, servants, and wife (Exod. 20:17); at the other end of the scale, Israel itself was conceived as a household: "The king presided over his house (*bayit*), the families and households of the whole kingdom. Thus, after the division of the monarchy the southern kingdom of Judah is referred to as 'house of David' (*byt dwd*) in the recently excavated stela from Dan, and probably . . . the Mesha Stela, just as the northern kingdom of Israel is known as the 'house of Omri' (*bit Humri*) in Assyrian texts" (Stager 1998: 151). The Benedictus (the Canticle of Zechariah in Luke 1:68–79), which many Christians say every morning, retains this ancient locution: "He has raised up a mighty savior for us, in the house of his servant David" (NRSV). The metaphor of the house retained its symbolic force long after the kinship group lost its political valance, because it had been engrained in the culture for centuries. In the early eleventh century BC, Israel consisted of roughly 75,000 ethnically similar people, living in networks of agricultural towns and villages in "U-shaped courtyard houses," unique perhaps to these settlers. These villages, unearthed by archeology, "clustered in groups of two to four, often sharing common walls . . . correspond closely with many narratives of daily life in . . . the books of Joshua, Judges, and Samuel, reflecting . . . a close-knit family and clan structure and an agrarian lifestyle. . . . The single-courtyard house represents the nuclear family dwelling; and the cluster of several such houses would then be the residence of the extended, or multi-generation family equivalent to the biblical *bet-ab*, or 'house of the father.' " While it may be an ideal farmhouse, the U-shaped courtyard dwelling was a long way from a palace (Dever 2002: 111–12). A man who had recently been publicly proclaimed as chief of a hitherto acephalous tribal people who lived by domestic agriculture in Early Iron Age conditions would not immediately have a palace to live in. Even if he dreamed of carrying out the threat of 1 Sam. 8:11–18 in full and surrounding himself with cooks, confectioners, charioteers, olive-yards, and vineyards, Saul had as yet no means of accruing these goods. Supposing the events of 10:17–27 had recently taken place, what else could Saul do except go back to tilling the soil with his herds?

Many parallels between 1 Sam. 10 and 1 Sam. 11 are embedded in the text: Saul is living in Gibeah (10:5; 11:4), Samuel is still playing the role of assembly caller and kingmaker, and there is no getting away from the grumblers (10:27; 11:12). It looks like, "new heart" apart, Saul is physically the same man as that in 1 Sam. 10 (Halpern 1996: 184). First Sam. 10–11 can be read with a hermeneutic of continuity, if we imaginatively consider Saul's political and economic circumstances. If 1 Sam. 8–15 made a family-based political economy morph into a centralized urban state at the drop of a hat it would be a self-evident fairy story. First Sam. 11 shows Saul coming in "after the herd out of the field" because it is a historically realistic text. It could be a much later urban author's idyllic image of his Early Iron Age ancestor initiating military maneuvers with manure on his sandals. But if it is comparable to the pastoral nostalgia seen in Theocritus's bucolics and Vergil's *Georgics*, it shows a decent acquaintance with the archeological verities. All we know is that the writer somehow succeeds in doing justice to the pace of historical change. Curiously enough, the only iron tool thus far to have been excavated from the Early Iron Age remains of the ancient fortress at Gibeah is a "single iron plough point" (McNutt 1990: 171).

Moabite kings lived in palaces (Judg. 3), but Saul has yet to achieve the wherewithal to build one; he has yet to acquire a standing army, lacking which the imposition of taxes and tithes is a tricky business. He is thus far a chief in name only. For commentators who regard 1 Sam. 10 and 1 Sam. 11 as the products of discrete sources, a compelling incongruity is that Saul seems to be made king once at Mizpah (10:21–24) and yet again at Gilgal (11:14–12:25) (Wevers 1971: 161). A history—rather than text-based approach—is required to harmonize the texts. Historically, ancient Near Eastern kings were first privately anointed, then publicly proclaimed, and then, only after proving themselves in battle, publicly crowned. Supposing that "the Israelite mythos of leadership dictated that YHWH's designee should prove himself, ideally in battle, before being confirmed," until Saul knocks out a Canaanite platoon, he has only notional status as king (Halpern 1996: 185). He has no standing army and must draw the people together by the spontaneous force of his personal acts, inspiring them with the symbolic act of the hewn oxen, rather than acting as an established king.

Saul has the look of a judge like Samson because charismatic kings retained the features of the savior-warriors who immediately preceded them. The notion that kings must achieve that status in various stages, including one in which the *nagid* demonstrated his charism by military prowess, is not an abstract theory thought up on paper and then applied in practice. It's not about kingship, the theory, but concrete acting kings. One must show that one is a king, really and in actuality a warrior who can muster all Israel to battle, before one can be crowned. *Being* and *doing* the king precedes having abstract kingship. The reason Israel's elders asked Samuel for a king was the constant threat of territorial encroachment from neighboring powers, especially the Philistines and the Ammonites. Israel's original "tribal democracy, governed . . . by its patriarchs' . . . influence over their families and clans" turned into a monarchy because of a military crisis (Halpern 1981: 235). The only way in which the tribes of Israel could surmount the threat was to act in concert. Therefore, the way in which the putative chief or *nagid* must demonstrate that he actually is a king of all Israel and not just a local savior-deliverer was to make all the peoples of Israel act in unison. This is how Saul as king differs from a judge: the charism of the king must enable him not only to kill a lot of Philistines, like Samson, but also to muster the whole people. When "the Spirit of the Lord" comes upon Saul, he sends the prophetic sign of the ox hewn "in pieces" round the tribes, exhorting them to rally to "Saul and Samuel": the effect of this is that "the fear of the LORD fell on the people, and they came out with one consent." The "messengers" are able to report to "the men of Jabesh-gilead" that "ye shall have help": and they tell Nahash what to do with his threat. Consequently, the Ammonites are met in battle not just by the men of Jabesh-gilead, but by a rousing "three hundred thousand" Israelites and "thirty thousand" Judeans (11:6–8).

Before the battle recorded in 1 Sam. 11, Israel was both a loose confederacy, existing more in the spirit than in the letter, and a cluster of independent tribes whose autonomy had become a liability. Their independency can be seen in Nahash negotiating with just Jabesh-gilead; their sense of spiritual unity is shown by their responding to Saul's signal. What Saul succeeded in doing was to make the spiritual unity a literal fact in hard military coinage: "A new development took place at that juncture which no charismatic war-leader could ever achieve. Saul managed to call up the militia 'as one man' from 'all the territory of Israel' (11:7–8)" (Ishida 1977: 36). In its context, "all the people lifted up their voices, and wept" (11:4) does not mean "all Israel": it means the people of Gibeah. It is only after Saul hews the ox and sends his signal that the people "came out with one consent." He thus demonstrated that he was in fact not just a savior-deliverer, but the man the elders were asking for when they petitioned Samuel for a king. The Spirit that comes upon Saul has made him a king capable of uniting all Israel. Those who think Saul was a dynastic, not a charismatic king from the outset affirm that "the people hailed Saul as king by acclamation when they recognized his victory as a sign of his designation by Yahweh. But the monarchy as a new regime had been prepared long before. . . . The people of Israel had designed the structure of monarchy as a political institution on the model of the neighboring countries before Saul appeared. They were simply looking for a man who would be able to function as a leader of the new institution" (Ishida 1977: 52).

It doesn't make sense to think of the institution as existing prior to the king, that is, of kingship preceding an actual king. Before Saul in the power of the Spirit caused the peoples to unite, there was no king in Israel (Judg. 18:1; 19:1) and hence no potential institution of kingship. The actuality of Saul's charismatic behavior as king created the potential for kingship as an institution. Samuel had to hand a "manner of the king" (1 Sam. 8:9, 11; 10:25), but laws are not a potential institution. Saul was not filling an empty slot but creating the kingship by being one. It is wrong to separate the facts that the people now see that Saul is a king, that he has already received his vocation to this role, at his anointing, and that this vocation has already been publicly recognized. It may work on paper, but it does not work in reality to say that "both divine designation and popular acclamation played essentially no part in determining the characteristic feature of the Israelite monarchy" (Ishida 1977: 52). The elite corps around Saul at Gibeah, when the messengers sped there, were insufficient to take on the Ammonites: he needed to rally "all Israel" to defeat Nahash. Saul does not defeat the Ammonites because the package of the institution of kingship included, in someone's mind, a standing army but because he succeeds in putting sufficient fear of God into the independent tribes to make them form a single army. "Needless to say," argue proponents of an originally dynastic kingship in Israel, "a powerful standing army cannot be sustained without a stable leadership. Thus, we can only assume that the people planned to build a hereditary monarchy, having realized long since that a stable leadership could be founded only on the hereditary principle" (Ishida 1977: 36, 52). When the elders ask Samuel for a king in 1 Sam. 8, they are asking for militarily unifying leadership, a king behind whom all his subjects will march, not hereditary leadership. That is why Samuel feels rejected by their request (8:7). Saul was a charismatic, not a dynastic, king.

It makes sense to do the historical and social anthropological work necessary to see that Saul ever remained something of a "charismatic leader of the old sort" whereas David's "kingdom had become an empire" (von Rad 1962: 36). This helps us to picture the difference between the religious culture of Saul's time and that of David and his successor, Solomon. We need to get the historical setting right in order to appreciate the theological demands made of Saul. Saul is a prepolitical figure, ruling in the twilight interim between the judges and the era of monarchic political compromise. The demands the Lord makes of him are therefore utterly uncompromising. The exigency of being entirely subject to the prophet Samuel is a requirement one can make of a person, but not of a political office. Whereas the political world tends to impersonality, personality is the engine of prepolitical and extrapolitical life. The theodicial questions relating to God's exacting treatment of Saul must be addressed to the particular kind of kingship that he held. It doesn't work to consider his tragedy as an abstract, esthetic, or philosophical question. In the sacramental, charismatic kingship to which Saul was historically consecrated, he was subject to Samuel as a monk is to his abbot. First Sam. 11 looks promonarchic because it is mildly nostalgic: the author knows that this is how kingship could have been and continued to be, if Saul had maintained this obedience.

Saul's defeat of the Ammonites is a high point in his drama, the scene where anger against the arrogant Nahash overwhelms his modest estimate of his own abilities, and the chevalier brings an army to the defense of the people of Jabesh-gilead (an event they do not later forget; 1 Sam. 31). This acme in Saul's career—the moment in which, under the power of the Spirit, he exercises free initiative, with the prophetic sign of the hewn ox, and assembles a vast counterinvasion force—is trumped only by the coronation scene itself: "And all the people went to Gilgal, and there they made Saul king before the LORD in Gilgal: and there they sacrificed sacrifices of peace offerings before the LORD; and there Saul and all the men of Israel rejoiced greatly" (11:15). According to Polzin, however, "the final rejoicing of Saul and the people (v. 15) is ironic in a tragic sense; and with the tragedy goes a sense of sympathy on the part of the reader toward them because of their missed opportunity" (1989: 115). The feeling that the rejoicing must surely be a dramatic irony, contrasting with the upshot of Saul's kingship, is not just based on foresight, on knowing that Saul will be rejected as king (1 Sam. 15), but on seeming hindsight, on knowing that Yahweh initially disapproved the request (1 Sam. 8). If Yahweh showed initial reluctance, the logical reasoning goes, then he must still be harboring his disapproval. This way of thinking fits the unchangeable Fate (Moira) of the Homeric epics and the character traits of their deities: Hera hates Odysseus all the way through the *Odyssey*. Israel's God may be impassible, but that does not mean that he is rigid or unaccommodating. A statically impassible God, immovable in the same way that Fate is immovable in Homer's epics and Herodotus's *History*, would disapprove of the kingship in a univocal way in 1 Sam. 8–15. All of the gestures toward accepting the people's demand made by such a God would be ironic or punitive. Since to speak of a "free fate" is an oxymoron, such a God, once having determined his attitude, would be bound to it. In fact, though, the Lord has adapted what he regards as acceptable law for his people ever since Gen. 3. He does so in acknowledgement of their moral and thus political decadence. It is not that his standard of right conduct has changed or that the ethical ideal has declined along with public morality, but that God is regulating for *this* historical people, not an ideal people.

Historically, a centralized monarchy did evolve in Israel over the eleventh century BC. The Lord acquiesces in this: "It was wicked to have demanded a king. But YHWH met the demand" (Halpern 1996: 194). We cannot understand the text or the history behind 1 Samuel unless we have developed a rough idea of its theology, its conception of God. The ideas that many critics have taken from scripture are not false but one-sided. Scholars get hold of the idea that Israel's God is transcendent, but then equate transcendence with frozen immobility (as if the Lord God were one of Plato's ideas). The equation of transcendence with immobility comes from thinking of transcendence as a marker for rationality and hence inferring that the God of scripture ought to be rational to us. The God of Exodus–1 Samuel is freer than that would make him; he can move *with* the people without being moved *by* them. Although such a conception transcends human rationality, "the God of the old covenant possesses a remarkable mobility, based . . . in his inconceivable inner freedom. It is . . . his 'glory' that wanders with his people in the wilderness for those who belong to him: indeed, he himself is the path. . . . To this outer mobility there corresponds an inner mobility . . . seen in the fact that he . . . personally commits himself at specific moments of history. He makes decisions, but he can also 'repent' (Gen. 6:6; 1 Sam. 15:11, 35)" (von Balthasar 1983–91: 6.223).

Van Seters argues that Greek and Hebrew history writing are fairly much equivalent, since "no cyclical view of time is evident in the Greek histories, whatever the philosophers might say, and there is no eschatology in the Israelite histories, whatever prophet and apocalypticist might propose." He thinks that 1 Sam. 11 is a "rather 'secular' story" given a theological gloss only by Saul's affirmation that "today the LORD has wrought salvation in Israel" (11:13) (1983: 8–9, 257). But the seeds of eschatology are present in texts just such as this, where "the Spirit of God came upon Saul," enabling him to rouse the whole people of Israel "with one consent" (11:6–7). The source of the idea, in Israel, that a great man could be a fighter, that the soldier is a sublime role for a man to play, is theological: it is the belief that God is a fighter, who defeats his enemies. In Ps. 74 the works of "God . . . my king" that are praised include having "divided the sea in your might, shattered the heads of the sea serpents, and pulverized the heads of Leviathan" (74:12–14, trans. Halpern). In Ps. 89 God's successful expedition against the forces of chaos has as its concomitant his handing over power to the human king: "I shall place his hand over sea, and his right hand over river" (89:26, trans. Halpern). The ideas of God as warrior and of the charismatic king as a holy warrior are analogous, the latter flowing from the former. One may even describe the king as an "avatar of the Divine Warrior": the "king in Israel was . . . the mundane counterpart and the individually powerless delegate of the Divine Warrior" (Halpern 1981: 65–66, 251, 174).

The biblical conceptions of God and of human beings make sense in relation to each other. They are analogous. Biblical characters are made in the image of a free God. They themselves are human images of the divine freedom. The heroes of the Greek epics have fixed epithets, like "many-wayed Odysseus," but it is otherwise for the biblical heroes: "Jacob is not 'wily Jacob,' Moses is not 'sagacious Moses' " (Alter 1981: 126). The hero of the *Odyssey* is expected to remain the same all the way through, whereas Saul or David are open to free change of direction. Auerbach famously put this comparison:

> Odysseus on his return is exactly the same as he was when he left Ithaca. . . . But what a road, what a fate, lie . . . between David the harp player, persecuted by his lord's jealousy, and the old king, surrounded by violent intrigues. . . . The old man . . . is more of an individual than the young man; for it is only during the course of an eventful life that men are differentiated into full individuality; and it is this history of a personality that the Old Testament presents to us as the formation undergone by those whom God has chosen to be examples. Fraught with their development . . . they show a distinct stamp of individuality entirely foreign to the Homeric heroes.[20]

One can see a change in Saul's character between 1 Sam. 9 and 1 Sam. 18, and this chapter highlights it. The men who had grumbled about his ascent to kingship have not gone away. The new king deals with the carpers with regal magnanimity: "The people said unto Samuel, 'Who is he that said, "Shall Saul reign over us?" bring the men, that we may put them to death.' And Saul said, 'There shall not

20. Erich Auerbach, *Mimesis: The Representation of Reality in Western Literature*, trans. Willard Trask (Princeton: Princeton University Press, 1974), 17–18.

a man be put to death this day: for today the LORD hath wrought salvation in Israel'" (11:12–13). This contrasts with the Saul who becomes determined to have David put to death. In between the Saul of 1 Sam. 11 and the Saul of 1 Sam. 18 lies a misuse of human free will. Just as Yahweh is not fate, so 11:12–13 expressly indicates that Saul is not simply fated.

The author could not write Saul's line, "There shall not a man be put to death this day," without knowing that, eight chapters on, "put to death" will be a leitmotif of Saul's recorded imperatives. But the author's tone is nearer to what Polish-Lithuanian poet Czesław Miłosz calls a "historical sense of humor"[21] than to tragic irony. Human character is free, flexible, and individuated in the Hebrew scriptures and depicted neither with cast-iron pessimism nor utopian optimism. Human political attitudes are also, as the narrator dryly records, a little fickle: "the people" who had acclaimed Saul in 1 Sam. 10 now have so little trust in their ruler, who had been elevated because they wanted a king to lead them in battle against invaders, that they "wept" (11:4) when they hear of the Ammonite peril; eight verses later these capricious people are demanding the death of anyone disloyal to the great leader (11:12) (Eslinger 1983: 66).

One cannot live in community with fate. Fate does not respect human free will, and thus, according to Polzin, the tragic irony of 11:15 is that "Saul and the men of Israel ... were being manipulated by Samuel's personal desires for power and prophetic control and by God's impelling desire to underline the dangerous re-sponsibilities of free will, [and] perhaps things might have turned out differently" (1989: 115). A historian can take a more balanced view, seeing that the prophet's role was "to ride herd on the monarchy," not to manipulate it (Halpern 1981: 234). But it may be that respecting the text's historicity is not sufficient to dislodge an interpretation of 1 Sam. 8–15 in which Samuel is motivated by self-interest and in which the Lord misuses Saul, making him a laughingstock in revenge for the impious request for a king. If we are imaginatively so determined, we will have to read the rejoicing of 11:15 in an ironic and tragic sense. It may be that it takes a theologi-cally inspired sympathy with God's accommodation of the people's request to see that his acquiescence is authentic and that he is willing to set his free will, his *ruah*, alongside that of the human Saul. First Sam. 11 exalts in what human initiative can do when it aligns itself with the will of God. The Lord is not inflexible fate, and this is expressed in his desire that his people live in community with himself.

Episode Six: The Rainman (1 Sam. 12)

First Sam. 12 is deemed by older critics to derive from the antimonarchic source. Samuel and the people both agree in 12:3–4 that his own impeccable judgeship is

---

21. Czesław Miłosz, *Native Realm: A Search for Self-Definition*, trans. Catherine S. Leach (New York: Farrar, Straus & Giroux, 2002), 245.

not the reason for wanting a king. Thus, 1 Sam. 12 pictures that, before passing the task of delivering justice on to the first king, Samuel makes it clear that kingship has not been called in to remedy a failure of the judges, but at the people's insistence. Recent exegetes stress the striking difference between 1 Sam. 12 and the preceding episodes. In 8:1–5 the mischievous character of Samuel's sons was the rationale offered up by the elders for the request of a king. Here, conversely, the portrayal of the sons is neutral: "I am old and grey-headed, and, behold, my sons are with you: and I have walked before you from my childhood unto this day" (12:2). A further "remarkably" jarring note thought to indicate that this chapter was pasted in after the exile is that the "Nahash episode is portrayed differently." In 1 Sam. 11 "no king is apparent before the victory over Nahash, and Samuel proposes kingship afterwards; here, it is fear of Nahash that causes demand for a king. In the preceding text, demand for a king is expressed in 1 Sam 8:4–5 on grounds of social justice. The king in 1 Samuel 10:20–25 depends on divine choice, by lot and oracle, not on victory over Nahash" (Campbell and O'Brien 2000: 246–47).

Our author marks the high points or turning points in his history with summative speeches that describe the past and relate it to the future, proposing how the people should go on the basis of an interpretation of their circuitous journey thus far. As the assembled tribes stood on the banks of the Jordan, waiting to enter the promised land, Joshua spoke to them of past and future (Josh. 1:12–18). Likewise, the changeover from Samuel to his successors, the kings, is marked by a farewell speech.[22] Samuel recapitulates the events of the end of Genesis and of Exodus: "When Jacob was come into Egypt, and your fathers cried unto the LORD, then the LORD sent Moses and Aaron, which brought forth your fathers out of Egypt, and made them dwell in this place" (1 Sam. 12:8). Then he symbolizes the events of Judges in one or two choice episodes, repeating the cyclical theme that apostasy is followed by subjugation to a foreign ruler, which will, in turn, be alleviated, if and when the people repent and return the LORD: "When they forgot the LORD their God, he sold them into the hand of Sisera, . . . and into the hand of the Philistines, and into the hand of the king of Moab. . . . And they cried unto the LORD, and said, 'We have sinned, because we have forsaken the LORD, and have served Baalim and Ashtaroth: but now deliver us out of the hand of our enemies, and we will serve thee.' And the LORD sent Jerubbaal, and Bedan, and Jephthah, and Samuel, and delivered you out of the hand of your enemies on every side, and ye dwelt safe" (12:9–11). Drawing the history of Israel to its close, before he interprets what it means for their future, Samuel mentions its most recent development: "And when ye saw that Nahash the king of the children of Ammon came against you, ye said unto me, 'Nay, but a king shall reign over us,' when the LORD your God was your king" (12:12).

Some think it odd that threat of enemy invasion should now become the pivot of the people's desire for a king, since the people asked for a king long before Nahash

22. Noth, *Deuteronomistic History*, 5.

threatened to put out the eyes of the men of Jabesh-gilead! But in a sense it is even odder to fix on the discrepancy, because of the existential rightness of Samuel's comment. When Israel was at peace with its enemies, the people wanted to emulate them and have a leader like theirs; in the aftermath of victory in war, they are beside themselves with enthusiasm at the prospect of a warrior chieftain. Samuel is speaking to the current exalted mood of the people. Rather than mechanically summarizing the steps that the people took toward this new form of leadership, Samuel's speech conversationally tracks what his people are now thinking and feeling. Since 1 Sam. 12 presents the third and final stage of the achievement of kingship, it was because of his successful muster against Nahash that the people regarded Saul's candidacy as confirmed and thus insisted that *this one* be publicly and finally crowned. The antithesis in the statement that "the king in 1 Samuel 10:20–25 depends on divine choice, by lot and oracle, not on victory over Nahash" (Campbell and O'Brien 2000: 246) misses the point that Samuel intends here to make the people acknowledge: victory over Nahash is a divine choice. *Hayyim* can mean both "life" and "blessing": so life itself is a blessing, a gift from God: the blessing of "life presupposes success, stability, and security, and makes itself manifest in joy, light, and *victory*" (Martin-Achard 1960: 9, emphasis added). From Saul's sleepwalking to his inevitable destiny at the house of the seer, to the lottery, to his charismatic transformation and courageous raising of a counterforce against Nahash, Saul has been God's choice. But the people who acclaim and thus confirm him are likely to think him their choice. Samuel therefore lays a decision before the assembly: will Saul be of God or of the people?

It is the time of the wheat harvest, the driest season in Palestine (Wevers 1971: 161–62). Samuel calls down a thunderstorm, the most startling and eye-opening event he can provoke: "'Is it not wheat harvest today? I will call unto the LORD, and he shall send thunder and rain; that ye may perceive and see that your wickedness is great, which ye have done in the sight of the LORD, in asking you a king.' So Samuel called unto the LORD; and the LORD sent thunder and rain that day: and all the people greatly feared the LORD and Samuel" (12:17–18). Terrified by this display of power and its symbolic demonstration of the potential retribution that the power behind it could wreck, "all the people said unto Samuel, 'Pray for thy servants unto the LORD thy God, that we die not: for we have added unto all our sins this evil, to ask us a king'" (12:19).

At first glance, it looks as if Samuel is contrasting two spectacles, the king (poor, excessively modest Saul who has to stand before the people's gaze and listen to these strictures) and the revenge that the Lord intends to take on the people for their insolent demand for a human rather than a divine king. For first, directing all eyes at the crowned Saul, Samuel says, "Behold the king whom ye have chosen, and whom ye have desired: and behold, the LORD hath set a king over you" (12:13). Second, announcing the miracle of the thunderstorm, the prophet again tells the people to look at a spectacle: "Now therefore stand and see this great thing, which the LORD will do before your eyes" (12:16), Samuel says, and delivers the "thunder and rain" (12:18), to the horror of the people, who think from the dual spectacles of Saul and the thunderous rain that they are about to be punished with death for requesting him.

If we follow the lead of the people's reaction to these twin spectacles, we will take the paired signs as testimony to God's intention to punish the request in the person of Saul. If we see the thunder and rain as symbolizing the punishment that will fall on Saul, then we may reflect that

> Yahweh the maker of plot makes Samuel the manipulator of people pale by comparison. The LORD commands Samuel to make a king (8:7; 9:22); the LORD chooses Saul (9:17); the LORD moves Saul to prophecy (10:10); the LORD publicly chooses Saul by lot (10:21); the LORD gives Saul victory over Jabesh-gilead (11:6); and the LORD cooperates with Samuel's fear-instilling display of thunder and rain (12:18). It is difficult to avoid seeing the LORD as the one who . . . sets up Saul for proximate rejection just as he will Israel for ultimate exile. The paradox of kingship, epitomised in Saul's abortive reign, is of an institution that came about through both obedience and disobedience to the Lord's command. The tragedy of King Saul, as of royal Israel in general, ultimately rests in the mysterious coexistence of divine omnipotence and human freedom. (Polzin 1989: 125–26)

It would seem then that Saul represents the human desire for human freedom, in the choice of the institution by which the people are governed, and that the thunder and rain represent an omnipotent God's irate answer to this insubordinate human propensity.

Before there were prophets there were priests, and before priests came shamans. The deal-breaker among shamanic skills, necessary for the people's survival and as a demonstration of his own *numen*, was the ability to call down rain. It was a practical necessity to have rain for crops, but it also exhibited the shaman's connection to the heavens: the shaman as rainman was literally a mediator between the heavens and earth. The ability effectively to address the heavens and the sky gods and to invoke the rains was literal and instrumental: the idea of the prophet as mediator has down-to-earth origins. The ability to produce rain at need was good: the rain-evoking shaman was doing something valuable. His demonstration of power, or *numen*, was not negative, but positive. It became a metaphor of his power, just as the ability to withhold or to supply life-giving rain was a metaphor of the life-giving power of the gods over humans. Rain long retained a symbolic value in the spiritual thinking of more intellectually articulate cultures. It comes to represent God's self-gift to the human soul. Origen wrote:

> The mighty deed Samuel is said to have accomplished through prayer is something that everyone who genuinely relies on God can accomplish spiritually even now, since he has become worthy of being heard. . . . For every saint and genuine disciple of Jesus is told by the Lord, "Lift up your eyes, and see how the fields are already white for harvest. He who reaps receives wages and gathers fruit for eternal life"

[John 4:35–36]. In this time of harvest the Lord does "a great thing" before the eyes of those who hear the prophets. For when the one adorned with the Holy Spirit calls to the Lord, God gives from heaven thunder and rain that waters the soul. . . . And Elijah, who shut up heaven for the wicked for three and a half years, later opened it. This, too, is always accomplished for everyone who through prayer receives the rain of the soul, since the heavens were previously deprived of it because of his sin. (Origen, *On Prayer* 13.5, in Franke 2005: 239)

Origen has taken a spiritual meaning from Samuel's calling down rain, because he has imagined the character of rain, what it means to us religiously.

Because we think of nature as a purely physical system, we think of miracles, such as Samuel performs here, as deviations within the physical system, and thus, if we think of God solely as the author of physical nature, we are a bit ashamed of them, as plot defects in a novel that the author couldn't bring to a desired conclusion in any other way than to subvert his own story. But in fact, most of the products of the storytelling art are pleasing precisely because they enable us to pass a moral: what happens, the physical events in the story, is structured so as to present right and wrong. Even when we find ourselves identifying with the criminals and against their lawful pursuants, it is because the author has made us see the criminals as fundamentally in the right and the detectives in the wrong. A character becomes the hero or heroine of a book, the one with whom we identify by being, in our eyes, the one who stands for the good. Because the event level of the story draws us into it through its appeal to our pleasure in discerning among the right- and wrongdoers and maintains our interest by making us ever more desperate to see right, or our hero, triumph, we are never just concerned to see how things turn out, but rather, how the persons who represent right and wrong turn out. When we are absorbed in a story, our wanting to know how things turn out is driven by the question of how good will overcome evil, and this is carried by the question of whether the persons with whom our conscience identifies or those whom it rejects will be the victors. Likewise, Newman says, nature operates in the service of a moral system, and a moral system is always represented by persons. In scripture, miracles are not presented as purely physical events, but as enabling right to be served and directing us to the person who performs them. They are there to show us which persons represent the author's heroes. Newman takes 12:16–19 as an instance of the "power of displaying" miracles being "entrusted to certain individuals, who stand forward as their interpreters, giving them a voice and a language": the thunderstorm of 1 Sam. 12 is not a dumb show, a voiceless miracle, but interpreted and explained by Samuel. It is here to personify Samuel's authority and to serve "the greatest of moral ends, a Revelation from God."[23] This explains the dry neutrality of Samuel's reference to his sons. "Behold, here I am," the prophet says (12:3): the speech is not about Samuel's sons, but initially about Samuel himself and his authority.

23. Newman, *Two Essays*, 18–19.

The spectacular signs performed by Samuel require, and are given, further interpretation by the prophet: we cannot understand them just by looking at them. Once having set Saul before the eyes of the people, Samuel tells them what his new kingship stands for: once the innovation of kingship is embarked upon, people and king will have to decide whether to use it well or sinfully. The kind of government is immaterial: what matters is theological ethics, whether the polity is directed toward or against God's moral law. In setting Saul before the people, Samuel sets before them a human free choice as to whether kingship will be good or evil. Immediately after telling them to "behold the king" (12:13), Samuel interprets this sign as meaning: "If ye will fear the LORD, and serve him, and obey his voice, and not rebel against the commandment of the LORD, then shall both ye and also the king that reigneth over you continue following the LORD your God. But if ye will not obey the voice of the LORD, but rebel against the commandment of the LORD, then shall the hand of the LORD be against you, as it was against your fathers" (12:14–15).

After the people quake in terror, at the sign of the "thunder and rain" and beg "that we die not" for the sin of "ask[ing] us a king" (12:19), "Samuel said unto the people, 'Fear not (ye have done all this wickedness: yet turn not aside from following the LORD ...): for the LORD will not forsake his people ... because it hath pleased the LORD to make you his people. ... Only fear the LORD, and serve him in truth. ... But if ye shall still do wickedly, ye shall be consumed, both ye and your king'" (12:20, 22, 24–25). The sign is interpreted by the prophet as representing a choice: they can "fear the LORD" or they can "do wickedly." Samuel is exhorting the people to use their freedom wisely, serving the Lord "in truth with all your heart" (12:24). Samuel uses the prophetic sign of the rainstorm in order to "set before [the people] life and death" (Deut. 30:19): "I will teach you the good way and the right way" (1 Sam. 12:23). It is not that Saul is foredoomed to be punished for the request or that the people themselves must ultimately be punished for it in the Babylonian conquest and exile. A free and open road lies before the people. Their identity and name is still God's people: "Because it hath pleased the LORD to make you his people" (12:22). God loves the people, and he will remain with them, in their monarchic enterprise, even knowing that this experiment is not the ideal of the promised land.

Noth observes that the Deuteronomic summative speeches contain two themes. First, there is divine retribution for misbehavior: Samuel's speech characteristically "interpret[s] the historical process showing ... how God's retributive activity takes its course against the whole people." There is also a "recurring emphasis on obeying the 'voice' of God" in its "demands upon human conduct."[24] Obedience cannot simply be antithetical to divine omnipotence. A God who despises human free will cannot require obedience to his moral law, because a robot cannot be obedient. A people whose freedom is at odds or in contradiction with the divine

24. Noth, *Deuteronomistic History*, 6.

omnipotence cannot be adjured to "serve [God] in truth with all your heart" (12:24). Samuel interprets the history of Israel down to and including the vindication of King Saul against Nahash as meaning that Israel can be the people of an omnipotent God so long as it freely wills to be a community consecrated to the covenant. God has freely set them apart from the nations—"it hath pleased the LORD to make you his people" (12:22)—and they will escape retribution on condition that they freely will to maintain a political kingdom set apart from the ways of the nations, one in which God is still king, however they are governed by men. Jobling pinpoints this accurately when he states that the Deuteronomistic History is neither promonarchic nor antimonarchic, as Martin Buber thought, but " 'balanced' between the two. It lets monarchy be seen for good and bad, and judgeship for good and bad; it also (though not very clearly) lets other possibilities be seen. Out of these elements, Israel is free to create its 'political theology'!"[25] The Israelites are neither automatically good nor ciphers for evil, like "Sisera, captain of the host of Hazor" (12:9): they apostatize, return, apostatize, and return once more. They stand for the freedom that consists in being able to choose for or against the God who has chosen them. It is being chosen, by God, as his people, that makes the Israelites free, individual human beings.

25. Jobling, *Sense of Biblical Narrative*, 86.

SERIES FOUR

DOWNFALL

1 Samuel 13–15

The elevation of classical Greece as the model for understanding biblical history took place in nineteenth-century biblical scholarship alongside calls for the de-Hellenization of Christian doctrine. Van Seters describes how eighteenth-century and nineteenth-century paradigms of the editorial production of Homer's epics out of independent oral songs and into the written, authorized texts of the *Iliad* and the *Odyssey* conditioned the conceptions of the emergence of the Pentateuch and Joshua-Samuel-Kings. Friedrich August Wolf not only led Greek scholars on a wild goose chase for the editorial interpolations in Homer's epics, but also, through his colleague J. G. Eichhorn at Jena, set biblical scholars on the road to making "the fragmentary, supplementary, and documentary hypotheses" articles of faith, "with the editor playing a key role in the compositional process" (Van Seters 2006: 141). Once having analyzed his text by the methods of Homeric scholarship, biblical exegetes illustrated the intentions of the Deuteronomist historian by comparing him to the historians of ancient Greece and Rome. It was thought that the Deuteronomistic History, from Joshua to Kings, treats of government much as the plot of Herodotus's *History* turns on whether Greece will preserve its democratic city-states or be governed despotically by the king of Persia. A method devised in relation to Greek and Roman literature was interpolated into the text of the Hebrew Bible, and, as the philologists say, corrupted it. Once they stopped treating the Old Testament as the letter to the gospel's spirit, scholars ceased to make it analogous to the gospel and instead equated it to classical culture.

The classicist bias thinks any one author would have a monologic perspective and fails to recognize that a primitive audience would enjoy the esthetic effect of a whole being formed through the intersection of perspectives. We know the Republican Roman historian Tacitus deprecated the rise of the Caesars and that the intention of Tacitus's *Annals* is to ironize the early Roman emperors. For all his stated aim of writing *sine ira et studio*, the *Annals* are biased against imperial government. The *Annals* contain little proimperial material because they were composed by a man who regretted the demise of Republican Rome. Herodotus's *History of Ancient Greece* sees the successful self-defense of the Greek city-states against their Persian invaders as the triumph of democracy over despotism. His *History* contains no pro-Persian despotism chapters. This is because of Herodotus's democratic governmental bias, in addition to the historical fact that Xerxes made a pig's ear of his invasion. Alas, when we turn from this clarity to the history of the Israelite kingdoms, we find ourselves in a twilight zone, where monarchy is alternately conceded and criticized. If one had not determined upon setting the Deuteronomistic History within the same monologic schema as that provided by Tacitus's *Annals* or Herodotus's *History*, the natural conclusion would be that the intention of the biblical author was not to make a specific governmental point. Herodotus was not an irreligious fellow. His account of the Delphic Oracle's words about Xerxes' invasion is ironic, but he believes the invasion was ill fated and notes omens to that effect.[1] Herodotus was a somewhat pious historian with a keen interest in politics. Our author was a historically minded theologian with a specialized interest in God's providence. The paradigm of Greco-Roman history writing and Homeric epic, with their sustained narratives, is too high minded to capture the osculating means by which he conveys this interest. The director of a television series, like David Simon, gets his script writers to supply different points of view for each scene, so that we see each side from within, as well as near, simultaneously viewing their juxtaposition. The director determines what the intersecting of the perspectives says or what its overall moral is. In the ancient world, they had to fall back on theater, since they did not have Home Box Office. Since, outside Aeschylus's *Persians*, ancient drama seldom represented political history, it was not taken as an analogy to Regum by classicist biblical scholars.

Those who took up Augustine's treatment of Regum in the *City of God* and saw Saul and David as precursors of the kingdom of God devoted rather cursory attention to the government of their earthly kingdom. The difference between the church fathers' approach to scripture and that of modern classicist biblical exegesis is that the fathers intended to absorb Greek wisdom into the scriptures, and not vice versa. Immersed in real, late Greco-Roman civilization, converts like Augustine could recognize the crudity of the Old Testament and appreciated that it is at most analogous—not identical—to Greek and Roman histories. Over the

---

1. Herodotus, *Histories* 7.59, 140–43, trans. Aubrey de Sélincourt (London: Penguin, 1954), 465, 488–89.

centuries, many aspects of Greek philosophy were baptized and exercised within Christian exegesis. But the father's disdain for the esthetic accomplishments of the Greeks and Romans, rehearsed in the first half of the *City of God*, left its mark. The Cinderella who was left out of the baptismal ball was Greek literature—the epics of Homer and the dramas. This oversight became apparent when in the late-nineteenth century classicist estheticism took up Greek tragedy as a positive alternative to the Christian ethos, for classicists had at their disposal not only an unbaptized but a modern, secularized conception of tragedy, which they turned against Christianity. Some contemporary exegetes read such an idea of tragedy into the downfall of Saul.

Tradition did not come to an end with the death of the last church father, and the traditions of the last four hundred years can also help us to listen to scripture. The church fathers tended to see Saul's downfall in black and white terms, as the condign consequence of disobedience. They underestimated the pathos of Saul. It marked a gain in the humane grasp of 1 Samuel when Handel represented Saul's descent into madness as humanly terrible and tragic in his oratorio *Saul*. Wellhausen approached literary insight into the Bible when he suggested that Saul is a "*vorspiel* to Samson,"[2] that is, a clumsy, failed hero. Von Rad displays his interiority with the Old Testament when he notes that Saul's story is the sole narrative in Israel's scriptures that has a "close affinity with the spirit of Greek tragedy" (1962: 325).

The perception of what tragedy means in relation to the stories of Saul and David shifted when critics elected to read what their predecessors had called the Deuteronomistic History purely as literature. Literary readings of scripture study the text in its final form and set aside mining it for sources within it or history beyond it. But when it came to imagining Saul and David, the supposed source history of 1 Samuel still has an impact on its self-professedly literary readers. Scholars who reject historicizing readings of the Bible imagine that adverse and favorable attitudes are juxtaposed in 1 Sam. 8–15. Even though they claim that they "are not looking for the historical facts of the matter" and that the "story of Saul . . . is put together far more like a novel than like a piece of modern historiography" (Good 1965: 58), recent literary appreciations of 1 Samuel are certain that what makes it a tragedy is its antitheses: a good Saul versus a bad Saul (Saul's light side versus his dark side), or a good king versus a bad king (Saul unfairly contrasted with David), and a good God versus a bad God (the merciful God who countenances David's rule-breaking and "the demonic side of God" [Exum 1992: 40], which punishes Saul for the same failures).

Literary interpretations of the text read King Saul as a tragic figure. Just like the source-critical readings of 1 Samuel, they do so because they think Saul is forced to represent incompatible themes: the need to establish a centralized state and

---

2. Exum 1992: 135: "Both are hailed as deliverers of Israel from the Philistines, both fail at the task, and both die seemingly ignominious deaths at the hands of their oppressors in the process."

the sense that there is something blasphemous about the emergence of a monarch. On this analysis, to carry off the persona of a tragic hero, Saul needs both greatness, or what traditional critics call a promonarchic source, and a terrible, fated or preordained fall from this height, with some "fatal flaw" (Good 1965: 56–57) inscribed in his personality, or what Noth viewed as the Deuteronomist's disapproval of the establishment of monarchy. In recent literary exegesis, the "tragedy of King Saul" is that of a good man destroyed by a political development he never asked to symbolize, used by God as a *pharmakos* or "scapegoat for the people's sin of requesting a human king" (Exum 1992: 38). Such tragic interpretations of Saul's fall are generated by interpreting Saul as torn between antimonarchic and monarchic imperatives.

For these recent critics, Saul is foredoomed to disaster from the moment Yahweh disapprovingly acquiesced in the people's demand for a king: as he set off innocently looking for his father's asses, Saul is proceeding to a doom as inevitable as it is unwarranted. The God-centered conception of his role and the political demands of his actual kingship are bound to collide. Saul has to "unite two incompatible conceptions of kingship," one in which he is like a judge, acting in obedience to prophetic oracle, and the other in which he does what is pragmatically required of the ruler of a state that has to hold its own against its neighbors and their armies (Good 1965: 56).

Since scripture is in fact both negative and positive about all aspects of human civilization, it may not be wholly off the mark to imagine that "the theological *ambiguity* of the establishment of the monarchy" is the heart of the story of Saul and of its tragedy (Good 1965: 58, emphasis added). The question is how to define tragedy. We better appreciate what tragedy is if we enter the ethical assumptions of its author. His assumptions were not so far from those of the classical tragedians, who were closer in time and in spirit to the author of Regum than are modern humanistic theorists of tragedy. In effect, two kinds of reader found tragedy in Saul's story. Some, drawing on a Greek understanding of tragedy, find him an enigmatic figure, whose self-loss and rejection by God is inexplicable. Others explain his plight with a theory that Yahweh in 1 Samuel is demonic and that Saul is the hapless recipient of his amoral resentment. This latter view would be more accurate if, instead of calling Saul a tragic hero, it named him as a melodramatic victim.

If we don't separate the esthetic appeal of 1 Samuel from its historical base, then we notice something. The Saul attested by the pro- and antimonarchic evidence is not struggling against someone else, David for instance: rather, he is wrestling with himself. Like Magritte's *Gigantic Days*, which depicts a woman assaulted by a man who is inseparable from herself, Saul is conflicted within himself. Though the explicit articulation of original sin by Paul ("for the good which I will, I do not: but the evil which I will not, that I do"; Rom. 7:19 Douay-Rheims), lay a long way ahead of him, our author's juxtaposition of the pro- and antimonarchic evidence evokes this human mystery. An integrated society, with communal politics as ordered as a Tibetan monastery, is a good to which our imagination naturally tends, and Saul wills it too, but the lure of evil and the lie is too great for him to be a good charismatic king. A tragic presentiment of original sin is present in the *Iliad*, in the homely scenes showing the love of Hector, his father Priam, and his wife Andromache: Homer recognizes that it is tragic that the archaic Trojan culture must be destroyed and superseded by that of the Greeks. In the *Iliad* the tragedy is a fight to the death between two opposing peoples. In 1 Samuel the springs of the sacral society are broken within the human heart. Saul's downfall symbolizes the historical fact of the autofragmentation of theocratic culture in Israel. Considering the text historically and thus seeing that monarchy means different things at different times helps us to identify the specific tragedy of 1 Samuel. This requires that we answer the question, "Did an institution such as a nondynastic monarchy exist?" in the affirmative (Ishida 1977: 2). The terms "promonarchic" and "antimonarchic" can make us think of any monarchy, Saul's or David's or that of Akhenaten. The reign of Saul was not the exercise of kingship in general. Historically, 1 Sam. 13–15 presents the self-destruction of one kind of kingship, its Hebraic, primitive, prestate, and thus prepolitical form: charismatic kingship. To uncover the universal significance of Saul's reign, we need to take note of its cultural specificity. The universality of his tragedy emerges within the particular kind of kingship that the scripture ascribes to him.

Episode One: The Mandate of Heaven (1 Sam. 13:1–14)

First Sam. 13 is linked to Samuel's instruction in 10:8. After Saul's private anointing, Samuel mentioned to him a "garrison of the Philistines" at Gibeath-elohim (10:5). Once imbued with the power of the Spirit, Saul is to "do what your hand finds to do, for God is with you" (10:7 ESV). "Then," Samuel instructs, "go down before me to Gilgal. And behold, I am coming to you to offer burnt offerings and to sacrifice peace offerings. Seven days you shall wait, until I come to you and show you what you shall do" (10:8 ESV). The withdrawal of the Lord's support for Saul's kingship will begin in Saul's decision not to execute this prophetic instruction, but instead to offer the sacrifice before the prophet arrives.

Saul and Jonathan, his son, who comes on stage for the first time here, have put their heads together in the U-shaped courtyard at Gibeah and come up with a U-shaped tactic to expel the Philistines. First, Saul musters three thousand men and divides the force, sending one thousand with Jonathan and retaining two thousand in Michmash (13:2). Then Jonathan takes a strike against the Philistine garrison at Geba: this provocation is intended, not to bring out their entire force all at once, but to spur them into troop movement (13:3) (Long 1989: 55–58). Meantime, Saul seems to withdraw the people to Gilgal. Ever since Wellhausen, the scene at Gilgal in 13:7–15 has been taken as a late interpolation. Scholars think it would have been military suicide for Saul to pull the mustered army back to Gilgal, in the Jordan valley, leaving Jonathan on the battlefield near Geba (Wevers 1971: 161).

One can adduce bad and good military reasons for the withdrawal of Saul's force to Gilgal. A good motive is that it was the best place for the larger contingent to gather, since Gilgal was outside the Philistine sphere of military dominance and offered attack and retreat routes into the hill country round about (Long 1989: 47–48). Dividing the troops permitted a pincer movement, with Saul in command north of the wadi and Jonathan directing a smaller force southeast of the dry river course. Even if it would have been a tactical blunder to move the larger portion of the army to Gilgal, this is a weak reason to rule out its historicity. The same criterion would lead us to deny the historicity of Gettysburg and Arnhem, strategic errors on the part of, respectively, General Robert E. Lee and the Allied commanders. Such errors often become the material of great drama, as in Ron Maxwell's *Gettysburg*, Richard Attenborough's *A Bridge Too Far*, and the "Operation Market Garden" episode of *Band of Brothers*. In our culture, defeat and near defeat is as much the stuff of legend as is victory, and both can be equally anchored in fact.

The people soon found themselves in proleptic concurrence with Wellhausen: the tactic of camping at Gilgal felt as precarious to them as it later would to the German exegete, and they began to sneak away home: "When the men of Israel saw that they were in a strait . . . then the people did hide themselves in caves, and in thickets, and in rocks, and in high places, and in pits" (13:6)—plenty of cover for them, but also many escape routes for deserters. Saul began to lose his mustered army: "And some of the Hebrews went over Jordan to the land of Gad and Gilead." Meantime, Saul was trapped at Gilgal with the "trembling" remainder of his force (13:7).

He had been told to wait "seven days" for the arrival of the prophet Samuel to set up the "burnt offerings," that is, to enact the prebattle ritual of sacrifice. At the end of the seventh day, "according to the set time that Samuel had appointed," there was no sign of the prophet: "Samuel came not to Gilgal, and the people were scattered from him" (13:8). Saul then did what any general in any time or place, excepting Saint Louis and Richard Coeur de Lion, would do: "Saul said, 'Bring hither a burnt offering to me. . . .' And he offered the burnt offering" (13:9). With stark inevitability, "as soon as he had made an end of offering the burnt offering, behold, Samuel came" (13:10). Samuel is the personification of the law, and it's like the moral law returning of its own accord and clipping Saul, because he has broken it.

In response to Samuel's "What hast thou done?" Saul gives three perfectly understandable reasons for flouting Samuel's instruction: the soldiers were deserting, the seven days were up, and the Philistines were visibly preparing to attack from Michmash (13:11). Against this reasonable self-exculpation, Samuel does not just rebuke Saul, but relentlessly pulls the rug of the kingship out from under him: "Thy kingdom shall not continue," but will be transferred to another

(13:14). Scholars are unanimous in condemning Samuel's irrationality in insisting on obedience to his instructions. Saul, says Good, was "prepared to fly in the prophet's face rather than lose his army, though he is not prepared . . . to tell Samuel to stop talking like a blithering idiot" (1965: 67). Militarily, says Wevers, "Saul is placed in an impossible position . . . and has failed to meet the arbitrary requirement" (1971: 161–62).

The text is punctilious in indicating that Saul followed the temporal half of Samuel's instruction to the letter and in allowing the listener to imagine the test to which the prophet's delay put the general: Saul "tarried seven days, according to the set time that Samuel had appointed" in 10:8, "but Samuel came not to Gilgal; and the people were scattered from him" (13:8). By specifying, not only his own presence but setting a time and failing to meet it, Samuel has heightened Saul's frustration. His army is draining away. Saul was timed out in an appalling situation, naturally lost hope, and took action. Saul was, if anything, overly meticulous about his cultic obligations, not lax in their performance: he was even ready to carry out the prebattle rituals in the absence of the prophet. The instruction, Gunn argues, was "ambiguous": it is unclear whether the essence is to wait "seven days" or to wait "until the prophet appeared," whenever that might be. Saul hinged everything on the seven days, whereas Samuel decided that the accent was supposed to be on his own presence. Gunn objects to Samuel's flatly ignoring the possibility of a misunderstanding. The automatism was funny when the servant had exactly the right money in hand, whereas now it is with a ghastly inevitability that Samuel walks on and catches Saul red-handed, burnt offering to the ready. It is the ineluctability of the process, with Samuel appearing on cue the moment the sacrifice is launched, that impels Gunn to consider that Saul "appears . . . as the plaything of fate." He is not being punished for anything he has done, but for what, Gunn thinks, "he represents," that is, a kingship toward which Yahweh is inveterately hostile (1980: 34–40, 68, 40).

Samuel as prophet is God's intermediary. If he said that warfare was not to be initiated without him, and the burnt offering was the immediate antecedent of the call to attack, then Saul had decided to conduct war without the presence of God in his spokesman. He had decided to conduct "godless war." Saul was setting himself above the word of the Lord, as personified by Samuel and his instruction. In choosing to carry out the sacrifice himself, the charismatic king fails to submit Israel's kingship to the prophet and thus to the kingship of God. Even in an emergency, Saul is not permitted to infringe the requirement that a prophet wield the power of the sacrifice. This seems morally unfair and militarily impractical.

To most historical critics, the situation of Saul's army is not militarily outcharioted, but historically impossible. The Philistine muster against the Israelite insurgency is usually taken to be unhistorical. The enemy is described by the author as mustering "thirty thousand chariots" (13:5). Chariots would have been worthless, we are told, on the steep slopes of the wadi (Wevers 1971: 161). One may protest against this that Assyrian inscriptions record chariots being carried to such difficult terrain, there to be deployed on the ground (Long 1989: 84). Chariots could be useful in instilling fear in hill country foot-soldier armies. The Hittites, neighbors to the original Sea Peoples' home ground of Anatolia, had pioneered the military use of the chariot to defeat the Egyptians at the Battle of Kadesh in the 1280s BC; Homer seems to preserve a recollection of this, though archeologists doubt whether Hittite technology for carburization was at that time up to speed.[3] The most well-known ancient example of the use of chariots in rocky and mountainous terrain is, of course, Xerxes' invasion of Greece in 480 BC, where the Persian soldiers are compelled to haul these heavy vehicles up- and downhill. The Greek city-states were assisted in their successful repulsion of the invasion by the Persians bringing such unsuitable vehicles as chariots to the mountains of northern Greece. But the value of a military tactic tells us little about its historical status.

The text does anything but downplay the difficulty of Saul's situation, with the people creeping into their hiding holes and the soldiers deserting. The scholarly criticism of Samuel's rejection of Saul is largely based on what 1 Sam. 13 tells them about Saul's position. The text does not just permit us to wonder whether anyone except a blistering idiot would have done as Saul did. It piles on the desperation of General Saul's position. The Philistines threaten the three-thousand-strong Israelite force with "thirty thousand chariots, and six thousand horsemen, and people as the sand which is on the sea-shore" (13:5). Herodotus would balk at thus numerically exaggerating the enemy faced by the Greek city-states. Greek history writing did not give rise to the genre of apocalypse. The terror of the people in 1 Sam. 13 is like that incurred in the book of Revelation after the angel has opened the sixth seal: "And the kings of the earth, . . . and the chief captains, . . . and every bondman, and every freeman, hid themselves in the dens and in the rocks of the mountains" (Rev. 6:15); "the people did hide themselves in caves, and in thickets, and in rocks, and in high places, and in pits" (1 Sam. 13:6). Not only the civilian population, but even Saul's people, his cadre of soldiers, were "trembling" (13:7). Our author hypes up the terrifying disequilibrium of forces and the consequent Israelite dread. The story is told in such a way as to pit an overpowering monstrosity against a humanly vulnerable people. It's like the battles in Peter Jackson's *Lord of the Rings*. This is how epic poets and moviemakers depict religious conflict. Epic poets and film directors display the good side as in peril of absolute annihilation by its foe. Given the leaden quality of some exegesis on this episode, one can only feel surprised that no one has ever questioned how the Philistines fed an army numerically equivalent to "the sand which is on the sea-shore" (13:6). The author is showing us what the conflict between good and evil feels like from within. Once Jonathan and Saul have "smitten" their garrison, "all

3. C. M. Bowra, *Homer* (London: Duckworth, 1972), 51; and J. D. Muhly, R. Maddin, T. Stech, and E. Özgen, "Iron in Anatolia and the Nature of the Hittite Iron Industry," *Anatolian Studies* 35 (1985): 68, 79.

Israel heard say . . . that Israel also was had in abomination with the Philistines" (13:4): the Philistines intend utterly to destroy the rebels, and the size of their army is a metaphorical signal of their intention to overwhelm Israel. The author is dramatizing the military maneuver as an existential event.

The people's desire to "be like all the nations; and [have a] king [to] judge us, and go out before us, and fight our battles" (8:20) on the one hand, and the Lord's command that this king should "obey his voice, and not rebel against the commandment of the LORD" (12:14) on the other, set Saul between a rock and a hard place. Saul is held to the requirements of some poetic spiritual warrior while inhabiting the world of prosaic flesh. As Gunn sees it, Saul has internalized the demands of the older tribal world, as the knowledge that cultic obligations must be met and sacrifice performed before battle is joined. But the Lord requires this new chieftain-general to obey him not only legally and cultically but personally, through the word of his prophet Samuel. He requires Saul to meet and wait upon himself as a person, an "I," and thus to be a king not only officially but as a person, a "Thou." The Lord's ethical requirements are absolute because they are personal to him, coming back to his "I say so." The Lord wants his king to be of another cut and caliber, a different make, to the kings of the pagan nations. With the terrifying coronation of Saul in 1 Sam. 12, the Lord has accepted chieftainship, but perhaps not prosaic politics and certainly not government-as-usual. Government combined with cult is the impersonal statecraft practiced by the biblical Egyptians and Philistines. It uses liturgy instrumentally, so its leaders do whatever is expedient, such as sacrifice and get the battle going before one has no army left with which to do so: cult is subordinate to power. But a personal, moral God is always above government and judges it. This is not an abstract, spiritual moralism that is remote from the drama in 13:1–7 as it grips an imaginative listener. Since the narrative itself depicts the opposing sides as an unequal combat between outsized evil powers and vulnerable human-sized ones, the only way in which the latter could hope to be successful would be by gracious "good luck," not by square-headed political pragmatism. It doesn't fit the story in the dramatic form in which it is told to think that Saul could have rescued his army by doing the expedient thing without doing the good thing, which was prophetically enjoined upon him. Now was the time, the story is telling us, for daring, courage, and respect for the *ruah elohim*. This is just when the characteristic comic élan that enabled the judges to overpower Jericho, Eglon, and Sisera is needed. Now was the time to believe, as Saul's namesake was later to say, "When I am weak, then am I powerful" (2 Cor. 12:10, author's translation).

First Sam. 13:1–7 exaggerates the numerical disproportion of the forces until they become a symbol of the spiritual polarity between them. The tale is telling us that Saul's embattled position calls, not for pragmatism, but for sticking precisely to the wizard-rainman's orders. Modern Christians are too prone to spout that what Saul really needed and lacked was faith, in a rather vaporized sense of the term. This lack of imagination is what evokes the countercharge of Samuel's unfairness and impracticality. If we think "wizard" then we think Gandalf and the author of "On Fairy Tales." Any reader of fairy stories knows that the success of their heroes and heroines depends on remembering and performing the precise words of the fairy. "Don't eat *anything*," says the faun in *Pan's Labyrinth*, "your life depends on it." The heroine's disobedience results in the death of two of her fairy guardians. Magic requires precise adherence to formulas. It is because they bring back memories of such fairy-tale enchantment that primitive cultures attract us. It would be more theologically accurate to say that Saul, the would-be hero of a sacred war, was insufficiently legalistic than that he lacked faith. "Expect me on the fifth day at first light," says Gandalf before the Battle of Helm's Deep: he means his friends to have sticklingly literal faith in his return.

Human beings have a moral conscience, and they enjoy those stories whose internal moral compass reflects and enlarges it. This moral compass is contained in the landscape of the story as a whole, but it is usually also concretized in one single figure. In most dramas, one character represents the ethical plumb line of the imaginative world that the story evokes. This figure need not be the protagonist or the ones who carry the narrative, and it need not be a character whom the audience spontaneously relishes. They instinctively identify this person as the one who gives this imaginative world its measure of morality. Within 1 Samuel, Samuel is this figure. The book began by presenting Samuel as the answer to Hannah's plea for a child. We are told that "his mother used to make for him a little robe and take it to him each year when she went up with her husband to offer the yearly sacrifice" (2:19 ESV). The intimate setting of his call in 1 Sam. 3 is a humanizing touch. In 1 Sam. 7, a near superhuman Samuel looms over the mountainside at Mizpah and repels the Philistine advance by offering a lamb in sacrifice: "As Samuel was offering up the burnt offering, the Philistines drew near to attack Israel. But the LORD thundered with a mighty sound that day against the Philistines . . . and they were routed before Israel" (7:10 ESV). In 1 Sam. 12, placing himself before the people at Gilgal, "old and grey-headed," and reminding them that "I have walked before you from my childhood unto this day" (12:2), a shamanic Samuel demonstrated his prophetic integrity. The author has laid down the markers to lead a reader to identify with Samuel as the moral compass of the story. Samuel functions like Tolkien's Gandalf.

The historical critics and the literary critics, with their antihistorical bias, seem to exchange places in their exegesis of this chapter. The historical critics note what they think are the militarily unfeasible features of 13:1–7 and on this basis write off the historicity of the affair, dealing with 1 Sam. 13 as if it posed purely textual problems, as a legendary interpolation into 1 Sam. 8–15. Their literal mindedness at least enables them to mark the mysterious elements of 1 Sam. 13. The literary critics disregard the dramatic, epic quality of the story and analyze Saul's behavior as if he were an actual historical figure, like a modern secular general. But it is the epic feel of the story that makes its theological morality imaginatively transparent. The odd thing about Good's claim that Samuel is "talking like a blistering idiot" when the prophet imposes the standards of Yahwistic kingship on a general in urgent danger of "losing his army" is that Good forswears his stance as an esthetic reader of the story and becomes an armchair strategist for a Late Bronze Age general. A reader who takes the story theologically has better access to it than either a purely historical or purely literary reader. The theological reader can imagine the historicity of the drama. But we should not overstate the requirement of supernatural faith for getting the sense of this military episode: there is a common human desire to understand war in ethical terms; or to understand our ethical lives as a combat between good and evil. The reason that Origen's interpretation of the battles of Joshua and Judges as really being about "spiritual combat" (Lubac 2007: 171, 212, 214–15) was not, along with many patristic shots at allegorizing the Old Testament, filed away among scholarly esoterica, but entered ordinary Christian spirituality is that it fits a human instinct to articulate the choice of good over evil as a battle against near-overmastering odds. It makes natural religious sense to think of the battles of the Old Testament, like that of 1 Sam. 13, as allegories of a struggle between good and evil, because, as in the rather ethereal battles of Peter Jackson's *Lord of the Rings*, it is not the dead bodies and the swordplay that really form the core, but the struggle of good to prevail against evil.

Saul is no "plaything of fate" in this episode (Gunn 1980: 68). He rehearses his mental processes before his interrogator: "Therefore said I, 'The Philistines will come down now upon me to Gilgal, and I have not made supplication unto the LORD': I forced myself therefore, and offered a burnt offering" (13:12). People wonder whether Saul is sincere, when he tells Samuel, "I forced myself": is this a self-exculpating exaggeration? On his own testimony, Saul made himself do it, that is, with reluctance he willed himself into willing to perform the sacrifice. He does not say "the Philistines made me do it" or "Yahweh made me do it." One half—the time length—of the instruction is fulfilled, but not the other half of the sign—the presence of the prophet. Saul would not reluctantly force himself if Saul believed, like Gunn, that there was an ambiguity in the two-sidedness of the instruction. The success of the maneuver at stake, Saul put the force of his volition behind an action he knew to be counter to the precise word of the prophet. It is a sorry tale, but Saul's loss of hope in Samuel's arrival and his entrusting himself to his own sacrificing and generalship is, on his own testimony, his choice. Although Saul is not the victim of fate in this episode, nor does he drive his own human free will. The choice is his, but it's not his own: "I forced myself." Freedom is self-possession (Thomas Aquinas, *Summa contra Gentiles* 3.2.112.2), whereas Saul pathetically allowed himself to be constrained by circumstances. What Saul means when he claims that he forced himself is that he permitted the material situation to take control of his human actions and designs. He gave away his freedom to act on the situation. He did not have it taken from him. This is a very common human experience.

As Gunn and others read the Gilgal story, Saul is really being punished, not for this one infringement of an arbitrary instruction, but for the people's impious

demand for a king, a request in which, as we saw in 1 Sam. 9, Saul was a passive participant. Yahweh has been fixed against him from the beginning, say some of those
who read Saul's story as a tragedy, and now Yahweh takes the opportunity for the
punitive retribution that has been impending all along. This is not the way Samuel
the prophet describes the Lord's attitude to Saul. Samuel says that Saul was given
the kingship, not temporarily and grudgingly but eternally and conditionally: "For
now would the Lord have established thy kingdom upon Israel for ever" (13:13).
The Lord would, Samuel claims, have kept his side of the bargain, in admitting this
kingship, if Saul had kept his side and ruled in subordination to God's spokesman,
permitting the Lord to preside as king within the human kingship of Saul.

A further reason for regarding the Gilgal episode as a late interpolation is that
Samuel will reject Saul again, after a further infringement of the divine word
(1 Sam. 15). Duplicate stories are commonly regarded by biblical scholars as
multiplications of one and the same event. There was, it is thought, a Gilgal version of Saul's rejection and a Mizpah one, and the Gilgal version has been pasted
in awkwardly here, three chapters after its starting point (10:8), where it breaks
up the flow of the story of the battle of Michmash Pass and where the event it
recounts will have to be replicated in its results two chapters hence.

There is room for doubt whether the two rejections are identical. Perhaps
Samuel is telling Saul here that his bloodline will not retain the kingdom. Some
claim that the wording doesn't bear this out, because "in both cases it is said
that Saul's kingship (*mamleket/memlᵉkût*) has been taken from him and given
to another, better than he" (Van Seters 1983: 261). But put the two episodes
alongside each other, and, despite the use of the same word for kingship, the
rejection in 1 Sam. 15 seems more drastic. In 1 Sam. 13 Samuel is not finally
stripping the kingship from Saul himself, as he will do in 1 Sam. 15, but denying
him the right of a father to pass on his status to his blood-heirs. Passing on the
kingship to his own sons would be the natural ambition of any leader: Eli and
Samuel passed on their status to their sons. The meaning of Samuel's "thy kingdom
shall not continue" (13:14) is thus: your kingship will come to an end in you, as
Eli's judging and priesthood did. This reading fits the pattern of repetition and
quasirepetition of similar stories in 1 Samuel: several episodes and part episodes
are analogous and echo one another. Eli's house has been deprived of the right to
continue because of the wickedness of his sons, Hophni and Phinehas, though
Eliades carry on functioning as priests until Saul and Doeg slaughter them in
1 Sam. 22. The messenger to Eli in 2:27–35 told him that his house would fall,
meaning both that his sons would die and that, eventually, his entire bloodline
would be rooted out. Samuel was told by the elders that a monarch was needed
because "thy sons walk not in thy ways" (8:5). Now, in an inverted reminiscence
of those narratives, Saul's *sons* will be deprived of the right to be king, because of
their *father's* malefaction.

Some recent historical critics concur that Samuel here "deprives Saul of the
long-term legitimacy of a dynasty." They think Samuel destroyed Saul's dynastic

hopes, not yet stripping Saul himself of kingship. But by the same token they feel charismatic kingship is to be ruled out, in relation to Saul. The argument for this is that "kingship is of its essence dynastic" (Campbell and O'Brien 2000: 250). It is not easy to make the case that, historically, monarchy has a single essence, given the variety of forms it has taken, from absolute monarchs to constitutional ones, including the Shogun emperors of Japan, Louis XIV, and Elizabeth II. In the person of the Dalai Lama, the bodhisattva rulers of Tibet transmit their kingship by means of reincarnation. It is deputed to the Panchin Lama to detect in which child the bodhisattva person of the Buddha has reincarnated itself.[4] This counterexample feels wrong fitting, but why? It seems an unfair example, because Tibetan Buddhists have a different conception of a human being: with their idea that, after its death, the karma of the self reincarnates in new bodies, allied to the Mahayana theory of the bodhisattva, they are able to conceive of the Dalai Lama as eternally recycling into new human forms. The Israelites had no such conception of the self to avoid dynastic kingship.

Ishida gives as the demonstration of his theory that all kingship in the ancient Near East was dynastic, so there was no phenomenon of charismatic kingship in Israel; in fact Egyptian, Mesopotamian, and Hittite kingship was dynastic. One of the sixteenth-century BC Hittite King Telipinu's inscriptions reads, "I have seated myself on the throne of my father." Instructions for the succession to the Hittite monarchy were laid down in King Telipinu's edict, which gave priority to a "firstborn son," followed by a second son, followed by the husband of the "firstborn daughter." It was hereditary: neither God nor popular acclamation came into it. In Mesopotamia, though, the hereditary principle was theologized: elected and "predestined by the gods to rule," any Babylonian king could say with Tiglath-pileser I, "Ye great gods . . . have decreed . . . that his priestly seed should have a place in Eharsagkurkurra forever." The Egyptian theology of kingship was even more religious: "Each reigning king was Horus, the legitimate successor to his father Osiris, and as he becomes Osiris when he died, the throne passed to his son Horus. . . . The authority of the Egyptian king was derived, in theory, solely from the king's divine ancestors. But in practice, too, the belief in the divinity of the royal blood was so strong that the heir apparent, if his lineage was not pure enough, sometimes had to marry his half sister who came of the legitimate line" (Ishida 1977: 16, 12, 15).

Like the Buddhists, though, the Egyptians and Mesopotamians may have had an idea of what a human being is different from the Israelites. It's arguable that they had an idea of humanity but no idea of personality in the biblical sense. For Israel, a person is someone called by God: each person attains identity and thus social status from vocation. Against this, some scholars see a common factor between

---

4. David Snellgrove and Hugh Richardson, *A Cultural History of Tibet* (London: Weidenfeld & Nicholson, 1968), 182–200; the medieval Dalai Lamas were clearly rulers in both the spiritual and the temporal sense.

other ancient Near Eastern monarchies and Israel's monarchy in the monarch being elected by the deity. "The notion of the election of Israel," Van Seters says, "is not so different from the notion of divine election of the king that is common in Mesopotamian thought"; and he argues that the Hittites, Mesopotamians, Egyptians, *and* Israelites hold the similar idea that the monarch is legitimized by "divine election" (1983: 59, 181). The Egyptian Thutmose III, Ishida notes, "tells how the god Amon chose him when he was a young acolyte in the temple of Amon. In Mesopotamia . . . every king ardently tells of his election by gods" (1977: 6).

Many religious cultures contain some idea of the election or adoption of a representative human being (the king) by God or the gods, because it is a widespread human aspiration to be a child of God. This desire derives from human beings actually being children of God, and feeling that heaven ought to be close, they sense its ringing absence in their souls. There is something loosely analogous between the Israelite idea of the person and the Egyptians' idea of human nature because God created all human beings and implanted in them a desire to know their Father. Despite this important analogy, the two can't be identified.

The believing reader of scripture has an advantage over someone who thinks scripture is on all fours with ancient Near Eastern mythology. He believes that Amon-Re did not exist and that the God of scripture does exist and that calling by this Lord really creates persons. It is a handicap not to appreciate that a primary difference between Israel's concept of the king as called and the Egyptian idea of the king as Osiris, the son of god, is that Amon-Re did not call Thutmose III: his calling is only the symbol of a human desire, not the reality. Believing that God called Samuel, Saul, and the prophets in historical reality refines our historical sense.

All ancient mythologies depict the gods as acting arbitrarily and therefore as electing favorites at will, but none of the historians who wish to show that "there is no evidence for an elective or nondynastic monarchy in the ancient Near East in the historical period" (Ishida 1977: 25) offer any instances of a deity's deselecting a royal bloodline or one of its occupants, outside 1 Samuel. The priests of Amon-Re had power struggles with the pharaohs, but when did they declare, "Now thy kingdom shall not continue" (13:14), or with yet more finality, "The Lord hath rent the kingdom of Israel from thee this day, and hath given it to a neighbour of thine" (15:28)? Even when Amenhotep IV moved his capital to Tell el-Amarna from Thebes, the power base of the priesthood of Amon-Re, and changed his name to Akhenaten as a sign of his sole devotion to the god Aton, the priests skulked in Thebes: they (and Amon-Re) had no right to depose the renegade monotheist. After Akhenaten's death, the clergy ensured the succession of a compliant heir and "excommunicated the memory of the heretic pharaohs Akh-en-Aton, Smenkh-ka-Re, Tut-ankh-Amon, and the short-reigned Eye";[5] but

5. John A. Wilson, *The Culture of Ancient Egypt* (Chicago: University of Chicago Press, 1951), 235.

they did not have the power of the prophet to mediate or to cancel the pharaoh's self-designated election. So, in the second place, there is a difference in kind between arbitrary self-election by mythological gods and Israelite calling. In one way, election by the gods of Egyptian, Hittite, and Babylonian mythology is more stable than the designation of the Israelite king, because the theory is just a ratification of the ruling political ideology. The only factor that can disrupt it is monarchic mismanagement. The ruling political religion distorts the genuine human desire to be elected by God into an ideology by which one family maintains power. But even the idea of one family gives away too much to the political religion of ancient Egypt. Over two millennia, the heads of twenty different dynasties held the title "pharaoh": the continuous factor was the ideal of the pharaoh as divine, not the dynastic principle.

The equation of the person of pharaoh with *maat* ("divine justice") entailed that "no codification of law, impersonally conceived and referable by magistrates without consideration of the crown" existed in Egypt: "There was . . . no impersonal and continuing body of law, like one of the Mesopotamian codes," or like Deuteronomy, in Egypt down to "Persian and Greek days; the centralization of the state in the person of the king apparently forbade such impersonal law." This contrasts with Deuteronomy, where the "right of the king" (Deut. 17) is followed by the command of obedience to the prophet in Deut. 18:14–22: "You must listen to him" (18:15 NIV). Such a juxtaposition in a legal context of king and prophet would have been unthinkable in Egypt, "where the state was summed up in the person of a god," the pharaoh, "ever present to voice the purposes and practices of the state by his divine utterances." Because "the law was personally derived from the god-king," charismatic kingship as 1 Samuel understands it could not be exercised.[6] No moral law stood above the Egyptian pharaoh as a criterion of his justice, so no priest or prophet could test or contest his charisma: the one who could say "I am *Maat*" could not be elevated to kingship by any other. This kingship was in a way no more dynastic than that of the Dalai Lamas: the pharaoh functioned as a (re)incarnation of the son of Re: this is why the ideology survived over twenty dynasties.

Charismatic kingship is also derivative: unlike the judges, the charismatic kings Saul and David are not directly called by God, but learn of their vocation from the prophet Samuel. The vocation of the king is literally a pale imitation of the calling of the prophet, and this is shown by its indirectitude. This gives the prophet preeminence over the king. Some feel that this idea of the prophet's superior prerogatives and his consequent right to give orders such as "seven days you shall wait, until I come to you and show you what you shall do" (10:8 ESV) is likewise an ideology, just one that favors prophets rather than kings. Interpreted as prophet-favoring ideology, narratives like Saul's anointing as *nagid* by Samuel in 1 Sam. 10 become late fabrications, produced by Samuel's domineering

6. Ibid., 49–50, 72–73, 173.

determination "to carry out his original plan of bringing the monarchy under his influence" (Ishida 1977: 49).

In Mesopotamia and in Israel, "the king ruled *for* the gods but not *as* a god. In Egypt the pharaoh ruled as the god who was upon earth and among mortals." The belief of Egyptians of the Old Kingdom that "the pharaoh was the physical son of Re, coming from the body of the sun-god"[7] speaks to the human imagination, because the idea is that the pharaoh as Horus son of Re is the macrocosm of the people, that his destiny is theirs. This is poetic symbolism: in reality, the pharaoh was the only son of the god, and the rest of humanity have no voice, no calling. In the Egyptian Old Kingdom, even the nobles had no *ba*, no soul or "continued function after death."[8] When, in creating a monarchy, Israel gave a certain weight to the people's acclamation of the king, it was satisfying the Israelite determination that the humanity of each of the chosen people be recognized. The Israelite determination went deep because it was consciously articulated in their religion. Large-scale history writing arose in Israel and not among the Egyptians, Hittites, and Mesopotamians, Van Seters says, because "at the point when the actions of kings are viewed in the larger context of the people as a whole . . . it is the national history that judges the king and not the king who makes his own account of history" (1983: 2). The nation judges the king in Israelite perspective because every denizen of the biblical religion is God-called and -created. There is something, therefore, that transcends the king: though pharaoh worship poetically touches on something elemental in human nature, the Israelite faith provides a more realistic articulation of it. This Israelite belief is not unique to Israel: it finds analogies in ancient Rome, "another society evolved from kin-group democracy into monarchy. There, the *lex quae dicitur de imperio Vespasiani* on the appointed *princeps*, had the right to delimit the power of the head of state. . . . The body negotiating the elevation of the monarch had the opportunity to impose conditions, to extract promises, and to level ultimata" (Halpern 1981: 222). It may antedate Vespasian, in fact, since Tacitus presents the senate sycophantically "debating" whether to ratify Tiberius's succession to Augustus (*Annals* 1.11).

A further example of an imperium that was, in theory at least, nondynastic is the Holy Roman emperor. Charlemagne was given this status at his coronation by Leo III in 800. Pope Innocent III "emphasized the right of the Germans to elect their king, but his promotion to emperorship was the exercise of papal judgment." When Emperor Otto IV annoyed him, in 1209, Innocent III pronounced, in the person of Samuel, "It repents me that I have set up Saul to be king" (1 Sam. 15:11 World English Bible). He excommunicated Otto and withdrew his imperium.[9] This biblically based insistence on the priority of the prophet over the king speaks to that in humanity that holds, as an exigency of human nature, that

7. Ibid., 45, 97, emphasis original.
8. Ibid., 86.
9. Walter Ullmann, *A Short History of the Papacy in the Middle Ages* (London: Methuen, 1972), 211, 213.

the "is" of kingship must be trumped by an "ought" of transcendence, that every human being really and not just poetically is a child of God. Of course, one can interpret Innocent III's papalism ideologically, just as one can interpret Samuel's prophetism ideologically. The interpretation of 1 Sam. 7–15, with its decisions to ascribe sources to an early or late date and thus the production of a "canon within the canon," a thread of supposedly early, authentic material, is largely driven by ideological factors. Those who take the scripture as it is given and do not devise a canon of their own have this to their reckoning, that, because they don't think that everything that happens historically, is ideology, from Thutmose III to Samuel, they leave open a space of transcendence within which the human, with its yearning to be called, can be itself and rest in a stable identity.

Thus, the idea that Saul's kingship was not dynastic but charismatic has something going for it. It does not rule out Saul's hoping that his sons would follow him: what father would not? Celibate Lamas may have few dynastic ambitions, but one could hardly say the same of Joseph Kennedy or George Bush I. In a kinship-based society like that of the ancient Middle East, a charismatic leader might hope to pass on his jurisdiction to his sons. There is precedent for this among the judges. Gideon's son, Abimelech, became "general" of Israel (Judg. 8–9), and Samuel made his sons judges. "Saul . . . is . . . portrayed in [1 Sam.] 8–12 not much differently from a judge"[10] and acts as a charismatic in 1 Sam. 10–11. Since government is based, not in logic but in what happens to come about in any one historical arena, there is no absolute contradiction either between Saul's being a king *and* a charismatic, or between his being a charismatic *and* hoping that his family will inherit his charism.

Both the absolute character of the obedience required from Saul and his being tormented by an evil spirit after his downfall, that is, the nature of Saul's life in its entirety, makes best sense by considering his kingship as charismatic. The backhanded suggestions that the author of Regum gives us about the character of Saul's monarchy are not unimportant, theologically speaking. By acting in Israel's history, God acts historically, and that means through characters and events that are each of them one-offs. That doesn't mean that Israel's kings lack broader resonance beyond their particularity but that their resonance resides *in* their particularity.

Saul's one-off charismatic kingship tells us something about that particular kind of kingship: it is tainted. Saul comes to grief and disobeys the prophet within the context of theocratic monarchy. We cannot go back behind the centralized, routinized states of later times to find some Edenic form of prepolitical kingship. In Saul's representative reign, even prepolitical kingship is shown to be fallen. The terrestrial city is fallen, as they say, all the way down; our only hope is the heavenly Jerusalem. The only moral criterion by which we can judge human political

---

10. David Jobling, *The Sense of Biblical Narrative: Structural Analyses in the Hebrew Bible* (Sheffield: JSOT Press, 1986), 87.

societies is an eschatological one, the city of God, not a historical one, some archaic sacral-monarchic society before politics got dirty. Human history, as represented by ancient Israel, offers us no elvish idol of unfallen kings and queens. All monarchy is tainted and broken by human error, and the fragmentation of Saul's dynastic hopes in this episode helps us to see this.

An interesting detail about the reference to Jonathan in this chapter is that, although it brings him on stage for the first time in 1 Samuel, it doesn't mention that Jonathan is Saul's son (Long 1989: 76):[11] "Saul chose him three thousand men of Israel: whereof two thousand were with Saul in Michmash and in mount Beth-el, and a thousand were with Jonathan" (13:2). It is not until 13:16 that we are explicitly told that Jonathan is Saul's son. We were not told before that Jonathan was Saul's son to keep the issue of sonship in the background. Now sonship becomes significant. Although we saw something of Jonathan's mettle in the strike against the Philistine garrison, we have yet to witness the scope of Saul's loss. In the subsequent episode, we will see precisely that: the would-have-been prince-in-waiting has the makings of a military hero and an Israelite judge-hero. Rather than intercepting the flow of the story into the Battle of Michmash Pass, the episode at Gilgal gives it a nostalgic flavor. We are learning what kind of guy has just lost the inherited right to "go out before us, and fight our battles" (8:20) when his father dies. We are shown that it is not just a loss for a father, as it would have been if Jonathan had been dull or unexceptional, but a poetic injustice. The man who has just lost the kingship is at center stage in the sequel to the Gilgal episode and now explicitly as Saul's son. This is, of course, acutely dramatic.

Episode Two: Jonathan on Display (1 Sam. 13:15–14:15)

The most evident feature of the Former Prophets is that it is a collection of beautifully told stories. Some religious readers may even secretly prefer the tribal battles, bum-warts, valor, and vengeance of 1 Samuel to the spiritual tension of the Epistle to the Romans. As Polzin observes, the "literary crafting of the story about the battle of Michmash Pass (13:15–14:23) is extraordinary" (1989: 132). This story is vigorous and enjoyable literature because it is a founding episode in the creation of Israel as a territory: in order to be a state, Israel first needed uncontested ownership of a piece of land. The question behind it is whether Israel will exist as a territory. As the problem posed itself in the eleventh century BC, either the Philistines would conquer and disperse the Israelite tribes, or the Israelites would push their adversaries back. The Israelite tribes were highlanders, inhabiting the northern hilly region about Shechem and Shiloh and also the southern hills near Hebron, down to the western side of the Sea of Galilee. They had arrived in these as-yet-unsettled highland regions a couple of generations before the Sea Peoples landed,

---

11. Long thinks the narrative is explicitly distancing Jonathan from Saul.

gained dominion, and set up their Pentapolis on the southern coastal plain. The Philistines were the lowlanders and the Israelites the hill people. So the Israelite tribes had one defense against conquest: it is very difficult for an army successfully to advance and attack *uphill*. Stager says, "Had the Philistines accomplished their military goal" of seizing the lands settled by the tribes of Israel, "it would have been the first time in recorded history that a lowland polity had succeeded in bringing the highlands under its control." The New Kingdom Egyptians had achieved "only nominal hegemony over this hilly, wooded frontier," and it was the "highland kingdoms, such as that of Shechem under Labayu during the Amarna age," that dominated "the lowlanders. Ignorant of these historical precedents, the Philistines made valiant attempts to turn these natural, long-term odds in their favor" (1998: 169–70). The story of the Battle of Michmash Pass turns on the question of fighting up, and down, hill.

To offset their geographical handicap, the Philistines had one crucial advantage, which made them appear to the Israelites as the top dogs in the contest. Whereas the weaponry of the Israelite highland farmers had stagnated in the Late Bronze Age, that of the Philistine technophiles had entered the Iron Age. Although their weapons may not have been especially useful in every situation, they were consistently terrifying. First Sam. 13:19–21 is of historical interest, in explicating the situation: "Now there was no blacksmith to be found throughout all the land of Israel, for the Philistines said, 'Lest the Hebrews make themselves swords or spears.' But every one of the Israelites went down to the Philistines to sharpen his plowshare, his mattock, his axe, or his sickle, and the charge was two-thirds of a shekel for the plowshares and for the mattocks, and a third of a shekel for sharpening the axes and for setting the goads" (ESV). A miniscule piece of evidence embedded carelessly in this text shows that the story cannot much postdate the exile of 586 BC. We are told that the Philistines had a monopoly on blacksmithing, so that the Israelites had to pay them for their ironmongering, such as sharpening their agricultural tools: "And the charge was two-thirds of a shekel for the plowshares and for the mattocks, and a third of a shekel [*pim*] for sharpening the axes and for setting the goads" (13:21 ESV). The shekel system for weighing coins was imposed by the Judahite monarchy during the reign of Hezekiah (715–686 BC). There are references to the abuse of this system in the writings of the prophets of this period, Hosea, Amos, and Micah: "Shall I acquit the man with wicked scales and with a bag of deceitful weights" (Mic. 6:11 ESV). The Judahite monetary system was abandoned after the fall of Jerusalem in 586, giving way, perhaps, to Babylonian "euros." The term "shekel" long outlived the usage of these coins, but not the words for two-thirds shekel and one-third shekel. It's as if a twenty-third-century British historian referred to "a ten bob note," a colloquial way of referring to ten shillings, which disappeared with the decimalization of the British coinage in 1972. The reference in 1 Sam. 13:21 is the only reference to the one-third shekel coin (Hebrew *pim*) in scripture. As Dever remarks, "The story about a *pim* weight in 13:21, told almost nonchalantly because everyone knew what a *pim* weight was, cannot . . . have been 'invented' by writers living in the Hellenistic-Roman period several centuries after these weights had disappeared and had been forgotten." It looks like "this bit of biblical text from an original Iron Age setting was handed down intact, although the unique, enigmatic reference to a *pim* was no longer understood" (2002: 227). First Sam. 13:19–21 highlights the strength of the Philistines against the vulnerability of the Israelites: dependent on the Philistines for iron, the Israelites are without swords or spears. The story of ill-matched armies makes for a titanic conflict: but the *pim* reminds us that these epical legends have an ancient foundation in fact.

First Sam. 13:19 claims that "now there was no blacksmith to be found throughout all the land of Israel, for the Philistines said, 'Lest the Hebrews make themselves swords or spears'" (ESV). Iron could be used to make, not only farmer's tools, but also weapons of war. Some biblical archeologists take this to indicate that the Philistines alone, in this region, had a hand in the arts of iron metallurgy. But 13:19 is not so easy to interpret: it could mean that, in the whole period under consideration, the Philistines alone had access to iron implements. Or, it could mean that at this time in particular, the Philistines controlled access to iron. A fifth-century Christian who retold the tale of Israel and the early church, Sulpicius Severus, elected the latter, temporally narrower reading: "The Philistines, as conquerors in the former wars, had deprived the Hebrews of the use of arms, and no one had had the power of forging any weapon of war or even . . . any implement for rural purposes" (*Sacred History* 1.33, in Franke 2005: 245).

The Biblical Hebrew word for iron, *barzel*, is a foreign loanword. Does this mean that iron itself was a loaned technology? In archeological surveys, a near equal number of iron tools and weapons have been excavated in Philistine and non-Philistine (including Israelite) settlements. On the basis of this evidence, McNutt argues that "iron was not relied upon" during the Israel-Philistine conflict "as a necessary material for promoting military or political advantages" (1990: 203–5). So why do the biblical texts, the Deuteronomist in particular, kvetch about their opponents' "chariots of iron" (Josh. 17:16, 18; Judg. 1:19; 4:3, 13)? A culture can be acquainted with a material technology without being especially proficient in deploying it. Possessing a certain material culture, such as familiarity with iron objects, is not sufficient: a society has to be imaginative in putting it to work. In the premonarchic period, before David's rise, the Philistines were the confident proponents of iron technologies, the Israelites the passive owners of iron objects. As Stager argues:

> A supposed Philistine monopoly on iron and steel is a modern myth, based on a misreading of 1 Sam. 13:19–22. But there is no mistaking their superiority in military organization and hardware. The Philistines were termed "chariot-warriors" in Egyptian inscriptions at Medinet Habu. They fielded expert bowmen (31:3) and crack infantry. Bronze linchpins for war chariots have been found at Ashkelon and Ekron, but nowhere else. The top half of the Ashkelon linchpin is in the form of a

Philistine goddess in the Aegean tradition. She leads and protects the elite corps of charioteers as they enter battle. These finds give substance to the biblical historiographer's lament that "Judah could not . . . take Gaza with its territory, Ashkelon . . . and Ekron. . . . Yahweh was with Judah, and he took possession of the hill country, but could not drive out the inhabitants of the plain, because they had chariots of iron" (Judg. 1:18–19). The war chariot was not made of iron, but a most essential part of it was—the axle, which stood for the whole vehicle. Homer describes the splendid chariot of the gods as having bronze wheels on either side of an iron axle (*Iliad* 5.7230). (Stager 1998: 168–69)

The Philistines were the abler and more resourceful military engineers, and here it is imagination, rather than material possession, that counts to advantage. If the Philistines were, for our author-historian, the Orcs of Early Iron Age Palestine, the Israelites were the dorks. They had to figure out how to turn their underdog status to their advantage.

The Israelites developed skills such as slingshotting and, by exploiting their weakness, became stronger than their foes, weighed down in their ironclad armies. Their lack of weapon power compelled them to take risks. The reason why we enjoy stories like that of the Battle of Michmash Pass is that we inherit them within the Judeo-Christian tradition. If the Canaanites had been consistently successful against Gideon, Jonathan, Saul, and David, and no Israelite kingdom had ever emerged, we might be taught to enjoy stories of the stronger grinding the weak into the ground. Winning by a trick, which happens here, is courageous, in our terms, because Jewish and Christian tradition gives us sufficient sense of humor not to overvalue brute force. The low-minded ruses of the judges aren't unique to Israelite literature: think of the Greeks, with their wooden horse. The Israelite tradition of vulgar, weak trickster heroes validates a human preference for the rube over the superman.

Saul is still at Gilgal, and when he counts heads, he finds the extent of the attrition cowardice has wrought: "Saul numbered the people who were present with him, about six hundred men" (13:15). The separate division commanded by Jonathan is at Geba of Benjamin (13:16). Moving out from their stronghold at Michmash, the Philistines are sending advance raiding parties into Israelite territory, to Shual, Beth-horon, and the Valley of Zeboim (13:17–18): they may intend to surround the Israelite camps. Having narrated the troop movements, the author backtracks to add the touch about want of swords and spears: only Jonathan and Saul are packing iron (13:22). One of the pair must take the lead. Having gathered all the ingredients for the adventure, the narrator opens the story of the battle: "And the garrison of the Philistines went out to the pass of Michmash" (13:23).

Jonathan decides to lead a foray among the mountain crags of Michmash. The narrator describes the scene very precisely: "Within the passes, by which Jonathan sought to go over to the Philistine garrison, there was a rocky crag on the one side and a rocky crag on the other side. The name of the one was Bozez, and the name of the other Seneh. The one crag rose on the north in front of Michmash, and the other on the south in front of Geba" (14:4–5 ESV). Since Jonathan's force has been at Geba (13:16), he and his armor-bearer seem to advance from the south. Jonathan realizes that nothing is to be gained by harping on their numerical weakness: they must fight the Philistines as they stand. It is not the material situation that counts in human life, but how one imagines what is happening. For Jonathan, their enemy is not a vast, overpowering sword-wielding force in an unassailable position on the slopes above the Israelite army but a bunch of pagans: "Come," he says to his armor-bearer, "let us go over to the garrison of these uncircumcised" (14:6 ESV). Jonathan imagines his opponents as uncircumcised, non-Israelite inferiors. Humanly speaking, the situation of the circumcised men is hopeless. So their only recourse is to hope in gracious good fortune: "It may be that the Lord will work for us, for nothing can hinder the Lord from saving by many or by few" (ESV). Rising above the material situation, Jonathan looks down on it, from a Yahwistic height.

The Philistines guarding the pass have the straightforward physical advantage of being on top of a mountain. Their position is strategically preferable because men can run faster downhill than they climb uphill. Jonathan and his armor-bearer plan to "cross over" to the Philistines guarding the pass and "show ourselves to them" (14:8 ESV). It is an important feature of the tactic that they show or display themselves to the Philistines. To attempt to creep up unseen was certain death: the alternative to this is the deception of self-display. Jonathan proposes a sign that will indicate whether the Lord is backing this deception: if the Philistines challenge them by saying, "Wait until we come to you," they will interpret this as a signal to retreat. For, if they were to "come to" Jonathan and his armor-bearer, the Philistines would do so charging downhill, an unassailable tactic. If the Philistines start pouring downhill, the intelligent course of action was flight. But if the guards arrogantly order the pair to "come up," waiting for them at the top and enabling them to climb up the craggy rocks without enduring assault from above, then, Jonathan says, "We will go up, for the Lord has given them into our hand" (14:9–10 ESV). The only thing that can topple the Philistines is excess self-confidence, the arrogant belief that they don't need sedulously to guard their position on the mountain, deluding them into ordering the Israelites to come up to them and thereby forfeiting their own advantage.

Jonathan conceals the plan for the exploit from his commanding officer: "One day Jonathan the son of Saul said to the young man who carried his armor, 'Come, let us go over to the Philistine garrison on the other side.' But he did not tell his father. . . . And the people did not know that Jonathan had gone" (14:1, 3 ESV). Why doesn't he discuss the strategy with the chief in command? We cannot get at the psychology of any such decisions, behind what actually happens on the stage. Jonathan's silence is a significant literary boon. Watching a military action unfold that a rather insubordinate subordinate commander has held to his chest and for which the main army can therefore supply no backup is more stirring than observing the effects of an agreed strategy. That is why thrillers use the stereotypical plot of the insubordinate detective, like Jimmy McNulty in *The Wire*, who is taken off the case and goes after the gangsters on his own. The secrecy builds up the listener's awareness of the hazard Jonathan is taking (biblical narrators have no sophisticated hesitations about laying it on too thick). Simultaneously, since Jonathan effectively makes his platoon incommunicado with the main army, the author lays a track for his ignorance of Saul's command to fast. The focus of this episode is not on Saul, but on dramatizing the character of Jonathan. Saul is passive or inactive, not because he is being shown to be an increasingly inept general—his military abilities are not at issue—but so that, with Jonathan center stage, we can see the would-have-been king in action.

As is common in biblical narrative, the subsequent events repeat narratively what has just been proposed dialogically (Alter 1981: 65): "Both of them showed themselves to the garrison of the Philistines. And the Philistines said, 'Look, Hebrews are coming out of the holes where they have hidden themselves'" (14:11 ESV). The Philistines see their enemy just as Jonathan wants them to do, as too pathetic to be worth taking cover against and killing outright. The arrogance upon which Jonathan counted is on full display: "The men of the garrison hailed Jonathan and his armor-bearer and said, 'Come up to us, and we will show you a thing.' And Jonathan said to his armor-bearer, 'Come up after me, for the LORD has given them into the hand of Israel.' Then Jonathan climbed up on his hands and feet, and his armor-bearer after him. And they fell before Jonathan, and his armor-bearer killed them after him" (14:12–13 ESV).

Jonathan has rightly intuited that the Philistines might have become overconfident in their superior stronghold atop the slope, but it would take more than that guess being right for the tactic to come off: the scales have to turn completely, in a military rout, for the trick to work. The exploit is blessed with more success than Jonathan could humanly imagine: "And that first strike, which Jonathan and his armor-bearer made, killed about twenty men within as it were half a furrow's length in an acre of land. And there was a panic in the camp, in the field, and among all the people. The garrison and even the raiders trembled, the earth quaked, and it became a very great panic" (14:14–15 ESV). Panic is a humanly possible consequence of an unexpected Israelite breakthrough, especially since Jonathan's "audacious design" could lead the Philistines to imagine he has brought a larger contingent than a single armor-bearer (Sulpicius Severus, *Sacred History* 1.33, in Franke 2005: 248). But an earthquake is evidence that it is the Lord who has tipped the scales in the Israelites' favor. Jonathan is presented as a "confessor of Yahweh," acting and winning Philistine scalps like a figure out of Joshua or Judges. Long notes that "Jonathan's bold initiative is to be understood as motivated not so much by personal bravado or derring-do as by the ideology of 'holy war'" (1989: 109). Jonathan is more than a James Bond knocking out twenty footless assailants. His audacious design is not just something conjured up by a hero who can kickbox his way into a garrison.

But in reading the story theologically, we have to be careful not to Christianize it in a way that doesn't fit the story itself. It is one thing to transform the figures and actions of the Old Testament scripture into types or symbols of something that is different but analogous to ourselves. It is another thing to take the Old Testament figures literally and make them into literal embodiments of Christian morality or spirituality. Jonathan's dangerous tactic is based on faith: "Nothing can hinder the LORD," he says, "from saving by many or by few" (14:6 ESV). On this Abrahamic faith he stakes his derring-do and is thereby enabled better to see the facts on the ground: *if* the Philistines ordered them to "come up," they could be in with a chance. For now the Philistines have lost their advantage.

Episode Three: Jonathan Accursed (1 Sam. 14:16–52)

That Jonathan has concealed the plan from the rest of the army now enables Saul's army to carry out the concluding link of his strategy. Having been withheld from the fray while Jonathan penetrates the Philistine camp and creates an opening, the whole army can swoop upon the enemy and force a retreat from Michmash Pass. Narratively, the thread of secrecy allows the author to show us what it looked like from close-up and as a wholly unanticipated scene. The camera pans away to Saul's men and zooms in: "And the watchmen of Saul in Gibeah of Benjamin looked, and behold, the multitude was dispersing here and there" (14:16 ESV). The Israelites realize that someone must have excited the Philistine panic, but can't see who: "Then Saul said to the people who were with him, 'Count and see who has gone from us.' And when they had counted, behold, Jonathan and his armor-bearer were not there" (14:17 ESV). They bring the ark, and Saul hands over to its clerical custodian his task of giving the sign for battle: as "the tumult in the camp of the Philistines increased more and more . . . Saul said to the priest, 'Withdraw your hand.' Then Saul and all the people . . . went into the battle. And behold, every Philistine's sword was against his fellow, and there was very great confusion" (14:19–20 ESV). In their confusion, the Philistines are killing one another, instead of their enemy. Some of the 1,400 Israelites lost to Saul's army had not, it seems, merely been deserters, but traitors. Now they figure out it is time to turncoat once again and mingle: "The Hebrews who had been with the Philistines before that time and who had gone up with them into the camp, even they also turned to be with the Israelites who were with Saul and Jonathan" (14:21 ESV). The others, who "had absconded to the marshes" (Sulpicius Severus, *Sacred War* 1.33, in Franke 2005: 245) also enter the fray, so that the army is massively reinforced: "When all the men of Israel who had hidden themselves in the hill country of Ephraim heard that the Philistines were fleeing, they too followed hard after them in battle" (14:22 ESV). The narrator attributes the victory to God: "So the LORD saved Israel that day. And the battle passed beyond Beth-aven" (14:23 ESV).

Having absented himself without permission in the earlier part of the day, Jonathan is ignorant that "Saul had laid an oath on the people, saying, 'Cursed

be the man who eats food until it is evening and I am avenged on mine enemies' "
(14:24 ESV). Famished after the hard fighting, Jonathan transgresses the prohibition, eating a honeycomb: "And his eyes became bright" (14:27 ESV). When the
people repeat the oath back to him, Jonathan reveals that his success has gone
to his head. He does what no second-in-command should do and criticizes his
commanding officer before the men: "My father has troubled the land. See how
my eyes have become bright because I tasted a little of this honey" (14:29 ESV).
Not content with criticizing the specific order not to eat anything, like honey in
the fields or their own rations, Jonathan justifies his transgression by suggesting
that the army should have been permitted to consume the Philistine's abandoned
supplies: "How much better," he tells his subordinates, "if the people had eaten
freely today of the spoil . . . that they found. For now the defeat among the Philistines has not been great" (14:30 ESV). This directly leads to the army's breaking, not just a personal proscription thought up by Saul, but Mosaic law, which
forbids eating food with blood on it (Lev. 17:10–14; 19:26; Deut. 12:16–24).
Being "very faint" with hunger and exhausted after driving the Philistines back
from Michmash to Aijalon, the "people pounced on the spoil and took sheep and
oxen and calves and slaughtered them on the ground. And the people ate them
with the blood" (1 Sam. 14:32–33 ESV).

Saul is criticized by commentators for his actions in the preceding scenes.
He is said to be compulsively obeying rituals, keeping the ark with him, having Ichabod the priest at his side, and laying the oath of fasting (Polzin 1989:
133–38). But these are rituals to which an Israelite king was expected to adhere.
Judaism is a ritual religion: it is one thing for a Christian theological reading
to take the rituals as trailers or types of its own rituals, and another to interpret
the use of such rituals in the Old Testament as an inherent indicator of legalism
or reliance on magic and superstition. The former actually takes the text in its
historicity, since some historical events are forerunners of later events, whereas
the latter prevents entry into the text in its historical reality. Saul's ban on eating
anything is defensible, because extending the Mosaic food laws was a safe way
of ensuring adherence to these laws during the heat of battle. When Saul is told
of the people's sin, he promptly forbids the misbehavior. Better sense is made of
the episode by the suggestion that an author who inhabited a later and less
primitive world is trying here to conjure up the aura of the battlegrounds of the
tribal days of yore, in which a soldier's conduct on the field was hedged around
with ritual prescriptions. In the narrative of the Battle of Michmash Pass, von
Rad claims, "the narrator brings every decisive event, military advantages and
setbacks as well as all human conflicts, into association with the world of the
sacral and the ritual": his aim is to put across the atmosphere of a battle fought
in the context of "pan-sacral faith." Perhaps by drawing on an "archaic military
account," the author imagines himself into the older culture of his ancestors and
thus presents the world of Saul and Jonathan as prepolitical, that is, presecular
(1972: 58–59).

Saul builds an altar: "It was the first altar that he built to the LORD" (14:35 ESV). The general wants to pursue the retreating Philistines, but his priest tactfully suggests that it would be a better thing first to ensure divine clearance for a nighttime assault. So "Saul inquired of God, 'Shall I go down after the Philistines?' . . . But he did not answer him that day" (14:37 ESV). Saul realizes that some "sin" must be preventing the oracle from speaking (14:38). Then he swears a second oath, like Jephthah's in Judg. 11:31: "Though it be in Jonathan my son, he shall surely die" (1 Sam. 14:39 ESV). When the choice comes down to either Saul or Jonathan, "Saul said, 'Cast the lot between me and my son Jonathan.' And Jonathan was taken" (14:42 ESV). Why was it not obvious to Saul that the culprit is Jonathan? Saul knows he didn't break the oath: he has to cast the lot one last time so that the ritual is carried through to its conclusion. When "the people" see that it is the hero of the day who has been taken, they appeal "to Saul, 'Shall Jonathan die, who has worked this great salvation in Israel? Far from it! As the LORD lives, there shall not one hair of his head fall to the ground, for he has worked with God this day.' So the people ransomed Jonathan, so that he did not die" (14:45 ESV). Saul is locked into the primitive mechanism of the lots, letting them decide for him: Jonathan bypasses the ancient practices, taking the people with him.

For many, Jonathan comes out of the Battle of Michmash Pass smelling like roses, and Saul comes out of it smelling of manure: "We begin to see," one exegete writes, "that something in Saul's character is inclining him to usages of Yahwistic ritual that border on sorcery and divination" (Polzin 1989: 136). It is natural to notice a contrast between Jonathan and Saul in the story, because both attempt to gather Yahweh's intentions from signs. Jonathan's efforts at reading the signs are successful, whereas Saul is answered with silence (14:37); and when he attempts to force the issue, he narrowly escapes having to execute his son. So one could read the story as supplying a negative comparison of Jonathan and Saul. But is God "not answer[ing] him that day" (14:37) an implied criticism of Saul? Some say yes, that Samuel's prediction of the tribulations that a king will bring upon the people is being speedily verified: "The LORD will not answer you in that day" (8:18 ESV) (Long 1989: 123–24). But 8:18 is the culmination of a series of monarchic offenses against the people that Saul has yet to perform. We are not told why God gave no answer to the question whether, if the Israelite army should chase the Philistines over the rocks in the dark of night, God will "give them into the hand of Israel" (14:37 ESV). The priest who suggested this delay might well imagine that the reason for the lack of a response was that it was a silly question. One might even think, as Saul does, that the cause of the divine silence is that someone has committed a sin: and we know that is Jonathan. By the terms of his first oath, Saul unwittingly implicated Prince Jonathan in an unwitting sin. By the terms of his second oath, Saul condemns his son to death.

Saul is a backup figure in the story, inactive and surrounded by clerics while his son plays the holy warrior against the Philistines. Polzin suggests that the purpose of the comparison of the two sign-gathering episodes, Jonathan with his sign from the Philistines and Saul with his lots, is intended to contrast a reliance on sheer faith with a passive dependency on semimagic ritual certitudes:

> Both accounts revolve around contrasting rituals of divine inquiry. Jonathan employs his ritual in hopes of concluding "We will *go up* for the LORD has given [the Philistines] into our hand" (v. 10); Saul inquires of God, "Shall I *go down* after the Philistines? Wilt thou give them into the hand of Israel?" (v. 37). . . . Jonathan's diffident "perhaps" (v. 6) results in God giving the requested sign (v. 10), but in Saul's [case] the certainty hoped for by inquiring of God is frustrated by God's refusal to answer (v. 37), which then explains Saul's move to find an answer by lot. Saul's rituals are sacral affairs seeking certainty from God either by official priestly inquiry or by a priestly casting of the Urim and Thummim. . . . Jonathan's ritual is a less confident, more secularized affair, which . . . embraces uncertainty from the start; Jonathan's "sign to us" from God is not to be coerced by only hoped for; Saul forces an answer by lot when none is initially given by sacral inquiry. (Polzin 1989: 133–34)

The contrast of Jonathan's "perhaps" with Saul's certitudes is onto something, but by itself it is not wholly convincing. When Jonathan proposes or invents the positive and negative signs of the Philistines' possible challenges to the approach of himself and his armor-bearer up the slope, his thinking is surely faithful and trusting beyond his actual material means, but because of that it's also empirically intelligent in a human sense. If the Philistines say "stay where you are," then, it's not just perhaps Yahweh is against this idea, it's a dead certitude, because the Philistines can chase them down the hill. And if the Philistines say "come up," then it is at least sure that Yahweh has sufficiently hardened their hearts to make them forget that their military superiority depends on physical elevation, above the pair. As signs, the Philistine challenges are as much what a young soldier would dream up, and tactically sound, as they are the thought of a would-be holy warrior or judge. Jonathan doesn't have faith in his faith, he has faith in what that tells him about his situation.

The lots give certitude, but at what cost Saul could tell better than any other. This time, the use of the lots horribly misfires, from Saul's perspective. He has just been told, at Gilgal, that his kingship "shall not continue" within his own bloodline (13:14). This means that Saul will not pass on the kingship to his son. Having just lost the kingship for his son, now Saul nearly gets Jonathan killed. The text tells us what that means to him, in words that are intended to show that Saul loved his son. Jonathan was not just a hero to the people, but beloved by his father. When Jonathan, finally forced into the open by the lots, says, "Here I am; I will die," Saul's response is, "God do so to me and more also; you shall surely die, Jonathan" (14:43–44 ESV). Saul says that God can and should punish himself with death and worse, for his oath-making. This is seldom remarked upon; it reflects creditably upon Saul and shows the pathos of the situation in which he has led himself, with his oath. It's like David's cry, on hearing of the death of his rebel son Absalom, at the hands of his own soldiers (Uncle Abner): "O my son Absalom, my son, my son Absalom: would God I had died for thee, O Absalom, my son, my son" (2 Sam. 18:33).

By the close of this episode, Saul has symbolically killed his son twice: first, by losing the kingship to him at Gilgal; and, second, by obstinately insisting upon carrying the oath through. At the close of 1 Samuel and the beginning of 2 Samuel, Jonathan dies, and all of Saul's male blood relatives are ruthlessly hunted down and eliminated by David's commanders. That was the fate of the scions of a failed royal family, as readers of Shakespeare's history plays know. The implication of Samuel's parting words to Saul, "The LORD hath sought him a man after his own heart, and the LORD hath commanded him to be captain over his people" (13:14), is that Saul's sons will not only fail to be kings, but are soon to be in danger of death. Behind the scenes throughout the battle, with his priests and the ark, the appropriate company for an Israelite chief, as our author believed, Saul is the hidden thread of the story. The point of the scene with the lots seems to be, not that Saul is in decline or is beginning to go mad or is a sorcerer, but that his family will be the first to be fragmented by the demands of politics. Having been ritually stripped of his dynastic hopes in 1 Sam. 13, now in 1 Sam. 14 Saul symbolically kills his son. Failure to keep his rule within the family, where it will bring honor to the family name after he himself is dead, is Saul's chiefly loss, thus far.

The heir apparent comports himself as a true Yahwistic warrior whose faith that God would tip the scales carried the day. Moreover, and here we see why Polzin is right to perceive a contrast of Saul and Jonathan, whereas the father does not work within the old sacral world and take it forward, imagining its potentials and broadening it, the son did have the genius to live within it inventively. Jonathan seems by his actions to stand for a younger, more vigorous culture than does Saul. But for Saul's faults, his legacy could have been passed to a contender. Charismatic kingship need not have been a one-off, historical anomaly in Israel's drive to become a territory. The tragedy of its failure is made apparent by the display of Jonathan at the Battle of Michmash Pass. The story denies the doctrine of historical inevitability.

Episode Four: The Bitterness of Death (1 Sam. 15)

Samuel declares, "Me big chief, you obey me." A literal Hebrew translation of "the LORD sent me to anoint thee to be king over his people, over Israel" (15:1) is "*me* Yahweh sent to anoint you king over his people, over Israel" (Long 1989: 135). The assumption is not a generalized "two-swords" theory entailing that, since God is above humanity, God's representative is above the monarch, but the particular presupposition that Saul's charismatic kingship hangs on God's commission. In the Middle Ages, there were many monarchs and an emperor, and there were corresponding generalized theologies of any ruler's relationship to the church.

But here, with the first Israelite ruler, one individual, local, personal chiefling is specifically designated as such by God, through his spokesman. Samuel received his call and vocation to be a prophet directly from God. Saul has a mediated vocation. His designation (naming) as king in 1 Sam. 9 and his installations in 1 Sam. 10–12 came through the prophet. The consequence of this is laid out in the second half of the declaration—"now therefore hearken thou unto the voice of the words of the LORD" (15:1)—and means "hearken to my voice," to Samuel's voice, which speaks the words of God: "Obey me, because I am God's mouthpiece." The assumption that King Saul is strictly subordinate to Samuel and must obey his injunctions meticulously is laid out explicitly in 15:1, setting the context for the story that follows. Despite this, some of the questions we may have about it follow not from the text, but from the false assumption that it presents generalizable political conceptions, rather than a historical event. The problem of theocracy versus the separation of church and state is interesting, but it is not conducive to grasping this text. It is misleading to read 1 Sam. 15 as a political text. The principles of Saul's calling and vocation do not lead us into modern or ancient principles of government or church-state relations. In the sixteenth century, the Dominican theologian Francisco de Vitoria wrote about the relationships of eternal (divine) law, natural law, and human law and by so doing founded modern international law theory. This sixteenth-century Thomist is unambiguous about the difference between extrabiblical kingship and biblical kingship. Ever since Noah's sons set out (Gen. 10), Vitoria observes, kingdoms have been created either by tyrants or by the consent of human beings: all extrabiblical kingship is a purely human construct. Though, according to Augustine and Aquinas, God "delivered imperial power to the Romans because of their justice and patriotism and excellent laws," we are not, Vitoria says, "to understand that they held their empire by divine institution . . . but that divine Providence brought it about that they should obtain universal empire by some other right, such as just war. . . . This was not the sense in which Saul and David received their kingship 'from God.'"[12] Vitoria means that Saul and David were and are the *only* kings who "received their kingship 'from God.'" Though they partake of natural law, since political sociability is natural to humankind, all kingships outside scripture are human inventions, not divine institutions; though these human kingships may be the object of God's providence, they are not specifically created by God. So they are not equivalent to the divinely elected kings of Regum. The kingships of David and Saul, Vitoria reminds us, are unique simply because their monarchies were divinely instituted. Vitoria recognized Saul's kingship as charismatic.

There is very little basis in medieval Christian tradition for the "bad literalism" (Lubac 2007: 430) that equates Saul and the conditions of his kingship with

12. Francisco de Vitoria, *On the Indians* Q. 2, A. 1, in Francisco de Vitoria, *Political Writings*, ed. Anthony Pagden and Jeremy Lawrance (Cambridge: Cambridge University Press, 1991), 254–55.

contemporary circumstances. Saul, with his charismatic kingship and divine order to commit genocide, was not taken in Western medieval Christian tradition as an example literally to be emulated. It was treated as the once-off historical event that it was. Saul's decision that God would really prefer him to sacrifice rather than to exterminate has for one twelfth-century abbot universality in the sense that Saul's disobedience is still recognizable in the way in which a monk "permits himself to pass beyond what is prescribed for him by his spiritual superiors . . . to follow the impulses of his own will." He thus "strives to ameliorate his own life by choosing rather than obeying, giving his patent disobedience a more virtuous tincture than his actual intention confers on it" (Pierre de Cava 2004: 85 §29.3). The only contemporary, generalizable analogy for the command given Saul and the psychologically subtle way in which Saul persuades himself he is being "more virtuous" by disobeying it that Pierre de Cava can think of lies in monastic life, not in an anachronistic political reenactment of a unique historical event. Those Western Christians who, from Augustine to Vitoria, understood the period of the judges and Saul as a failed effort to achieve what would be ultimately wrought, not in politics, but in the church, read the Old Testament literally, as a story about the past. The drama of this text is not political at all, in the sense of having a generalized resonance with human governance in postbiblical times. The drama of this text is the question of Saul's obedience to God's instruction.

Samuel's instruction is preceded by an explanation, an abbreviated mnemonic that religious readers who knew Exodus by heart could expand for themselves: God can "remember that which Amalek did to Israel, how he laid wait for him in the way, when he came out of Egypt" (15:2). In Exod. 17:9, "Amalek" attacked the assembled Israelites at Rephidim. The ensuing battle is remembered, chiefly, if at all, for the key role that the position of Moses's arms plays in the victory. As Joshua goes out to lead the troops, Moses stands on a hill, and when he raises his hands, the Israelites overcome, but when he lowers them, the Amalekites overcome. Since Moses is old and his arms tire, his two seconds, Aaron and Hur, stand on either side to ensure that his hands don't drop (17:11–12). After Joshua forces the Amalekites into retreat "by the edge of the sword" and battle is done, "the Lord said to Moses: Write this for a memorial in a book, and deliver it to the ears of Josue: for I will destroy the memory of Amalec from under heaven" (17:13–14 Douay-Rheims).

Amalek is the name of the leader of this people (Exod. 17:13 speaks of "Amalek and his people") and is also used collectively to designate the tribe (17:10–11). God's vow of vengeance against Amalek has the collective entity in view (17:14). The action that links Exod. 17:9–14 to 1 Sam. 15:2–3 is recollection: in 15:2 God says, "I remember that which Amalek" did to Israel; in Exod. 17:14 God vows that he "will destroy the memory of Amalec" (Douay-Rheims). God intends to use Saul to carry out this vow of blotting out the memory of Amalek. The intention behind the vow is not to eradicate the Amalekites because they pose a threat to Israel or because they are Baal worshipers or because they corrupt the

Israelites with their habit of consorting with fertility trinkets. The intention is to erase Amalek, here reduced to a collective singular, from memory. So often in the biblical text, when Yahweh remembers, it is because the people's sigh has come up to him (Israel in Egypt in Exod. 2:23–25; Hannah in 1 Sam. 1:11, 19) and he intends to help them. Here God intends to eradicate a bad memory. When he remembers the people and saves them from oppression, God is remembering the covenant. When he remembers Amalek, he is remembering his vow to eradicate it, as a collective unit.

From Exodus through the miraculous battles of Joshua and Judges and down to 1 Sam. 15, the Israelites have been settling in the promised land for many generations. They have, as Exodus through 1 Samuel tells it, fought their way tooth and nail to a still vulnerable possession against the aboriginal peoples and the neighboring tribes. This part of the Old Testament is currently taken to have little foothold in fact, since archeology yields little evidence of a violent conquest of the land such as described in Joshua and Judges (Dever 2002: 62–63, 121). But the next stage of the narrative, the move from a vulnerable tenure to established conquest and the emergence of a centralized state, can be inferred from the archeological data. First Sam. 15:1–8 is a reflection of this process. Israel is symbolically expelling the first of its enemies. The rationale for the instruction to eliminate the Amalekites is original enmity, as shown from the reference to Exod. 17:9–14. Historically, Israel did become the predominant ethnic-religious group in the region. This piece of history is symbolized in 1 Sam. 15:1–7 by the command to eradicate the Amalekites, considered as an original and thus perpetual threat to Israel.

First Sam. 15:1–7's reference to the elimination of representative threatening tribes, clearing the way for state organization, is shown by the detour in which an original alliance is recalled. The Kenites were *gerim*, or what we would call Bedouin: the Old Testament thinks of the Kenites (Hebrew *haqqeni*, "the *qeni*") as metalworkers and musicians descended from Cain (Hebrew *Qayin*), who, marked with God's protective sign, went to live in "the land of Nod" (Gen. 4:16), which means "wandering land" (McNutt 1990: 240–42). As Saul's army goes forth, with its marching orders to waste all comers, Saul enables the Kenites to escape the approaching massacre, because they were original friends to Israel: "Depart," he tells the Kenites, "for ye showed kindness to all the children of Israel, when they came up out of Egypt" (1 Sam. 15:6). Saul is not only remembering and repaying a past kindness. Like the abbreviated mnemonic of Exod. 17 in 1 Sam. 15:2–3, 15:1–8 is a condensed historical recollection of how Israel rose to dominance in this region: by destroying hostile peoples and by enjoying nonaggression pacts with peaceful tribes. What Saul is instructed to do, and does, by way of warfare and peace deals in 15:1–8 is a telescoped way of describing the end of the beginning of the continual warfare between the interloping Israelite people and their neighbors, in their promised land. Historically, whether the fantastical battles described in Judges came into it, in the Late Bronze Age of the thirteenth–twelfth centuries BC, the Israelites were on a level with other tribes, while later, at the time of this episode, in the nascent Iron Age of the early eleventh century, they achieved cultural predominance. Although it looks like it's about vengeance, repaying an ancient slight by an unprovoked assault on Amalek generations later, 15:1–8 is about recollection, remembering the end of the beginning.

In 1 Sam. 13, Saul has already been told that the kingdom will not pass to his sons. Now comes the crime for which Saul's punishment is extended from the loss of a dynastic legacy to the withdrawal of the divine commission to himself as chief. Saul's kingship actually did pass to another family. Saul was a real, historical person, and there is good evidence that he lost his kingdom to David. As the best literary critic of the Bible puts it: "There really was a David who fought a civil war against the house of Saul, achieved . . . sovereignty over the twelve tribes, conquered Jerusalem, founded a dynasty, created a small empire, and was succeeded by his son Solomon" (Alter 1981: 35). That Saul had remitted his kingship to David was common, folkloric knowledge for the author's audience. This story specifies why it happened. A good archival historian, the author is one of those historians who present a pattern in history. For him, the pattern is God's providence. First Sam. 15:8–35 gives the reason why God decommissioned Saul.

Having seized "Agag the king of the Amalekites alive, and utterly destroyed all the people with the edge of the sword" (15:8), Saul has already broken the vow that the Lord intended to be carried out by him. He was to have been the instrument of God's vow in Exod. 17:14, and fulfilling it entailed taking no prisoners. Saul tarnishes his crime by slaughtering the inferior Amalekite animals but taking the finer specimens: "But Saul and the people spared Agag, and the best of the sheep, and of the oxen, and of the fatlings, and of the lambs, and all that was good, and would not utterly destroy them: but everything that was vile and refuse, that they destroyed utterly" (1 Sam. 15:9). There is reason to suppose that this episode contains a recollection of faithful Yahwists' first grievance against the institution of monarchy. The first sign of alteration to the ancient sacral culture was not the cult, the ritual of journeying to the sacred places, or the oral traditions of the law, for the kings did not, perhaps dared not, lay a hand on these. In all historical likelihood, the first place where sacral culture was tested against political expediency, and government won, where rite gave way to policy, was the army (von Rad 1962: 60). Whether premonarchic Israel had a thoroughgoing, explicit ideology of holy war, heroic cultures impose greater religious-ethical constraints on warfare than secular cultures do.

First Sam. 15:9 inculpates "the people" alongside Saul. Later, when confronted by Samuel, Saul will protest, "The people took of the spoil, sheep and oxen, the chief of the things which should have been utterly destroyed, to sacrifice unto the LORD . . . in Gilgal" (15:21). Much has been made of this, as if "the people" were a significant actor in the story. One is sometimes encouraged to read 15:8–35 as if Saul, having been made king at the people's behest, is now simply their cipher. As a king, victorious in war, he must play the role that people expect of a king and share out the war spoils. This is the way the kings of the nations behaved, and so that is how Saul is required to behave in this socially constituted role. When Samuel comes looking for the miscreant king, he is told, "Saul came to Carmel, and behold, he set him up a place" (15:12). This possibly refers to Saul's setting up a victory stele at the Amalekite encampment, a conventional regal gesture. Thus, it is equally likely that sparing Agag reflects the same impulse, to have a living trophy of his victory (Long 1989: 140). If so, then it is not unreasonable to suggest that, in taking the Amalekite king prisoner and sparing the best animals, Saul "cared more for his 'public image' than for his royal responsibility." This could be reinforced by Saul's final plea to Samuel: "Honour me now, I pray thee, before the elders of my people, and before Israel, and turn again with me, that I may worship the LORD" (15:30). Saul's condemnation is not yet public knowledge: Saul is begging Samuel not to disgrace him in front of the "elders of my people, and before Israel." In that case, one might infer that public relations comes before his responsibilities to Yahweh in Saul's priorities (Good 1965: 72). If the place mentioned in 15:12 is a victory stele, it is common sense to suppose that Saul's relationship to the people played a part in his downfall.

But let's make certain that the people do not play a greater role in the imaginations of readers than they do in the text. There are four references to the people in 1 Sam. 15. The first shows that Saul and the people were in it together: "Saul and the people spared Agag, and the best" of the Amalekite animals, "but everything that was vile and refuse, that they destroyed utterly" (15:9). But there is no indication in this verse that the people pressured Saul to seize a prisoner and to pillage some livestock. The second reference may strike us as yet another example of the human propensity, ever since Gen. 3, to shift the blame: Saul tells Samuel, "The people took of the spoil, sheep and oxen, the chief of the things which should have been utterly destroyed" (1 Sam. 15:21). Saul is at the excuse-making stage of his spiel. First Sam. 15 is no more a funny story than Gen. 3, but it is leavened with black humor. The third reference occurs when Saul's story turns into a confession: "I have sinned: for I have transgressed the commandment of the LORD, and thy words: because I feared the people, and obeyed their voice" (1 Sam. 15:24). This seems to be the clinching passage. It is unlikely that this is a piece of self-exculpation on Saul's part, because the "voice" and the "words" of the LORD are given a commanding position in 15:1. Here the divine word is solemnly contrasted with the human voice. Perhaps the difference between 15:21 and 15:24 is intended to show a progressive acknowledgement on Saul's part: instead of saying "they did it, not me," Saul is admitting that, torn between the people's voice and that of God, he has taken the easier course. This could be the heart of the matter: he has become the people's king instead of God's king.

The final reference to the people is Saul's request to Samuel, to "honour me now, . . . before the elders of my people, and before Israel, and turn again with me" (15:30). Samuel has utterly refused to pardon Saul's crime. Saul has pled for mercy, first verbally (15:24–25) and then physically, by wrenching Samuel's mantle, and the prophet has relentlessly insisted that the kingdom is torn from him. But now, at this third request, Samuel yields: "So Samuel turned again after Saul; and Saul worshipped the LORD" (15:31). Samuel has obediently performed an instruction he evidently dislikes (15:11, 15; 16:1), but he will not go so far as to destroy Saul's public face. In the ancient world, the face was the man, with little distinction between the person's public status and his private psychology. Samuel was willing to strip the kingdom from Saul, but not his personal public honor. In this final reference, instead of saying "the people," Saul speaks of "my people," indicating the close continuity between himself and them. The psychological idea of Saul's excess concern for his public image gets this wrong: heroic societies are societies in which honor is a high and socially objective value: among the Yoruba of West Africa, honor is the ability to hold other people's gaze (Iliffe 2005: 67–68).

When we read this text, we mentally paraphrase "Amalek" as "the Amalekites." The name of the king, who led his "people" into a unsuccessful assault on Moses's host in Exod. 17, is given to the people by God in 1 Sam. 15:2–3. Even though the people's king is now Agag, they are Amalekites, Amalek's people. The king is the people and the people the king. Their fault is his, and his is theirs. The collective Amalekites are "sinners" (15:18) as partners in Amalek's sin. In Saul's initial attempts to conceal what happened from Samuel, he tries to make the people a separate entity from himself: "The people took of the spoil" (15:21). In his act of contrition, he tells that he listened to the people's "voice" instead of the "words" of the Lord (15:24). That doesn't mean that, weighed down by the social pressures of kingship, Saul listened to someone else's voice. Rather, it means that, collectively, the king and his people listened to their own voice. They did what they wanted. Jointly and collectively, chief and people took prisoners and booty, instead of doing what the Lord, through Samuel, told them to do. The chief was the people's representative. Because of the significance of blood ties within it, which make brothers equivalent to cousins, the segmentary tribe "is a superperson, and its members are as one" (Sahlins 1968: 11–12). In the narrative, Saul is as much the people's representative as Amalek is. When we are told that "Saul smote the Amalekites from Havilah until thou comest to Shur" (15:7), that doesn't mean he engaged in single-handed combat against their armies. The narrator renders the theme by simply lumping king and people together, as partners in crime: "Saul and the people spared Agag, and the best of the sheep, ... but everything that was vile, that they destroyed" (15:9). Saul is singled out for punishment for a crime that is his and the people's together, because he is their representative. The idea of collective guilt is commonplace throughout the Old Testament: but so is the idea of representative guilt. The two are similar but not identical: collective guilt entails that a group is in it together; representative guilt entails that one person is guilty on behalf of the others. The narrator makes the representative criminality look fair: Saul and the people together participate in the decision to conduct a human war of despoliation, a war for glory and gain, not the war of remembrance that Yahweh specified.

What sort of war, precisely, was Saul supposed to conduct? The Achilles' heel of von Rad's matchless genius for historical reconstruction was, perhaps, his genius for matchless imaginative historical reconstruction. Von Rad created large imaginative and hypothetical *Gestalten*, like schools of scribes at Solomon's court and, as is apposite here, the idea of holy war as a general activity embarked upon by the Yahwistic tribes. Later scholars argued that the idea of holy war was invented by the Deuteronomist after the exile.[13] The endeavor to bring Saul out of this episode as a tragic victim of an arbitrary God begins from the argument that von Rad claims too much generality for the concept of holy war. We know less of the details of holy war in ancient Israel than von Rad imagines.

First Sam. 15 does not specifically mention holy war. What we know from the text, and what Saul knew, was that he was to "utterly destroy all that [the Amalekites] have" (15:3). "Utterly destroy" translates the Hebrew *hrm*. But did Saul know to interpret *hrm* as meaning destroy in the straight sense of annihilate then and there? Gunn suggests that *hrm* could mean "something like 'devote to a god by destruction.'" On this interpretation, the ambivalent notion of *hrm* is "akin to the notion of sacrifice (*zbh*)" (1980: 45). Only the best meat could be used in sacrifice. King and people would not utterly destroy the best of the animals, because on this analysis their highest priority was to take the finest specimens to sacrifice to Yahweh. Gilgal was the place of sacrifice. Why go there, unless it was to sacrifice? That could be the only reason for going there, Gunn argues. In that case, Saul did the right thing, taking the best animals to sacrifice to Yahweh at Gilgal. That is what he originally claims he has done: "The people spared the best of the sheep and of the oxen, to sacrifice unto the LORD thy God; and the rest we have utterly destroyed" (15:15). Why not take him at his word? Should we not say it all comes down to a misunderstanding about the meaning of *hrm*? There may be sound reasons for not doing so.

At the outset of the dreadful confrontation, Saul acts as if he were blameless. He goes blithely to meet Samuel saying, "Blessed be thou of the LORD: I have performed the commandment of the Lord" (15:13). Given how strictly law-abiding Saul was in the previous episode, immediately rectifying the sin of the people's eating the animals with the blood on it and being willing to remain faithful to his oaths to the bitter end, "his self-defence deserves at least a hearing."[14] If Saul is to be found a tragic victim, we may want to say that Saul is stripped of his kingship because of committing a cultic impropriety of which he was unaware (Gunn 1980: 55): he didn't realize, Gunn contends, that he was supposed to eradicate

13. Others argue that holy war does occur in early documents, but didn't occur in actual fact, since the model of holy war is "separated not only from the reality experienced in the field of battle, but also from an ideology that could actually influence war leaders in the premonarchic period"; A. de Pury, "La guerre sainte israélite: réalité historique ou fiction littéraire?" *Etudes théologiques et religieuses* 56 (1981): 5–38 at 35.

14. Bernard P. Robinson, *Israel's Mysterious God: An Analysis of Some Old Testament Narratives* (Newcastle upon Tyne: Grevatt & Grevatt, 1986), 44.

the Amalekites, not sacrifice them. Is it just moralizing to argue, to the contrary, that "Saul is bluffing" (Long 1989: 146)?

Several things may prevent us from regarding this as a tragic misapprehension. One of them is a feel for the comedy of it. When Saul greets Samuel with the statement that he has been obedient to the commands, his claim is promptly disproved, and unless we have no sense of humor, we have to take the bleating, lowing, grunting, and mooing of the fatlings, lambs, sheep, and oxen as a live giveaway. Samuel's line—"what meaneth then this bleating of the sheep in my ears, and the lowing of the oxen which I hear?" (15:14)—is funny-satirical, because animal noises are subhuman, uncontrollable, and physical, reducing the man who gives vent to them, or is given away by them, to his lowest denominator. Samuel's reference to "bleating" and "lowing" could hardly be spoken by an actor without raising a smile in the most grim-faced audience. The amusement is not there for the reader's delectation, but as a precognitive signal that Saul is morally remiss. The author selects the animals, rather than the untoward appearance of Agag, as the evidence tendered to Samuel that the *hrm* has been, as Gunn imagines, misinterpreted. The noisy, uncontrollable appearance of the animals is funny in a way that that of King Agag would not be. That's because the animals are not frightened of Samuel, whereas Agag might reasonably be so; a frightened man is not amusing.

First Sam. 15:1 sets the dramatic context for the story. There is a chain of command: Saul reports to Samuel, because Samuel was "sent" by "the LORD . . . to anoint thee to be king." Saul's role is a diminutive one, to listen and do. Then, springing from God's decision to fulfil the oath of Exod. 17:14, comes the terrifying order: "Go and smite Amalek, and . . . slay both man and woman, infant and suckling, ox and sheep, camel and ass" (1 Sam. 15:2). The biblical story claims that as a result of divine providence Israelite culture achieved uncontested possession of the region. As the agent of God's vow, Saul is set under "monastic" obedience.

The text accentuates Samuel's dismay: "It grieved Samuel; and he cried unto the LORD all night" (15:11). We are not told what precisely grieved Samuel. We may imagine that he was piously horrified to hear that Saul had broken God's "commandments" (15:11). Samuel had let the judge system pass, after God had assured him that "they have not rejected thee, but they have rejected me" (8:7). He had then been given a new mission: no longer to rule as judge, he was to be the anointer of God's king. This will be his identity and his providential place: "*Me* Yahweh sent to anoint you king," Samuel had told Saul in 15:1. By undoing Saul's kingship, by telling Samuel, "It repenteth me that I have set up Saul to be king" (15:11), Yahweh has simultaneously undone Samuel's mission. Samuel grieves in recognizing that what God has given, God can take away; providential history does not add on, cumulatively, in an endless linear progression, but changes direction. Samuel grieves not only for his own mission but for Saul, perhaps in the way that God grieved for Israel's monarchy, given and then taken away.

John Cassian began his spiritual journey among the monks of Egypt, fled from theological controversy there, lived for a time in a monastery near Bethlehem, and spent the last thirty years of his life founding a monastery near Marseilles, bringing the culture of the Egyptian desert monasteries to the West. He was well placed to interpret 1 Sam. 15 as a warning against fossilized ethical and spiritual attitudes, thinking that our mission will remain unchanged. "These texts declare," Cassian wrote, that

> we should not cling stubbornly to our promises, but that they should be tempered by reason and judgment, that what is better should always be chosen and preferred and that we should pass over without any hesitation to whatever is proven to be more beneficial. This . . . judgment also teaches us . . . that, although each person's end may be known to God before he was born, he so disposes everything with order and reason and, so to say, human feelings, that he determines all things not by his power or in accordance with his ineffable foreknowledge but, based upon the deeds of human beings at the time, either rejects them or draws them or daily pours out grace upon them or turns them away.
>
> The choosing of Saul also demonstrates that this is so. Although, indeed, the foreknowledge of God could not be ignorant of his miserable end, he chose him from among many thousands of Israelites and anointed him king. In doing this he rewarded him for his deserving life at the time and did not take into consideration the sin of his future transgression. And so after he became reprobate, God as it were repented of his choice and complained of him with, so to speak, human words and feelings, saying, "I repent that I set up Saul as king, because he has forsaken me and not carried out my words." And again: "Samuel grieved over Saul, because the Lord repented that he had set up Saul as king over Israel." (John Cassian, *Conference* 17.25.14–15, in Franke 2005: 254)

God, "so to speak," changes direction, integrating the actions and choices of human beings into historical providence. Saul, who had once been "deserving" afterward fell away, and so the path of providence passed from him.

Samuel is, as he says in 15:1, "the voice of the words of the LORD," the mouthpiece of divine providence. Perhaps the reader of 1 Sam. 15 is supposed to neither sympathize with Samuel nor take what he does personally: "To see humanity in Samuel," one interpreter says, "is to mistake his role. He is like Teiresias in Sophocles' *King Oedipus*. He is the mouthpiece and agent of forces beyond him. He has no choice but to give effect to the intractable demands of the divine decree, the dictates of fate" (Gunn 1980: 72). One might say, conversely, that the stress on Samuel's grief, mentioned here and in 15:35 ("Samuel mourned for Saul") and again in 16:1, sparks a sympathy for Samuel and for the God whose voice he is: we have three times been told that it tore his entrails to undo the kingship. What does it mean to weep all night? John Cassian has no hesitation in ascribing feelings to God. Perhaps, like the prophet who is his intermediary and earthly symbol, God weeps to undo this first kingship of Israel. We are told that in 1 Sam. 15 only by analogy. The drama must have one figure holding firm to the decision to undo the monarchy, to repent or draw back the gift of the monarchy, and the other figure protestingly mourning. It is two sides of one and the same God, who, because he is God, loves human beings, including Saul, and, who, because he is God, disavows sin. Neither Samuel nor God function in 1 Sam. 15 like an ironclad fate. This is why Saul's rise and downfall is not melodramatic, but genuinely mysterious. The author gives us a sufficiently rounded picture of the historical Saul for us to grasp his plight. Because his history writing was realistic, he gives us a theologically realistic, and therefore mysterious, image of God.

When Samuel catches up with his appointee at Gilgal, Saul greets him with a statement—"I have performed the commandment of the LORD" (15:13)—that directly conflicts with God's account: "He . . . hath not performed my commandments" (15:11). From what we know of Saul's character, do we have grounds for thinking that this declaration to Samuel could not be "brazenly dishonest self-justification" or "humbug"?[15] Samuel's immediate taking him up on the noise of the animals (15:14) seems to be satirical, a prelude to the prophetic diatribe of 15:22–23: Samuel is mocking Saul's pretensions, bringing him down from the heights to which he has risen in his imagination by knocking the nomadic Amalekite tribes back "from Havilah until thou comest to Shur" (15:7). The entire dialogue between Saul and Samuel is thus a slow unraveling of the image of himself that Saul has built. Saul begins by trying to dig deeper under the luggage: "They," he says, not I, "have brought them from the Amalekites: for the people spared the best of the sheep and of the oxen, to sacrifice unto the LORD thy God, and the rest we have utterly destroyed" (15:15). Saul is not claiming that it was his own lack of grasp upon the meaning of *hrm* that has brought the animals here, but that "the people" interpret *hrm* to mean "sacrifice." If Saul wants to play hide and seek, the upshot will be the same as at Mizpah, since God is all-seeing: "I will tell thee what the LORD hath said to me this night" (15:16), says the prophet. Samuel looks back to the scene at Mizpah, where the tallest man in Israel tried to hide under the bags, when he reminds Saul of who it was that made him king: "When thou wast little in thy own sight, wast thou not made the head of the tribes of Israel, and the LORD anointed thee king over Israel?" (15:17). Saul had been avowed to "utterly destroy the sinners the Amalekites . . . until they be consumed" and has, Samuel declares, taken them, not killing them as "sinners," but consuming them as "spoil" (15:18). As Pierre de Cava observes, there is a fine paradox in Samuel's statement: "Even while convicting the king of pride, one recalls the time when he was chosen, to make him understand that his heart was not puffed up when he was chosen, but has developed following on his elevation, because he was placed above others. He was good when the Lord chose him, but just as he was enlarged by his elevation, so he has been decreased by his pride. So the prophet said, 'When you were small in your own eyes, you were placed at the head of the

15. Ibid.

tribes of Israel. Now you have turned upon the booty, and you have done evil in the eyes of the Lord.' Otherwise put: 'Your true humility made you worthy of kingship, but now, since you are humble in appearance but proud in reality, you lose the kingship'" (2004: 75 §26.1).

Saul now tries a third ruse: dividing the blame. He takes responsibility for bringing Agag, who is mentioned here for the first time in the dialogue, but continues to shift responsibility for the animals to his subjects, "the people" (15:20–21). Saul has actually begun to admit that the object of the taking of booty was not just sacrifice. Perhaps he mentions Agag because he realizes Samuel must know about that too. Agag doesn't quite fit into the spiel about sacrifice. By now, Saul is ready to admit to Agag, but is stonewalling on the animal sacrifice. It is plausible that Saul and the people decided to believe that God would like them to sacrifice the animals to him at Gilgal rather than just destroy them where they found them. Although recent literary interpretations of Saul's downfall are misled by overeagerness to deflect any censure from Saul, it does have the merit of picking up Saul's obliviousness to what he has done. This helps us see that Saul had lied to himself before he lied to Samuel. Once having decided to believe that God would really prefer sacrifice to extermination, Saul has become so willingly self-deceived that he no longer recognizes the difference between truth and fiction.

The prophet Hosea criticized animal sacrifice. His word from the Lord about it was short and to the point: "I desired mercy, and not sacrifice; and the knowledge of God more than burnt offerings" (Hos. 6:6 KJV). Jeremiah's God is brutally sarcastic: eat it yourselves, he says; "Thus says the LORD of hosts, the God of Israel: 'Add your burnt offerings to your sacrifices, and eat the flesh. For in the day that I brought them out of the land of Egypt, I did not speak to your fathers or command them concerning burnt offerings and sacrifices'" (Jer. 7:21–22 ESV). For Saul and the people, sacrifice was the pleasanter option to slaughtering the animals where they stood, because sacrifice cooked up a meat feast. "Eat it yourself," then, Jeremiah's God spits it back. In his answer to Saul, Samuel speaks just like these prophets: "Hath the LORD as great delight in burnt offerings and sacrifices, as in obeying the voice of the LORD? Behold, to obey is better than sacrifice, and to hearken than the fat of rams" (1 Sam. 15:22). Samuel is not just "championing the necessity for the strictest formal observance of sacred *rites*," like the miniscule difference between *hrm* and *zbh* (Gunn 1980: 55). Why has Samuel switched from criticizing Saul for having the animals there at all (15:14) to denouncing sacrifice? Is it because, unlike the prophets, all he cares about is getting the instruction right and performing the ritual of *hrm* where appropriate and of *zbh* where that is? Short of calling down a miracle from the Lord, Samuel cannot disprove Saul's claim that the animals were brought to be sacrificed. It is probably true and not made up to explain the lowing and bleating. Samuel and the reader or listener know that this noise is untoward, but Saul really does not. He is in a trance, hypnotized by his own self-deception. To an audience, that is, from an onlooker's perspective, Saul has been given away, but he himself only very dimly realizes this. They did take the animals to Gilgal to sacrifice them and afterward enjoy a slap-up supper of sheep, oxen, fatlings, and lamb (15:9).

Saul and the people have not just invented a lie on the spur of the moment: they have been deceiving themselves about the divine commandment ever since they took the animals. This explains the aura of innocence that leads many to feel that Saul is a tragic victim of a misunderstanding. Saul could not circumvent God's command without telling himself that God really wanted him to do what Saul wants to do. Gunn's stress on the ambiguity of *hrm*/*zbh* clarifies this episode, because it enables us to see how Saul could disobey while telling himself he was being obedient. He slid from *hrm* as "eradicate" to *zbh* as "sacrifice" by telling himself it was fairly much one and the same. What the tragic reading obscures, though, is that most sin involves self-deception. It doesn't see this because it doesn't accept Samuel as the authorial plumb line in the story. The lowing and bleating in Samuel's ears is funny-chilling, because it ought to wake Saul up and doesn't. In the dialogue between Samuel and Saul, there is a step-by-step stripping away of the self-deception: "Thou hast rejected the word of the LORD" (15:23). Rather than nail him on a cultic detail, Samuel is bringing him back to the truth of the event, by showing him that his circumlocution, switching destruction into sacrifice, was disobedience to "the word of the LORD." By rejecting God's word, Saul has separated his human freedom, as chief, from the divine freedom. He is living in his own world, the world of the lie, in which "destroy" means whatever he prefers it should mean.

The freedom of the divine king and the freedom of the human monarch having come unstuck in Saul's deceitful action, the consequence is inevitable: "Because thou hast rejected the word of the LORD, he hath also rejected thee from being king" (15:23). There is a one-to-one correspondence here: Saul has rejected God so God rejects Saul. There is a direct, antithetical correlation between Saul's action of turning away from God and God's turning away from him. God relieves him of his commission as chief because he has ceased to enact it as a divinely commissioned chief. Saul is in that sense both the author and the executioner of his own charismatic kingship. This is the plain meaning of the story. The wool he has placed on his eyes having been torn away, Saul finally admits his guilt: "I have sinned: for I have transgressed the commandment of the LORD, and thy words: because I feared the people, and obeyed their voice" (15:24). Again, in the contrast of obeying the voice of God (15:1) and that of the people (15:24), divine and human freedom are shown to have gone their separate ways. Human freedom has ceased to be itself. Good says that Saul's "personal insecurity prevents his actuating the greatness that he has in him and that his office requires" (1965: 72). Saul "feared the people, and obeyed their voice" because he was too "small in his own eyes" to grasp the powerful potential of his human freedom and unite it to God's freedom. As at Gilgal in 1 Sam. 13, he has become an unfree man and therefore a disobedient one. He is imprisoned by the people's desire just as he was imprisoned by material circumstances, the imminent attack of the Philistines, at

Gilgal. The people are here an extension of his material self, his ego. Saul cannot rise above himself, or above the people as representing an extension of himself, or above his circumstances, because he cannot be himself.

The author expects us to experience the pathos of Saul's thrice-repeated pleas for mercy in 15:24–25, 27, 30. We know it is hopeless, because 15:1–3 frames the episode. Dramatically, Samuel's command to obey himself as God's mouth followed by the evocation of God's oath to blot out all memory of Amalek, followed by the terrifying instruction utterly to eliminate all trace of the Amalekite people, soldier and civilian, man and woman, adult and child, edible and transport animals (15:3), is too absolute to leave any leeway to come back from disobeying it. The command sets the context for the episode in the way that God sets the context for everything in creation. First Sam. 15:2–3 is a statement of God's nature. It is an expression of what in God hates sin. God's nature is unchangeable. The chapter is about God's unchangeability all the way through: at the start, we learn that having made a vow in Exod. 17:14 God now wills for it to be fulfilled, and at the end we see that not even a sight as heart-tearing as the fall of Jerusalem in 586 BC, that of Saul clutching Samuel's robe, can alter God's resolve. That is why, rejecting Saul's entreaties, Samuel says: "The Strength of Israel will not lie nor repent: for he is not a man, that he should repent" (1 Sam. 15:29). The intent of the story is not to teach its readers that "Yahweh is not a consistent God of command and . . . consequence" (Brueggemann 1997: 370–71). The consequence is the extension of the command, in this case. Saul was instructed freely to be an extension of God's arm: he failed to be so and is therefore cut off. He wills to have a chiefdom that is not of God, and God withdraws his appointment.

Saul makes Pierre de Cava think of those who "are strong during the battle, but fall after the victory" (2004: 38 §5.1). The king changes many times in the story, from powerful obedience to the command (15:6–7) to self-deceptive disobedience (15:8–9) to the slow unmasking of his self-delusion by Samuel (15:13–23) to contrition (15:24) to the wretch who begs for mercy (15:25–30). His will turns and turns about. First it is directed by God. Then his volition is turned in upon himself and becomes a lie. Finally, Saul is overpowered by Samuel and becomes contrite and self-abnegating: he is a man of broken will. It is with such human mutability that Samuel contrasts the divine unchangeability: "The Strength of Israel will not lie nor repent: for he is not a man, that he should repent" (15:29). But did not the Lord tell Samuel, "It repenteth me that I have set up Saul to be king" (15:11)? Having begun with a flaming declaration of unshakeable divine resolve, the chapter concludes: "And the LORD repented that he had made Saul king over Israel" (15:35). Doesn't what Samuel says about God conflict with what God in 15:11 and the narrator in 15:35 say about God—that he does repent? God's actions toward individuals are expressions of God's eternal nature. The consuming fire of love that is God's eternal nature cannot be resisted: it is all-powerful, sweeping all in its way, utterly destroying all that is in enmity to it. This God cannot be true to himself if he retains the disobedient Saul as his representative. If being true to himself means letting Saul go and letting Israel's monarchy go by the board in 586 BC, then, if it tears God's heart, he does it. For Yahweh is free to be himself.

The word "repentance" (Hebrew *nhm*) "captures the concerns of this chapter" (Polzin 1989: 140). The episode draws out Saul's slow awakening to his guilt, his confession, and his pleas for mercy so as to contrast them with Yahweh's immovable resolve. Far from "evidenc[ing] no curiosity about why penitent Saul cannot be forgiven" (Brueggemann 1997: 370), the narrative is focused on exactly that question. The narrative contrasts Yahweh's unchangeability and Saul's changeability. But we shouldn't picture the divine will and the human will as competing for space, as if they were larger and smaller instances of the same sort of thing, struggling for survival in the same territory. It's against such naïve anthropomorphism, such humanlike pictures of God, that Samuel says, "The Strength of Israel . . . is not a man," not like a human being only larger and much more powerful, like the villain of a melodrama.

Augustine is not interpolating a Greek, Platonist idea of God into this scene when he argues that "though God said 'I repent,' it is not to be taken according to the human sense" (*On Various Questions to Simplician* 2.2.5, in Franke 2005: 255). He means that, though these words can't be allegorized out of existence, neither can they be taken with flat-footed literality. Brueggemann contrasts what happens to Saul when he ignores the injunction of Exod. 17:8–16 and Deut. 25:17–19 that the Amalekites deserve the *herem* with the praise heaped on David for plundering the Amalekites, not exterminating them (1 Sam. 30:19–20, 23–25). He notes that after sending Uriah, whom he is cuckolding, into the frontline of battle and getting him killed, David is forgiven: "After the massive indictment of David by Nathan, . . . David also responds directly, 'I have sinned' (2 Sam 12:13). That is all. David does not, like Saul, appeal for forgiveness. But forgiveness is . . . promptly granted by Nathan: 'Now the Lord has put away your sin; you shall not die' (v. 13)." These are, Brueggemann thinks, just a few of many "incongruities in the life of Yahweh," all caused by "Yahweh [being] inordinately and irrationally committed to David" and this "causes Yahweh to act in odd and unreliable ways" (1997: 369–70, 367).

Interpretations of 1 Sam. 15 that contrast God's inflexibility toward Saul with his lenience toward David's crimes already existed in Augustine's day. They were composed by Gnostics and Manicheans, who regarded the God of the Old Testament as the villain in the melodrama of a cosmic battle within creation. The repentance of God is a different sort of repentance from that which issues from human changeability, and the judgment and the mercy of God are likewise different from human judgment and mercy, because God is all-knowing, omniscient. Seeing into the heart of Saul and of David, God appreciated the difference between the two: the words "I have sinned" are not univocal, meaning exactly the same thing when Saul says them and when David says them. They cannot be equated just because they are the same words. Writing against the Manichean scholar Faustus,

Augustine observes that Saul, like David, admitted under Samuel's reproof that "I have sinned.' Why, then, was he not considered fit to be told, as David was, that the Lord had pardoned his sin? Is there favoritism with God? Far from it. While to the human ear the words were the same, the divine eye saw a difference in the heart. The lesson for us to learn from these things is that the kingdom of heaven is within us and that we must worship God from our inmost feelings" (*Against Faustus* 22.67, in Franke 2005: 258).

The meaning of the words comes from the heart of the speakers, and knowing the difference between David and Saul, God acknowledges the contrition of the one as authentic and the other as inauthentic. The meaning and nature of two chemical reactions might be equivalent, identical apart from the circumstance of occurring in different places. The meaning not only of human words but of human actions is always personal, and the same external actions can have quite disparate moral connotations. Schooling in imaginative literature teaches us that, and Augustine knew his Vergil, though he famously disparaged both his classical education and his tears for Dido (*Confessions* 1.13). Though he interpreted this passage as teaching us, through Samuel's prophecy, to "turn our attention to the stock of David, from which sprang, by physical descent, 'the mediator between God and men, the man Jesus Christ' [1 Tim. 2:5]" (*City of God* 17.7), Augustine has a great deal to teach literary readers of the books of Samuel about the imaginative grasp of its characters.

Like P. D. James, who thought that if Myra Hindley actually repented her crimes, she would have wanted to stay in prison, Pierre de Cava thinks that the falsity of Saul's repentance is shown by his asking to be given a clean slate and return to the kingship: "It is like this," he says, when people "go spontaneously to confession, but they don't weep for the faults of which they accuse themselves in themselves, but beg others to do penitence for them. They think they are saved by faith alone" (2004: 105 §38.4). That is, the abbot thinks of Saul as a free actor, an author of his destiny, who wants to be relieved of the responsibility that his freedom carries.

If we picture God's actions anthropomorphically, then it may seem that the point of 1 Sam. 15:29 "is to combat the erroneous idea that it is easy to talk God round, and that his threats and promises need not be taken seriously" (Eichrodt 1961–67: 1.216). If we imagine God and Saul set alongside each other, in the same metaphysical dimension, then we have a sad contrast of Saul's repentance and God's lack of mercy for him, and an unfair contest, since God is larger *and* inventing the rules of the game as he goes along. This compels us to picture the episode as "one of a number of seeming incongruities in the life of Yahweh" (Brueggemann 1997: 369). For Brueggemann, the incongruity and inconsistency is that David will later manage to "talk God round" and is regularly forgiven for similar offenses, like his Amalekite campaign in 1 Sam. 30, whereas Saul fails at the same bar.

If we picture God and the humans in his story, like David and Saul, as occupying or trying to occupy the same space as God, then divine and human freedom are in competition. It is a zero-sum game: the more divine freedom, the less scope for human freedom, and since God is omnipotent, he must necessarily restrict human freedom to a minimum. In his fine and thought-provoking analysis of Saul's rejected repentance in 1 Sam. 15, Polzin argues that "this second account of God's rejection of Saul as king is a profound meditation on the human foolishness that believes humans can restrict divine freedom even in the context of human freedom.... The destiny of Saul ... shows how human repentance, however good and necessary, does not limit God's freedom to act, however mysteriously, in ways that do not correspond to human understandings of mercy" (1989: 140, 146). This episode seems to be about, not *God's* denial of human freedom but the *human's* abnegation of his own freedom. Good captures Saul's failure really to stand up and be a free man, when he says that "Samuel pins Saul to the wall with an observation ... which ... forms the psychological centre of the ... Saul story: 'Though you are little in your own eyes, are you not in fact the Chief of the tribes of Israel?' [15:17]." Saul has failed to recognize his value: "The greatest fact of Saul's life, his kingship, ought to, but does not, override his self-deprecation" (1965: 70–71). Saul has failed to grasp his human identity, as king. This episode goes as far as it is imaginatively possible to explain why mercy is, in this context, not dramatically or theologically possible. God wills to be free alongside and in cooperation with human freedom: he has gone so far in this intention as to appoint a human chieftain. God cannot change his mind or repent because he will not override Saul's having stripped himself of his human personhood, by failing to be free. Given that his persona is kingship, he loses both simultaneously. He has not been just a bad chief, and therefore had the chiefdom taken from him as a punishment. Rather, having been a blank slate at the beginning of his tale, the only personality he has is invested in this calling. Having failed in his vocation, he loses his identity, and with it his kingship.

God is, as Polzin says, "mysterious," and without limiting that mystery, the episode makes it imaginatively explicable why God cannot make Saul back into a king. First Sam. 15 doesn't force us to agree with it, as sacred scripture. It doesn't demand that we make a purely moral choice between sympathy for God and sympathy for Saul. Rather, it combines what Polzin calls the "authoritative word" and the "internally persuasive word": the Deuteronomic "History's obvious claim to authority may be the truth, but it is ... not the whole truth. For within its supremely authoritative pages we find an ever-present fusion of 'authoritative word' with what Bakhtin calls 'the internally persuasive word.' Texts that succeed in uniting both authorial consciousnesses within them are rare: ... that the type of first-millennium narrative represented here by the history did it first and perhaps does it as well as any since. It is this profoundly successful integration of the authoritative word with the internally persuasive word that constitutes the first significant feature of that remarkable generic innovation represented by the Deuteronomic History" (1989: 149).

First Sam. 15 has been ascribed to an antimonarchic source. But that doesn't mean that the text is about whether Israel should have a king. Both the text rejecting the continuation of the Saulide monarchy in Saul's successors (1 Sam. 13) and this text, rejecting Saul himself as king, contain declarations that God has elected another to be king. Saul is told here that "the LORD has rent the kingdom of Israel from thee this day, and hath given it to a neighbour of thine, that is better than thou" (15:28). In 1 Sam. 15 "monarchy per se is no longer in question . . . Saul's occupancy of the throne . . . very much is." The story of Saul's rejection "is neutral toward the monarchy but negative toward Saul" (Long 1989: 166). This episode is not about a generalized theology of monarchy, like the medieval and early modern *De Regnum Principes* and *De Monarchias*. It is about Saul's divine commission to the kingship. The story, from 15:1, which restates the terms and very conditional quality of Saul's kingship, to 15:35 ("and Samuel came no more to see Saul until the day of his death . . . and the LORD repented that he had made Saul king"), which underlines the withdrawal of the prophetic word to Saul and the withdrawal of the divine commission, is about one particular, historical king, not kingship in general. The sources the author used may have come from varied interest groups, some hostile to Saul, others friendly to him. Once they are assimilated into it, the series in 1 Sam. 8–15 is no longer for or against monarchic government. Rather, it uses particular literary means (telling the story of Saul) to describe a particular historical event.

SERIES FIVE

MEMORY AND HISTORY

1 Samuel 16–20

The stories about David raise new theological questions. Saul is still in the story, leaving open the problems about divine providence and human free will. We tend to ask less about David's free will and more about his humanity as a whole. Whether Saul is a tragic hero or just a glum fellow, few wish to emulate him. People have always liked David and seen him as their contemporary. Saul is history. David seems to be alive. David's "story possesses what . . . Gadamer describes as 'a kind of timeless present that is contemporaneous with every age'" (Flanagan 1988: 34, citing Hans-Georg Gadamer). It is this that raises the problem of David's historicity: How precisely is he alive, and how is he a historical character? What theological act makes David live millenniums after he died? Perhaps the question of free will is not a dangling thread left us by Saul: perhaps that theological act comes back to human *and* divine free will.

Interpretation is part of the life of Christian believers. How is it that their interpreting can give a contemporaneity to an Early Iron Age warrior-chief? In 1 Sam. 16–20 David will offer crude physical insults to Goliath before murdering him. He will kill dozens of Philistines, returning to Saul with basket loads of their foreskins as a dowry for Saul's daughter, Michal. When Saul decides to murder the upstart, David goes on the run. Since the "red thread guiding us through" 1 Sam. 18–26 "is the theme of escape" (Lemche 1978: 8), the series could be subtitled "David on the Lam." He will break into a sanctuary and eat consecrated shew bread; the priest who protects him dies for his trust in David's half-truths. Still betrothed to Michal, David will pick up a second wife, Abigail, in the course of an aborted revenge attack and a third, Ahinoam, at some, disputed, stage in the proceedings. He will fake madness to escape execution. It is not immediately evident how these exploits coincide with our theological concerns. Supposing we take the act of interpretation as a provision of theological meaning, then believers interpret the David of 1 Samuel into life: their interpreting makes him alive today, in all theological relevance and vigor. One way of conceiving the theological interpretation required to turn this alien figure to theological account is as a kind of colonization.

The church fathers believed the Old Testament's claim to historical truth. And, because the Old Testament's historical truth was accepted, the biblical history lived on in the memories of generations of Christians and was repeatedly reinterpreted.[1] Augustine interprets the five stones that David picked up to use against Goliath as the five books of the law, and David killed Goliath with just one stone because grace transfigured the Pentateuch into the gospel. The problem with this interpretation understood as a provision of meaning is the implication that the natives didn't understand their own story, or that "only Christians could understand the hidden, New Testament meaning of David's actions" (Gosselin 1976: 19). The idea of hiddenness directs us to what is questionable about this kind of allegorical reading. Latency implies a code, so that such exegesis seems to turn the Old Testament into a secret code that only Christians can decipher.

The decoding will make the Old Testament mirror Christian experiences. One of the commonest historical parallels between David's story and that of the church has been persecution. In line with tradition, Thomas Aquinas connected the symbolism of the persecution of Christ and therefore of the church to the persecutions of David.[2] But for those who equate interpreting with giving meaning, the very word "persecution" is a giveaway. If we translate David's escapades on the lam from Saul into persecution we are filtering them through the analogy of the sufferings of Christians under civil leaders. It seems to follow that we are overlaying our meaning on his. We are colonizing his bandit period for our persecutions.

It may seem that there are good colonizers and there are bad. The bad colonizers do not really like being abroad and make a poor fist of living among foreigners with their strange manners, unfunny jokes, weird attitudes to women, revolting language, and unspeakable cuisine. All the bad colonist notices about the natives is their foreignness. When the bad colonist ventures into the Old Testament as a Christian interpreter, his only defense against the savages is allegorization. He knows that, in principle, all of this ought to be meaningful to him, and allegory is his way of making it so. Caesarius of Arles felt that, in the "ten cheeses" that David was given to deliver to the embattled army at Shochoh (17:18), "we recognize

---

1. Erich Auerbach, *Mimesis: The Representation of Reality in Western Literature*, trans. Willard Trask (Princeton: Princeton University Press, 1974), 16.

2. P. C. Spicq, *Esquisse d'une histoire de l'exégèse latine au moyen age* (Paris: Vrin, 1944), 149.

the decalogue of the Old Testament" (Sermon 121.1–2, in Franke 2005: 268). Eisegetical allegory so extensively deodorizes the heroic cheese-bearer that it seems preferable to some simply to regard David as someone like ourselves. No allegorizer, the good colonist is unworried by differences of language and custom and recognizes a Bronze Age hill fighter as a regular guy like himself.

Good colonization may be felt to correspond to reading the 1 Samuel stories in their literal, historical intensity. A literal reading of the David stories appeared, for instance, in the fourteenth-century Franciscan exegete Nicholas of Lyra, who pictured David as a parallel type to bishops. In this kind of typology, one looks for literal parallels, like David as leader and episcopal leadership. Nicholas of Lyra wrote that *bonus prelatus per David figuratus*, the good bishop is "figured" by David, meaning David models the good bishop. What matters in this kind of interpretation is not that David was a forerunner or prophecy of the good bishop, but that he in his own time and we in ours act in equivalent ways. Nicholas of Lyra does not so much interpret David as having prefigured "popes, prelates, and kings" as having had "*parallel experiences* to theirs" (Gosselin 1976: 34, 29, emphasis added).

Unlike the bad colonist, who can only hold his nose at this unwashed Bronze Age womanizer and allegorize him into something he never intended to be, literal typology is thought by many to take David's Hebraic character seriously. They feel that the least bad way a Christian colonist can give David interpretative meaning is to recognize that the Old Testament was "theologically valid and could stand alone without the New Testament" (Gosselin 1976: 70). Rather than providing David with the meaning of a shadow of the church to come, the good colonist is said to have given David one and the same faith to that which he himself held. The introduction to Calvin's Psalms commentary is cited as an example of the Swiss Reformer's good practice in this regard (cited in Gosselin 1976: 69). Calvin does indeed claim that his own sufferings have given him access to the woes articulated in David's Psalms: "The small measure of experience which I have had by the conflicts with which the Lord has exercised me, has in no ordinary degree assisted me . . . in . . . comprehending the design of each of the writers. And as David holds the principal place among them, it has . . . aided me in understanding . . . the complaints made by him of the internal afflictions which the church had to sustain through those who gave themselves out to be her members, that I had suffered . . . similar things from the domestic enemies of the Church." He thinks his "Godly reader" will be able to discern that "in unfolding the internal affairs . . . of David . . . I discourse upon matters of which I have familiar experience" (1845–46: 1.xxxix–xl, xlviii).

Did Calvin himself think he was giving David less of a Christian patina than the fathers had done? Or is the idea of Calvin as superior to the patristic allegorists itself an act of modern colonization? Augustine's reading of the Psalms lies at the back of Calvin's feeling of intimacy and comradeship with David. For Augustine, commenting on Ps. 55:2, "David himself figuratively stands for Christ, in virtue of being Christ's carnal ancestor": "So David represents Christ." *And* "Christ is both head and body, and we must not think ourselves alien to Christ, since we are his members. Nor must we think of ourselves as separate from him, because 'they will be two in one flesh. This is a great mystery . . . but I am referring it to Christ and the church' (Eph. 5:31–32). Since, then, the whole Christ consists of head and body, we must understand that we too are included in David" (2001: 54).

Calvin says, for instance, that, since "it is the will of God that he should be known in his gracious character, not only of one or two, but generally of all men, whenever he vouchsafes deliverance to any of his children, it is a common benefit that all the faithful ought to apply to themselves when they see in the person of one man in what manner God . . . will act toward all his people. David . . . asks nothing for himself individually but what pertains to the whole church" (1845–46: 2.110, on Ps. 40:16). When Calvin sees David's experiences as the mirror of his own calling, he does not think he is interpreting David or giving him meaning, but rather the reverse: "Whatever the most illustrious king and prophet suffered, was exhibited to me by God as an example for imitation" (1845–46: 1.xl). David was his contemporary because Calvin's own life was given meaning by David's sufferings.

It may seem that, whereas Augustine in his sermon on Ps. 55 makes christological and ecclesiological doctrine central to his interpretation of David, Calvin lets David speak for himself. Unlike Augustine, Calvin seems to avoid decoding David's meaning through the filter of an ecclesiology of the mystical body of Christ. There's no question that Calvin appeals directly to the humanity of David and is drawn into the Psalter by the appeal of that vivid and warm humanity. For Calvin, it is not a matter of David standing alone without the New Testament: it's about David's humanity. For Calvin and the Christian tradition, David's humanity has an especial resonance because this is the humanity that is united to the divinity of Christ. Calvin is not staking out a secular position, based in the interpretative stand-alone value of David. He is taking a theological position, which goes back to Augustine's reading of the Psalms: as *man*, Christ is "son of David," and as *God*, he is "Son of the Father." As Augustine puts it, "In one respect Christ is the son of David, and in a different respect he is David's Lord: son of David according to the flesh, but Lord of David in his Divinity" (2001: 54, on Ps. 55:2). Our enjoyment of David's all-too-human personality, with his escapades and great escapes, is a legacy of that Christian tradition that gave individual human personality value, by making the union of human and divine in Christ a dogmatic teaching. David is important to Christian tradition as the historical humanity that was drawn up into the divinity of Christ.

How can we tell that Calvin's perception of David was under the sway of an Augustinian Christology? One way to tell is by comparing his characterization of David with that of peoples who had the opportunity to emulate the warrior-chief of the literal stand-alone Old Testament. Something analogous to the heroic culture of Judges and Regum existed in medieval Ethiopia, where, instead of "restraining the heroic ethos, Christianity tended to be absorbed by it. Saints acted like heroes rather than heroes acting like saints." The Ethiopian chronicler who compiled the tale of the warrior-emperor Amda Seyon "specifically compared his hero to Saul and David." He tells how his most Christian emperor "called out to his soldiers, 'Stand in patience . . . and see how I fight and how I die, and (see also) what God will do to-day by my hand.' . . . He . . . struck so hard that he transfixed two men as one with a blow of his spear, through the strength of God. . . . Men's blood flowed like water, and bodies lay like grass on the earth." This pitched battle was fought against Muslim neighbors. Lacking a Chalcedonian Christology and therefore setting the Old Testament on the same spiritual footing as the New, "unlike the medieval European Church, that of Ethiopia created little ritual to discipline the military life, other than blessing and absolving armies before battle" (Iliffe 2005: 55–56). Calvinist Presbyterianism never left the soldier David wholly unbaptized.

It would be idle to insist that Chalcedonian Christology has always been at the forefront of Christian Old Testament exegesis. Making literal connections between David and ourselves is a recurrent feature of our exegesis. Watching Melanchthon give his inaugural lecture at Wittenberg in 1518, "Luther remarked that the audience . . . 'saw in him only the David who was destined to go forth against the Goliath of scholasticism'" (Gosselin 1976: 68, citing Robert Stupperich). For Augustine too, David was "in the Old Testament" but not "of the Old Testament" (*Expositio Epistolae ad Galatas* 43), or as Origen about David: "They were no longer little children in Christ but already evangelical men" (*Contra Celsum* 1.48) (both cited in Lubac 2007: 302). Augustine could speak of David as if there was no temporal disjunction between David and the church: "Those saints," he said, "delivered the Old Covenant as was fitting for their times, but they themselves belonged to the New Covenant" (Augustine, Patrologia latina 33.540, cited in Lubac 2007: 302). Augustine gives David citizenship rights in the Catholic church.

Such constructions are questionable. If the similarity between attitude and belief in Old and New is overstressed, it is difficult to see in what sense the former is the Old Testament. Both the bad colonizing of excess allegory and the good colonizing of literal typology can scarcely avoid missing the difference between David and ourselves. Hence, "a better informed historical sense prevents us today from sharing . . . fully" in Augustine and Calvin's embrace of David as a man after their New Covenant hearts. The literal typologist imagines that it is the Jewish historicity of David's exploits and attitudes that make them continuous with us, because our times are in a historical continuum with his. One flaw in the idea of a level historical continuum between us and David is that it entails that the Christ event makes no incisive mark on time. A second drawback is the failure to notice that continuity is not the only historical category: change and difference are just as historical. "Continuity and discontinuity," as Lubac says, "are both historical categories" (2007: 302, 306). There can be no history without temporal fissures, because historical figures as such have disappeared into the wash of time. There is no temporal disparity between ourselves and Dido or Aeneas because, unlike David, they are not historical figures, but imaginative archetypes who have never entered the flow of time. Any person who belongs to history appears and then disappears into the past. If an event is part of the string of history, eventually it is a past event and hence in discontinuity with ourselves. Moreover, those historical events that make a mark effect a change from what has gone before. The first two modes of interpretation, allegory and literal-historical typology, must be applied carefully if they are not to deny to David his historicity, by making him our contemporary, in the same way that Plato's Socrates or Vergil's Aeneas can be our contemporaries.

A third interpretative maneuver wants to make David's adventures speak to our ethical concerns. For such readers, the spiritual significance of the David stories is practical: Nicholas of Lyra's use of David is "more heavily pastoral than theological." Thinking that David's actions are "worthy of repetition," "the Franciscan exegete employed . . . a 'David moralisé' who served as an example to the Christian faithful" (Gosselin 1976: 31–32, 67). Such Franciscan preaching constitutes the bulk of the homiletics to which the present writer has been subjected. Putting pastoral *actualité* at the heart of our interpretation of David risks ascribing our own concerns to him. When he indicates the signs for move and retreat before assaulting the Philistine garrison (1 Sam. 14), Jonathan is endowed by many readers with a touchingly baseless faith, whereas in the geographic reality of hillside combat, his signs were good strategic thinking. His military tactic doesn't fit the modern psychological categories of insecurity versus certainty. Many preachers assure us that David's unarmored combat with Goliath is a mark of unself-reliant faith, whereas, as we will see, being able to move fast is David's best natural asset. The "something like this happened to me" school of homiletics updates the scripture at the risk of making our morality and idea of faith come between us and David's morality and faith. This is an occupational hazard of pastors, preachers, and biblical scholars. Interpreting is not necessarily giving meaning, but it can come within a hair's breadth of doing so. A *David moralisé* can easily become a figment of our contemporary imagination.

For some biblical theologians, that is fairly much what David is. Too large to be contained in any one cycle of stories, "his memory and presence keep generating more and more stories," from 1–2 Samuel to Chronicles and beyond. "David is the engine for Israel's imagination," says Brueggemann, and, as he takes it, that means he must always be for us a construction, someone imagined in literature, not someone who lived and died in the Early Iron Age. For Brueggemann, David is in this no different from anyone else. He is not an imaginative figure because *he* is especially archetypal, but because *we* are ever imagining our forebears: "Historical persons are never 'historical' but always constructions and portraits, partly done for us and to us, and partly done by ourselves, as we are always busy constructing ourselves for the sake of appearance and for the sake of self-understanding. Those constructions are . . . strange combinations of fidelity and deception."[3]

3. Walter Brueggemann, *David's Truth in Israel's Imagination and Memory* (Minneapolis: Fortress, 1985), 14, 17.

Brueggemann is on to something important. There's a difference between how, say, Bede and Calvin see David, and it corresponds to the relative lack of historical consciousness in the former and the relative degree of it in the early modern reformer. It's like the archetypality of Norman portraiture, in comparison to the naturalism of seventeenth-century Dutch painting. The terms "ancient" and "modern" originate around 1600. The modern chap wants his portrait to look like him, because the emergence of "historical consciousness was involved intimately . . . with the development of . . . personal understanding, or self awareness, or self-consciousness."[4] The link between the two is that, if who I *think* I am contributes to who I am, then my historicity goes into my makeup. So a character like David cannot be understood from without his perspective on where he stood. The great thing about personal awareness—awareness of one's unique standing as a person, with one's own, historical, perspective—is to keep it personal and not to allow it to sink back into an impersonal theory. Overly theorized, the sense of historicity transmutes into historicism. The evolution of personal consciousness was the result of concrete historical events, relating to the specific personhood of Christ. Deprived of that theological basis, personal and historical consciousness descends into an ideology of history. Thus dehumanized, personal and historical perspective ceases to be a means of sharing in insights between generations, a function of our shared humanity, and turns into the dogma that perspective is imposed between ourselves and historical events. Then the idea of interpreting as "giving meaning" comes into the open, a calculated embrace of subjectivity in interpretation.

This fourth interpretative strategy is like what Halpern calls "negative fundamentalism," that is, "the denial of any historical value" to "such historical books as Judges, Samuel, and Kings, concerning which skepticism has reawakened today." Where the "positive," confessional fundamentalist interprets scripture like a "map" that always contained all of the cities we know to exist today, "negative fundamentalists . . . date the whole map by its latest elements" (1996: 4). Both kinds of fundamentalism are "antihistorical," ignoring that the map developed over time, the one wanting it to be all there at the outset, the other thinking it was all invented "after it didn't happen." To interpret David as one invented by our imaginations is to make him an allegory we construct of ourselves, his humanity a projection of our own.

When Halpern claims that, for "negative fundamentalists" the scriptural "map reflects a view from" later times and so "cannot be used to get at earlier times" (1996: 4), he is referring to the revisionist biblical scholars who think the David stories were invented in late Hellenistic times. Minimalism takes the Deuteronomistic History as a fiction in its entirety. Lemche claims that likening "the Bible's tales about David with Early Iron Age Palestine is like comparing the story of Gilgamesh with Bronze Age Uruk, Homer with ancient Mycenae . . . , Arthur with early medieval England, or . . . Wagner's Siegfried with a Germany of the

---

4. John Lukacs, *Historical Consciousness; or, The Remembered Past*, new ed. (New York: Schocken, 1985), 14.

early Middle Ages."[5] One piece of evidence Lemche gives for ascribing 1 Samuel to the genre of fiction is that the story is biased in favor of David (1978: 3). The author is prejudiced because he wants to make David, his invented founder of the monarchy, as lustrous as the antique state of Israel itself. For Lemche, both are equally fictive. Lemche thinks it is circular to argue from the tribes uniting around a monarchy centered in Jerusalem to David as the founder of Israel's united monarchy: "States of Israel and Judah certainly existed in ancient Palestine. The Bible's story was the necessary story of their origin. . . . The argument rests . . . on the romantic expectations we have of history: all great institutions need comparably great origins. If ever there was an example of a story accepted as history because we needed it, the Saul-David story was it."[6] Lemche does not note that, since science is the search for the causes of known facts, it is only unscientific or circular to argue from the united monarchy to David as its cause, if we already know that the united monarchy is a fiction.

The model of the composition of the books of Samuel and Kings used by biblical historians from J. G. Eichhorn onward was that, first, in the Solomonic enlightenment of the tenth–eighth century BC, old source documents and oral legends were put together in the archives of old shrines like Shiloh in some semblance of a narrative, and, second, inspired by the seventh-century Josianic reform the Deuteronomic editor performed yet more pasting and cutting to turn them into something close to the canonical books of Samuel and Kings. Exaggerated claims about this enlightenment assumed the status of facts. During the latter half of the twentieth century, this model was subject to multiple criticisms. The notion of a Solomonic enlightenment was gravely deflated. The idea of the Solomonic enlightenment had given an explanation of how the Deuteronomistic History was written in the seventh century BC but had had access to reports of events a half millennium earlier. Though some of the features of this enlightenment have reappeared in the scholarly pursuit of the professional "scribal culture" that turned "the oral culture of Israel" to produce the "books of the Bible," it has been resituated, in the seventh century and in postexilic times (Toorn 2007: 75, 77–101). If the editor(s) of Regum were not drawing on source documents or materials, what *were* they doing, when they told stories about Samuel, Saul, David, Solomon, and his heirs? One element of proof in history is evidence close to the events described, and the source documents had played that role. Once the documents' existence began to be doubted, the revisionists drew the conclusion that the Deuteronomist editor was a fiction writer, not a historian. At just the moment when scholars were taking an interest in the esthetic qualities of the Hebrew scriptures, a mass of negative evidence appeared to show that the editor(s) of the Deuteronomistic History were *solely* interested in producing literary artifacts.

5. Niels Peter Lemche and Thomas L. Thompson, "Did Biran Kill David? The Bible in the Light of Archaeology," *Journal for the Study of the Old Testament* 64 (1994): 3–22 at 18.
6. Ibid., 17–18.

On a methodological level, revisionism and rigorously esthetic treatments of scripture are working on the same lines. There is an immense esthetic quality in the stories about David. Brueggemann wants to say something valuable, but the way in which he uses the ambiguous term "imagination" tends to imply "fictivity." His idea was put better by Auerbach, half a century ago: "In the stories of David, the legendary . . . imperceptibly passes into the historical."[7] David straddles the region between legend and history. David is partially a legendary figure because the Jewish authors who recounted the tales about him were groping toward something new, something that has "no parallel in ancient times." Neither the Orientals nor the Greeks attempted to make theological claim out of a historical claim: "The Bible is . . . the first to anticipate the appeal to the surviving record of the past that characterizes modern history telling. Such relics abound on the narrative surface itself. . . . Customs are elucidated, ancient names and current sayings traced back to their origins, monuments and fiats assigned a concrete reason as well as a slot in history, persons and places and pedigrees specified beyond immediate needs, written records like the Book of Yashar or the royal annals explicitly invoked. In terms of communicative design and force, it is the novelty of the gesture toward historicity that matters."[8] By weaving theology out of history, and staking the truth of the theology on the truth of the history, the author of the David stories was doing something new, discontinuous with ancient narrative.

A human head could not conceivably lie behind such an undesigned and malformed script as the Deuteronomistic History has come to be represented by source critics. The literary-historical reconstructions of the production of this history have become party to antihistorical interpretations of the aims of 1 Samuel–2 Kings because they so "often imply that the editors of our documents did sloppy and illogical, even nonsensical work." Recent historical critics often treat 1 Samuel–2 Kings as if it were an aimless archeological deposit left in the sands of the ancient Near East, not a document written by persons for other human persons: "This is possible, but it is not likely. What survived is not a group of idiosyncratic documents but a group of documents around which a community was organized. Someone in that community should have been able to point out the problems, even if the 'editors' were the morons that some modern scholars imply" (Halpern 1996: xxv). Once the sources were separated from an author who deliberately cites them, the separate units were treated "as if the traditions they contain had a life of their own" (Van Seters 1983: 16).

Source-critical analysis often ties hypothetical documents to hypothetical motivations: readers of the David stories are seldom allowed to forget that anti-Saulide texts come from promoters of a Davidic ideology. The reductionist take on this is that, in approaching the biblical history, we must always ask "why is

7. Auerbach, *Mimesis*, 20.
8. Meir Sternberg, *The Poetics of Biblical Narrative: Ideological Literature and the Drama of Reading* (Bloomington: Indiana University Press, 1985), 31.

this story being told?" and the answer cannot be "because it happened," since "something happening does not of itself provide adequate reason for telling it. Literature is a form of persuasive communication . . . literature is ideology. If so, historiography, as a branch of literature, is also ideology." "No story," the revisionist Philip Davies claims, "is ever an innocent representation of the outside world. All story is fiction, and that must include historiography."[9] What is followed to a logical conclusion here is a shying away from history always passing through human hands, as though the humanity of history consistently contaminates it into ideology. "Perspective," as Ortega y Gasset said, "is one of the components of reality. Far from being its deformation it is its organization."[10] Christians spontaneously avoid the term "historiography" in reference to the biblical texts, because they sense that the author was inspired in his humanity, that he presented his interpretation of David for a human religious community, and did not write as an autonomous "scientist."

It may seem that one concedes the perspectival quality of the biblical history only to arouse a worse specter than accusations of ideological bias. The specter is historicism, that is, conceiving the biblical history as begotten by the mind of its era and therefore true only for its own era. But historicism is itself an ideology of history, the "most German and idealist . . . recognition of the presence of history" in "so categorical and abstract" a state "as to become abstract." The minimalist neurosis—its fear of the perspectival quality of human perception—produces the urge to become that oxymoron, a true historicist, with a final, abstract solution to the problems of historical thinking and existence, that is, to eliminate the biblical historians and replace them with inventive ideologists. By contrast with historicism, a humane historical consciousness is merely "the recognition of the historical character of human reason and reasoning." Whereas a few intellectuals may have a philosophy of history or an ideology, our biblical author presents us with that more humane and more prophetic thing: historical thinking. Minimalists are worried about how history, the past, gets into our heads. If we take a step back, we can see that all human life is historical and thus perspectival: the point is "how the events of history are 'made' by their participants . . . not how the 'past' is spun out of minds *post facto* but how the past is made by people into their 'present.'" Because human beings put their historicity into all of their actions, "*every* novel is a historical novel, in one way or another."[11] If we were just looking for the apparent ideal of archeo-scientific history, end products without human aims and motivations, we could not find a single human artifact, for "history is not what happened. What happened . . . was sequential direction, velocity, and acceleration of particles. History is our way of organizing particle configurations into perceptible fictional blocks, such as individuals, groups, and the environment.

9. Philip R. Davies, *In Search of "Ancient Israel,"* Journal for the Study of the Old Testament Supplement 148 (Sheffield: Sheffield Academic Press, 1992), 13.
10. Cited in Lukacs, *Historical Consciousness*, 113.
11. Ibid., xxx, 151, 153, 342.

... Historians deal with people, and with societies, as though these were the atoms of causation. The historian's job is to expound human causes to the reader—to organize a sequence of subatomic events, so that we can understand them in a human way.... So, like everything else human ... all history is flawed, in the sense that it is all metaphoric" (Halpern 1996: xxxiii). That ancient conversations and conversions and mad, intemperate fits cannot be captured by "radiocarbon dating, neutron activation analysis," or "aerial photography" (Dever 2002: 59–60), and that these events were set down by someone with human motivations and perceptions, no more prevents them from being history than the fact that a doorway is really made of subatomic particles hinders it from being a doorway. The humanity of the author is his doorway into the humanity of his protagonists, for the "nature of our perception helps us get through the doorway without banging into the walls" (Halpern 1996: xxxiii).

As any clever undergraduate can see, in the reductionist search for motivated ideologists, there is always someone who thinks he escapes contamination, the professor who sees through the motivations of others. Though editors, as we understand the term, did not exist until the Renaissance, the original biblical scholars were all textual critics, and when they "began to imagine how the biblical texts first came into being, they used themselves as the models for the persons who brought these texts together." It was in the sixteenth century that the profession of comparing and amending texts in order to distribute a critical text came into being: it thus "*becomes highly anachronistic to consider ... anyone ... in antiquity as editors.*" Taking themselves and their own work as the prototype and realizing that editing always alters a text "led, by erroneous reasoning, to the conclusion that ancient revisions and interpolations in a text likewise resulted from the activity of editors" (Van Seters 2006: 15, 18, 19, emphasis original).

We have considered four interpretative schema by which to grasp the David stories, and we seem to be back where we started. The first, the allegorical embrace of the Old Testament by Christian theological tradition, stands accused of having "reinterpreted the entire Jewish tradition as a succession of figures prognosticating the appearance of Christ."[12] Second, the literal-historical typological approach sees David in parallelism with ourselves and smoothes over the discontinuities between this Jewish king and modern Christians. Third, the moralizing pastoral approach makes his faith Christian rather than Jewish. Fourth, the esthetic interpretative paradigm is methodologically in harmony with the revisionist historians who imagine David like King Arthur, that is, as nonexistent. And, as it seems, the revisionists themselves are reliant on an anachronistic model of how the Bible was composed or edited, decoding the Bible through the filter of the printing press and regarding its original editors as having miraculously prefigured textual scholars like themselves. The story of Samuel's anointment of David is a salutary reminder that historical, moral,

12. Auerbach, *Mimesis*, 16.

and imaginative parallels have the drawback that "man looks on the outward appearance," is literal and materially minded; only the vision transformed by Christ "looks at the heart" (16:7 ESV). Given that interpreting is so easily conflated with providing meaning, it might be better to move away from the idea of an interpretative paradigm.

The advent of Christ doesn't give us a special way of thinking about David. Rather, it changes who and what David was. Halpern is right to criticize as unhistorical a fundamentalism that imagines that the whole map was there from the start. For Christian theology, the terrain did not just evolve along the same line but underwent an earthquake at the coming of Christ. That made, not just for epistemic change, but a factual alteration. It was not a paradigm shift, it was a shift in the lay of the land. With the birth of Christ, David was not reinterpreted, but *became* something he had not been before, the ancestor of the world's redeemer. Israel's first king became the progenitor of the Messiah of Israel. The David stories did not all along contain a dormant spiritual sense, within their literal sense, which was decoded by Christian interpreters. Christ gave a spirituality to this history that it had not had before. As Lubac puts it:

> It is thus not an explanation on the intellectual plane that "opens" the Old Testament. It is an effective fulfillment, and the result of that fulfillment is its assimilation to the New. . . . After Christ, the old Scripture in a way lost its literal meaning. Once very real, henceforth . . . it is outdated. That is literally true for the legal prescriptions, which no longer correspond to the will of God for us. But . . . it is also true in a certain way for the accounts themselves. For history is essentially something that passes. The events recounted in the Bible thus, so to speak, exhausted their historical role as they were unfolding, in order to live on only as signs in view of our edification. "The old things have passed away: behold, they have become new." . . . If we think back to the time before Christ, we should say that at that time this Scripture had still to acquire its spiritual sense.

Lubac cites Origen: "Before the coming of Christ, the law and the prophets did not yet have the proclamation of what is clearly defined in the Gospel, since the one who was to clarify their mysteries had not yet come. But when the Savior had come to us and had given a body to the Gospel, then, *through the Gospel, he made everything similar to the Gospel*." Christ's historical act of preaching the kingdom changed David's kingdom. So, " 'prophecy' arose in a way from its own fulfillment. The marvelous harmony that the two Testaments makes the ears of the faith hear is not, if we take the point of view of empirical history, a preestablished harmony: it was necessary for Christ to come in order to unite them with each other, in order to make of them a single harp and a single song" (*Commentary on John* 1.8, cited in Lubac 2007: 311–14, emphasis original).

The christological paradigm does not abolish interpretative paradigms: it grounds them. If Christians from the church fathers to contemporary African believers find much that is relevant to themselves in the biblical and Davidic themes of "martyrdom, oppression, and exile,"[13] that is not because there is a general, transhistorical analogy between their times and ours, but because the church is the body of Christ, experiencing persecution as Christ did. When Augustine sees in the fall of the house of Saul and the anointing of David a prefiguring of the kingship of Christ, he does not take this to be the allegorical meaning of 1 Samuel, but its literal meaning. Before Christ came, that might have been a potential allegory hovering over the text, but now it is really and literally what the text means. It is not that we can now uncloak this meaning in it, but that it is now literally there, because Christ's kingship makes the event new. If there are historical analogies between David, Christ, and the church of yesterday and today, it is because the historical alchemy of the advent of Christ changes what was and is. If it matters that David is the one through whom a cultural shift is engineered, that "the legendary David stood in the storm's eye" of "a transitional period characterized by exceptional social traumas and internal political turmoils" (Flanagan 1988: 33), this is not important because cultural progress is good in itself or because we can make sense of him by relating our cultural upheavals to his, but because Christ himself transforms all cultures. This is an elemental analogy by which we can understand this hero of the Early Iron Age.

Episode One: Sight for the Blind (1 Sam. 16:1–13)

Discontinuity is a mark of all history. Once he became an ancestor of Christ, we understand David's particular discontinuity in a special way. He is not just one of the many new steps that occur in history: he is a historical rupture because he was chosen by God to be so. Thomas Aquinas notes that it was fitting that Christ had both Abraham and David in his lineage, because Abraham symbolizes the circumcision and David symbolizes God's choice: "Circumcision had its beginning in Abraham: while in David God's election was most clearly made manifest, according to [1 Sam.] 13:14: 'The Lord hath sought him a man according to his own heart.' And consequently Christ is called in a most special way the Son of both, in order to show that he came for the salvation both of the circumcised and of the elect among the Gentiles." The flesh, that is, the humanity of Christ, comes to Christ from Adam through David, his elected precursor (*Summa theologiae* III Q. 31 A. 2 reply).

In the lectionary (Fourth Sunday of Lent, Year A), both epistle and gospel shed light on the Old Testament story. The epistle is from Eph. 5:8–14: "For at one time you were darkness, but now you are light in the Lord. Walk as children of light (for the fruit of light is found in all that is good and right and true), and try to discern what is pleasing to the Lord. Take no part in the unfruitful works of

---

13. Philip Jenkins, *The Next Christendom: The Coming of Global Christianity* (Oxford: Oxford University Press, 2002), 217.

darkness, but instead expose them. . . . But when anything is exposed by the light, it becomes visible, for anything that becomes visible is light. Therefore it says, 'Awake, O sleeper, and arise from the dead, and Christ will shine on you.'" This Pauline passage contrasts living as light and living in darkness. Those readers who have felt that Saul's predicament is unjustly grim have cottoned on to something in the feel of 1 Sam. 8–15. Overall, the episodes in 1 Sam. 8–15 have a gray, shadowy tonality. Here, in 1 Sam. 16, it is as if crepuscular twilight has awoken into the full light of day. Just as the epistle contrasts people of the light and people of darkness, the gospel reading for this day is about blindness and sight. Jesus gives sight to the man born blind (John 9). Read alongside these New Testament passages, 1 Sam. 16:1–13 is about a fresh start, a sudden and complete break in the path of events: "The old things have passed away: behold, all things have become new" (2 Cor. 5:17 Darby). Light breaks in upon the darkness.

The New Testament passages about light direct us to the most important verb in 1 Sam. 16:1–13: *raah* ("to see"), which occurs six times (16:1, 6, 7 [4x]). Samuel is still grieving for Saul. The prophet is refusing to see things the way they are. God tells him to look at the reality—to leave Saul behind. Samuel is told to go to the house of Jesse of Bethlehem to anoint a new king. Since Samuel is afraid of featuring in an act of treason, God tells him to personate the performer of a sacrifice. We know from 9:12–13 that traveling from village to village to perform the sacrifice was one of the seer Samuel's conventional roles. Saul pretended to be just sacrificing in the previous scene. Now God tells Samuel to conceal the anointing behind staging a sacrifice. Saul can hardly "kill" (16:2) Samuel for doing what he called "perform[ing] the commandment of the LORD" in 15:13 (ESV). Anointing the king that God has chosen is God's idea of a true sacrifice. Samuel had told Saul "to obey is better than sacrifice" (15:22 ESV). The meaning of the anointing is obedience to God's will.

Samuel is not called to see for himself what to do next or whom to anoint. God tells him, "I will show you what you shall do; you shall anoint for Me the one I name to you" (16:3 NKJV). Jesse's eldest sons gather round the sacrifice. When Samuel "looked at Eliab" he says to himself, "Surely the LORD's anointed" right there! (16:6 NKJV). The episode gently mocks Samuel's "blindness" by contrasting his human way of looking with God's insight. Eliab must be a big husky guy, for God tells Samuel, "Do not look at his appearance or at his physical stature, because I have refused him" (16:7 NKJV). Whereas in patristic and medieval times, Christians sometimes drank too deeply of philosophies that exaggerated the separation between body and spirit, today, they are as likely to be influenced by antidualist ideologies. We are even told that differentiating the internal and the external is just Platonism or Cartesian dualism and has nothing to do with Christianity. But this text clearly and simply distinguishes the external, physical look of persons from their interior self, characterized as their heart. It contrasts the blindness of Samuel, who is impressed by what's on show—the visible height and stature of Eliab—with the insight of God, who sees the truth of a human being. God tells Samuel, "The LORD does not see as man sees; for man looks at the outward appearance, but the LORD looks at the heart" (16:7 NKJV). This, as we saw in the previous episode, was Augustine's explanation of the discrepancy between God's treatment of Saul and David. The human heart evades literal analysis. It is a wayward thing that humans can know only partially, by contemplation, and that only God can see in full. The heart symbolizes what is personal to the human agent, because it is the concealed force directing all human action. Two more sons, Abinadab and Shammah, are lined up for viewing and passed over. After seven sons have been displayed, Samuel asks if there are any more in the offing. There is, Jesse says, "the youngest," out "keeping the sheep," too junior to be recalled from work and invited to the sacrifice. This naïve pantomime parade, a childish story of the passing over of the outstanding eldest for the insignificant youth, is put on to show that God is making a break with the natural run of things and starting over, as only God can start over, from the spirit or inside out. The contrast between external spectacle and invisible interior worth is telling us that the authentic measure of sight is God's way of seeing. God can see someone that everyone else has forgotten or doesn't know about: and when they brought the youngest in, "he was ruddy, and withal of a beautiful countenance, and goodly to look to" (16:12). Up the sleeve of the divine providence was a boy who even looks better than his elder brothers. Maybe Samuel was cheered up by this divine joke against himself.

The story presents a subtle contrast and harmonizing of the inner and the outer person: on the one hand, David is overlooked, and the elder sons are evidently presentable, but on the other, David is good-looking (16:12). If we exaggerate the former and overplay the imperative "do not look at his appearance or at his physical stature" (16:7 NKJV), we adopt a Jansenism or Puritanism that writes off David's physical charm. If we underplay the imperative and stress the physical charm, we are susceptible to spiritual utilitarianism, as if the good looks make the person. Pierre de Cava seems to get it about right. He begins, rather allegorically for our tastes, by reading "there he is, keeping the sheep" (16:11 NKJV) to mean that David is "abject in his own eyes, but not in those of God . . . the humble man nourishes simple thoughts by contemplating his eternal inheritance." This detour into the "eternal and celestial pastures" shows its exegetical worth when the abbot of Cava asks about the apparent conflict between David's having slipped the mental sight of his family and yet being the most visually striking: "Why does it remark on his beautiful deportment, when it has made us notice his interior contemplation?" Commenting on the Vulgate's *erat autem rufus et pulcher aspectu decoraque facie* ("he was red, with a beautiful face and a charming carriage"; 16:12), Pierre de Cava argues, not that "the body *sums up* the real person," but more precisely that one's exterior is the exhibition of one's spirituality, which rises up from elsewhere: "He has a beautiful face, so as to say, that it shines with the beauty of the vision which he has in his interior contemplation. . . . It is by the face that each one is known. And the beauty of the face is the manifestation of a way of life which does one honor. Someone effectively puts forward a charming visage when he somehow shows his splendor in all the movements of his body. It is thus love which makes him red, knowledge which gives him a beautiful face, and good conduct which does him honor and gives him a charming carriage." An inner attention to God makes David glow with a "ruddy" (16:12) light, making his body translucent with a light from outside it, like the stained glass window, which is dark unless the sun shines through it. The contrast being drawn is not between visible and invisible but between the man who is set in the light of God's election and the man who is not. David's "charming face" reflects, the abbot says, "the beauty of charity," the theological virtue par eminence: "The other virtues are the body of justice, but charity can be considered to have a right to be called the face of the body." Charity is the greatest of the theological virtues, the virtues of grace: "When a pastor is thus red (i.e., *ruddy*), when he has a beautiful visage, that is to say a high contemplation; when he has a lovely face, the whole force of his conduct and the sublimity of his contemplation makes us see the divine majesty, like the imprint of the unspeakable beauty of charity" (2004: 197–99 §90.1–3, §99.2; 201 §92.2). David has always been the mirror of human beings, because he is a mirror of God. With his twelfth-century Platonic esthetics of light, Pierre de Cava captures that fairly precisely.

On God's instruction, Samuel anoints David, and his name is then shared out too: "Samuel took the horn of oil and anointed him in the midst of his brothers; and the Spirit of the LORD came upon David from that day forward" (16:13 NKJV). No ugly duckling, David is the jolt to the system that the all-knowing God had selected. The Psalms speak of the striking innovation of this election, which overturns the traditional familial hierarchy known to all tribal cultures:

> I made a lad ruler in preference to a warrior, I exalted a youth above a
> hero.
> I found David my servant, with my holy oil I anointed him. (Ps. 89:19–
> 20, trans. Flanagan 1988: 201)

A transition is occurring within Israel's religious self-understanding, bound up with its cultural self-understanding and with the self-understanding of all peoples after Christ. To modern Western readers, instructed by countless fairy tales, bypassing of the elder sons for the youngest is about as surprising as the appearance of an unlikely hero in a Disney movie. Our culture has been steeped in the Christ event for so long that it takes an imaginative effort to see that, because Samuel's culture was one in which "the elders were an important component of the social stratum" and the "gods of the progenitors," their own "ancestors influenced the Israelites to structure themselves hierarchically according to age. To be a *gibbor* ('firstborn') accorded a son special status, not because the firstborn was stronger, wiser, or more experienced, but because he was the closest one in line to the ancestors." What we, no less than the "African and Israelite communities

... organized along family hierarchical structures,"[14] have to learn from the up-heaval and transformation represented by the anointing of the youngest son is that Christ, and like him his forefather David, creates a change in the register of God's action. In the world of the patriarchs and the tribal cultures of the judges, where God acted in the seen (the naturally beautiful), the order and beauty of the family and tribe, henceforth God will often act in the unseen (the invisible and yet providential gesture). There are no miracles in 1 Sam. 16–31. God's working has gone underground, and hence a signature theme must be the contrast of the heart and the externals that mortal family members can see. According to von Rad, "In this story we are . . . listening to a late interpretation, one which introduces the Davidic dynasty into a set of concepts which was originally alien to it, namely the antecedent designation of Jahweh's elected by a prophet. Historically, the pious story is . . . in error. But . . . it is the one which most strongly emphasises the ele-ment of the completely unexpected and incomprehensible in this new action of God, since the strangeness of this act . . . went beyond what the charismatically inspired Samuel could grasp." The choice of David as king, first over Judah (2 Sam. 2:4) and then over Israel (5:3), "was due, as the accounts make clear, to human initiative, namely that of the 'men of Judah' and later on that of all the 'elders of Israel'" (1962: 309). This is a hitherto unknown kind of anointing, different from that of the judges, down to Samuel. It even differs from the selection of Saul, the "big man." David is an "archetypal mediator" between the old and the new, because in his anointing, his "displacing Saul" and ultimately "moving the ark" to his capital city, Jerusalem (Flanagan 1988: 207), tribal culture is come to an end. A new world of politics has commenced.

In the breviary 1 Sam. 16:1–13 is twinned with the gospel passage in which Jesus's disciples break the law, and to answer Pharisaic kvetching about it, Jesus reminds them of the lawless behavior of David on the run: "One Sabbath he was going through the grainfields, and as they made their way, his disciples began to pluck heads of grain. And the Pharisees were saying to him, 'Look, why are they doing what is not lawful on the Sabbath?' And he said to them, 'Have you never read what David did, when he was in need and was hungry, he and those who were with him: how he entered the house of God, in the time of Abiathar the high priest, and ate the bread of the Presence, which it is not lawful for any but the priests to eat, and also gave it to those who were with him?' And he said to them, 'The Sabbath was made for man, not man for the Sabbath. So the Son of Man is lord even of the Sabbath'" (Mark 2:23–27 ESV). A comparison between David and Jesus is important to Christians.

Pierre de Cava uses the text as an example of the selection of priests and prelates in the church. In his Vulgate, the Lord tells Samuel, "Anoint the one which I will

14. Temba L. J. Mafico, "The Biblical God of the Fathers and the African Ancestors," in *The Bible in Africa: Transactions, Trajectories, and Trends*, ed. Gerald O. West and Musa W. Dube (Leiden: Brill, 2000), 484.

show you." Pierre de Cava asks, "Does this mean that those who set others at the head of the church must be prophets? They can recognize the one whom God has provided, if, in order to detect which person has been chosen as priest, they can consult the sacred Scriptures. In effect, it is as if God spoke to show them, when one chooses a pastor such as the sacred Word recommends." It takes the prism of scripture as a whole, not just one-on-one parallels, to imagine how later figures could be envisaged as operating as Samuel did. Noting that bad priests still get anointed, the abbot asks, "When those who anoint men who are not designated by God, that is when they permit themselves to be guided by carnal affections when they place those whom they want to ordain at the head of the church, does not that happen, not because they discern merit in them but because they are respecters of persons? They anoint the 'kings,' but not those whom God has designated. They play their role, but they relieve God of his. For it is God to whom it belongs to designate the person, and to the one who is ordained to confer the unction. In choosing for themselves those whom they will ordain, and in ordaining those whom they chose, they refuse to have God as their collaborator" (2004: 155 §62.3; 173 §75.3).

The comparison with Mark 2 helps us to see that 1 Sam. 16:1–23 is not just an ugly-duckling-into-swan fable, but touches on God's freedom to overturn customs, since he is their author. God is not a public fiction useful for grounding our social and political traditions. Rather, traditions exist only for the sake of God who creates and can revoke them. We don't need God because without a God, public and political morality would decline. In this story, God sits loosely to public order and political morality: he tells Samuel to use sacrifice as a camouflage for anointing a new king while King Saul still holds the power of life and death over mortals like Samuel. We need God because only God can enable us to rise above mere human political orders. God in 1 Samuel is not interested in political order but in individuals, whose hearts he can see. He is not the last link in the chain of the earthly political establishment. Rather, he is sovereignly free to upset it.

Episode Two: The Stringman (1 Sam. 16:14–23)

If you just hear it, the repetition in 16:14–15 is odd: "But the Spirit of the LORD departed from Saul, and an evil spirit from the LORD troubled him. And Saul's servants said unto him, 'Behold now, an evil spirit from God troubleth thee.'" This is disconcerting to a modern lector, who first reads that Saul is visited by an evil spirit and pictures that and then has to say that the servants explained to Saul that he is visited by an evil spirit. Why does Saul have to be told? One could pass over this quickly by relating it to the literary adage of the show-and-tell style of Hebrew narrative, the way it repeats in dialogue what has already been noted in narrative form. This can rapidly become subversive, as we wonder what the servants were up to, insinuating to Saul that he is demonically possessed and presenting

David as the cure. Those who tire of the fragmentation of the text into the voices of its characters insist, conversely, on the centrality of the omniscient narrator, emphasizing that if "we dispense with the controlling frame of the narrator's voice in our pursuit of the meaning of a narrative, we dispense also with the existing narrative." First Samuel isn't built up out of divergent voices: it is not a collage of subjective perspectives on the fortunes of Saul and David. It is not given to us to select what we think is *the* authentic voice and use it to generate a theory about what is *really* happening behind the scenes of this narrative about Saul's court. Such a theory would be just as subjective as the "multiple perspectives" of the voices (Eslinger 1983: 69).

It is true both that the omniscient narrator is the linchpin of the narrative *and* that he is counterpointed by the voices of the speakers. This gives us a narrative that has a kind of objective perspectivalism. These scenes, with Saul and his evil spirit and with David playing with his hand on his harp, are not filmed by a detached camera's eye outside or above the story—there is no omniscient narrator for modern readers. What happens here is neither purely objective nor subjectively perspectival: it's realistically perspectival. We see and hear the evil spirit and David musically exorcising it simultaneously from the outside, as a literal given situation, and from the inside, from the characters' reactions to it. This narrative style makes it a simple given, an objective problem that the servants have to handle: an evil spirit is visiting Saul and David's music making can expel it. At the same time, the style draws the reader into the situation, making its objectivity something we gather from within it, among the characters' reactions to the situation. It follows from the narrative's objective perspectivalism that we know the truth of the drama only from within it.

For a reader or for a hearer, moreover, the two sentences "an evil spirit from the LORD troubled him" (16:14) and "Saul's servants said unto him, 'Behold now, an evil spirit from God troubleth thee'" (16:15) are fractionally distinct in time. One way of conceiving what the author is doing for his preliterate audience, when he expounds narratively what he has just relayed in dialogue (or vice versa), is to transpose the dialogue on top of the narration, just as a comic book has pictures *and* speech or thought bubbles. This way of telling the story recreates with immediacy the experience of conversation, when we simultaneously hear and see the interlocutors. The comic-book esthetic of the author gives his prose an immediate configuration with felt experience, which anchors it in reality, for its audience.

By being drawn into the truth of this drama, we are drawn into the truth of God. The episode tells several times that the evil spirit is "from God/the LORD" (16:14, 15, 16, 23). For hard-hearted ancients, like Tertullian, it was easy to deal with God sending an evil spirit into a person: "The right to tempt a person," he claims, "is granted to the devil, either for the sake of a trial . . . or for . . . the reprobation of a sinner, who is handed over to the devil as to an executioner. This was the case with Saul. 'The spirit of the Lord departed from Saul, and an evil spirit from the Lord troubled and stifled him'" (*On Flight in Time of Persecution* 2.6–7, in Franke 2005: 264). Conversely, some contemporary commentators regard this sending of an evil spirit as an effect of the darker side of God's nature.

If we hear the episode from within the drama, we hear it differently. Christian tradition has reflected on the strange fact of the stay of doom upon Saul. Saul's charism has been excised, and David has been anointed. From here on, Saul's days are numbered. This story is the first of several episodes in which disaster is averted from Saul by the hand of David. The withholding of punishment from Saul is an expression of God's mercy, and it is effected by David. In other words, whereas modern exegetes consider it problematic that a just God would torment Saul with an evil spirit and stress the theodicial aspect of the story, an older Christian tradition of exegesis thinks it merciful of God to delay Saul's death and stresses the providential aspect of the story. Commenting on one of David's many deliverances, Calvin writes that David's "soul is filled with admiration of the providence of God, which extends itself to the whole human race" (1845–46: 2.89). Christian tradition has seen the stay of writ upon the psalmist-king's predecessor as showing that God numbers the days even of fallen Saul. The theme of divine providence is not acutely dramatic in this episode. It is a setback being troubled by an evil spirit, but the courtiers treat the problem as soluble, not mortal. Saul is not yet placed in danger of the death that alone will enable David to be publicly established as king. It is only later in the story that we can look back and see that the theme of a delayed providence has been introduced here, with David's entrée to the court.

Ever since the seventeenth century, David has been a gift to defenders of the musical and poetic arts against the puritanical objections to the esthetic side of religion. David the musician and David the sublime poet are examples of literal or historicizing typology. The parallel is central to the iconography of David: you don't need to be a medieval art history buff to pick David out in Romanesque capitals and Gothic windows: he's the one carrying a harp. The harp is the sign that, down the ages, has seemed to connect us best with the Late Bronze Age shepherd. David's musicality is something that we can identify with without projecting ourselves into him. David's musicality links us up with him, because this is the talent that makes him universal in his humanity. Human beings are not the only musical animals: David's musicality makes him not only everyman but representative of all sentient creatures. Just as the romantics thought of the poet as the antennas of the human spirit most attuned to the divine spirit, so David is pictured in 1–2 Samuel "as a mediator always remembered for being in the betwixt and between . . . between north and south, between the Judahites and all Israel, . . . between egalitarianism and monopolized force and, like the ark, between human and divine realms" (Flanagan 1988: 271).

The nineteenth-century romantic poet Robert Browning imagined David as an archetypal artistic genius. By itself, the literal type of David as the musician or the poet is too narrow, because it comes at his universal human appeal the wrong way round, from his humanity. From Augustine to Calvin, David is not simply a poet: he is a psalmist. What sort of harpist did the servant recommend to Saul? The servant tells his master that he knows of a man, "a son of Jesse the Beth-lehemite," that is, a Benjamite warrior like Saul "that is cunning in playing, and a mighty valiant man, and a man of war" (16:18). Christian tradition has imagined David using his harp to celebrate the Lord's providential succor only because it has conceived David as the author of the psalms ascribed to him in the Psalter. If we imagine the David of 1 Samuel with a harp, singing to enhance his own military prowess but as no psalmist, singing to praise God's merciful assistance, we have perhaps taken our first step toward the many modern portrayals of David as an egotistic bandit. Without the David of the Psalter, the piety of the David of 1 Samuel is easily demolished. A David who sings no hymns will be no choirboy. Christian tradition never questioned that David is the author of a portion of the Psalter because it interpreted him christologically. Christ puts the Psalter into the hand of David. Adherence to Chalcedonian Christology makes us see the warrior-griot of 1 Sam. 16 as a psalmist. This is the backdrop to that very important monument of the human imagination, David the poet.

David is the desirable human type, the perfection of humanity, because "the LORD is with him" (16:18). David is esthetically absorbing because he is inspired by the Spirit. Origen is closer to our Old Testament text than the seventeenth-century Anglican poetasters or the nineteenth-century romantics when he argues that the Christian scripture is "a single instrument of God, perfect and well adjusted, transmitting with varied sounds a single salutary voice for whoever consents to hear it, soothing and holding in check the malignant spirit, just as the music of David suppressed the evil spirit that had taken possession of Saul. Everything in them is unified by the one Logos to which the one Spirit leads" (cited in Lubac 2007: 346). David's singing and playing is assimilated by Origen to the Logos, to the works of reason, and with sound scriptural testimony, since "the teachings of Israel's wise men," the Proverbs, "are all composed in a poetic form, . . . are poetry" (von Rad 1972: 24). But is it equally sound to assimilate David to Christ?

Today, our greatest fear about typological linkups between David and Christ is that the image of Christ will be superimposed upon that of David. Christians want to avoid spiritual imperialism. But in fact, their linking works the other way as well. When we authentically link David the ancestor of Jesus of Nazareth with the Christ of Christian faith, we know more about Christ than we would otherwise. It is David who puts the harp into the hand of Christ. We would never have known that the Logos sings had it not been for the legacy that David passes to him and, through him, to us. The idea of an esthetic, musical analogy for inspiration is taken by Origen from David's playing the harp. For Origen, it is not only the esthetic side of faith, but also the beauty of divine inspiration apparent in David and emerging in its revealed fullness in the face of Christ.

David has always been appealing to humanists because he is one of the very few culture heroes in the Bible. The biblical heroes can sometimes seem to be a grim, puritanical lot. Likewise, some biblical scholars claim that the Bible is uniformly positive about unsettled, nomadic shepherds and consistently negative about cities and urbanites, those centers of human civilization.[15] There are those who believe that the monarchy founded in David is an absolute and intrinsic departure from authentic Yahwism: "Not until the *destruction* of state and temple," Mendenhall claims, "was there a possibility of rediscovering the Mosaic oneness of God, and the recognition that God is more than merely a political symbol of unity" (1973: 152, emphasis original). David with his harp, as the legendary author of the Psalms and as Israel's great monarch, seems to offset such austere opinions, in favor of human culture. He seems to represent God's blessing on human artistry. The first reference to a harpist in the Bible is Gen. 4:21: Cain's grandson Jubal is "the father of them that play upon the harp and the organs" (Douay-Rheims). After that the Bible goes mute on musicians: no character plays the harp again in the Pentateuch or in Joshua or Judges. Cain's descendants, including Tubal-cain (the "hammerer and artificer in every work of brass and iron"; Gen. 4:22 Douay-Rheims), were construed as the nomadic Kenites. The natural inference from this is that Israelite culture was remembered as having been no richer in musicianship than it was in metallurgy. Our second biblical reference to harpists is near the outset of Saul's story: Samuel tells Saul that "thou shalt come to the hill of God, where is the garrison of the Philistines: and . . . when thou art come . . . to the city, . . . thou shalt meet a company of prophets coming down from the high place with a psaltery, and a tabret, and a pipe, and a harp before them; and they shall prophesy" (1 Sam. 10:5). In the episode that gave rise to the saying "is Saul also among the prophets?" there is no musicality in Saul's charisma: "A company of the prophets met him, and the Spirit of God came upon him, and he prophesied among them" (10:10). So one difference between Saul's prophesying and David's inspiration is that with David, the divine gift flows into a human artifact, the harp, transfiguring it by inspiring his playing, whereas the spirit that Saul takes on is tone-deaf. It does not enter the forms of human culture, as it does with both the wild hillside prophets and David. David is a cultured prophet who has the imagination to borrow the use of the harp from Israel's hostile, neighboring tribes. In that respect, there is something of a romantic in David.

Nonetheless, the romantic idea of David as the type of the poet is one-sided. It conceives of the poet as someone who has the gift of imagination, whereas it may make more sense to speak of David as a man who has the gift of inspiration. We are not literally told here that David's harping is inspired. We hear that Saul's men think that music might calm what they designate as Saul's demonic possession: "Saul's servants said unto him, 'Behold now, an evil spirit from God troubleth thee. Let our lord now command thy servants, which are before thee, to seek out a man, who is a cunning player on a harp: and it shall come to pass, when the evil spirit from God is upon thee, that he shall play with his hand, and

15. The best treatment is Herbert Schneidau, *Sacred Discontent: The Bible and Western Tradition* (Berkeley: University of California Press, 1977).

thou shalt be well'" (16:15–16). If we go literally from this text alone, it is only a superstitious impulse, though a fairly solid one, that leans us toward thinking that David is inspired: we infer that, since David's playing can expel the "evil spirit from God," he must have a gift akin to that of the musical company of prophets of 10:5. Saul's servants seem to have the same superstitious idea that the musician is one possessed: when they decide to send for "a cunning player on the harp," they seem to imagine that one can counter evil possession with good possession. This soundly primitive idea shows why the romantics were all too modern in their conception of artistic gifts: even on a nontheological level, and simply as telling us about the religiosity of the characters who people 1 Samuel, music making is conceived as a kind of shamanism, or spirit possession, not as plying the humane power of imagination. Shamanism and exorcism are live realities in the Christian communities of the southern hemisphere.[16]

Saul's spirit possession does not run over into human cultural artistry, whereas David's does. But on the other hand, it really *is* possession that enables David to ply his harp so well that it can drive an evil spirit away. Like the highland bagpipers, David is putting the instruments of human culture, or imagination, at the service of divine inspiration. As the founder of Israel's monarchy, who united the tribes and made Jerusalem the capital city of their state, David is the Bible's central image of good urbanity, the positive side of human culture and civilization. Israel's enculturation in ancient Palestine, with its borrowings of such human arts as metallurgy and musicianship, was positive to the extent that it laid these gifts in the service of its covenanted Lord. David's united Israel gave the ancient world one great artifact, the Psalms. It is in singing those Psalms that Israel was at its most devout: "Israel is happy when it sings" (von Balthasar 1983–91: 6.211). It is because David is his ancestor that we imagine Christ as the lord of civilization and the king of human culture.

So did the evil spirit come from God or didn't it? Jerome effectively equates the evil spirit with the absence of God, God's permission of its evil activity: "Does God, then, have an evil spirit? Not at all. God had withdrawn so that afterwards an evil spirit might trouble Saul. In that sense, the spirit of God is called evil" (*Homilies on the Psalms* 9, in Franke 2005: 264). The text does tell us four times (16:14, 15, 16, 23) that the evil spirit was "from God." Tertullian's blunt concession that God hands persons over to the devil for testing or punishment seems closer to the spirit of the text, given that we read 1 Sam. 16 within the later development of the notion of the devil in Israelite theology,[17] that is, given that we read it within Jewish and Christian tradition as a whole. Prior to the postexilic evolution of the notion of angelic powers hostile to God, the earlier Israelite theology wanted to exhibit the truth that everything that happens, good or ill, comes from God. The

16. Philip Jenkins, *The Next Christendom: The Coming of Global Christianity* (Oxford: Oxford University Press, 2002), 122–29.

17. A classical treatment is D. S. Russell, *The Method and Message of Jewish Apocalyptic* (London: SCM, 1964), chap. 9: "Angels and Demons" (235–62).

later theology recognized that something in God's good creation has elected to oppose God. The simplest answer to the theodicial problem raised by 1 Sam. 16's evil spirit is that Christ alone conquers the devil. Nicetas of Remesiana, who hailed from Yugoslavia, a country long rich in oral song cycles, tells us that "you will find plenty of men and women, filled with a divine spirit, who sang of the mysteries of God." David "became the prince of singers. . . . He was still a boy when his sweet, strong song with his harp subdued the evil spirit working in Saul. Not that there was any kind of power in the harp, but, with its wooden frame and the strings stretched across, it was a symbol of the cross of Christ. It was the passion that was being sung, and it was this which subdued the spirit of the devil" (*Liturgical Singing* 4, in Franke 2005: 265).

Episode Three: The Slinger (1 Sam. 17)

None of the scenes of single-handed combat in Homer's epic of war or in Vergil's Roman successor has achieved the mythic universality of this historical, biblical tale. One reason is that it is much simpler and more naïve. Both Achilles' fight with Hector in the *Iliad* and Aeneas's climactic defeat of Turnus in the *Aeneid* are psychologically and artistically complex. Achilles and Hector, kings of the Greeks and the Trojans, and "Trojan" Aeneas and Turnus king of the indigenous Sabines, are evenly matched in their social status and military prowess. The deaths of Hector and Turnus both have tragic overtones. They participate in the grandeur of the epic milieu from which they spring. No Greek or Roman epic poet would dream of matching a shepherd against a giant. As against the tragic endings of the Homeric and Vergilian epics of war, the slaying of the hulking Goliath by the youthful shepherd is a straightforward happy dénouement.

At the same time, all is not quite what it seems, and we know that. It is not the uneven conquest of a Philistine champion by an anonymous boy that it looks like on the surface. Few are taken in. It is not about a *habiru*, a socially marginal migrant, taking on a terrifying tyrant,[18] and anyone who has read the preceding chapters of 1 Samuel knows that. In this story, a secretly anointed king throws down the gauntlet to a representative member of the most God-mocked tribe in sacred scripture. A Martian who had thus far read only from Joshua to 1 Sam. 16 could grasp that David is a prince-in-waiting and the Philistine a booby. The Israelites are in danger from the Philistines from Joshua to the end of 1 Samuel, where Saul dies at their hands, but the supremacy of God's chosen heroes over these enemies of God is an edge-of-the-seat affair in a way similar to that of Jason Bourne over his amoral assailants in *The Bourne Identity* and its sequels: thrilling, but not unanticipated. You don't have to know God's injunction to Samuel, "Man looks on the outward appearance, but the LORD looks on the heart" (16:7

18. Brueggemann, *David's Truth*, 31.

ESV), to intuit that this is what the story is about. It is the secret of its universal, mythic appeal, because everyone knows that appearances are deceptive and because everyone likes it that way. Or, they'd like to like it that way. The truth that Plato wrote a philosophy to expound is told in 1 Sam. 17 as an adventure story. But Platonists are not all that sure that the deceptiveness of appearance is amiable. It is a conundrum for them, and a tragedy: Socrates was a martyr to truth over the common opinions of the Athenian jurors, their susceptibility to false appearances. Whereas, for the Bible, the deceptiveness of appearance is weighted to winning: it launches the heart to triumph over the appearance. It is because we yearn to believe that "strength is made perfect in weakness" (2 Cor. 12:9) that the inspired authority of scripture is humanly gripping. That weakness is deceptive is what launches the underdog to victory. This is why David is a great comic hero, and the biblical vision is ultimately a comedy.

This story bridges the staging of the signature theme of the "vision of the heart" in 1 Sam. 1:11–20 and 1 Sam. 16 and the overt presentation of David as a wise man, that is a wisdom figure, in 1 Sam. 24–26. The contrast of externals and true reality was important to the wisdom tradition of the Hebrew proverbs, because these are concerned with presenting a "radical concept of God's guidance," which is neither sacral nor secular in the modern senses: God is determining events, but invisibly. And it follows from the invisibility of God that we cannot literally, empirically see God acting: we must use the eyes of the mind and the heart, not our physical eyesight to perceive his works. It thus becomes both a less and a more than simple thing to know God. So, we cannot know for sure what God will do: "The teachers take a man out of the security of his perceptions" (von Rad 1972: 98–99), teaching us that

> A man's steps come from Yahweh,
>   how then can a man understand his way? (Prov. 20:24, trans. von Rad)

This perception that human beings are reliant on trust in God comes from Israel's wisdom tradition. Wisdom does not set faith and reason against each other. Rather, it recognizes that a reasonable person accepts the dimension of faith in human life.

To succeed as literature, a story about optical illusions must be intensely visual. First Sam. 17:1–3 gives us a field that is most satisfying for the eye, that is, a left-to-right contrast. In the middle, a valley, with opposed armies arrayed on either side: "The Philistines stood on a mountain on the one side, and Israel stood on a mountain on the other side: and there was a valley between them" (17:3). On strides Goliath, clanking in his armor. We are made to see him from top to toe, before we hear him: "six cubits and a span" tall, "a helmet of brass upon his head," "a coat of mail" weighing "five thousand shekels of brass," "greaves of brass upon his legs," "a target [body shield] of brass between his shoulders." Every inch the new Iron Age warrior, Goliath carries a "spear . . . like a weaver's beam," weighing in at "six hundred shekels of iron." He has need of a "shield" carrier, leaving both arms free to wield his ton weight of spear (17:4–7). It's a lesson in how to look invincible.

The symbol of Iron Age Philistia asks to meet the representative Israelite: "Am not I a Philistine, and you servants to Saul?" (17:8). In terms of his armor, Goliath is no different from his Bronze Age Mycenaean forebears, who, on the Warrior Vase wear long-sleeved tunics under corsets of steel, "greaves that reach just above the knee, and protective helmets" (Stager 1998: 169). But in terms of his weapons, his sword and spear, Goliath is bedecked with the tokens of an Iron Age warrior. Having left behind the crude weaponry of the Bronze Age, the Philistines were culturally ahead. The Israelites have just made their first gesture toward advancing beyond an acephalous Late Bronze Age culture. Our author uses anaphonics, the ventriloquism of Israel's theology by pagan speakers. You are "servants to Saul" (17:8), Goliath says, sounding like Samuel at his most sarcastic; designating himself as a "Philistine," Goliath identifies his antagonists not as "Israelites" but "Saul's people." If your man can "kill me, then will we be your servants," the Philistines and what were once the tribes of Yahweh, all "servants to Saul." And conversely, "if I prevail against him, and kill him, then shall ye be our servants, and serve us" (17:9). Goliath is channeling the Samuel of 1 Sam. 8: first servility to kings, followed logically by enslavement to foreign overlords. Goliath has made championing the "servants to Saul" sound like a contradiction in terms: a "heroic servant." "The Philistine said, 'I defy the armies of Israel this day.'" Goliath stands for his people: which of the heroic servants will represent the servant-tribe: "Give me a man, that we may fight together" (17:10)? The proposed single combat does not so much replace the battle between the two forces as it symbolizes its outcome: the victory of either man will be a sign to one army that their gods prevail. And Israel has been designated, not as "the people of Yahweh," but as the "servants to Saul."

Leaving "Saul and all Israel . . . dismayed, and greatly afraid" (17:11), the next plate in the storyboard depicts Jesse's homestead. The author paints in what was sketched but not specified in the previous chapter: Jesse is reckoned an old man, too old to fight or to farm, "Eliab [is] the firstborn, and next unto him Abinadab, and the third Shammah." The eldest of the sons are in the battle lines, but David "the youngest" has been sent back from entertaining Saul's court to tend "his father's sheep at Beth-lehem" (17:12–15). After briskly returning to Goliath's daily repeated taunts on the battlefield—the "forty days" (17:16) of Goliathan insults give the hero a realistic interval to scuttle from Bethlehem to Ephes-dammim—the cue for David comes in reported speech. Jesse orders his youngest to take bread and "ten cheeses" (17:18) to the Israelite captain and find out how his soldier brothers are holding up: the retired farmer is in such tranquil ignorance of events that he doesn't know that "the Philistine" (17:16) is waiting to be matched with an Israelite.

Being made to glide from one story arc to another makes the auditor feel like a participant observer. David doesn't just vamoose by magic and reappear at the scene. He has responsibilities: he leaves "the sheep with a keeper" and gathers up the supplies "and took, and went" (17:20). The proliferation of verbs in the chapter—David doesn't just go, he takes first—both give the story drive *and* slow it down, permitting the audience to savor every detail and making this savoring of the details unleash the significance of the conquest of the armed man by the boy.

Now we see the opposed, left-to-right armies again, as David observes the scene for the first time: "Israel and the Philistines had put the battle in array, army against army" (17:21). He hears the same words that we have heard before, from "the Philistine of Gath, Goliath by name" (17:23). David sees, as we have, "all the men of Israel" retreating in fear from this man. The episodes have pointers to their sequels. This is a lead-in to the later tale of David becoming Jonathan's friend. It is important to their friendship that David derogates Goliath just as Jonathan had deprecated the Philistines at Michmash. "Come, let us go over to the garrison of these uncircumcised. It may be that the LORD will work for us, for nothing can hinder the LORD from saving by many or by few" (14:6 ESV), Jonathan had said at Michmash, and David likewise is utterly unimpressed by the spectacle of Goliath. He brushes aside the idea that a reward is being offered for taking on an enemy of God: "What shall be done to the man that killeth this Philistine, and taketh away the reproach from Israel? for who is this uncircumcised Philistine, that he should defy the armies of the living God?" (17:26). For David, the question is not how much, for killing him, but who does he think he is, to challenge God's army? Like Jonathan, David imagines the circumstance theologically rather than materially, and this enables him to see the empirical facts better than those who look at the facts on the ground. With the wisdom teachers, David recognizes that "a man's mind thinks out his own way, but Yahweh directs his step" (Prov. 16:9, trans. von Rad 1972: 100).

A fanciful element enters, from the people's gossip, a populist enlargement on the news: "The man who killeth him, the king will enrich . . . with great riches, and will give him his daughter" (1 Sam. 17:25). Saul's promise of promotion to a challenger has aroused Israelite fantasies without rousing their courage. People would rather think about anything than the present situation. Instead of feeling angry with Goliath or angry with his torpid brothers-at-arms, Eliab turns his ire on David:[19] "Why [is] this—thou hast come down! and to whom hast thou left those few sheep in the wilderness?" Eliab claims to see through David: "I have known thy pride, and the evil of thy heart—for, to see the battle thou hast come down" (17:28 Young). Eliab's honor is wounded that David should witness his older brothers as partners to a defeated army. We were shown the layout, then we saw it again through David's eyes, and now we see Eliab reacting to being caught out in this mess by his younger brother. The theme is seeing and being seen by.

David keeps repeating his contempt for an uncircumcised enemy of God from one group of soldiers to the next until his attitude is reported down the lines to

19. Ibid., 32.

Saul himself, who calls David in and tells him, it's impossible: "Thou are not able to go against this Philistine to fight with him: for thou art but a youth, and he a man of war from his youth" (17:33). Just as 17:1–24 paints a graphic scene, so David's reply to Saul gives a visual picture of his own past experience in combat (Polzin 1989: 169): "A lion, and a bear . . . took a lamb . . . and I went out after him, and smote him" and rescued the lamb from its jaws, and, when the beast reared upon David, "I caught him by his beard" and struck and killed it (17:34–35). David is not just boasting. He is showing us—and Saul—that he can see this challenge, get the measure of it, by analogy to his brawls with wild animals. Wisdom thinking is about learning to see reality truly. To see reality with one's imagination is to see the hidden thread connecting things: "Like vinegar to the teeth and smoke to the eyes, so is the lazy man to those who send him" (Prov. 10:26, trans. von Rad 1972: 120). Proverbial wisdom is full of comparisons because likening one thing to another teaches us to "bring out analogies" (von Rad 1972: 120). David has an analogical imagination, shown by his use of this proverbial analogy to dramatize the likeness between his God-given power over animals and that over Goliath. The analogy enables him to liken Goliath to an animal and to see that the power of God makes the two cases analogous.

To David's imagination, Goliath is not a representative of an advanced culture, but just like a hostile wild beast. David explicitly parallels the two: "Thy servant slew both the lion and the bear: and this uncircumcised Philistine shall be as one of them, seeing he hath defied the armies of the living God" (1 Sam. 17:36). This is the first time the expression "the living God" has occurred in 1 Samuel. A fighting army is violent, and so it is hugely energetic: in the Deuteronomistic History, it is as fighters that God's chosen ones express the vitality and energy of the God who is. Half the psalms in the Christian Psalter are about the God of battles (not that I've counted); you can hardly read or say the Psalter alongside 1 Samuel without seeing that it is the *same* God. Both speak of God as a fighting victor in war so as to give a picture of God's active energy. The one Lord is not statically omnipotent, but actively triumphant. To David, the opponent is subhuman, not because David himself is a member of a master race, an *Übermensch*, but because "the LORD [hath] delivered me out of the paw of the lion, and out of the paw of the bear, he will deliver me out of the hand of the Philistine" (17:37). So Saul sent him to it.

Saul puts his own armor on David, an eminently practical but also a symbolic gesture. David is to go as Saul's representative, and Saul is making him an extension of himself. The narrator does not make Saul suggest the idea of his armor or make David take a look at it and refuse it. David actually tries the armor on, becoming Saul's replica. The narrative combines speed and leisurely pace. Saul's daughter has been promised to the victor, and, clothed in the king's armor, David is already stepping into the role of surrogate son. He promptly steps out of it, with a tactful subterfuge. Is David's polite refusal—"I cannot go with these: for I have not proved them" (17:39)—a piece of diplomacy, not his full reasoning?

We cannot know that yet. We just get a hint of what we will repeatedly find in 1 Sam. 18–31, that David uses language sparingly and cunningly, as the wise men taught. It would not in fact be the best idea to make a trial to the death turn on an experiment with unaccustomed armor. As John Cassian recognized, "put[ting] on Saul's manly and heavy armor . . . would . . . have imperiled the boy" so "he chose the kind of weaponry that was appropriate for his youth and armed himself . . . with the projectiles that he himself was able to fight with" (*Conference* 24.8.1–2, in Franke 2005: 272). So David is not being dishonest, but he is not telling the whole truth. David cannot see himself in Saul's armor, helmet, and chain mail. He could not know that without putting them on. "David put them off him" (17:39): David will not sally forth as a replica of Saul, but as himself.

The episode is about being conned by images, by externals: "When the Philistine looked about, and saw David, he disdained him: for he was but a youth, and ruddy, and of a fair countenance" (17:42). It was arrogant Philistine contempt for Jonathan and his batman that gave the pair their leg-up at Michmash. There, the Philistine watchmen despised what they saw as two more cowering Israelites. Goliath sees the absence of soldier's gear and sees no man of war before him. He picks up exactly what David needs him to notice, the unarmed pretty boy. If he had looked anything like Michelangelo's David, Goliath might have taken a second look, whatever his sexual proclivities (or perhaps not, being, after all, a Philistine).

"Am I a dog?" Goliath asks, "that thou comest to me with staves? And the Philistine cursed David by his gods" (17:43). David does in fact see Goliath as an animal, by dint of comparing the living God to the lifeless images to which the heathen ally themselves. David is controlling the moment, imposing his way of seeing on the opponent. Why demean one another verbally before the physical assault begins? The greatest epic of the griot of West Africa is the *Epic of Sundiata*, the legend-history of Sunjata, founder of the Mali Empire in the thirteenth century. Sunjata's defeat of the sorcerer Sumanguru is his pivotal step to chieftainship: "Before they joined battle, Sunjata and Sumanguru exchanged conventional boasts and challenges, for, as the griot observed, 'One does not wage war without saying why it is being waged'" (Iliffe 2005: 24). David and Goliath exchange abuse to express their reasons for fighting. The Philistine threatens to feed David to the birds and the beasts. David curses "in the name of the LORD of hosts," in whose power he goes forth to slay and decapitate Goliath (17:46).

With a volley of verbs—thirty-six in seven verses—17:48–54 suddenly accelerates the action. The Philistine *arose, came, drew nigh*; David *hasted, ran, put, took, slang, smote*; the stone *sunk*; Goliath *fell*; so David *prevailed, smote* and *slew, ran* and *stood* over his felled opponent, *took* the other man's sword, *drew* it, *slew* Goliath, and *cut off* his head; the Philistine army *saw* and *fled*; in counterpoint, the Israelite armies *arose, shouted, pursued*; and as the Philistines *fell* their conquerors *spoiled* their supplies; and David *took* Goliath's head and *put* his enemy's valuable bronze armor aside for himself. The living God of whom David spoke has brought the Israelites to life in David.

David has stated why the fight is his to win: "The battle is the LORD's, and he will give you into our hands" (17:47). It is not only a Protestant impulse to turn the David and Goliath story into a fable about the unmerited imputation of grace. It is not just a Christian quirk. It is not even just an obvious experiential lacuna on the part of scholars who have never stabbed anything more than a keyboard in anger. In the first century AD, Josephus, who had taken part in the Jewish uprising against the Romans in 66–73, tells the tale as if David himself had imparted nothing to it. In his retelling of 1 Sam. 17, the Jewish historian wrote that when David encountered Goliath, he was "accompanied by an ally invisible to the foe, and this was God." Josephus's "paraphrase deftly excises the Deuteronomist's recurrent suspicion that human actions have some natural consequences of their own."[20]

Wevers cites a traditional opinion, when he states that, in this combat, David is no more than an "instrument" in God's hands (1971: 164), and it may seem willfully provocative to run counter to this widespread judgment. But we may have a sneaking suspicion that Maximus of Turin's desire to put "a spiritual sword" (Sermon 85.3, in Franke 2005: 274) into David's hand is rather effete. Even our Martian, with his droidlike total recall of Judg. 20:16 (the Benjamites who "could sling a stone at a hair and not miss" [ESV]), when he sees David pick up "five smooth stones" and slip them in the "shepherd's bag" that he carried for such tackle and observes that "his sling was in hand" (17:40), knows that the contest has evened up. We know that the two men will meet on a valley between two steep slopes and that a boy who is disencumbered of armor can run much faster than a man dressed like a tank, whose armor and weapons are so heavy than he needs a second to carry his shield. With its thirty-six verbs, the battle scene is about speed. In his retelling of the tale Heller's David explains, "I would spend whole mornings and afternoons practicing with my sling in order to help the time go faster. I knew I was good. . . . And with Goliath that day, I knew that if I could get within twenty-five paces of the big son of a bitch, I could sling a stone the size of a pig's knuckle down his throat with enough velocity to penetrate the back of his neck and kill him, and . . . I knew if I was wrong about that, I could turn and run . . . and dodge my way back up the hill to safety without much risk from anyone chasing me in all that armor" (1985: 90). Another reader who seems to attend to the voice of this text is Mather Byles, a Protestant minister who preached on it in 1740, before the Massachusetts Artillery:

> Not a man, not a Captain bold enough to issue from their Ports, and engage the brawny Champion: they all shrunk behind their Entrenchments, and retreated from the thundering Defiance. Thus it was that David . . . heard the menace of the godless Giant, and a generous Indignation fired his Breast. . . . The Rosey Warriour

20. Jan Wojcik, "Discriminations against David's Tragedy in Ancient Jewish and Christian Literature," in *The David Myth in Western Literature*, ed. Raymond-Jean Frontain and Jan Wojcik (West Lafayette, IN: Purdue University Press, 1980), 23, citing Josephus, *Jewish Antiquities* 6.189.

... with a Sling, and a few Pebbles, runs out to the glorious Expedition. ... The mighty Philistine hasted onward, and David rushed to meet him ... while the Sling in his Hand whirled round, and away sung the Victor-Stone toward the broad Front of the Enemy. It strook, it crushed, it sunk, and down the proud Boaster thundring to the Plain. This was the Courage, and this the Success of David; and Devotion and Religion was the Spring and the Basis of all. A Zeal for the God of Israel inspired his glowing Breast, and a firm trust in Him animated him, undaunted in the Undertaking, compounded of Religion and Enterprize.[21]

Turning his "Undertaking" into a "compound ... of Religion and Enterprize" may seem to us to make it say that the living God only added some vim to David's native cunning and slinging skill. The fear of a compound makes us retreat and entrench ourselves in a picture of David as a helpless boy-child, no running dynamo, but a passive implement of divine providence who goes humanly naked into combat. If we expect the patristic and medieval commentators and artists to be replete with christological interpretations of David, we will be surprised at how little taken they were by the image of David's physical exploits. David and Goliath first captured the imaginations of artists at the Renaissance. It was at the Renaissance that David's great humanity was heroized and lauded. David came to the foreground of the biblical story as a humanist hero for a humanistic age. In reaction against this recent addition to our tradition, many Christians have some distaste for interpreting the story as a tale of human courage against a stronger foe, backed up but not enabled by God.

The text that Byles is preaching on was 17:45, the "ardent reply" of David to Goliath's insults: "Thou comest to me with a sword, and with a spear, and with a shield: but I come to thee in the name of the Lord of Hosts, the God of the armies of Israel, whom thou hast defied."[22] David's want of a sword is repeated by the narrator after the first strike has left the giant flat on his face: "David prevailed over the Philistine with a sling and with a stone ... but there was no sword in the hand of David" (17:50). It may be better to take on the powers of evil in naked fear and trembling, but it seldom feels like the right move at the time. Whatever he knew intellectually about slings and speed, it took courage to step out without a sword, and David's courage was activated by the living God, with no "buts" about it. "He who trusts in himself is a fool, but he who walks in wisdom escapes" (Prov. 28:26, trans. von Rad 1972: 102). Because it inculcated the invisibility of divine wisdom to the naked human gaze, and therefore that a human being "must always remain open for a completely new experience" since

21. Mather Byles, *The Glories of the Lord of Hosts, and the Fortitude of the Religious Hero: A Sermon Preached to the Ancient and Honourable Artillery Company June 2, 1740* (Boston: Thomas Fleet & Joseph Edwards, 1740), 8–9, cited from Marie L. Ahearn, "David: The Military Exemplum," in *The David Myth in Western Literature*, ed. Raymond-Jean Frontain and Jan Wojcik (West Lafayette, IN: Purdue University Press, 1980), 113–14.

22. Ahearn, "David," 113–14.

"this life of yours is determined . . . by God," Israel's wisdom tradition taught that "self-glorification cannot be combined with trust in Yahweh. . . . Wisdom itself can never become the object of trust, never become that upon which a man leans his life" (von Rad 1972: 106, 102–3).

If there are no "buts" about the God-givenness of David's courage, there is an "and." It is a God-given "and." David's appearance deceives the Philistine because Goliath despises him: the Jew is a representative of a backward culture. He's looking at a throwback, someone using a Bronze Age weapon. It may be true that, as he "lumbers forward like a peasant with a pitchfork," Goliath "never has a chance to close with David," but no one at that time considered the slingshot the cutting edge of conquest in the Early Iron Age. It's with Helleresque hindsight that Halpern recognizes that David's slingshot was still "state-of-the-art weaponry in Iron Age warfare" (1996: 41); he appreciates now what no one on the scene perceived, that David's sling is a match for Goliath's iron spear. By making the first and exemplary combat of David turn on antiquated weaponry, the Jewish scripture pays tribute to the living presence of memory. For the Jews, the past and its culture was not a dead letter, but ever refreshed and ever reborn. David steps forth with no iron spear or sword not because he is going weaponless, but because God wills to activate the ancient tradition in him. God activates the tradition, and David lives the tradition. Memory comes to life in his actions, and perhaps in those of one or two of his heirs. David's use of an antiquated sling against a modern man with contemporary iron weapons symbolizes God's bringing the tradition to life. With its repetitions, sometimes discounted as interpolations but integral to its literary texture, the Hebrew narrative works by doing the same thing over, with a little difference. For instance, David's story is like Jonathan's, but more so. The Hebrew scriptures think in verbal, dramatic analogies. The way that the ancient memory of how to fight and win is brought to life in David's enterprising action is analogous to what the living God himself is like. David in his single combat at Ephes-dammim is an expression of the character of the living God. We are not meant to think about apportioning weight to God or to David in this story. David's surprising means of victory is a symbol of what God is like. This is the God who brings the dead to life. This is the God whose might is his mercy, the Father of Jesus Christ.

Saul has apparently lost any memory of David's musical appearances at his court. First Sam. 17:15 ("but David went and returned from Saul to . . . Beth-lehem") has been regarded as a negligent redactional slip, because the Saul of 17:55–58 does not seem to know the boy. The conclusion is taken to be "another version of David's introduction to the court," because "Saul again does not recognize David—in spite of verse 31!" (Wevers 1971: 164–65). Saul turns to Abner and says, "Ask thou whose son this [is]—the young man" (17:55, trans. Polzin). This is the first time someone sees the worth of another in the episode: "What's *this*?" Saul is asking: "Will you look at *that*?" The demonstrative pronoun "this" is used in a derogatory form throughout the episode. The Israelites call Goliath "this man" and "this Philistine" (17:25, 26, 32, 33); Eliab asks David slightingly, "What is this coming down of yours?" (17:28, trans. Polzin); David set aside Saul's armor, saying, "I cannot go with these" (17:39). Saul's "this," the first nondeprecatory demonstrative in the episode, shows that a narrative about mutual derision has just turned into one about amazement. It is the first time the emphasis has come off the "this" and onto the absent verb: who the heck *is* this guy? Saul is pushing the question of paternity. Asking three times "whose son," twice to Abner and then directly to David (17:55–56, 58), "is a compelling directive for the youth to call him father, just as he would later call David son (24:16)" (Polzin 1989: 172–73, 175). When von Rad designates 1 Sam. 16, 17, and 18 as "three mutually exclusive stories," he neglects what he himself taught so well about the self-restrained literary genius of the authors of these narratives (1962: 309). Far from forgetting their encounter in 17:31–39, where Saul kindly explained to David that "thou art but a youth" (17:33), when Saul asks David, "whose son art thou, thou young man?" Saul is prosecuting with paternal "self-irony" (Polzin 1989: 174) his own conviction for having been taken in by appearances. Theologically, the story is about memory come to life in David, in the memorial arts of war, and in the memory of the faith of Abraham, Samson, Gideon, Hannah, and Jonathan: the best literary means of conveying a memory brought to life is to make everyone from Jesse to Eliab to Saul somnolently forgetful of who he is. The sleight of Saulide memory enables our author to do what he loves best—to identify the protagonist out of his own mouth with an epiphanic flourish at the conclusion of an episode: "David answered, I am the son of thy servant Jesse the Beth-lehemite" (17:58).

This would be a corny story if David came on as the first-class harpist from the previous episode who now surprisingly demonstrates that he is just as brilliant with a sling and stone! Episodes in comic books and in television series have to stand alone as well as link up with their predecessors and sequels. The main actor who could realistically puncture the necessary narrative incognito of the boy-versus-giant theme is Saul, since David demonstrated his musical talents at court. As his namesake was to say a thousand years later, "a veil was over" his eyes (2 Cor. 3:15), because Saul's ignorance of the boy's identity is a prerequisite of the episode's independence. Saul's recognizing his armor-bearer from 16:21 and asking, "what you, back here again?" would detract from the theme. The independence is crucial here, because its theme is truth versus appearance, and someone with even more talents than he hitherto displayed is not the ideal candidate to show this. It would undermine the graphic simplicity of David's truth versus Goliath's appearance. With Goliath, all is show, presentation: "The Philistine . . . presented himself forty days" (17:16). With David, nothing is on show. David must be incognito, not only as anointed king, but even as harpist, even though the reader who has followed the whole series knows that the Spirit is with David. The author can create stand-alone episodes because he doesn't see them only temporally, coming one after another, but also sees them, in the simultaneity they would have in a set of wall paintings or on a storyboard.

What do we mean by saying that the David and Goliath episode is a victory of truth over deceptive appearance? Some would like to see it as about God's truth versus human truth. It is very natural for theologians to want to win David back for God. Ever since Michelangelo's 1504 statue of David, theologians have worried that David is being spoiled by secular Egyptians and made to represent human perfection. He stands in that famous statue naked, unadorned, one arm resting, the other raised as if carelessly to scratch his shoulder blade. As this David gazes into the distance, there is no sign of the bloody combat in which the hero has lately been embroiled, in which as the Deuteronomist crudely records, David takes Goliath's sword "and cut off his head therewith" (17:51); Michelangelo's David does not come before us as he came "before Saul with the head of the Philistine in his hand" (17:57). The head that had been the sign of David's triumph in Do-natello's 1432 sculpture and in Verocchio's 1475 clothed David has been excised from Michelangelo's bloodless Renaissance hero. David was won as a secular hero for early modern humanists at the cost of cauterizing the combative Late Bronze Age humanity allowed to him by the Deuteronomist and Donatello. The theologian does not need to recover David for theology by further denuding him of his humanity. It is in his humanity that David is a living memorial of the God he serves. In the statues of Donatello and Verocchio, the severed head is at David's feet. He has put his enemies under his feet. Truth triumphs over deception in this episode as good triumphing in battle over evil. Truth is not simply seen or intuited intellectually, but wrested out of swift, energetic combat with its enemies. Effortlessly vanquishing in unshielded innocence and carrying his footless foe's head away to prove it, David is the braggadocio of the living God.

In their ritual exchange of threat before hand-to-hand combat commenced, David had threatened to "give the carcases of the host of the Philistines this day unto the fowls of the air" (17:46). An Ethiopian Christian was inspired by these Old Testament verses to celebrate Amda Seyon in this praise song:

> Emperor, gainer of victory,
> His ancestor was the striker of Adal.
> When he appeared in Adal,
> The entrails [of the enemy] fell out
> Like a hyena that has eaten poison.
> Vulture, David's vulture,
> Follow behind me here!
> I shall give you shredded flesh to eat,
> I shall give you red blood to drink . . .
> We are called the Emperor's Jackals.

For this non-Chalcedonian version of Christianity, the "standard was that of the Old Testament, to which the Ethiopians attached the same veneration as the new" (Iliffe 2005: 54–55). It shows why we cannot draw on literal, historical typology in our construal of the story. This story, which captures the imaginations of all children, has been lost to adult Western Christian readers by the combination of a false respect for the literal meaning of the Old Testament and an inability to take that to its logical conclusion, as Ethiopian Christianity does. We thereby lose the imaginative dynamite of the story.

Of course the story is about Christ vanquishing Satan. Caesarius of Arles recognizes that the *new* thing Christ did, the leap into a new state of affairs achieved in Christ's conquest of Satan, lies behind this story. David's unprecedented courage is a shadow of an event as yet to come. "Why," asks Caesarius, did the Israelites "not dare to" fight "against their adversaries"? "Because David who typified Christ had not yet arrived. . . . Who was able to fight against the devil before Christ our Lord freed the human race from his power? Now the word *David* is interpreted as strong in hand; and what is stronger, brothers, than he who conquered the whole world, armed with a cross but not a sword" (Sermon 121.5, in Franke 2005: 268–69). The duel between David and Goliath, which Lemche unsurprisingly imagines "may never have taken place" (1978: 4), is not just reinterpreted by Christians to mean Christ's defeat of death. The combat between an apparently weaker hero and his overweening opponent becomes something new, because of Christ's conquest of the evil one. Caesarius's love of the doctrine of Christ's descent into hell is reputed to have led to the insertion of the line *descendit ad inferos* into the Apostles' Creed.[23] This victory, no less historical and no less a triumph of apparent weakness over apparent dominion than David's defeat of Goliath, was, Caesarius says, "prefigured in David" but "accomplished by our Lord Jesus Christ; for he strangled the lion and the bear when he descended into hell to free all the saints from their jaws" (Sermon 121.4, in Franke 2005: 271).

Episode Four: Friendship (1 Sam. 18:1–5)

As we inherit them in our Bibles, the chapter breaks are the invention of thirteenth-century biblical exegete Stephen Langton. First Sam. 18:1 is the next line following on David's self-identification: "I am the son of thy servant Jesse the Beth-lehemite" (17:58). Jonathan's "soul" is "knit with the soul of David," and he "love[s] him as his own soul" (18:1) because he has just seen him kill Goliath and provoke a rout of the Philistine army.

Friendship is a special kind of human love. Friends share a common interest. Whereas companions do things together, like plan battles, friends pick something out of their cooperative task as the important part of it. "Friendship arises," C. S. Lewis says in *The Four Loves*, "when two or more of the companions discover that they have in common some insight or interest or even taste that the others do not share and that, till that moment, each believed to be his own unique treasure

23. J. N. D. Kelly, *Early Christian Creeds* (London: Longmans, Green, 1950), chap. 12: "The Apostles' Creed (= T)."

(or burden). The typical expression of opening friendship would be something like, 'What? You too? I thought I was the only one.'" David and Jonathan are friends because they are both fighting Yahwists, with a common love of biffing Philistines. The text depicts the befriending as an immediate reaction to the vision of David holding the head of Goliath: "When he had made an end of speaking unto Saul" (18:1). At the sight of David the conqueror of the Philistine who had insulted "the armies" "of the Lord of hosts" (17:45), Jonathan is bowled over and recognizes a soul friend. Friendship has an element of "you too!" of finally escaping the loneliness of singular tastes and beliefs. At his appearance in 1 Sam. 14, Jonathan was the only figure who is both fighter and righteous Yahwist. He recognizes the same quality in David: "When two such persons discover one another, when, whether with immense difficulties . . . or with . . . amazing and elliptical speed, they share their vision—it is then that Friendship is born. And instantly they stand together in an immense solitude."[24]

Saul "took" David and "would let him go no more home to his father's house" (18:2). David has exchanged families. David and Jonathan "ma[k]e a covenant," because Jonathan "loved [David] as his own soul" (18:3): they become sworn friends, allies in this rural court. Jonathan strips off his own regal gear and hands it to David. Since the clothes are the man, Jonathan is symbolically giving him his own identity, with the status it carries. By handing him his own badges of honor, the insignia of a prince, Jonathan is honoring David as the true prince in Israel. The episode is making Jonathan the anchor of the story, the measure of the right reaction to David's defeating Goliath and instigating the Israelite army to a spirited assault on the Philistine camp. David's kingship is not just imposed by God, but recognized as right by the characters in 1 Samuel.

Since Saul had offered David his clothes, and David tried them on but rejected them, it is natural to compare the Jonathan and Saul scenes. It could look like David rejects Saul's gift of clothes but accepts Jonathan's (Gunn 1980: 80–81). It is not that simple, because the situations are not equivalent. David would have been a fool to go into the lists wearing the heavy armor of an older man. Nor are we shown David dressing in Jonathan's "garments, even to his sword, and to his bow, and to his girdle" (18:4). David inspires naked love, complete self-giving. Some think it important that we are told that Jonathan loved David, but never that David loved Jonathan (Polzin 1989: 178). This story shows David in the eyes of Jonathan, not because their friendship is not mutual, but because it's about how David looks to others. This story further characterizes David as a man beloved by the best in Israel, Jonathan, and "accepted in the sight of all the people, and also in the sight of Saul's servants" (18:5). The author is building a bridge between the all-too-human edifice of David's kingship in 2 Sam. 2 and 5, which "was due, as the accounts make clear, to human initiative, namely that of the 'men of Judah' and later on that of all the 'elders of Israel'" (von Rad 1962: 309), and the divine

24. C. S. Lewis, *The Four Loves* (London: HarperCollins, 2002), 78–79.

election of David in 1 Sam. 16. David is the king that God selected, and human beings spontaneously want him to be king, as symbolized by Jonathan's handing over to him his regal attire. Like grace, like the spirit of God, David is the object of natural human desire, what we most deeply want, and David is given to us by God. He is the point where the ends of human culture, which ultimately reaches for divinity, and God's providence meet.

Episode Five: King's Daughters (1 Sam. 18:6–30)

"Saul eyed David from that day and forward" (18:9) is the keynote of the story. It carries forward from the previous two episodes. The Goliath story was about display. David's giant-slaying had an immediate, efficient effect, provoking a rout of the Philistines by the hitherto torpid Israelite army. David had constructed a successful *gestalt*. One can appreciate a spectacle in more ways than one. The Jonathan episode was about David's figure in the eyes of love, and this, its antithesis, is about the single-minded eye of hatred.

The king returns home from the victory at Ephes-dammim to be greeted by women, "singing and dancing... with tabrets, and with joy, and with instruments of music" (18:6). Saul had once become king by public acclaim. He's not necessarily exhibiting paranoia when, hearing the women chant, "Saul hath slain his thousands, and David his tens of thousands" (18:7) he says, to no one in particular and as if in a direct aside to the audience, "What can he have more but the kingdom?" (18:8). The women's song makes a comparison, and the verse parallelism could be intended to mock. And yet, flowing from the author's faith that God's historical providence is inscribed in the hearts of men and women, a core theme of 1 Samuel is the deceptiveness of outward looking. The wise person knows that appearances are not everything, because one has, at the least, to be able to perceive analogies between things in order to track God's purposes, and knows that this probing inevitably carries us into mystery. Saul is deceived by David's appearance into conceiving him as a danger to himself.

The Saul of 1 Sam. 13–15 is literal and objectivistic. Saul lets himself be taken over by verbal automatisms, that is, by objective mechanisms that play themselves out willy-nilly. In 1 Sam. 14 he took two oaths. The first, that the people fast until battle was won, spun out of his control, because not everyone knew about it. The second oath was that he would execute the man who had broken his eating ban, even if it was his own son. Then, using the gadgets of the Urim and Thummim to finger the culprit, he came just short of having to kill Jonathan. He has made a third oath at Ephes-dammim, aiming to use it to get a taker for Goliath by the promise of his daughter (17:25). With his oaths and use of lots, Saul evidences a "certain *mechanical inelasticity* just where one would expect to find the wide-awake adaptability and the living pliableness of a human being." It is quite funny when people who are addicted to gadgets fall victim to their working, willy-nilly of human control, because one buys gadgets to be in control, and the impulse boomerangs. In Jacques Tati's film *Mon Oncle*, the sophisticated technology of the modern house takes control of its owners. It is the inflexible person who becomes the object or butt of a practical joke, just because, lacking "the living pliableness of a human being," he cannot change course.[25]

The very next day, after coming home to the women's song, "the evil spirit from God came upon Saul, and he prophesied in the midst of the house" (18:10). Saul is watching David play the harp, "as at other times" (18:10; 16:23), when Saul was overwhelmed by moody fits, but this time, "there was a javelin in Saul's hand." The javelin takes on its own momentum, like the oaths and the lots that brought Saul near to killing his son Jonathan. Saul does not hold a javelin, but rather, it's there, in his hand. The use of the impersonal form, "there was a javelin," indicates no advertence, but that the spear took over, like the oaths and the lots: things get the better of Saul. So "Saul cast the javelin," remarking, "I will smite David even to the wall with it" (18:11). David got out of the way, not once, but "twice." David's escape further terrifies Saul: "Saul was afraid of David, because the LORD was with him, and was departed from Saul" (18:12).

This scene raises a theological question. The problem is that *God* makes Saul lose control. We are explicitly told that an "evil spirit from God came upon Saul, and he prophesied in the midst of the house." The second clause makes the meaning of the first inescapable, since prophesying is an effect of the spirit of God, a divine inspiration. The attempt to nail David to the wall with his javelin seems to issue right from the madness instilled by the "evil spirit from God" (18:10). Josephus saw the problem in the first century and attempted to smooth it away by the simple device of eliminating the evil spirit and making what the author plainly calls Saul's divine-demonic possession into psychological madness. Josephus "suppresses one of the episodes about Saul's madness (which corresponds to 1 Sam. 18:10ff.) and explains another (. . . 1 Sam. 19:9ff.) quite rationally. . . . Josephus first mentions that Saul's jealousy for David had been aggravated by his recent success against the Philistines. The 'evil spirit' he then describes as haunting Saul could be taken as simple narrative hyperbole for insane jealousy. . . . Josephus removes whatever he can of any hint of demonic possession."[26] He does this because he didn't want to give his Roman readers a poor impression of the rationality of the Jewish scriptures.

Christianity is not a philosophy, but a revealed religion. No religion, revealed or otherwise, is entirely rational. David Hume was right to brush aside the Josephus-like efforts of eighteenth-century Christian theists to demonstrate that their system came up to rational criteria. The real question is not whether the story can be rationalized, for evidently it cannot, but what to make of the "curious

25. Henri Bergson, *Laughter: An Essay on the Meaning of the Comic*, trans. Cloudesley Brereton and Fred Rothwell (London: Macmillan, 1911), 10, emphasis original.
26. Wojcik, "Discriminations against David's Tragedy," 213–22.

conjunction of human failing and divine mystery" articulated in "Saul's prophesying" and the murder attempt that seems to flow from it (Polzin 1989: 179).
For many, since the intense portrayal of the madness in Handel's opera *Saul*, the
doomed king has been a tragic figure who in the nineteenth century stood for
Byronic defiance of a villainous deity. Our Christian communities teach us these
stories about David, Jonathan, and Saul in an infantilizing way, and so we never
learn to imagine them as adults. When we try to exercise an adult imagination
upon them, we may have mature theories and ideas about theology, but we don't
have the affective and imaginative maturity to match. In that case, we may see
the haunting of Saul by an "evil spirit from God" as what we call a tragedy. Exum
writes that "the tragic hero is haunted by demonic forces both from within and
without. We witness as Saul, driven by petty fears and jealousies, becomes a disintegrated personality, but most disturbing is the realization that the evil spirit
which torments him and makes his plight even more desperate is the agent of . . .
YHWH. In this acknowledgement of the root of Saul's distress, we discover why
Saul alone of biblical heroes attains a truly tragic stature, and we reach the core
of the tragic vision: the problem of evil."[27]

This reading sees itself as tragic, but is actually crudely melodramatic. Within
melodrama, a dastardly villain is often pitted against an absolutely innocent victim-
hero. Exum's reading projects this melodramatic vision into the Saul story. This
interpretation imagines God as the villain and Saul as the innocent victim. Thus,
Exum claims that

> Saul encounters God's dark side. . . . Saul . . . knows the demonic side of God not
> only through divine absence, but also, paradoxically, through YHWH's persecuting
> presence in the form of an evil spirit. YHWH and YHWH's spirit take possession of
> Saul immediately after his anointing. God gives him another heart (1 Sam. 10:9),
> the spirit of God makes him prophecy (10:10), and when he hears of the plight
> of Jabesh-gilead, the spirit inspires him to come to their aid (1 Sam. 11:6–7). . . .
> Divine possession leads to bizarre deeds. But we do not recognize it as especially
> problematic until after Saul's rejection, when we are told pointedly, "the spirit of
> YHWH departed from Saul and an evil spirit from YHWH tormented him" (1 Sam.
> 16:14). Under the evil spirit's influence, Saul tries to kill David . . . (18:10–11;
> 19:9–10). (Exum 1992: 40)

This is rationalistic, because it is reasonable, at least in one way, to think of
God as split into a dark side and a good side: from sheer objective or empirical
observation it would be reasonable to think that God is like a force within the
known universe, and a God who was a thing like an object in this world, a vast
force or power, would have two converse or opposed sides to his character. In the

27. J. Cheryl Exum and J. William Whedbee, "Isaac, Samson, and Saul: Reflections on the Comic
and Tragic Visions," in *On Humour and the Comic in the Hebrew Bible*, ed. Yehuda T. Radday and
Athalya Brenner (Sheffield: Almond, 1990), 153–54.

story as we have it in 1 Sam. 18, God is not an evil spirit. God *sends* an evil spirit upon Saul. God in 1 Samuel does not have two opposed sides, one evil and one good, as in the Manichean religion or the melodramatic universe.

That leaves open the question, still, of why God seems to compel Saul to act badly, through the evil spirit he sends upon Saul (Polzin 1989: 179). Saul looks like a puppet in God's hand in this scene. Why is God doing this? God is mocking him. "We laugh," Bergson writes, "every time a person gives us the impression of being a thing." Saul has the proclivity to become a thing, and God is satirizing him through this, through his becoming the javelin in his hand and turning into a human weapon of murder.

If we have a mental picture of Saul, it is perhaps in this gesture of lunging with a javelin that we capture him. Bergson argues that "instead of concentrating our attention on actions, comedy directs it rather to gestures." An action would take forethought, like a knife in the ribs. A gesture is that lunge with the heavy javelin, Saul dissolving into impersonal rage. Saul becomes the inhuman gesture, the thinglike propulsion of a spear. The realm of comedy spans heaven and hell—fulfilled desire and the abandonment of hope. It can go in either direction. This wide realm extends from the comic perspective, which is heaven bound, to the comical, which is satirical or infernal. What makes a hero comic, like David, is an ability to triumph over external circumstance, a certain uplift. What makes a character comical is "the ready-made element in our personality, that mechanical element which resembles a piece of clockwork wound up . . . and capable of working automatically." Imitation is often comical, and when we go on autopilot, we imitate ourselves, becoming a parody of what is most inflexible in us and uncontrollably repeating formulas. Saul has become fixed on certain ideas: first he is "wroth" (18:8) about being adversely contrasted with David; he then becomes anxious that David will take the kingdom (18:8); and finally he becomes "afraid" (18:12, 15). Fixed on his fear and fixated with David ("Saul eyed David from that day and forward"; 18:9), Saul becomes the "man who withdraws into himself," the man who "is liable to ridicule, because the comic is largely made up of this very withdrawal."[28] God is making Saul to make a fool of himself, just as the ark made a laughingstock of the Philistines in 1 Sam. 4–6. This is a transcendent God who acts from without the human frame. Whereas the comic hero cooperates with a lucky chance (divine good fortune), the comic butt is penalized. Saul is being punished by a transcendent God. God is in control of events: as Saul rightly intuits, David escapes his javelin throwing because God is with David and not with Saul (18:12).

Exum argues that Saul does not deserve the punishment God sends: "Saul's downfall is of his own making. . . . But whereas Saul is guilty, he is not really evil. . . . The hero's punishment exceeds any guilt."[29] Let's consider this assessment in

28. Bergson, *Laughter*, 58, 148, 138.
29. Exum and Whedbee, "Isaac, Samson, and Saul," 154.

relation to the ensuing scenes. Saul concocts the first of a series of plots with which to kill David. The first is to entangle David in fighting the Philistines by making it the condition of marriage to his elder daughter, Merab. Saul seeks to turn the oath he made when his army was threatened by Goliath, that the champion would have the king's daughter, to his own account. He tries to play the original verbal mechanism out further, by twisting what had been originally the promise of a daughter to the victor over one Philistine to a conditional offer of a daughter, dependent upon further military engagement: "Saul said to David, 'Behold my elder daughter Merab, her will I give thee to wife: only be thou valiant for me, and fight the LORD's battles.' For Saul said, 'Let not my hand be upon him, but let the hand of the Philistines be upon him'" (18:17). He wants to use the Philistines, like things, and to instrumentalize them as David's executioners, rather than having the blood of a popular hero on his own hands. This connivance is of a piece with Saul's earlier recourse to objective verbal mechanisms. Where Saul's primitive objectivism in 1 Sam. 13 was innocent, it has now become destructive, because it represents regression and rigidity.

We are told twice about David's wisdom, once that he *is* so, and again that Saul *perceives* him thus: "And David behaved himself wisely in all his ways; and the LORD was with him. Wherefore when Saul saw that he behaved himself very wisely, he was afraid of him" (18:14–15). David the wise guy easily slips the noose Saul has prepared for him. He uses the device of play humility. David may actually be humble, but in this episode he also turns his own humility to his advantage. He makes his humility a strength, as he had done with the sling. He pleads insufficient status to be married to a king's daughter: "Who am I? and what is my life, or my father's family in Israel, that I should be son-in-law to the king?" (18:18). Having turned a promise into a conditional, Saul breaks his word: "When Merab Saul's daughter should have been given to David, . . . she was given to Adriel the Meholathite to wife" (18:19).

The younger daughter presents a greater complication, and perhaps temptation: like Jonathan, "Michal Saul's daughter loved David" (18:20). Saul is delighted, because that gives him a new and better opportunity to get David clipped. A girl who loves a man is less easily turned aside than the anonymous, probably ugly, Merab. We are told "the thing pleased Saul" (18:20), that is, Saul was made happy by the possibility of repeating the gesture: "I will give him her, that she may be a snare to him, and that the hand of the Philistines may be against him" (18:21). This time, Saul sends his servants to give David the offer, because he realizes that this is a better way of spying out what David thinks. Turning his servants into informers, he tries to make David his dupe: "Commune with David secretly"—pretend I don't know about this—"and say, 'Behold, the king hath delight in thee, and all his servants love thee'"—the silly girl—"'now therefore be the king's son in law'" (18:22). What happened to the Saul who went back to his farm in Gibeah? We are in the court, where rumors of the king's favor go here and there, and servants report back on secret messages. Nixon's Whitehouse may have been like this, and

Stalin's inner circle, but this story is not saying, "this is where *politics* gets you." The milieu around Saul is not a political world, but a family despotism. In fact, "in contrast to David," Saul "is . . . *not* launched on a wide-open field of political action. His enormous tragedy belongs to another field of forces." Saul "represents the painful transition from the period of the Judges to that of the Kings" and belongs primarily "to the line of direct charismatics" (von Balthasar 1983–91: 6.106, emphasis original). This is both a theological and historical judgment and explains why the effort to detect pro- and antimonarchic sources within 1 Sam. 8–15 is a wild snark chase. Rather than being political, Saul belongs to the old world of the household economy. With the generation of his chieftainship, this domestic milieu has turned into something like the infernal, amoral world of the *Sopranos*, where mobsters set up smaller fry to get their enemies "popped," and no official detection can ever trace the disappearance back to the instigator.

David again tries out the "poor man" line (18:23). Once David's reply is reported to him by the dutiful servants, Saul has time to think how to outwit the plea of poverty. He sends the servants back with the suggestion of a slender dowry: "The king desireth not any dowry, but a hundred foreskins of the Philistines" (18:25). Moral sensibilities vary, but it may strike many readers as quite wicked to retract a promise (17:25), into a conditional (18:17), to use the conditional as a means of camouflaging murder (18:17), to break the promise (18:19), to instrumentalize a second daughter's love as a vehicle of tempting a rival to marriage (18:20–21), to use servants as a dirty tricks brigade, and to invent a "dowry" that one hopes will get the putative son-in-law killed. This is an evil plot: "Saul thought to make David fall by the hand of the Philistines" (18:25). This is not like loosing control and throwing a javelin. It took slow calculation and premeditation.

The comic hero bounces back. There is nothing David would rather do than gather Philistine foreskins. He hates Philistines because they are enemies of God's people, and so of God. His earlier answers were not just fake humility. We know that because it is when Philistine foreskins hove into the picture, when the servants repeat back the words of Saul about the foreskin dowry (18:26), that David wants to be a son-in-law: "It pleased David well to be the king's son in law: and the days were not expired" (the time limit was not yet up on the promise). Saul has fallen into a trap of his own devising, which is what one would expect of the mechanized comic butt. It is in character, since his earlier plots with the oaths and the lots likewise entangled him in their own automatism. He is in this episode the plotter outplotted and the God-mocker mocked. Hebrew proverbial theology would later teach that "the fear of Yahweh is training for wisdom, and before honour comes humility" (Prov. 15:33, trans. von Rad 1972: 66). David knows that God is not mocked. What was to have been a trap for this comic hero is his favorite pastime, and what he does best.

That's "another thing," Heller's David observes, "that pisses me off about the Michelangelo statue of me in Florence. He's got me standing there uncircumcised!" (1985: 60–61). If circumcision and its opposite is beyond one's vulgarity

threshold, one is bound to make David a universal man at the expense of his Jewishness. Josephus was perhaps the first to be embarrassed about this: he delicately
translates the Philistine foreskins of 18:25–27 into six hundred Philistine heads
(*Jewish Antiquities* 6.198). Lacking Josephus's Hellenized theological refinement,
the author knows that circumcision stands for Jewishness and uncircumcision for
pagan godlessness. Why are the foreskins in particular such an appealing game
to collect? Because, for the circumcised Jew, circumcising the uncircumcised
Philistines is like slapping yellow stars on the bodies of S.S. men. It is poetic
justice for their godlessness. God is not mocked: he is the power by which David
escapes Saul's plots and by which he returns victorious, with the foreskins of "two
hundred" Philistines. David has tallied, not a mere hundred as commanded, but
double it. He hands the whole lot over, the braggart: "They gave them in full tale
to the king, that he might be the king's son-in-law" (18:27). And this is funny.
Through the power of God, David has made a laughingstock of Saul, and he has
won the hand of the fair maiden: "And Saul gave him Michal his daughter to wife."
Contemporary studies of David often delight in presenting him as a devious figure.
A moderate application of this line in interpretation is the comment that "David
uses Michal to gain optative affiliation with Saul's family. The practice allows married couples to choose affiliation with either parental group, and they usually elect
residence among the one that bestows the higher status. The practice is a form
of adoption that enables the husband to stand in for his wife and to inherit from
and succeed her father. . . . When the direct line son and a collateral line traitor
(Abner) are eliminated, the way is open for David to succeed Saul legitimately
as leader of Israel" (Flanagan 1988: 243–44). Where the cynic conceives David
as instrumentalizing circumstances to his own advantage, a comic and Christian
perspective recognizes that those with the humility to disguise themselves are
successful, because God himself works hiddenly and in humble disguise. The wise
man not only thinks but acts analogically: he taps the reality of the God created
world and in so doing imitates God and rises toward his desires.

Saul is trapped doubly, by the ploy of the servants' whispers, for the well-known
promise could not be broken. Trapped triply, because he has lost his daughter to
David: "Saul saw and knew . . . that Michal Saul's daughter loved" David (18:28).
Trapped quadruply, because he knew too that "the LORD was with David." So the
episode ends, with Saul "yet the more afraid of David" (18:29). Horrible things
happen to Saul in this story, and we can well ask whether the impression that Saul's
punishment exceeds his crime would be the spontaneous reaction of anyone who
read this story without theologizing bifocals. A Christian reader has a right to ask
why God cannot just extend mercy to Saul for his past crimes and misdemeanors.
Why this never-ending mockery? Or, as Exum puts it, "The hero's punishment
exceeds any guilt. The question is not why is Saul rejected. The question is why
is there no forgiveness."[30] What God's mockery actually makes happen to Saul

30. Ibid.

is to get David as a son-in-law. This is not all that bad, in reality. It could be seen as a kind of teasing forgiveness. At the end of all his plotting and manipulative mind games, what Saul is made to achieve, by God's omnipotent Spirit, is to give Michal, the people, and David what they want. It goes without saying that it is not quite what Saul wants. As he "eye[s] David" (18:9), the women's hero is an enemy, a potential usurper. But David never shows any sign of enmity to Saul. The narrator doesn't tell us anything, or put any words into David's mouth, to make us imagine him a threat to Saul. Saul decides he's a threat, when he takes the women's song as a put-down. The problem and the punishment live and have their only reality in Saul's eyes, in his mind. Saul's punishment is in his mind, his way of imagining events. As Chrysostom observes, "such is the nature of envy"; Saul "knew that he was saved, yet he would rather have perished than see him that saved him have honor" (*Homilies on 2 Corinthians* 24.4, in Franke 2005: 278). Given the description of Jonathan's, the heir's, surrender of his patrimony to David in 18:1–5 and the upshot of the present episode in David's joining the Saulide line by marital right, we have no way of knowing what might have been if Saul had not been rigidly determined on interpreting David as a punishment.

Although it looks as if it were engaging with the mysterious quality of this scene, the tragic reading of Saul's prophesying and javelin throwing is a twentieth-century example of the rationalist interpretations of scripture that have captured a section of the popular imagination since the eighteenth century. The way we know this is a rationalist reading of the scripture is that it imagines there can be tragedy without transcendence. If there is no transcendent, absolute rightness, there can be no tragedy. It is not tragic that Saul should lose his humanity if his humanity is not ultimately valuable, that is, valuable in the sight of a being who transcends this world. When the romantics call the doomed Saul tragic, what they really mean is that his plight is, to them, supremely melodramatic. Melo-drama is a secular genre that first appeared at the end of the eighteenth century. For the melodramatic imagination, a tragic hero is one who defies God. In this context, Saul becomes a sort of damned soul, like Heathcliffe. Thus, for Exum, Saul "displays heroic greatness in his refusal to acquiesce in the fate prophesied by Samuel, taking extraordinary steps to hold on to his kingdom. A lesser man, a man without hubris, might merely accept his destiny. Saul . . . wrestles against it."[31] If Saul accepted his destiny, which at the present point in the narrative is David as son-in-law, he would have forgiveness, because he would be able to rec-ognize himself as forgiven. This Saul does not and cannot do. To live is to change. Saul has become a lifeless figure, and if "rigidity is the comic, and laughter . . . its corrective,"[32] he has become, not a Byronic God-deifier, but an involuntary tool whose conspiracy to murder is the unwitting lever of a vulgar comedy in which foreskins rain down from heaven and a wedding is won.

31. Ibid., 155.
32. Bergson, *Laughter*, 21.

Episode Six: Getaway (1 Sam. 19:1–17)

In the previous episode, Saul brought in his servants as informants and Philistines as potential executioners. Now he tries to get Jonathan's complicity, telling "Jonathan his son, and . . . all his servants, that they should kill David" (19:1). Saul is so impassioned that he is telling everyone and has inadvertently addressed his murderous thoughts to a sane person of rank who is a friend to David. Jonathan wisely tells David to "abide in a secret place, and hide thyself " while he talks his father out of it (19:2). When he speaks "good of David unto Saul," Jonathan tries to get his father to see the reality, that he is living in a happy ending, a good world brought about by David, not in a punishment that exceeds his crime: David "hath not sinned against thee, . . . his works have been to thee-ward very good [literally: his deeds have been to you good; he has only done you good]. For he did put his life in his hand," he risked his life, "and slew the Philistine, and the LORD wrought a great salvation for all Israel." You saw this with your own eyes and acclaimed it (19:4–5). Jonathan tries to help Saul see that he has no reason to be made miserable by David: why "slay David without a cause?" (19:5). His father returns to reality, so far as a mechanized automaton can, and makes yet another oath: "Saul swore: 'As the LORD liveth, he shall not be slain' " (19:6). The content and form are comically ill adjusted: swearing a thundering oath that an "innocent" man shall "not be slain" undermines swearer's integrity and credibility.

The same situation, the same result: another war, the Philistines in flight from David, "great slaughter" (19:8), and the warrior harpist once more a target for Saul's javelin (another misthrow). Not leaving it there, Saul "sent messengers unto David's house, to watch him, and to slay him in the morning" (19:11). Hearing of this plot, "David's wife" warns him, and "Michal let David down through a window: and he went and fled, and escaped"; the episode in 19:10b–17 combines "dangerous escapes with comic effects" (von Balthasar 1983–91: 6.111). As in the Goliath episode and "king's daughters," the narrative contrasts a negative character's comical absurdity with a comic hero's seizing his good fortune: "Out the window I went, like some hairylegged clown in a dirty burlesque" (Heller 1985: 205). The next scene could grace a Molière comedy: "And Michal took an image, and laid it in the bed, and put a pillow of goats' hair for his bolster, and covered it with a cloth" (19:13). Like many comic heroes, disguise suits David. His lack of armor camouflaged his threat when he presented himself to Goliath. Now, David's absence is disguised as a statue ("an image") wigged with "goats' hair" and covered with a blanket. "And when Saul sent messengers to take David, she said, 'He is sick' " (19:14). David makes his getaway while Saul's servants see an imaginary David, lying stiff as a statue, under the covers. Undeterred and absolutely single-minded in his automatism, like a maniacal Mr. Bean gone bad, Saul's reply is, "Bring him up to me in the bed, that I may slay him" (19:15). St. Thomas Aquinas and Calvin found in Saul's persecution of David a historical type of the persecution of the church. Sometimes David is in real danger, but other episodes are farcical relief. It is esthetically obtuse to equate them all. The early church and the French Huguenots were in real danger of death from their enemies, whereas Saul's persecution of David is, in this episode, a consistent series of luckless misfires. Saul's *idée fixe* does succeed in uncovering the imposture, since the soldiers draw back the coverlet, and "behold, there was an image in the bed, with a pillow of goats' hair for his bolster" (19:16). The laconic repetition of the exact phrase enables us to see the servants unmask their deception. Like all promise breakers, Saul cannot bear to be lied to, and often is: "Why hast thou deceived me so?" he demands of David's wife. Knowing that Saul sees David as a walking death threat, Michal easily persuades the one-tracked man that David had threatened to murder her: "He said unto me, 'Let me go; why should I kill thee?'" (19:17).

The theological theme of the invisibility of God's action and the shortsightedness of going on appearances blossoms into comedy. Just as the virtue or vice of words and actions depends, like their meaning, on context, so lying and deceit depend for their moral tone on the generic, imaginative world in which they occur. Deceit, like disguise, is the humble weapon of self-preservation of comic heroes and heroines the world over. Disguise works, and deceives, in comedy, because its world is one in which things are ampler and richer than they seem, and knowing this is wisdom and happiness. Michal's act of "let[ting] David down through a window" (19:12) has been interpreted as a symbolic giving birth, and she figures here as mother to David. Like many comic heroes, David draws to him female rescuers and helpers. Everything conspires to save him. In a comic cosmos, like that of the Hebrew-Christian scriptures, being a wise guy is not boring, but hilarious.

Episode Seven: As Sounding Brass, or a Tinkling Cymbal (1 Sam. 19:18–24)

David goes for protection to Samuel at Ramah. He has the sacred power of the prophet behind him. God turns the prophetic power against Saul. Saul sends one set of messengers to "take David" from Samuel, and, with Samuel "standing" over them, "the Spirit of God was upon the messengers of Saul, and they . . . prophesied" (19:20). We find these scenes in which Saul prophesies perplexing. For us, prophesying is plainly and simply something good, God sending true information about the future via his chosen. This idea of prophecy has a venerable ancestry. Augustine wrote that "'the days of the prophets' is a name given . . . especially to the era beginning with the prophetic activity of Samuel, who at God's bidding first anointed Saul and then, when Saul proved unsatisfactory, David himself, from whose stock the whole succession of kings derived" (*City of God* 17.1). But Augustine realizes that this definition cannot be applied indifferently to every outburst of prophetic charismatism in the scriptures or in Christian history.

In a sermon about this episode, Augustine compares Saul's messengers to bailiffs, sent by their superiors "to drag someone out of the church; he dare not act against God" by arresting their intended victim, "and in order not to face execution himself he stays there, in the place where he was sent, to haul someone out of it. So . . . pleasantly surprised and relieved, . . . these men suddenly became prophets because they were innocent; the very gift of prophecy bore witness to their innocence. They came because they were sent, but they weren't going to do what the bad man had told them to do." As each group of bailiffs arrives to arrest the churchgoer, "the Spirit of God leaped on them too": "let them all be innocent." Augustine applies the final case to Saul himself: "Was he also sent by some authority, and not ill-intentioned of his own free will?" Evidently not. "Yet the Spirit of God leaped on him too, and he began to prophesy." The bishop explains the difference between the prophesying of the "innocent" messengers and of Saul by reference to 1 Corinthians: "Saul is prophesying, he has the gift of prophecy, but he has not got charity. He has become a kind of instrument to be touched by the Spirit, not one to be cleansed by the Spirit." As the ancients understood it, the prophet is an instrument of God, to be used as God wills: being made an instrument of God is the heart of prophetic speech, considered as a God-given action. Augustine concludes that Saul evidently made ill use of his charism: "Did Saul have charity, who persecuted the one by whose hand he had been delivered from his enemies, so that he was guilty not only of envy but of ingratitude? So we have proved that it is possible for you to have prophecy and not to have charity. . . . Prophecy does you no good, according to the apostle: 'If I do not have charity,' he says, 'I am nothing.' He doesn't say, 'Prophecy is nothing,' or 'Faith is nothing,' but 'I myself am nothing, if I don't have charity'" (Sermon 162A, in Franke 2005: 287–88).

Defining prophecy by relation to the divine instrumentalization of the speaker helps us to see why, in itself, prophesying is not simply a good thing. Phenomenologists of religion speak of the sacred as, in one aspect, simply power. When we think of prophets or shamans as instruments of the divine, we can think of prophecy as the power or energy of God acting through a person creatively or destructively. According to van der Leeuw, religions channel power or energy into forms.[33] Saul can appreciate that power comes on the prophet, but he cannot direct this dangerous "electricity" into a cable that could carry or communicate it. He cannot enable prophecy to come into conjunction with human artistry, whether imaginative or strategic. The raw power of the sacred of which van der Leeuw speaks is what Christians understand as love, the heart of God.

Noting that the episodes of "ecstatic prophecy" (*wayyitnabbe*) in 18:10 and 19:18–24 are parallel to the story of Saul's first appearance as a charismatic king in 1 Sam. 10, one scholar argues that the implied polarity is not the result of

33. Gerardus van der Leeuw, *Religion in Essence and Manifestation: A Study in Phenomenology*, trans. J. E. Turner (London: Allen & Unwin, 1938).

both stories coming to the writer's hand, but rather "the second episode was put forward by Dtr, the author of the Story of David's Rise, to negate the positive attribution of the first. He wants his readers to interpret the saying 'Is Saul also among the prophets?' in the most derogatory fashion as madness and disgusting behavior" (Van Seters 1983: 266). Lemche thinks the episodes showing Jonathan and David united against Saul are unfair to the original king, who, he thinks had the political *nous* to grasp the peril embodied in his son-in-law. David, Lemche argues, was a wily political climber who "deliberately worked his way up to the highest positions. In his high military position and as the personal friend of the heir to the throne he was guaranteed the second highest position next to the king when Saul died, and in case anything should happen to Jonathan David would be in an advantageous position as claimant to the throne." The naïve Jonathan missed the potential menace that the elder man appreciated. Hence his efforts "to get rid of David. The author of 'David's Rise' has thrown a veil over Saul's real motives by explaining Saul's hatred against David as something originating in Saul's insanity. In reality ... if Saul and his dynasty were to be secure in their position they sooner or later had to liquidate David" (Lemche 1978: 8). In reality, if we discount Saul's insanity, he comes over even worse as a political strategist. His madness is the only mitigating factor in his politically disastrous obsession with eliminating David. Saul is obsessive about the obstruction that David represents because he cannot think of creative means through which to harness his power and to stabilize his authority in enduring forms. Saul acts the control freak, bleeping *exterminate!* like a Dalek. In his hands, God-sent prophecy becomes a destructive force. Because of his character, Saul becomes a sorcerer's apprentice when he comes into contact with the unpredictable and transcendent force of prophecy. He's like the greedy man in the fairy story who sees that something can be gotten out of the magical talisman for himself, but has no idea how to channel this sacral and therefore dangerous thing.

As we've seen in each episode in which Saul tries to get control through some mechanism, it rebounds on him. The minute his first group of messengers saw Samuel's "company of prophets prophesying," they went into mimetic hypnosis and "also prophesied" (19:20). Repetition of identical actions or "symmetrically identical" situations is one of the commonest features of comedy.[34] Saul can't change tactic: hearing that his executioner-messengers have turned into prophets, "he sent other messengers, and they prophesied likewise. And Saul sent messengers again the third time, and they prophesied also" (19:21).

Where does providence come into the satirical reduction of Saul's murderous messengers to helpless, hysterical prophesiers? God is using the prophesying power that he channels through Samuel to protect David. Prophesying is a force, an energy, that can be creative or destructive. David is alive, and Saul, the story is telling us, is like a dead man. The story gives Saul the character of a

---

34. Bergson, *Laughter*, 91.

comic automaton, a marching Cleese figure, in order to contrast his deathliness with David's liveliness. By contrasting a comic butt and a comic hero the author compares death, with which prophecy freezes, to life, with which prophecy is creative. Where there is no charity, there is no life. Comedy corrects and penalizes rigidity precisely because it is on the side of life, and life is not automatic, but spontaneous, innovative, and particular. The mechanical can be imitated just because it is hardened into stereotype; it can reproduce itself in identical replicas because it lacks the unpredictability of love—or life. In itself, life "never goes backward and never repeats anything. . . . A continual change of aspect, the irreversibility of the order of phenomena, the perfect individuality of a perfectly self-contained series: such . . . are the outward characteristics . . . which distinguish the living from the merely mechanical. Let us take the counterpart of each of these: we shall obtain . . . *repetition, inversion,* and *reciprocal interference of series.* . . . These are also the methods of light comedy."[35] When Saul, having exhausted his supply of messengers and so profoundly trapped in his *idée fixe* that he can't see what's coming, goes himself to get David and Samuel, "the Spirit of God was upon him also, and he . . . prophesied . . . and . . . stripped off his clothes also, and prophesied before Samuel . . . and lay down naked all that day and all that night" (19:23–24), we are meant to see in this robotic frenzy the meaning of death. The truly dead, those who are removed from the presence of the living God, become like machines, ventriloquist's dolls or "effigies of evil": "It is only because they are effigies that they can be looked at," for these images have no objective reality in themselves (von Balthasar 1983–91: 3.99). Saul's epigraph is repeated at the end of the chapter, as an epitaph: "Wherefore they say, 'Is Saul also among the prophets?'" (19:24). Saul, the flesh-and-blood human being with whom many readers feel a natural sympathy, long ago disappeared, to be replaced by a parody of himself. Where Saul himself is, only God knows.

Episode Eight: Covenant Friendship Renewed (1 Sam. 20)

We strain to get the hang of what is supposed to happen in this episode. By the end, nothing seems to have happened: one may tend to assume that the firing of the arrows is supposed to be a signal between friends who may henceforth be incommunicado, but in fact David doesn't flee immediately; when he gets the prearranged "flee" signal he instead meets up with Jonathan before he heads for the hills. So what was the point of this playacting with the arrows? It seems to take forty-two verses for David to learn from Jonathan what he already knows and states clearly at the beginning, "There is but one step between me and death" (20:3). There are other oddities. Why are both Jonathan and Saul so naïve? How could Jonathan honestly not yet know that his father wants to kill David and

35. Ibid., 88–89, emphasis original.

think he would tell him if he was planning to do so: "My father does nothing
. . . without disclosing it to me. And why should my father hide this from me?"
(20:2 ESV). And how can Saul be surprised when David doesn't come for dinner
at the new moon festival (or any other time)? Why should David think that, if
Saul was plotting to get him whacked, he'd tell Jonathan? One obvious way to
resolve such conundrums is to say that this chapter has been spatch-cocked into
the narrative from an alien source that knows nothing of the previously indicated
inclinations of Saul to David and was left looking just the way he found it by its
redactor (Polzin 1989: 187–88).

One way into this episode is to think of it as one that does not intend to take
the plot on further. It's like a sleeper episode in a long series, where the plot stills
and the writers let the characters show themselves without involving them in
thrilling action. Because it is about the Mafia family, the Sopranos' world is in
some ways analogous to prepolitical tribal culture, with the important difference
that the prepolitical world was not, in itself, corrupt by dint of not yet having
achieved civil society, whereas the Mafia represents a regression that is not merely
prepolitical but subpolitical. The boss of the family, Tony Soprano, orders execu-
tions and takes part in murdering enemies and aberrant employees. It is a "family
drama." One of the plot lines is his daughter Meadow's coming to terms with what
her father is. She knows on one level that he is evil, but on another level evades
this, consistently denying that her father ordered the killing of her friend Jackie
Aprile Jr. (third season): in the concluding episode, she becomes complicit, a
collaborator who is tied to her family for life (sixth season). Meadow cannot rise
above "the family principle." This episode in 1 Samuel has the opposite outcome.
It is about Jonathan putting friendship above domestic loyalty. We have seen
Jonathan complain to the other soldiers about his father mismanaging the battle
at Michmash (14:28–30), but this was adolescent impatience, tearing at the bit
of paternal authority by publicly disparaging the commanding officer, not coming to grips with his father on any deep level. In growing-up stories, not much
happens, but an individual on the verge of real adulthood makes a decision and
learns something about herself or himself. If we don't quite get the stage business
about the arrows, it is because we start from the false premise, that the episode
is about Jonathan helping David to escape his father, whereas it is really about
David helping Jonathan to escape his father.

The episode is about family ties and their transcendence both in relation
to Jonathan and even to David himself. In tribal cultures, as with "the great
chief in his domain, the father is in his own house a sacred figure, a man of
superior *mana* . . . chieftainship begins at home: the chief's due is no more than
elaborate filial respect" (Sahlins 1968: 64). Jonathan must put his law-abiding
"covenant" above his lawless family, and that means more than psychologically
transcending his allegiance to his father, because this allegiance is not a matter
for the tribesman of subjective, personal devotion, but of quasiobjective sacrality. Scripture commands to "honour thy father and thy mother" (Exod. 20:12),

and this chapter does not abrogate that commandment: it is a matter of which culture this prescription operates in: a healthy tribal one (as in the times of the patriarchs), a late, regressive tribal culture (as in the early chapters of 1 Samuel), or the political culture being born with David. David too had become a "son" to Saul, effectively from the time of his victory over Goliath, when he entered Saul's family ambiance, and in fact from the time he married Michal, for marriage into a superior family could be a "form of adoption" (Flanagan 1988: 243). Three times here, Saul revokes that adoption, describing David in distancing terms as "the son of Jesse" (20:27, 30, 31). Saul himself is causing the family as tribal culture understood it to fragment, destroying it by not rising above it. David is wise to this: but is Jonathan?

When David asks Jonathan, "What is my sin before your father, that he seeks my life?" (20:1 ESV), in one way, he may be asking for information, but in another way he's trying to put the situation as it is before Jonathan's eyes. His friend refuses point blank to see it that way: "Far from it! You shall not die. Behold, my father does nothing either great or small without disclosing it to me. And why should my father hide this from me? It is not so" (20:2 ESV). It's a series of unconvincing exclamations, not a reasoned response. "You shall not die," Jonathan says, which means, "I don't want you to die"; he does not utter the unthinkable words: "My father would not kill you." The exaggeration "either great and small" is followed by a giveaway that Jonathan is closing his mind to what father does: the adamant conclusion—"it is not so"—is unnecessary, if he believes what he just said. David tries to help his friend overcome his self-imposed naïveté: "Your father knows" you think well of me, "and he thinks, 'Do not let Jonathan know this, lest he be grieved.'" David "vowed," trying to get his friend to look evil in the face: "As the LORD lives and your soul lives, there is but a step between me and death" (20:3 ESV). David wants to get his friend to do what most men avoid: to accept that some people, even beloved family members, are evil, and he needs to arrange that fast, because he is inches from death. It is right to see continuity between Jonathan's candor in this episode and the frankness he exhibited at Michmash (Polzin 1989: 188–89): a candid person might wrongly assume candor in others. It is also right to take bravery as a key feature of Jonathan's character: "Prince Jonathan is the most daring hero of all (1 Sam. 14); unwittingly he violates his father's vow, and when the oracle declares him to be the guilty party, he exclaims, 'I am ready to die'" (von Balthasar 1983–91: 6.110). Candid with others, Jonathan has yet to be candid with himself about Saul; it is easier to take an "uncomplicated view of people and events" (Polzin 1989: 189) than to acknowledge that his father wants to kill his friend. The Jonathan who led a two-man assault against the Philistine watch at Michmash Pass without telling his father (14:1–14) and the boy who cheerfully handed his patrimony over to David in the symbolic surrender of his robe (18:1–5) has a carefree impulsiveness that has yet to be earned. He is a daredevil, but he doesn't yet fully appreciate what the stakes are. He has faced death, but he has not faced up to human murderousness. He is what Saul once called

David, a "stripling" and a "youth" (17:33, 56). David has learned what the stakes are; Prince Jonathan is an innocent.

David implicitly trusts his friend. He trusts that he has a good will toward himself, because, like himself, his friend is generous. As Bishop Ambrose of Milan, who converted Augustine, says, "Good will . . . goes together with generosity. . . . So . . . any one trusts himself to the counsels of a man of good will rather than to those of a wise one, as David did. For he, though he was the more farseeing" and appreciated Saul's evil designs, "agreed to the counsels of Jonathan, who was the younger" (*Duties of the Clergy* 1.32.167, in Franke 2005: 289). David does not need to make a trial of Jonathan's good will or generosity. Nonetheless, David cannot yet know where he really stands with his friend, for Jonathan has not made an existential decision between David and Saul. Jonathan still inhabits a prepolitical world in which the deviousness that comes naturally to David is unknown. The episode contrasts David's deviousness—he suggests the lie about his own whereabouts—with Jonathan's straightforward and open character, characteristics reinforced by his representation in earlier episodes (Polzin 1989: 192, 188). Jonathan knows that a ruse can be necessary as a military tactic, but he has not entered the world in which deceit is part of peacetime politics. He does not realize that, as John Chrysostom puts it, "not in war only, but also in peace the need of deceit may be found. . . . The daughter of Saul would not have been able to rescue her husband out of Saul's hands except by deceiving her father. And her brother, wishing to save him whom she had rescued when he was again in danger, made use of the same weapon as the wife" (*On the Priesthood* 1.8, in Franke 2005: 285). Jonathan has yet to draw the lesson, which later writers adduce from this episode. So David, who will not gain much new information about Saul's fluctuating intentions, proposes a trial of friendship for Jonathan. He will stay away from new moon supper, and Jonathan can test out his father's plans. What David needs to learn from this is not whether Saul wants to kill him, but whether Jonathan will tell him what he knows. Jonathan might be swayed by his father and collude with his fantasies: David begs him, by the "covenant" they have made together, "kill me yourself," rather than giving away his whereabouts to his father (20:8) and letting Saul do the deed. David seems to get the answer he needs from Jonathan: "If I knew that it was determined by my father that harm should come to you, would I not tell you?" (20:9 ESV). Jonathan is admitting that he may have to take sides between, on the one hand, the authority of his father, a crucial moral and cultural benchmark for a people that called its ancestors "the fathers" and that made honor to "father and mother" its fifth commandment (Exod. 20:12), and, on the other hand, fidelity to his covenant with a friend.

David presses the point, because his life may depend on this friendship being deeper than an impassioned impulse. So he repeats the question from another angle, "Who will tell me if your father answers you roughly?" (1 Sam. 20:10 ESV). The emphasis is on *who*: will you yourself give away your father's intentions? Jonathan replies, "Let us go out into the field." He intends to reaffirm the covenant made in 18:1–5, and he does not intend to do so in the whispering gallery of an Early Iron Age domestic house, where the only place for private conversation was also, in daylight, the most conspicuous—the roof. In "Iron Age I highland villages, the heartland of early Israel," families like David's and even Saul's lived in "multiple family compounds," "comprised of two or three houses set off from their village surroundings by enclosure walls" that "formed the basic socioeconomic units of the community": "In such villages, the extended or multiple family unit was the ideal type. Such a household may have constituted a minimal 'house of the father' (Hebrew *bet 'ab*), or a small patrilineage" (Stager 1998: 135–36). "House" is a literal synonym for "family": "The physical structure of the house is symbolically accommodated to clan organization. Divided into socially 'higher' and 'lower' spaces, it makes a perfect exoskeleton for the differentiated family organism. In all family activities—eating, sleeping, or just talking—the men of the family spatially dispose themselves in the house according to their seniority" (Sahlins 1968: 64).

In the field, Jonathan swears: by "the LORD, the God of Israel. . . . When I have sounded out my father . . . if he is well disposed toward David, shall I [that is, I myself] not then send and disclose it to you? But should it please my father to do you harm, the LORD do so to Jonathan and more also if I do not disclose it to you and send you away" (20:12–13 ESV). The sustained and still undented quality of Jonathan's self-delusion about his father is perhaps exhibited in his expressed hope, that, if David gets away in safety, "may the LORD be with you, as he has been with my father" (ESV). This might be an extraordinary piece of authorial irony at Jonathan's expense, for the Lord has *not* been with Saul for some time. An alternate interpretation is that Jonathan means, "May the Lord elevate you to the kingship, as he raised my father" (ESV). Jonathan's follow-on comments might make us lean to the latter: "If I am still alive"—once you are king—"show me the steadfast love of the LORD, that I may not die; and do not cut off your steadfast love from my house forever"—when you and my father exchange places—and "when the LORD cuts off every one of the enemies of David from the face of the earth" (ESV). In the field, away from listening ears, Jonathan has now exposed his genuine appreciation of the situation. It is close to becoming a battle to the death for the kingship, between Saul and David. Jonathan perhaps recognizes this for the first time, when he articulates the thought in renewing his covenant with David.

Jonathan is a pious Israelite. "Friendship love" is about seeing or caring about "the same truth" above and outside both parties: "Lovers are normally face to face, absorbed in each other; Friends, side by side, absorbed in some common interest."[36] The Lord is the same truth that David and Jonathan share. It is because he puts the one Lord above king and kin that Jonathan is able to put his friend before his father. Jonathan wittingly abdicates as prince-in-waiting, when he says, "May the

---

36. Lewis, *Four Loves*, 79, 73.

LORD take vengeance on David's enemies" (20:16 ESV). Jonathan makes David swear, in turn, "for he loved him as he loved his own soul" (20:17 ESV): he insists on the reciprocity of the covenant, not out of self-interest, but out of love. What holds David and Jonathan together, the true covenant binding them, is their God: "Behold, the LORD is between you and me forever" (20:23 ESV).

Such friendship makes politics as such possible. To understand why this is so, we have to recognize that it is false to regard prepolitical society as more personal than political, as for instance in the claim that "we see the conflict between . . . two kinds of ethical systems with the beginning of the monarchy. . . . The conflict is really between two different kinds of community, the face-to-face personal relationships based upon a common value system and the impersonal power structure of the state which can hardly do more than maintain a delicate balance between conflicting interests" (Mendenhall 1973: 208). In fact, to the contrary, because it does not come back to literal, visible kinship but to trust, political society depends on personal relationships in a way that tribal cultures never could. The culture in which the kinship group "is a superperson, and its members are as one" (Sahlins 1968: 12) is more impersonal and anonymous than political cultures, the kind of cultures in which texts like 1–2 Samuel, with their thumbnail sketches of unique personalities, were composed. The notion of friendship as a basis for the city-state is present in Aristotle. It is in scripture too, because the history of the Jewish people incorporated a development from an archaic, acephalous society based in family and clan loyalty to a monarchic state. Unless people can form reliable friendships and relationships of trust outside their own bloodlines, and unless they can set these friendships above their own families, there can be no civil society. So long as the domestic or family principle is the single mainstay of a culture, it is impossible for its members to put the common good, the good of society as a whole, above what is good for their own clan or family. They tend to take the law into their own hands because they perceive the law as a vehicle of benefit for their own clan, not as representing the good of society in its entirety. They also tend to twist or break the law when it does not serve their family interests. We can still observe, in some countries, politics breaking down into clan rivalries or mobsterism.

What is happening, historically, in this episode set in antiquity is that people are moving beyond a family-based culture into a society in which the state is the more ultimate custodian of moral order. By making this covenant, sworn in the name of the God of Israel, Jonathan and David are symbolically creating the basis for a genuine, stable political culture, a monarchy. That cannot happen until people recognize that public law, founded in the Lord, has more authority than the private loyalties of the family. The kingships of Saul and David were probably something like chiefdom, that is, at a transitional stage between tribal and state organization (Hackett 1998: 201). Perhaps, empirically, Saul's chiefdom stumbled and disintegrated because he didn't know how to sustain a transition from a family-based culture to a civil society and created a familial despotism, not a state. This episode symbolically presents the historical shift from one kind of culture to the other. It shows through one symbolic friendship that, in the earlier culture, the father was the earthly representative of God, whereas, in the later culture, the representative of God is not only the father, but also the king, and that this transition was enabled by friendships in which the common truth of God came before kith and kin.

Then come the unduly complicated system of signals, designed by Jonathan. If David sees him "shoot three arrows to the side" of the rock behind which David is concealed and hears him shout out "go, find the arrows" to his servant, "as the LORD lives, it is safe for you and there is no danger" (20:20–21 ESV), but if he hears Jonathan call out, " 'Look, the arrows are beyond you,' then go, for the LORD hath sent you away" (20:22 ESV). This is much more complex than the "come up" or "stay where you are" signs that Jonathan invented at Michmash Pass. They are not even strictly necessary, since, as we see at the end, the friends meet and converse after Jonathan sends the danger signal; so he might as well just have walked over to the rock behind which David is concealed and told him. As Sternberg says, scripture combines and is regulated by three principles—ideology (or theology), history, and esthetics—and it is not always easy to tell which principle is uppermost in its intentions. What we see as the realism of history might actually be the narrator striving for an artistic effect: "Does the avoidance of black-and-white portrayal reflect the historian's scrupulosity, the artist's eye for intricate characterization, or the doctrinal tenet that all men exercise free choice, so that no man can be wholly righteous . . . throughout his life?"[37] On a historical level, the author makes this rigmarole with the arrows part of the conclusive sealing of the pact between Jonathan and David because, believing that Jonathan had in fact done this, he describes it. Like his father, Jonathan is a "Benjamite." Given that tribe's skill as archers, to "shoot three arrows to the side of" David's hiding place, "as though I shot at a mark" (20:20), would be child's play for the historical Jonathan. The signal system devised by Jonathan is in historical character. In its esthetic dimension, Jonathan as marksman is a symbolic demonstration there is something of Saul in Jonathan. The narrator may be showing us that the Benjamite Jonathan is not entirely unlike Saul, and thus that he is making a sacrifice, leaving a part of himself behind, when he binds himself to David.

Some readers are perplexed that Saul can't imagine why David would not want to come to dinner with him. But we have to remember that, in Saul's paranoid imagination, David is a threat to him, not vice versa. He doesn't recognize himself as a threat. Although all his acquaintance know him to be a cold-blooded killer, Tony Soprano can ask, nonrhetorically, "Am I a toxic person?" (series three). *The Sopranos* is not difficult literature: it's a television series and quite lucidly represents the idea that evil people don't recognize themselves as such. If we find it puzzling to conceive of Saul's behavior here, it may be because we are conceiving

37. Sternberg, *Poetics of Biblical Narrative*, 45.

it too puzzlingly and not in a literal and direct way, as it might be represented on television. If we try not to think the situation but to dramatize it, we can imagine Saul doing that, and we can, simultaneously with this exercise of imagination, see why Saul behaves like this: he himself does not see his own evil, as those round about him do. The presentation of the first entrance of the "evil spirit" helps us to understand the point. There, Saul was told by his courtiers that he had a problem: "An evil spirit from the LORD troubled him. And Saul's servants said unto him, 'Behold now, an evil spirit from God troubleth thee'" (16:14–15). Saul's predicament is witnessed from the outside, not grasped internally by Saul himself. He can't name the problem, because it's himself.

Saul can't bear to imagine that David would not present himself for supper. Observing that "David's place was empty," he does not remark on it the first night to Abner or to Jonathan, "for he thought, 'Something has happened to him. He is not clean; surely he is not clean'" (20:25–26 ESV). The thought captures Saul's nail-biting anxiety. Saul hopes that the reason David is away is that he has incurred some ritual uncleanliness and cannot eat with the others, but he fears other possibilities. On the second day, he finally asks, and Jonathan repeats the lie that David had dreamed up, that he is celebrating the feast with his family in Bethlehem. Saul's reaction shows that, for him, Jonathan has become a traitor to the Saulide dynasty: "You son of a perverse, rebellious woman, do I not know that you have chosen the son of Jesse to your own shame, and to the shame of your mother's nakedness?" (20:30 ESV). Saul recalls him to his blood ties and tells him he disgraces the mother who gave birth to him by preferring a member of another family to his own clan. Saul imagines this as a political matter: "For as long as the son of Jesse lives on the earth, neither you nor your kingdom shall be established. Therefore send and bring him to me, for he shall surely die" (20:31 ESV). Saul tries to get Jonathan to see that it is in his own self-interest to put his family before his friend. In the short term, it might have been. But kings who elect to murder innocent men whom they imagine to be a danger to themselves or to their heirs tend often enough to be disestablished by their own promotion of lawlessness. What Saul cannot see is that, in the new cultural situation he has entered, unless persons put the law above self-interest, no kingdom can be established.

When Jonathan puts that point to Saul, by asking, "Why should he be put to death? What has he done?" (20:32 ESV), his father answers him with a spear: the rule of the family is ultimately the rule of egos, under no rule. Saul could never quite leave the Bronze Age: it's because they were still there, Heller's David says, that "you find us doing so much smiting all through the Pentateuch, and so little thrusting, hurling and shooting. Smiting is just about all you can do with an axe or a club or a curved sword molded like a sickle and with just the exterior edge whetted. The only spears and javelins we possessed were the . . . captured ones in . . . brushes with the Philistines. . . . But who knew how to use such weapons? Saul missed me with his javelin all three times he sought to kill me, and I was seated off guard no more than twenty feet away. He missed Jonathan too across the dinner table" (1985: 84). There is no crime in being in the cultural rearguard any more than there is intrinsic virtue in the avant-garde. Progress has little inherent spiritual value. Yet 1 Samuel captures David in a snapshot of the triumph of political over tribal society. For Christians, the leap forward from Saul to David symbolizes the leap forward into a universal church: "The city of God . . . developed down . . . to the time when Saul was rejected and David first ascended to the throne, so that his descendants . . . reigned in the earthly Jerusalem. . . . This change was symbolic; it was an event that pointed prophetically to the future. . . . It betokened the change that was to come in the future in respect of the two covenants, the old and the new, and the transformation of priesthood and monarchy by the new and eternal priest-king, who is Christ Jesus" (Augustine, *City of God* 17.4).

After this last murder attempt, the narrator laconically remarks, "So Jonathan knew that his father was determined to put David to death" (20:33 ESV). This is the son's moment of recognition of what his father is, a lunger with a javelin. Now consciously acknowledging that "his father was determined to put David to death," Jonathan cannot eat, "for he was grieved for David, because his father had disgraced him" (20:34 ESV). The truth he could not bear to think was that his father could be such a man as this. Jonathan's naïveté about his father in this episode is not due either to its being an interpolation by another hand or to the candid quality of Jonathan's personality. Jonathan's grief at the shame brought upon him by his father's actions suggests that he has not been open with himself and has repressed his own awareness of his father's evil. The emergence of this recognition in the form of grief forces him to take the final step, out of his family.

So, Jonathan fires the warning signal, calling out, "Is not the arrow beyond you?" to his servant. Sending the boy home, Jonathan goes to meet his friend, his mission of verifying his covenant completed. David "bowed three times," in appreciation of Jonathan's altruistic gesture. We are not told that "David loved Jonathan," but we are told that when the two men "kissed one another and wept with one another," it was "David weeping the most" (20:41 ESV). David is weeping with gratitude that his friend has shown himself capable of preferring their covenant to the authority of his father. Jonathan sees it as a mutual protection pact, between the Saulide dynasty and the Davidic: "Go in peace," he says to David, "because we have sworn both of us in the name of the LORD, saying, 'The LORD shall be between me and you, and between my offspring and your offspring, forever'" (20:42 ESV).

SERIES SIX

WISDOM AND FOOLS

1 Samuel 21–27

First Sam. 21:1–28:2 traces the elliptical path taken by divine providence to guide David toward his monarchic role. The working of historical providence here is a game of chess. David escapes from Saul to the shrine of Nob, where he makes the priest believe he is on a secret mission from the king, and thence on to Gath, where he feigns madness as a gesture of unthreatening submission to the Philistine chief (1 Sam. 21). David's antics rebound on the clerical townsfolk of Nob, when Saul's men murder the remnant of the Eliades in lieu of the refugee (1 Sam. 22). David rescues the people of Keilah from the Philistines. When he flees that stronghold on God's instruction, Saul's men come within an ace of capturing him. David and his desperados hide from Saul in the wilderness, but forgo several chances to kill him (1 Sam. 24; 26). The fugitive gets a foothold in Hebron (1 Sam. 25), but remains a freebooter, putting his militia at the service of the Philistine Achish (1 Sam. 27). David is moved backward, until he lands outside Israel and among Israel's hostile neighbors, and this turns out to be where he needs to be to achieve power over both Israel and Judah. The miracle is that David's retreat *is* the way forward.

Because David's rise and Saul's fall is historically based, it lives on in the events and persons to which it leads. Because he is a real historical figure, David has no avatars. Because historicity is important to it, historical reenactment should have no place in theological exegesis. David lives today in what he wrought. "History . . . is essentially what passes on," and therefore "the events recounted in the Bible

. . . all exhausted . . . their historical role at the same time as their factual reality: in its entirety . . . history" as such "is a preparation for something else" (Lubac 2007: 322). Or, as Stephen Freeman puts it, "You are not a Bible character."

Many authors have advised their sovereigns to the contrary, endeavoring to discover a literal recurrence of David's feats in their contemporary political situations. In 24:1–28:2 the apparent usurper but real king is pitted against the pretender but holder of the throne. This contest excited attention in the sixteenth century, when the rights of Christians were topped by the divine rights of persecuting kings, and again in the seventeenth century, when Royalists faced off against Puritans. Both appropriated different aspects of David's demeanor to their own cause, the Royalists noting his unceasing reverence for Saul's anointing, the Republicans observing the persecution of this vagabond by the royal house, each "interpreting to their own purposes the significance of David's refusal to slay the Lord's anointed."[1] Theology has attempted to breathe life into David by denominating a favored politics as "Davidic."

The understanding of a situation far separated from the interpreter in time and space requires making an analogy between present and past. If the men and women of the Early Iron Age had no similarities to us, we would not find them incomprehensible, but understanding them would be like understanding an ant colony, an exercise in scientific observation rather than humane empathy. Hypermodern subjectivists apart, most people think there is some kinship between historically distant peoples; we take an interest in historical figures because we empathize with them. Anachronism—or imagining distant peoples as literally folks like us—is funny because it is true. In historical fiction and movies, anachronism makes us laugh because it hits the spot: it strikes the intuition that our ancient forebears were like we are. Historical analogies work because human beings are ever subject to the same affective and existential exigencies and freedoms: "A modern woman may understand many things about Cleopatra . . . : because human nature does not change, because she may understand some of Cleopatra's personal characteristics, her femininity, her problems, because she belongs to the same genus and species as her sister." Theology likewise uses analogy. Theological analogy turns on Christ. David's analogies to us are linked to his kinship to Christ. The reason why it is easy to conflate historical and theological typologies is that Christ is our brother; the reason why it is dangerous to confuse theological and historical analogies is that Christ's brotherhood to any individual historical person is more concrete and temporally specific than their kinship with any other human being. Though "each of us may have at least *one drop* of Cleopatra's blood in his veins," each of us bears the whole image of Christ in a unique way, in our time-bound vocation. It's unwise to link real contemporary situations to David's, because the

1. Raymond-Jean Frontain, "Transformations of the Myth of David," in *The David Myth in Western Literature*, ed. Raymond-Jean Frontain and Jan Wojcik (West Lafayette, IN: Purdue University Press, 1980), 6.

analogy is often the less embodied one of history, not the more richly incarnate theological analogy. The "poetic truth about the unity of mankind, living and dead,"[2] tends eschatologically toward a more solidly esthetic truth, the hilarity of the universal body of Christ.

Both the historian and the theologian treat the events as typical. But the typologies have different sources: for the historical case, the analogy is generated by distant folk having been our ancestors. Having caused us, they are usually similar to us. In the theological case, the analogy is generated by Christ's action in transforming all citizens of his kingdom into the Jews of the New Testament and so making David and Saul our ancestors. Historical analogy looks to a set of causes behind us, whereas theological analogy is prophetic and eschatological and looks to the transformation of history by an event above history.

The type of David as proto-royalist or proto-Puritan is literally there in the scripture. With their propositionalist conception of revelation, the early moderns may have been inclined to think that the letter of scripture should be literally repeated in the circumstances of their day. In this respect, the theology of the last hundred years, which sees divine revelation as much in the general pattern of the events of the Old Testament as in its propositions, is at an advantage in descrying a genuine typology. One general pattern in 1 Samuel is that material culture is not normative in itself; it is the vision of the city of God that generates cultural forms, and not vice versa. David's advantage over Saul is that he has the imagination to put monarchy on a new footing, rather than trying to rest it in the old tribal culture. He sees that the imagined, ideal event transforms the material circumstance, rather than material circumstances dictating events. The spirit of David's actions was not made to be teleported into yet another physical body, real kings or generals or poets, because it was not generated by material circumstances: David was the resourceful creator of situations. Origen appreciated that it is wrong to think "the historical events are types of other historical events, and the physical actions are types of other physical actions; rather, the physical actions are types of the spiritual; and the historical events are types of the intelligible" (Origen, *Commentary on John* 10.13, cited in Lubac 2007: 324).

The liturgical meaning of the Old Testament types is not a literal one. When they become types of the Christian sacraments, the Old Testament scenes are reborn within the souls of Christians; finished and gone as history, they live again in the Christian spirit. In the liturgy of baptism, the crossing of the Red Sea is no longer about the historical event of the liberation of the Israelites from Egypt. It is an anticipation of the spiritual event of the liberation of Christ and Christians from death.

The exegesis of 1 Samuel is not given much guidance by liturgical tradition, since no scene in 1 Samuel is used in the sacramental liturgy of the church. The

2. John Lukacs, *Historical Consciousness; or, The Remembered Past*, new ed. (New York: Schocken, 1985), 248, emphasis added.

sacramental liturgy of the church is its model for how to exercise typological exegesis, and nothing in 1 Samuel became a sacramental type. Rites for the coronation of Christian kings were developed between the eighth and tenth centuries. The consecration of Charlemagne as Holy Roman emperor by Pope St. Leo III on Christmas Day 800 speeded their evolution. The coronation of kings by their bishops was modeled on the coronations of Saul and David by Samuel. But extrabiblical coronation is not a sacrament per se, not one of the seven sacraments of the church. It is a broadly sacramental action, like blessing a church building. Rather than one of the seven sacraments, the anointing of kings is what Catholics call a "sacramental," like the blessing of meals, holy objects, icons, or buildings. Coronation belongs with the generalized meaning of "sacramental" that Alexander Schmemann used when he spoke of "the sacramental universe," not to the focused meaning of a liturgical sacrament that generated patristic biblical typology. Since it is sacramental, not a sacrament, instead of making a literal parallel between David's kingship and that of their contemporary monarchs, exegetes do better to be a bit imaginative about the analogy.

In the coronation ceremony, the king is crowned by the bishop, and since this action is not a sacrament, it is not axiomatic for our interpretation of scripture in the same way as, for instance, the use of the Passover scene in the liturgy of the Pasch, with its baptismal rite, determines the Christian understanding of the exodus. It does not follow that this tradition gives us no help at all in obtaining a historical and theological grasp of 1 Samuel. The image of the king as crowned by the bishop, the representative of God's church, enables the modern reader to keep the political aspect of 1 Samuel in perspective. The image of Christian coronation reminds us that monarchy "is not strictly a political institution," since it represents the moral elements in "national life which transcend the political plane, but without which a purely political system cannot function satisfactorily."[3] Reading 1 Samuel against the backdrop of the consecration of kings by bishops and of emperors by popes makes our imagination expand beyond its description of governments to the author's theological implication. Bishops and popes conceived their role in consecrating kings on the model of the prophet Samuel anointing Saul and David because the prophets are the predecessors to the apostles and the bishops are successors to the apostles.

Liturgical typology can teach us about how to read scriptural episodes that are not the foci of the church's sacraments. The first thing the church does with scripture is to enact it in baptism and the other six sacraments. Second, and dependent upon this, it preaches it. It is because "the typology of the liturgy" is "always spiritualizing" (Lubac 2007: 443) that preaching has a spiritual meaning. The sacraments are not historical reenactment but spiritual enactment. The church brings the scripture to life by enacting it. One sort of spiritual enactment of scripture

3. Christopher Dawson, "The Tradition of Christian Monarchy," *The Month* 9 (1953): 261–66 at 264.

that is extrasacramental is the moral behavior of believers. When it informs their moral vision, Old Testament history is spiritually reenacted in people's lives. This valuable way of bringing the scripture to life has its drawbacks, as a hermeneutical key. To think of the sacramentally relevant parts of scripture as performed in the liturgy but of its history as conveying moral examples may abstract the histories from their concrete, esthetic base, especially if we think of ethics as prohibitions and injunctions. This runs the risk of legalism. When, for instance, Melanchthon used the notion that David "restrained himself and did not kill Saul" to illustrate that tyrannicide is alien to faith he makes David a particular case to which a lawyer can refer. Even though the natural law would "allow that a manifest tyrant may be killed," Melanchthon comments that the faithful David would not kill a king (cited in Gosselin 1976: 94–95). Though Melanchthon is right about that moral point, one needs to be careful to steer clear of biblical-case citation and to avoid making ourselves Bible characters in an abstract legal sense. What legal cases have in common is what can be abstracted from the particular case, the rules that atemporally apply to all. Practical Christian ethics is dramatic, because no two cases are alike. It is about the believer's free interpretation of his calling, the use of the role God gives him. The commonality between ethical situations lies not in the rules but in the concrete role images. High drama in the original event, the exodus remains dramatic in its sacramental, liturgical form: the historical Jews and the Christian baptized take on the role of liberated ones.

Coronation is a broadly sacramental action, a piece of political theater, in which the king receives his role at the hands of the bishop and is publicly acknowledged in it by the people. In that sense, theater as such can be a sacramental action, and the performance of a play can be a sacramental event. One way of keeping the moralizing exegesis of the histories in contact with the sacramental exegesis of liturgically oriented texts is to conceive biblical ethics dramatically. Shakespeare made a good spiritualizing exegesis of the David stories when he reinterpreted them in his plays. Addressing questions similar to the David stories as the early modern exegetes, but without making Hamlet an avatar of David, Shakespeare gives his reconfiguration of the biblical stories a universal quality. The "similarities between the story of David and the tragedy of Hamlet . . . suggest how universal issues . . . tend to realize themselves in similar forms."[4] Biblical revelation has its own, dramatic natural-law theory or universal-moral typology. Shakespeare creates a moral story analogous to the biblical exemplar, not its one-to-one repetition.

The postfiguration of a biblical character who inhabits its moral vision and dilemma does not look literally like his exemplar.[5] The player is aiming morally

---

4. Gene Edward Veith Jr., " 'Wait upon the Lord': David, Hamlet, and the Problem of Revenge," in *The David Myth in Western Literature*, ed. Raymond-Jean Frontain and Jan Wojcik (West Lafayette, IN: Purdue University Press, 1980), 82.

5. The term "postfiguration" was coined by Murry Roston to describe Elizabethan dramas; see *Biblical Drama in England: From the Middle Ages to the Present Day* (London: Faber & Faber, 1968), 69.

to create an after-figure of David and the rest, not a copy. Just as Christ is prefigured by David, so he is postfigured by the Christian disciple. The locus of all the analogies is Christ. Whereas the archetype of the expectation of one-on-one repetitions of biblical events in contemporary dress is the literal interpretation of revelation as a prediction of the millennial kingdom, the archetype for theological analogy is Christ's decision spiritually to recapitulate Old Testament history in the creation of a new kingdom of God. It is in his messianic consciousness that spiritual readings of the tales of the Davidic monarchy are first born and to which they must always return. It is Christ's act of turning the image of the Davidic kingdom into the kingdom of God that makes the Old Testament live today as a Christian moral vision. The stories of David have become universal exemplars of moral action by entering the mind and imagination of David's heir and being recast there as the city of God. The first person in whom the Old Testament is spiritually internalized and transformed is Christ. This is our authority for reading these stories allegorically. Any millenializing or politicizing reading not centered on Christ and that looks, not for postfigurations of Christ, but for generalized moral aims, has lost the plot. In Christ's interpretation of his role as the new David and of his mission as enacting a new kingdom, "the passage from one Testament to another is carried out, the alchemy that transforms the one into the other" (Lubac 2007: 465–66).

Episode One: Economical with the Truth (1 Sam. 21)

Resealing his covenant with Jonathan gave David a single safe port in a sea of enemies. It does not quite do to call him stateless, because a stable state did not yet exist. Nor can we say he is outside the law, since it would be a stretch to see lawfulness in Saul's kingdom. Better to call David at Nob and in Gath estranged, since most around him are hostile: there is a price on his head for any Israelite who fears the name of Saul, and he is not exactly a hero to the denizens of the Philistine Pentapolis. He has exchanged the role of harpist-warrior for that of refugee. He would not be asking the Israelite priest at Nob for five loaves of bread unless he and his followers were out of cash and rations. Why barter rubricist jokes with the priest to get a few loaves unless you are hungry and need them? With no direction home and no sign that his ship will come in, David is yet buoyant. The priest turns out to be an admirer who has treasured up the sword with which David decapitated Goliath. The good luck of finding a priestly fan who, with clerical fastidiousness has "wrapped" the trophy "in a cloth behind the ephod" (21:9) gives David a piece of weaponry.

If not prohibited by Mosaic law, keeping a bronze sword in a holy place was at least cultically risqué. Exodus 20:25 prohibits using iron tools for building a place dedicated to God. The Deuteronomic 1 Kgs. 6:7 knows this prohibition: the stones for the Jerusalem temple were prefabricated "at the quarry, so that neither hammer nor axe nor any tool of iron was heard [at the temple] while it was being built" (ESV). Since the most likely cause of this prohibition was that tools of iron were linked to weapons of iron (McNutt 1990: 218–19), keeping a sword in a sanctuary infringes the spirit if not the letter of the law. This temple priest seems to be no innocent. Ahimelech is not, perhaps, the naïve victim of David's wordplay that Lemche imagines when he asserts that "David deliberately tricked the poor priests into helping him": the priest against whom, as Lemche thinks, the cunning fugitive perpetrates a "fraud" (1978: 9) is himself no stranger to living outside the law.

Nob is not a safe harbor: "fear of Saul" drives David to "Achish the king of Gath" (21:10). We know from the ark stories of 1 Sam. 4–6 that Gath was a Philistine stronghold. Was the sword of "Goliath, of Gath" (17:4) what drew David to flee to that city: "Where does a wise man hide a leaf?" "In the forest."[6] The legend of his triumph precedes David and gives him away. Achish's servants remind the king, "Did they not sing one to another of him in dances, saying, 'Saul hath slain his thousands, and David his ten thousands'?" (21:11). He has been a defenseless stripling and a statue, and now David puts on a new feint—as a madman. Having found a bit of safety and a sword with Ahimelech, David hits a low point in Gath.

Although David does not ply his harp in this episode, one of the psalms was taken by Christian tradition to be David's song of his plight in Gath. Psalm 56 identifies itself as a prayer "of David, when the Philistines seized him in Gath": it prays for help from God, "for man tramples on me; all day long an attacker oppresses me." A downtrodden psalmist complains that "my enemies trample on me all day long; for many attacked me proudly" (56:1–3 ESV). The church fathers and the medieval monastic theologians expended a river of ink on the Psalms for every half pint they gave to the history recounted in the four books of Regum. Theological commentary on the Psalms abounded because the liturgical cycle and thus the thinking prayer of the monasteries revolved around the Psalter. When he touches on the Davidic kingdoms in book 17 of the *City of God*, Augustine hopscotches through a couple of episodes in 1–2 Samuel and leaps from 2 Samuel into the Psalms of David, upon which he lavishes his attention. The medievals interpreted David's life through the latticed rood screen of the Psalter. They read the Davidic psalms christologically. Augustine figures that "Gath" means "press," as in winepress. He understood David's being "trodden underfoot" in Gath as sacramentally referring to the crushing of the grapes, in a winepress from which flows the metaphorical wine of Christ's true, eucharistic blood. David's adventure in Gath is taken as a symbol of the passion. Augustine writes:

> "There held him," then, "Allophyli in Geth." We find indeed, brethren, David himself, son of Jesse, king of Israel, to have been in a strange land among the Allophyli [the

6. G. K. Chesterton, *Father Brown*, "The Sign of the Broken Sword."

Vulgate term for Philistines], when he was sought by Saul, and was in that city, and with the king of that city, but that there he was detained we read not. Therefore our David, the Lord Jesus Christ out of the seed of that David, not alone they held, but there hold Him still Allophyli in Geth. Of Geth we have said that it is a city. But . . . this name . . . signifieth "press." . . . How . . . is He held in Geth? Held in a winepress is His Body, that is, His Church. What is, in a winepress? In pressings. But in a winepress fruitful is the pressing. A grape on the vine sustaineth no pressing, whole it seemeth, but nothing thence floweth: it is thrown into a winepress, is trodden, is pressed; harm seemeth to be done to the grape, but this harm is not barren; nay, if no harm had been applied, barren it would have remained.

. . . Fear not because man hath trodden thee down: have thou wine, a grape thou hast become in order that thou shouldest be trodden. . . . And let him faint not in this treading down, knowing Him on whom he is calling, and by whose example he hath been made strong. The first cluster in the winevat pressed is Christ. When that cluster by passion was pressed out, there flowed that whence "the cup inebriating is how passing beautiful!" [Ps. 23:5]. Let His Body likewise say, looking upon its Head, "Have pity on me, O Lord, for man hath trodden me down: all day long warring he hath troubled me." "All day long," at all times. Let no one say to himself, There have been troubles in our fathers' time, in our time there are not. If thou supposed thyself not to have troubles, not yet has thou begun to be a Christian. . . . But when thou hast begun godly to live in Christ, thou hast entered into the winepress; make ready thyself for pressings; but be not thou dry, lest from the pressing nothing go forth.

. . . A grape I was, wine I shall be. . . .

Let not the Body disdain that which hath gone before in the Head. (Augustine, cited from Library of the Nicene and Post-Nicene Fathers 8.219–20)

"The first cluster in the winevat pressed is Christ": David's sufferings at Gath prefigure those of Christians because they foreshadow the passion of Christ. Since the meaning of Gath as "press" is not central to this scene and is not adverted to in 1 Sam. 21 or Ps. 56, one may feel that Augustine is overegging the pun. He seems to be thinking about the fruitfulness of the passion, about the eucharistic wine, the blood of Christ, not about David in Gath. Augustine seems to be squeezing or treading the Old Testament underfoot. Exhibiting a "distaste for a literal understanding of the Psalms and David, which could only be detrimental to the worth of the Old Testament," Augustine may be thought to have "taken a historical fact and made of it a prophetic message," subjecting "David's experience at Gath" to being "squeezed" in his "exegetical press" (Gosselin 1976: 15–16).

If we concur in this disparaging assessment of Augustine's exegetical technique, we will probably accord the same criticism to a modern theologian who seems likewise to read 1 Sam. 21 through a christologized Psalter. Von Balthasar sees in this chapter an upswing followed by a knock-back that deposits David into utter humiliation. He says that "with deceptions (21:2f.) that unwittingly unleash terrible consequences (22:6–19), and yet in the end turn to the advantage of this eternally happy-go-lucky man," David the survivor in the Ahimelech episodes falls into the abyss in Gath: "At the low point of his flight he has to play the lunatic and so invite contempt" (1983–91: 6.111–12). We may feel that von Balthasar here excessively "miserabilizes" David, just so that he can force his exploit into parallel with the passion. For isn't David once again playacting? Isn't he *still* the survivor, even at Gath, when he seizes on the camouflage of lunacy: "He changed his behaviour before them, and feigned himself mad in their hands, and scrabbled on the doors of the gate, and let his spittle fall down upon his beard" (21:13)? Disguising himself by diminishing himself is successful, just as it had with Goliath: these Gathites likewise discount David as a danger to themselves: "Said Achish unto his servants, 'Lo, you see the man is mad: wherefore then have ye brought him to me? Have I need of madmen, that ye have brought this fellow to play the madman in my presence? Shall this fellow come into my house?'" (21:14–15). Achish doesn't want David around: "Philistine doctrine back then insisted that madness was contagious, and subsequent scientific studies have proved this primitive superstition largely correct" (Heller 1985: 225). In Achish's imagination David has become a nuisance—"have I need of madmen. . . . Shall this fellow come into my house?"—that is, a time waster, not a threat. David's willing invitation of "contempt" (von Balthasar 1983–91: 6.111–12) may seem to resolutely cheerful readers to be nothing to be pitied, but rather the piece de résistance of David's many stage triumphs. Achish even seems to realize David is acting—"ye have brought this fellow to play the madman in my presence." Achish so arrogantly despises the actor that he takes him at his own presentation. Isn't this intelligent ploy for escaping with his life a good joke at Achish's expense on David's part? Can't we keep von Balthasar's characterization of David as an "eternally happy-go-lucky man" and relegate the "low point" idea to the margins?

No, since David *is* a comic hero, and since the epic that sings his deeds is a theological comedy, the lighter side of life cannot be all there is to comedy. Comedy isn't just about a string of funny things happening, although Hollywood makes that its most obvious feature. It's when comedy, with its happy ending, is rigidly demarcated from tragedy, with its fated fall, that both genres morph into melodrama. If we think of comedy as fun and games and of tragedy as relentlessly grim, then comedy turns into mechanically optimistic melodrama, and tragedy becomes the pessimistic melodrama of a blameless victim beset by evil. Scripture study is packed with scholars who, having had their fill of melodramatizing Saul as a victim of evil forces, take to turning David into a devious, melodramatic villain. Whence Lemche's somewhat humorless opinion that, in this story "of how David came on the Philistine payroll," the would-be usurper of Saul's throne wickedly "had no . . . scruples about transferring his allegiance to his former enemies": "David turned to the Philistines to be on the safe side and perhaps to get a new starting point for his comeback" (1978: 10). There's no way back to a plain unbiased assessment of the historical facts about David, because we have to decide with what moral tonality to imagine him. Those who find David's amoral exploits funny will do so because he is the human great-grandfather of the one who "redeemed us from the curse of the law" (Gal. 3:13): to the Christian, David's comic good fortune represents grace. We have to choose between standing outside scripture and reading it through the lens of melodrama or standing within its objective perspective and reading it theologically. If we house our reading within the scripture, we enable its drama to remind us what comedy and tragedy actually are. In reality, since both tragedy and comedy are equally serious and each in its own way deals with evil, comedy and tragedy are close to each another, analogous. Reading 1 Sam. 21 theologically means reading it christologically, because the life of Christ is the founding image of the comic hero, miraculously bouncing back and defeating his foes, and the original tragic hero, subject in his passion to contempt and death. This is not just a gesture of interpretation: by holding tragedy and comedy together, in his death and resurrected generation of a church, Christ makes the tragic and the comic creative only by reference to one another. That is, he makes the tragedy of his passion and the comedy of his eucharistic, inebriated church analogous to one another. He *is* the analogy of the two genres: "The first cluster in the winevat pressed is Christ." By rescuing the world from trivial lightheartedness and fated doom, he rescues it from melodrama.

Christ does this incognito, in disguise, "veiled in flesh," as man (Charles Wesley, "Hark the Herald Angels Sing"). David is likewise incognito throughout this episode. For here, explicitly and implicitly for the first time since his anointing, David is a king. For those who want to see David as a clever rascal, his lie to Ahimelech is a good hook. To the priest's question, "Why art thou alone, and no man with thee?" (21:1), David replies, "The king hath commanded me a business, and hath said unto me, 'Let no man know anything of the business whereabout I see thee, and what I have commanded thee: and I have appointed my servants to such and such a place'" (21:2). Although David's spiel is in a sense duplicitous, his words are deceptively simple not simply deceptive, for David is a secret king, a king who is moreover in hiding, and he has, as it were, given himself the order to conceal his business from all around him. In fact, "David's deceptive statement is accurate: few Israelites are yet aware of David's true position as the one charged by the LORD to be king over them" (Polzin 1989: 194–95, 203). Achish's servants seem to know the truth of the matter, "Is not this David the king of the land?" (21:11) they say, ineffectually trying to warn Achish against him.

Thomas Aquinas cites Jerome to the effect that dissimulation isn't always wrong: "David 'changed his countenance before' Achish king of Geth. Therefore not all dissimulation is a sin," he notes in the second objection of his question "Whether all dissimulation is sin?" Unimpressed by this example, Thomas maintains that "dissimulation is properly a lie told by the signs of outward deeds" and is always sinful. But he follows Augustine in seeing that to pretend is to lie only when the pretense means nothing else than what it literally means: "To pretend is not always a lie: but only when the pretense has no signification, then it is a lie. When, however, our pretense refers to some signification, there is no lie, but a representation of the truth." In other words, if a statement corresponds to no real state of affairs, it is a lie. It is a lie because it is empty of reference. But not all simulative statements are lies: as Augustine says, a figure of speech is not a lie, and when one's deeds are acted figures of speech and capture some metaphorical reality, they are not lies, because one's acting does correspond with some reality. Hence, Thomas concludes, "David's change of countenance" before Achish "was a figurative pretense" (*Summa theologiae* II–II Q. 111 A. 1 ad 2 reply and ad obj. 2). David's line to Ahimelech and his figurative pretense before Achish are dramatizations of the truth. He is acting, but David the actor is presenting a metaphorical figure of a reality. Far from feeling mildly embarrassed by the church's reverential reading of David's actions, we should recognize that our tradition's ability to distinguish empty and meaningful dissimulations shows more sophistication than the moderns who lump together all deceptive actions as lies.

For the everyday, quotidian comic hero, dissembling madness is par for the course of pratfalls, for the everyday comic hero has not far to fall. But for a man who recognizes himself and is recognized by others as a king to let "spittle fall down upon his beard" (21:13) is to drop from a great height. David begins the episode riding the crest of the wave of his triumph over Goliath, and it metonymically carries him as far as Gath, where it is recalled and endangers him: he has to drop from this pedestal to save his life. His regal invitation to "contempt" (von Balthasar 1983–91: 6.111–12) is an invitation to pity. It shows as it creates the seriousness of the comic hero, his proximity to death and shame. There is nothing funny about it. It is miserable "to play the madman in [the] presence" of the Philistine king of Gath (21:15).

The pious Homeric heroes offered "prayers, vows and sacrifices" to their gods.[7] In another comic epic, set in the same epoch as Regum, a heroic king repeatedly disguises himself in order to return home to his rightful kingdom. Unlike the tragic heroes of the *Iliad*, Odysseus uses guile (*metis*) rather than force (*bie*) to secure his aims. Odysseus's use of lowly disguises, like the beggarly costume he adopts once in Ithaca, constitutes a breach with the heroic world, in which a man's honor is the acceptance of his status by others, his reputation. "Odysseus' affinity to disguise" is a source of "the capacity for endurance that is expressed in his characteristic epithet, 'πολυπτας,' 'much-enduring.' It represents the ability to endure a suspension of recognition—both in the narrow sense of recognition of identity, and in the broader sense of recognition of achievement and status—that other Homeric heroes were unable to tolerate."[8]

Calvin observes that according to 1 Sam. 21 David avoided being apprehended by Achish "by feigning madness; but this psalm proves that he must have been engaged in fervent supplication, and that faith was secretly in exercise even when he betrayed this weakness" (1845–46: 2.347). David prayed when he rolled frothing on the ground? That may seem to put an excessively pious gloss on our comic hero.

7. Jasper Griffin, *Homer on Life and Death* (Oxford: Clarendon, 1980), 148.
8. Howard W. Clark, *The Art of the Odyssey* (Englewood Cliffs, NJ: Prentice-Hall, 1967), 5.

But David's discounting his status is his tapping his own source of endurance, his moment of truth in which he makes himself wholly and simply reliant on God's promise. In Greek myths and the Homeric hymns, "disguise is typically not a human but a divine strategy": the gods disguise themselves as shuffling elders when they visit the earth. So for Odysseus to conceal his true name is simultaneously a discarding of his proper status, the humility that gives him a saving endurance, and a transcendence of normal human limits, by which he shows himself to be "like the gods for him the experience of mortal limitation is a form of playacting."[9] The *Iliad's* tragic tale of the fall of Troy relates the impassible deafness of the Fates even to the petition of the gods and to the "tears of blood" wept by Zeus, father of gods and men, over the impending death of his son Sarpedon (*Iliad* 16.425–61). Conversely, the *Odyssey* presents the approachability of the gods, and through Athena's near inability to resist Odysseus's prayers for her assistance (*Odyssey* 13.324–55), it shows the mutability of the gods, their closeness to us.

If we find it difficult to imagine that David was praying for help while he mimicked a madman to save his skin, we might ask ourselves if we rate prayer for help as rather low in our hierarchy of spiritual exercises. Do we regard the prayers of the foxhole as the practice of half-believers who have yet to grasp God's disdain for such worldly concerns as mere physical survival? If so, then we have set the vulgar *is* at too great a distance from the spiritual *ought*: for David's world, as for the world of the *Odyssey*, and in the real world in which we live, the good is simultaneously the right and the enjoyable, like fair-trade double-chocolate cookies. Even Calvin is a little nervous about conceding that David's fear of murder by the Philistines cooperated with his faith, when he mimicked the madman: "He would not appear to have been under that inordinate agitation of mind, which instigates men to adopt methods of relief which are positively sinful; but in the desperate emergency to which he was reduced, he was compelled through fear to employ an artful device, which might save his life, although it would lower his dignity in the eyes of the world. . . . It is . . . apparent from this psalm, what a strenuous contest there was between faith and fear in his heart" (1845–46: 2.347).

And yet, God's providential care for his chosen is so humble in itself that it can accept even an artful device as a petition and a prayer. Comedy teaches us the humility of the divine, the proximity of divine good to human good, by presenting us with heroes whose near-disasters are averted in such extravagantly unlikely ways that we can only call the comic hero graced. It is funny that the Philistines fell for David's artful device, his figurative playacting. It is funny because it rewards the everlasting human hope that "ought" (the just and the right) and "is" (survival and enjoyment). Without a prayer of survival, David prays by throwing himself on the truth of his identity, the author of his kingship, God. David can pray, can return to the truth of his human identity, because he is humble. It gives him access to God when severely pressed. When he "feigned himself mad in their hands, and scrabbled on the doors

9. Ibid., 11, 14.

of the gate" (21:13), David does not assume a cunningly deceptive appearance of humility: as he *does* humble, so he *is* humble, for the hiddenness of God is not just the external appearance of humility, but the most authentic humility.

Episode Two: Consequences of Economy (1 Sam. 22)

This episode has stimulated the imaginations of those patristic and medieval theologians who discerned in Saul's pursuit of David the persecution of the church. Some theologians' imaginations may even seem to have become overstimulated by the apparent parallels. They have found apocalyptic overtones in it. Cassiodorus saw Doeg the Edomite as "the foe of David, just as antichrist will be the enemy of Christ. Doeg destroyed priests; antichrist will make martyrs" (*Expositions of the Psalms* 51.1–2, in Franke 2005: 298). Such apparently exaggerated efforts to find christological meaning in the text provoke an equally forceful counterreaction. Some modern literary readers have countered the determination to find meaning in Doeg by noting how contingent his presence is in 1 Sam. 21: he is, for some, representative of the way in which the Hebrew scriptures resist imposition of typological meaning, because, as the narrative seems to present him, he is a trace or residue of meaninglessness, someone who just happens to be there, witnessing David's conversation with Ahimelech by chance. Is Doeg the lord of the world, or is he some random guy? Is providence present in this episode?

It may seem to overdo things to see raw evil set against pure good here, because, looking back at 1 Sam. 21, we can see that David brought this about himself, with his twofold concealment of the truth. Unlike those Christians who, as the book of Revelation and Christ's own apocalyptic warnings teach, will face persecution by satanic powers in the last days, Ahimelech is not a fully knowing or willing believer. The parallel between David and Christ seems to fall through here, because David deceived his follower. David had soothed Ahimelech's anxious inquiries about what he was doing traveling "alone" by claiming to be on the "business" of the "king"; the pretender gilded the half-truth and forestalled further interrogation by claiming that the king had ordered him to keep his mission secret (21:1–2). Ahimelech thus unearthed Goliath's sword and gave it to the "king's messenger," innocent of David's interpretation of the word "king." Falling in with the story, the unworldly priest is also persuaded to supply David with the "hallowed bread" for which the runaway had come foraging, by David's endowing himself and his men with the character of priests and the food with the character of "common bread" (21:4). Ahimelech accepts this line of reasoning without question. He does not seem to act with intention to save David from Saul. Whoever the Christian confessors of the last days will be, they will not be dupes or ingénues.

The present episode seems to show that Ahimelech is not complicit in David's plan. When Saul asks the priest, "Why have ye conspired against me, thou and the son of Jesse, in that thou hast given him bread, and a sword, and hast inquired of

God for him, that he should rise against me, to lie in wait, as at this day?" (22:13), Ahimelech assures him of his loyalty, claiming that he merely assisted the king's "faithful" servant, Saul's "son-in-law" (22:14), and denies the king's embellishment of his crimes: no ritual inquiry occurred under his hands (22:15). The reward for Ahimelech's truthfulness is Saul's blunt, "Thou shalt surely die, Ahimelech, thou, and all thy father's house" (22:16). Not only Ahimelech and his family suffer the consequences of David's duplicity in flight, but also the villagers who live round about the rural shrine: "And Nob the city of the priests smote he with the edge of the sword, both men and women, children and sucklings, and oxen, and asses, and sheep, with the edge of the sword" (22:19). The *ḥrm* of total extermination that Saul neglected to perform against the Amalekites is executed against the innocent priests of Nob and its villagers. At best, Ahimelech seems to have been caught up in a conflict that he did not initiate, "a sort of vendetta between the Saulides and the Shilonite priesthood from which Samuel sprang. Saul . . . accuses the Shilonites, now at Nob, of abetting David" and "obliterates their sanctuary" (Halpern 1981: 238). Ahimelech is thus a victim of David, Saul, and, ultimately, of the Lord's decision to uproot the Eliades.

But is Ahimelech as guileless as he at first appears? The name means "brother of the king," and he is kin to "king" David in his use of words. He foregrounds one aspect of the truth, that David is Saul's "son-in-law," and his answer to Saul weaves around the charges that are actually true, that he knowingly gave the outlaw the hallowed bread and the sword. Like many a purveyor of relics ever since, he even seems to have a stock of "Goliath swords" in the hold and gives one to Saul (22:10).[10] If we call David's words to the old priest "lies," then Ahimelech himself is likewise deceptive in the interests of survival. They are apparently brothers in deception when it comes to escaping Saul's threats. Several patristic writers sought to exculpate David from appearing to lie in 1 Sam. 21. To the literal-minded reader, some of the exegesis smacks of desperation, such as Ephraem the Syrian's suggestion that David really "was a priest, because he was a temple of the Spirit" (*Commentary on Tatian's Diatessaron* 5.24, in Franke 2005: 293). Augustine claims in one passage that, since Christ was "both . . . king and . . . priest," so too, in retrospect, was his venerable ancestor David, and David therefore could legitimately "represent the role of a priest, although he was patently a king, when he ate the show bread. For it is not lawful for anyone to eat that, except the priests alone" (*Harmony of the Gospels* 1.3.5, in Franke 2005: 294). That might seem to be pushing the boat out at bit, even if we accept his theory of the figurative pretense. An ancient interpretation that moderns may find more convincing, since it takes into account both historical development and the historical actor's own intentions, is John Cassian's explanation of how David's deception was acceptable in its time: in the early history of God's dealings with humanity, certain things that would later be called sinful were not abhorrent to God. Cassian argues that

10. Doubtless a textual corruption!

greater things were permitted them because it was a time of beginnings. For what is there to wonder at that when the blessed David was fleeing Saul and Ahimelech the priest asked him, "Why are you alone . . . ?" he replied . . . , "The king gave me a commission. . . ."? And again: "Do you have a spear or a sword at hand? For I did not bring my sword and my weapons with me because the king's business was urgent"? Or what happened when he was brought to Achish, the king of Gath, and made believe that he was insane and raging . . . ? . . . They lawfully enjoyed flocks of wives and concubines, and no sin was imputed to them on this account. . . . They also frequently spilled their enemies' blood with their own hands, and this was held not only to be irreprehensible, but even praiseworthy. We see that, in the light of the gospel, these things have been utterly forbidden, such that none of them can be committed without very serious sin and sacrilege. . . .

We believe that no lie, in however pious a form, can be made use of by anyone in a pardonable way, to say nothing of praiseworthily, according to the words of the Lord: "Let your speech be yes, yes, no, no. Whatever is more than these is from the evil one" [Jas. 5:12]. (John Cassian, *Conference* 17.18.1–2, in Franke 2005: 292–93)

John Cassian's point is that the ethical bar has been raised since Christ's preaching. His account takes note both of the historical actor's conscious experience of what happened (both Ahimelech and David intentionally withheld part of the truth in order to confuse their interlocutors) and of the newness of the gospel teaching.

Although Cassian's account is satisfying if taken narrowly in relation to 1 Sam. 21, it does not do full justice to it and especially not in relation to the follow-on episode in 1 Sam. 22. Two aspects of this story are mysterious, even if a lower standard of ethical behavior was expected of the patriarchs. The first is the sheer evil on display in Doeg the Edomite. The man turns up by chance in 1 Sam. 21: when David and Ahimelech met in the temple at Nob, "a certain man of the servants of Saul was there that day, detained before the LORD, and his name was Doeg, an Edomite, the chiefest of the herdsmen that belonged to Saul" (21:7). The silent overhearer was set there in order to return in 1 Sam. 22. When Saul, hot in pursuit of David asks the Benjamites, have "all of you conspired against me, and there is none that showeth me that my son hath made a league with the son of Jesse, and there is none of you that is sorry for me, or showeth unto me that my son hath stirred up my servant against me, to lie in wait?" (22:8), the inadvertent spy turns deliberate informer: "Then answered Doeg the Edomite, which was set over the servants of Saul, and said, 'I saw the son of Jesse coming to Nob, to Ahimelech the son of Ahitub.' " Doeg does not simply spill the beans but elaborates: "He inquired of the LORD for him, and gave him victuals, and gave him the sword of Goliath the Philistine" (22:9–10). Saul's men cannot stomach the order to murder Ahimelech and the priests, but the silent witness willingly prosecutes the crime: "The king said unto the footmen that stood about him, 'Turn and slay the priests of the LORD, because their hand also is with David, and because they knew when he fled, and did not show it to me.' But the servants of the king would not put forth their hand to fall upon the priests of the LORD. And the king said to Doeg, 'Turn thou, and fall upon the priests.' And Doeg the Edomite turned, and he fell upon the priests" (22:17–18). Those whom Doeg is to kill are given away by their clerical dress: he "slew on that day fourscore and five persons that did wear a linen ephod" (22:18). Doeg relishes the king's order down to the embellishment of the letter, slaying the townsfolk, who are absorbed into the clergy by their contiguity to the temple: "Nob the city of the priests," where the families of the priests dwelt, "smote he with the edge of the sword, both men and women, children and sucklings, and oxen, and asses, and sheep, with the edge of the sword" (22:17–19). Doeg does not merely slay, he *falls* on his human victims. Since priests and civilians are unarmed and cannot fight back, his sword comes "down" on their cowering bodies. Doeg's action is mysterious because it represents bottomless evil, evil beyond rational explanation.

David is conscious of responsibility for this onslaught. This is a second reason why excusing David's deception by setting it early in the economy of salvation, before higher standards of truthfulness were set by Christ, doesn't quite match the case. David acknowledges to Abiathar, the one priest who escapes to tell the tale, "I knew it that day, when Doeg the Edomite was there, that he would surely tell Saul: I have occasioned the death of all the persons of thy father's house" (22:22). David, who blithely deceives Achish and takes what John Cassian called "flocks of wives and concubines" (*Conference* 17.18.1–2, in Franke 2005: 292), recognizes *his* responsibility for the consequences of his meeting with Ahimelech. The beginning and end of the chapter show two antithetical sides of David's charisma. At the outset, the powerless are drawn to David: "David . . . escaped to the cave Adullam. . . . And every one that was in distress, and every one that was in debt, and every one that was discontented, gathered themselves unto him" (22:1–2). The merry gathering of outlaws is caught by Heller's paraphrase: "It began to look as though every deadbeat, misfit, rascal, and freebooter in the land was ambitious to throw in with me" (1985: 229). David draws people *up* into his charisma. But then, at the end of the episode, we perceive that to know David is also to draw a sword *down* upon oneself: "I have occasioned the death of all the persons of thy father's house" (22:22).

David draws to him, not only good fortune but bad. It is like the tragic paradox that, the more the light of Christ is preached and spread throughout the world, the darker grows the hatred for Christ and his followers. The light of Christ "not only uncovers the nature of darkness, it drives it from its hiding place and intensifies it." The enmity that Christ evokes falls both upon his conscious disciples and upon those who represent him by blamelessly falling in its path. To know David, as to know Christ, is to participate in the tragic aspect of divine providence. To know David isn't a superficial happy ending: it brings the characters he encounters into the arena of a drama, a conflict between good and evil, in which one suffers the mystery of evil. "At this point," where the knowledge and presence of the light evokes the ever greater resistance of evil, "we stand at the very core of drama and of tragedy."[11] This interpretation is that it is not solely prophetic: it does not only take David in his aspect as a forerunner of Christ, pointing forward, but also leaves him precisely where he is, in the economy of salvation, in what John Cassian calls his own "dispensation" (*Conference* 17.18.1–2, in Franke 2005: 292), for the degree of evil that David draws down on his followers is immensurably intensified in the persecution of Christ and his disciples. Relatively innocent in his own time and place, David is not wholly sinless; unlike Christ, he is still caught up in the evil that he contests. David's encounters with evil persons are not univocally matched by Christ's meeting and overmatching the evil one. His stories are shadows of the light to come. Divine providence does not roll ahead in a linear way, but as it were, spirals, accumulating instances, in expanding circles.

Thus interpreted as a fully historical parable of the struggle between holy innocence and those who despise it, this episode is one act in the continuous conflict of good and evil, or of what Augustine calls the city of man and the city of God. As Augustine puts its, "This Doeg, who had betrayed David's whereabouts . . . was a single person, but he represents a whole class of people. Similarly David embodies both king and priest, like one man with a dual personality, though the human race is one. So too at the present time and in our world let us recognize these two groups of people. . . . Let us recognize Doeg still with us today, as we recognize the kingly and priestly body today. . . . There is an earthly kingdom in this world today, but there is also a heavenly kingdom. Each of them has its pilgrim citizens . . . the kingdom that is to be uprooted and the kingdom that is to be planted for eternity" (*Explanations of the Psalms* 51, in Franke 2005: 298).

Precisely as a casual bystander turned informer turned collaborator in sin, Doeg is a typical representative of fallen humanity in its enmity to God and to other human beings. He acts the part of every sinner. The priests, in their linen ephods, and their families who die because they are all identified as a single group are set apart as holy people and, guileful or not, represent objective holiness and innocence. The people of Nob are like Christ's holy innocents: as Ephraem the Syrian says, the "priests were slain because of David, and the infants because of our Lord [Matt. 2:16]. Abiathar escaped . . . as John did from the infants." In Abiathar's person "the priesthood . . . of Eli was brought to an end, and in John the prophecy of the sons of Jacob was terminated" (*Commentary on Tatian's Diatessaron* 3.3, in Franke 2005: 298–99). David's words to Abiathar are an acknowledgement of blame, but also an indication that the prophecy to Eli (1 Sam. 2:30–33) has been unwittingly brought to its conclusion by his actions: the house of Eli has fallen "by the sword" (2:33 ESV). Within this terrible tragedy there is a mysterious, providential promise of protection. David tells Abiathar, "Abide thou with me, fear not: for he that seeketh my life seeketh thy life: but with me thou shalt be in safeguard" (22:23).

11. Hans Urs von Balthasar, *Theo-Drama: Theological Dramatic Theory*, vol. 5: *The Last Act*, trans. Graham Harrison (San Francisco: Ignatius, 1998), 201.

Episode Three: Trusting Oracles (1 Sam. 23)

This story is about faith and hope. It makes its hero's virtue of faith and infinite propensity for gracious good fortune imaginatively appealing. "They told David" (23:1) that Philistine militias are looting the people of Keilah, and he asks God whether this anonymous report is a call to assist them. His first thought is not to dash chivalrously to the rescue, but to find out from God what the meaning of the situation is for him. He does not just act or, upon acting, receive a military charisma, like some of the judges; nor is he the passive recipient of a prophetic oracle from a priest or prophet as he was in 22:3–5. Rather, "David takes the initiative" and receives an "unmediated or . . . unspecified communication" from the Lord (Polzin 1989: 202). David's people naturally advise him against it: the heat we're in now will be nothing if these gangsters draw fire from the Philistine armies: "Behold, we be afraid here in Judah: how much more then if we come to Keilah against the armies of the Philistines?" (23:3). So David asks God "yet again," and the Lord repeats the instruction, with an assurance of help: "Arise, go down to Keilah," leave the safety of the hills, "for I will deliver the Philistines into thy hand" (23:4). God is telling David that he must enter a place of greater danger. The self-help books might recognize this as a good gambit, since one sometimes has to take a risk in order to become a "highly effective person." But David's prayers do not evoke a promise of success in his own purposes; rather, the hero is assured that he will achieve the Lord's purpose. The outcome seems to be a tactical advance: David and his men have substituted their vulnerable cave hideouts for the fortress walls of the city of Keilah. By the tenth century, cities were encompassed by benched walls, and their gates had strong iron bolts, whose holes are still there for archeologists to see. It is to this apparently impregnable fortress that Abiathar the priest escapes, "with an ephod in his hand" (23:6), bearing the tool of his trade, the implement by which the Lord's will is made known. Saul conceives David's apparent safety as a net in which the outlaw has caught himself: "God hath delivered him into my hand: for he is shut in, by entering into a town that hath gates and bars" (23:7). The author knows about iron-bolted gates, which were a feature of Middle Eastern cities in the tenth–eighth centuries but had disappeared from view by the fourth century BC, when some revisionists set the "invention" of Regum (Dever 2002: 199–202).

David himself recognizes that city walls can lock a man in as much as they can lock an army out. Grateful as they are for their delivery, the people of Keilah could well hand over their savior, if the alternative was starvation under siege. So, with the ephod on tap, he asks God about his hunch that Saul is coming and that the Keilahites will betray their deliverer, and he receives the laconic, "He will come down" and "they will deliver thee up" (23:11–12). Sometimes the best answer to prayer is hearing what one didn't want to know. The ephods transmitted yes/no answers, and the author has translated the two yeses into the terse divine rejoinders of 23:11–12. Rather than asking for the bad news to be wrong or deflected, David prays well, because he asks for the bad news. He asks for what he has "certainly heard" (23:10) to be confirmed in the divine inquiry. God's reply reinforces David's conviction that his enforced position is one of greater weakness, all too pregnable, because it relies on trusting the Keilahites.

So David and his "six hundred" scatter "whithersoever they could go": they make the best of a bad situation and head for "the wilderness of Ziph" (23:13–14). Whereas the people of Keilah would have delivered him over to Saul, "God delivered him not into his hand" (23:14). God is not just guiding David, but deliberately countering Saul's intentions. Saul is doubly disempowered, unable to trust in God or in his eldest son for his grip on power. Jonathan slips to his beleaguered friend and rallies him with the confidence that "thou shalt be king over Israel, and I shall be next unto thee; and that also Saul my father knoweth" (23:17). Jonathan "strengthened [David's] hand in God" (23:16) by assuring him that destiny will carry him to the heights. Thus Jonathan helps David to believe in his divine appointment. Though Lemche doubtless has reasons for his certitude that the "sequence of events" in 23:16–18, where "Jonathan expresses the confidence that David was going to be king after Saul . . . has no historical value" (1978: 11), its psychological insight is fine. In their lowest moments, we do not tell our friends that they will get out of the woods with their bare skins, but make extreme and ridiculous predictions, promising them that their wildest hopes will be fulfilled.

The episode is structured around trust and betrayal. The Ziphites counter the narrator's exposition of the friends' aspirations with a word to Saul about "all the desire of thy soul" (23:20): the informers give a precise location for the hideaway. Knowing that moving his troop to one spot could give the unencumbered bandits time to escape, Saul tell the Ziphite agents to go and make sure of the location: "See therefore, and take knowledge of all the lurking-places where he hideth himself, and come ye again to me with the certainty" (23:23). Saul is matching David's cunning with his own and closing on him. David heads out for "the wilderness of Maon" (23:25); so does Saul, on his heels. The opponents come nearly face up: "Saul went on this side of the mountain, and David and his men on that side of the mountain," and with his more numerous troop, the chief can send his men round both sides (23:26). At this cliff-hanger, word comes to Saul that "the Philistines have invaded the land" (23:27). Just when he has pincered his prey, Saul is compelled to undertake more pressing business.

It is small wonder that generations of beleaguered Christians have seen themselves in David, "as in a mirror," taking the runaway king as their forerunner in persecution and looking to him as a sign of hope in times of oppression. David's kingship has been most real to Christians in the period of his life when it was real and yet still to be hoped for. Calvin sees his face in David's, because he believes "that whatever that most illustrious king and prophet suffered, was exhibited to me by God as an example for imitation" (1845–46: 1.25–26). The David whom he believed it was given him to imitate and whom he took as his model was not the overtly illustrious king in Jerusalem, but the resourceful-vulnerable outlaw in Ziph. Most believers from Augustine to Calvin to the contemporary persecuted Christians of India and Africa have believed in the historical reality of David because, by participating in experiences like his, they have participated in the suffering of Christ and have therefore known the faith and hope in which this real but powerless king lived and died. Taking Ps. 54 to be occasioned by David's betrayal by the Ziphites, Augustine remarks that we are discouraged in keeping the commandments of God by the blooming success of those who don't. Despite this poetic injustice, Augustine asks his congregation:

> Wouldest thou also wish to be a Ziphite? They flourish in the world, wither in judgment, and after withering, into fire everlasting shall be cast: wouldest thou also choose this? . . . If the flower of the Ziphites were to be desired, would not Himself thy Lord also in this world have flourished? Or indeed was there wanting to Him the power to flourish? Nay but here he chose rather amid the Ziphites to hide, and to say to Pontius Pilate, as if to one being himself also a flower of the Ziphites, and in suspicion about His kingdom, "My kingdom is not of this world" [John 18:36]. Therefore here He was hidden: and all good men are hidden here, because their good is within, it is concealed, in the heart it is, where is faith, where charity, where hope, where their treasure is. Do these good things appear in the world? Both these good things are hidden, and the reward of these good things is hidden. (Augustine, cited from Library of the Nicene and Post-Nicene Fathers 8.206)

For Augustine, the authentic David, like the authentic Christian, is the one who must "hide himself" (1 Sam. 23:19) from dangerous enemies. In books and movies where the allegory is too explicit, the message overwhelms its concrete medium and becomes false to flesh-and-blood experience. This is why people dislike overt allegory: it has so much of a design on us that it neglects what actually touches us, the concrete detail. The idea of David's persecution by Saul as an allegory of the experiences of the members of the city of God in its pilgrimage through history fits our human experience, because Christians learn through persecution that the kingship of Christ on earth is a matter of faith and hope in God's promise and providence. Calvin comments that the psalms recording David's flight from the treacherous Ziphites were set down by him "to teach us that we should never despair of divine help even in the worst situation. Surrounded as he was by hostile troops, and hemmed in on every side by apparently inevitable destruction, we cannot but admire the rare and heroical intrepidity that he displayed in committing himself, by prayer, to the Almighty. It might have appeared just as credible that God could bring the dead out of the grave, as that he could preserve him in such circumstances; for it seemed impossible that he should escape from the cave where he was concealed with his life" (1845–46: 2.321).

One reason why even skeptical moderns can make sense of an episode like this is that the author does not present David as eluding his pursuer in a way to which a historian could object. Because the narrative does not make use of what is to us the deus ex machina device of miracles, David's narrow escape is genuinely suspenseful. Saul and his men very nearly trap their prey in an entirely realistic way by surrounding the bandits when both groups are collected on opposite sides of the same hill ("Saul and his men compassed David and his men round about to take them"; 23:26), and Saul is called up short from the pursuit by a large-scale attack by a neighboring tribe, a setback that could and did happen to ancient Near Eastern chieftains. The reason for this narrative realism seems to be that the author is relatively rationalized himself. Whether or not one posits a Solomonic Enlightenment on the analogy of the Athenian one at the back of this, it seems to make sense to say, with von Rad, that the author or earlier sources that the author is using are confronted with a new and secularized notion of reality, one in which, rather than working through intermittent miracles, God acts in "every department of life, the wholly secular as well as the sacral," and for which, following the basic Yahwistic idea to its root, God is identified as the "cause of *all* things," even, as here, the attacks of the Philistines on Keilah, followed up by a full-scale invasion of "the land" (23:27). Rather than working through "wonders or . . . charismatic leaders," as in the biblical history down to the end of the era of the judges, from Samuel's resignation on, "events apparently develop in complete accord with their own inherent nature." The protagonists of the narrative are likewise depicted with psychological realism, like Saul's bursting stream of words to the Ziphites about his hated rival, because the author especially locates God's work in "the human heart," without confining it there, but rather, depicting God as using human designs as the means by which to take "control of history." The David of 1 Samuel is perhaps more believable and accessible to skeptical moderns than the blue-eyed David of Chronicles (which discreetly commences his story at the outset of David's kingship in Jerusalem). The David who "dealeth very subtly" (23:22) is accessible even to modern nonbelievers, because however pious he may be, he is acting to his own advantage and building up a stock of loyalties, alliances, and territories that could make for good leverage if Saul were out of the way. Even though our author's theology has it that God achieves his ends from within human impulses, this does not turn his protagonists into "religious characters": quite the reverse, "they are . . . passionately and doggedly pursuing their own aims" (von Rad 1962: 53, 316). And though God acted through miracles in biblical times and does so still today, it was a great and enlightened theological achievement to recognize the all-encompassing power of God at work as much in the secular as in the sacred world. In this narrative, God acts through the laws of the cosmos that he created, on the analogy to a human king's acting, not arbitrarily or through temperamental whim, but through the structure of law. And though it wins our hearts by presenting David's kingship at its least regal, and thus confirms the proverbial injunction "put not your trust in princes" (Ps. 146:3), our minds must know, too, that the author's regal concept of God's omnipotence found an analogy in the political achievement he credits to David, wielding the tribes of Israel together into a monarchic state.

Not that our author has any deistic concept of a God who is bound by his own laws: rather, like a human king, he uses the law to achieve his ends. It is persons and not the structure of their law who make things happen, in divine and human governance. The theological principle behind the narrative is thus thoroughly anthropic: God elects David from among all others to reign. The personal is thus drawn up into the political.

It is false to imagine that the idea of law that preceded the state is more Hebraic and superior to that which succeeded it. It is not accurate to claim that, with the monarchy, Israel exchanged an idea of law as "mutual understandings among human beings, culturally determined and relative—as well as changeable" for a "Greek idea of law." It is wrong to imagine that, with the monarchy that David inaugurated, Israel replaced a culture in which the "foundation of the community had nothing to do with a social agreement concerning divine legitimacy of social power structures" for one like that of the ancient Sumerians, in which "the political power structure derives from . . . the world of the gods from which," the Sumerian kings claimed, "kingship was lowered down from heaven" (Mendenhall 1973: 189, 195). Far from espousing a pagan mythology of kingship and power drawn from its Near Eastern neighbors, this episode lets us see David warts and all, hiding in woods, fields, and caves. As von Rad says, "Unlike the Babylonian dynasty" the "Davidic dynasty . . . did not 'come down at the beginning from heaven.' . . . No mythic dignity of any kind attaches to it. The historical texts allow the decisive political phases which led finally to David's elevation to the throne over all Israel to be clearly seen. The historical work which gives us the account of David's rise to power (I Sam. xvi.14–II Sam. v.12) sets before us with very matter-of-fact realism the tortuous path trodden by this erstwhile warrior in the service first of Saul and then of the Philistines, until he attained to the dignity of king over all Israel. . . . There is no possibility of regarding *him* as an incarnation of the deity, as . . . the Egyptian mythology of the king does!" (1962: 308–9, emphasis original).[12] That David the not-yet king, the David of faith and hope, is presented as an outlaw, a *habiru* or "troublesome parasocial element" (Lemche 1978: 11), and yet one and the same passionate personality as David the monarch, entails that all the prepolitical anarchism that he represents is drawn up into the monarchy, to enliven it and give vitality to its legal forms. With Saul the old tribal culture dies, and in David all that brotherhood meant to it is resurrected within the state. Far from a "divine legitima[tion] of social power structures . . . enter[ing]" Israelite culture "from paganism with David and Solomon" (Mendenhall 1973: 189, 195), David's monarchy represents the inclusion of "every one that was in distress, and every one that was in debt, and every one that was discontented" (22:2). As persecuted Christians have seen, this historical text prophesies that kingdom in which the poor are blessed and the hungry satisfied (Matt. 5:1–13). This episode inspires faith and hope because the wretched man in the woods

12. Van Seters 1983: 68–92 has a different assessment of Babylonian history writing.

(1 Sam. 23:15, 18–19) *is* the cunning man who becomes king in Jerusalem. This is the deep analogical and comic imagination of the scripture: outlaws with their hunger for justice are not set in contradiction to the law-keeping state or even paradoxically contrasted with it, as in jokes and satirical humor, but satisfyingly united to it in the figure of David.

Episode Four: Divine Providence Delayed (1 Sam. 24)

Hot on his rival's heels, Saul enters the "cave" "in the wilderness of En-gedi" (24:1, 3) in which David and his men are sheltering. "Three thousand . . . men" (24:2) would have given noisy warning of their approach. In a scene worthy of the *Odyssey*, the fugitives file into "the sides of the cave" (24:3), while Saul once again sleepwalks toward his destiny (cf. 1 Sam. 9). David's men believe that providence is on the side of their captain: "Behold the day of which the LORD said unto thee, 'Behold, I will deliver thy enemy into thy hand, that thou mayest do to him as it shall seem good unto thee'" (24:4). According to Melanchthon, these speak for "providence as natural law": they urge David to put God's promise into practice. David's cutting of the chieftain's skirt is a symbolic act in a primitive and therefore poetic society. To cut and appropriate a piece of the royal robe is to cut and appropriate a slice of the chieftain's charisma. This is why "David's heart smote him" (24:5): he has trespassed upon the sacral dignity of his chief. When David "cut off the skirt of Saul's robe" (24:4), however, he has performed a symbolic satire, not the real satirizing that the Lord performs on his foes: David has shown symbolically that he believes himself the true king, but he has not cut at Saul's body and seized the kingdom. One of those who get a grip on themselves "before proceeding to sin" (Chrysostom 2003: 21), David playacts the seizure of the kingdom but does not carry the metaphor over into reality: the plight of Saul is emphasized by the echo of the scene in which, begging Samuel not to remove his kingship from him, Saul had ripped the prophet's robe: "As Saul tore the skirt of Samuel's robe (*kenap mecilo*), David now cuts off the skirt of Saul's robe (*kenap hammecil*). The first action and its effect are ragged, the second sharp and incisive" (Polzin 1989: 209). David's delicate deliberation is contrasted with Saul's desperation. For all his precision tailoring, David restrained his hand from murder.

There are those who say that, historically, that was the only thing David could have done. Some revisionists claim that the traditional reading of David's gesture as an exercise in self-denial is wrong, because restraint was the only move open to David. Lemche argues, for instance, that "if David had killed Saul in the cave at En-Gedi, he would without doubt have lost his own life as well since Saul's army . . . , including Abner, was camped before the entrance to the cave" (1978: 10–11). It is indeed interesting to imagine what would have happened if Saul had failed to reappear among his army, the soldiers had sought him, found the right cave, and discovered him dead before his assailants had made a getaway. The "three thousand . . . men" might have massacred David and his smaller force. Or else, Abner, Saul's uncle, who, as 2 Samuel indicates, was a brutal and militarily efficient fellow, might have done a deal with David. We don't know whether his army would have wanted to kill David, once Saul is no longer in command. There is no telling how an army may react to the death of its general, especially when he is the LORD's anointed: the murder of the king might have been taken as either a sacrilegious act to be punished forthwith or as a divine indication of the ill-omened character of Saul's pursuit of David. All we can be sure of is that we know what did happen better than what would have been.[13] One might as well ponder what David's men might have done to him when they discover he has *not* killed Saul: "Even if" David "chose to . . . spare his assailant, it was likely he was also afraid they might slay him in the cave for undermining and betraying their safety and saving the life of their common foe" (Chrysostom 2003: 18).

Empirically, it is very rare indeed for a lone man backed by a desperado force voluntarily to seek contact with the leader of three thousand men intent on killing him. Statistically improbable, like many historical turning points, the scene between David and Saul dramatizes what is in the balance in the contest between the two men. The question at stake is both who is the anointed king of Israel? and who is the fitting ruler of the kingdom? Augustine points out that the issue is the kingdom as well as the king when he writes that

> the kingdom of Saul himself, who was certainly rejected and cast aside, was a shadow of the future kingdom that was to continue for ever. . . . The oil with which he was anointed—and because of that chrism he was called the anointed [*christus*]—is to be taken in a mystical sense and interpreted as a great sacrament. . . . David himself had such reverence for this sacrament in the person of Saul that he was smitten to the heart and shaken with dread when . . . he secretly cut off a tiny piece of Saul's robe from behind, so as to have a proof of how he had spared him when he could have taken his life. . . . David was filled with terror in consequence, for fear that he should be guilty of violating so great a sacrament in the person of Saul, simply because he had so treated even his clothing. (*City of God* 17.6)

For Augustine, the sacrament foreshadowed by King Saul is the kingdom announced by the true anointed, Christ. The question is thus: who has the moral right to rule the kingdom? The dialogue makes this clear. In reporting his rejection of his soldiers' advice, David seems to give a royalist explanation of why he stayed his hand, "I will not put forth my hand against my lord, for he is the LORD's anointed" (24:10). He calls Saul "my father" (24:11), which is not only an affective term but denotes the authority of the "daddy-chief" of the tribe. His verbal exaltation of "the LORD's anointed" (24:10), "the king of Israel" (24:14), highlights the disparity with his own nugatory status as "a dead dog, . . . a flea" (24:14). David wants to show Saul that he has nothing to fear from him: "David's

13. My thanks to Christopher Brittain for pointing this out to me.

purpose was to remove from Saul's mind the suspicions that led him to pursue the holy David with violence, supposing him to be his enemy" (*City of God* 17.6). For David, both the "flea" and "the LORD's anointed" king are together suing for judgment from the gate of heaven: "The LORD judge between me and thee, and the LORD avenge me of thee: but my hand shall not be upon thee. . . . The LORD therefore be judge, and judge between me and thee, and see, and plead my cause, and deliver me out of thy hand" (24:12, 15). David reminds Saul that, though administration by judges has had its day, deliverance of justice by the judge of all has not. In return, responding to this personal appeal, Saul—and not David—names the character of David's act. David has the right to rule the kingdom, Saul says, because he has shown mercy: "Thou art more righteous than I: for thou hast rewarded me good, whereas I have rewarded thee evil. . . . Thou hast dealt well with me: forasmuch as when the LORD had delivered me into thy hand, thou killedst me not. For if a man find his enemy, will he let him go well away? wherefore the LORD reward thee good for that thou hast done unto me this day. And now behold, I know well that thou shalt surely be king, and that the kingdom of Israel shall be established in thy hand" (24:17–20). With Saul's acknowledgement of David's persona as a man of mercy, the positions of the "dead dog" and "the king of Israel" are reversed, and Saul asks David for mercy: "Swear now therefore unto me by the LORD, that thou wilt not cut off my seed after me, and that thou wilt not destroy my name out of my father's house. And David swore unto Saul" (24:21–22).

It is, as Melanchthon noted, much more natural to us to conceive of God's providence in terms of condign punishment than of mercy. An aboriginal conception of divine justice in the Old Testament is the returning of like for like: we have seen this pattern in 1 Sam. 5–7. Divine justice ensures that, as a man sows, so shall he reap. In the wisdom tradition cited by David, "Wickedness proceedeth from the wicked" (24:13) and not only proceeds from the wicked, but rebounds on them. This rational, natural-law conception of providence works very well on the stage because it is enjoyable for an audience to see the working out of poetic justice. Late medieval tragedy, "which traced the rise and fall of great men, originally were studies of the fickleness of fortune, but soon came to illustrate God's punishment for sin, so that the concept of fortune gave way to the concept of providence. Applied to the rise and fall of kings and nations, the theme of the disasters that befall sin comprehends practically all of Renaissance tragedy."[14] A large subset of Renaissance tragedy is the revenge play: "God's revenge is the general theme dominating all the tragedies of the period; the revenge play is concerned with one variant of this theme, that of private revenge in its relation to God's revenge."[15] Shakespeare's *Hamlet* seems to reverse this theme and likewise to echo

14. Veith, "Wait upon the Lord," 81.
15. Lily B. Campbell, "Theories of Revenge in Elizabethan England," *Modern Philology* 28 (1931): 281–96 at 293.

the example of David. Hamlet forgoes the opportunity to murder Claudius, in parallel to David's staying of his hand against Saul in 1 Sam. 24 and 1 Sam. 26.

Both David and Shakespeare's tragic hero feign madness, and both meditate on the real nature of the divine providence when rendered homeless: "Hamlet, though thirsting for revenge" against Claudius, who has murdered his father and taken the throne, "is stymied in his actions and, like David, exiled." Sailing to England, he discovers that Rosencrantz and Guildenstern carry an execution order on his head. Telling the tale to Horatio, he says that "though experienced as free will, he now perceives" his random act of foraging through their papers "as being guided":

> Praised be rashness for it—let us know,
> Our indiscretion sometimes serves us well,
> When our deep plots do pall; and that should learn us
> There's a divinity that shapes our ends,
> Rough-hew them how we will.[16]

It is when he escapes death by a random hair's breath that Hamlet discovers what it is to have faith in God's guidance of events. Hamlet sends his minders to the death intended for himself, enabled to do this by his chance possession of his father's seal:

> Why, even in that was heaven ordinant.
> I had my father's signet in my purse.

Hamlet still knows that it is his duty to avenge his father's murder and knows that his own death is therefore imminent. But he no longer seeks to allocate the time and the place. He tells Horatio:

> We defy augury: there is a special providence in the fall of a sparrow. If it be now, 'tis not to come; if it be not to come, it will be now; if it be not now, yet it will come—the readiness is all. Since no man owes of aught he leaves, what is't to leave betimes? Let be.[17]

Whereas the heroes of other revenge tragedies plot their enemies' downfall, Hamlet on his return from England gives up devising murder scenarios and simply awaits the moment: it is Claudius, who by arranging the duel and poisoning the daggers, inadvertently stages his own demise. The purpose of the slow move to checkmating the king in 1 Sam. 24–31 is to test the thesis that providence is not in human hands, but in God's: "Hamlet, like David, eventually assigns vengeance to the Lord, who providentially—in what might seem accidents—brings justice

16. Veith, "Wait upon the Lord," 81, citing *Hamlet* 5.2.7–11.
17. Ibid., 82, citing *Hamlet* 5.2.209–17.

to pass. . . . When David and Hamlet spare their royal enemy, their motives are as different as their personalities, but both see the king in terms of the judgment of God, to whom they ultimately consign their cause."[18]

Down to the book of Job, at least, the Old Testament makes a literal connection between doing good and achieving happiness: "Honour thy father and thy mother," it enjoins, "that thy days may be long upon the land which the LORD thy God giveth thee" (Exod. 20:12). For overtly irreligious moderns, such a connection between the good and physical goods, between doing the right thing and earning a reward, is utilitarian. We find it difficult to picture, so that the idea of sin rebounding on the sinner evokes send-ups like the Australian song "My Boomerang Won't Come Back," by Charlie Drake. Even religious moderns find it difficult to pinpoint the connection between right doing and this-worldly happiness. Modern Christians tend either to disjoin them altogether, rejoicing in the disparity between "ought" and "is," with Kant, or to connect them in a mechanical way, with the prosperity gospel. Like its ancestor, the revenge play, the prosperity gospel is the product of an antireligious mentality in which, crucially, justice and therefore success are really conceived as being the product of human undertaking. By contrast, the linkage of doing right and achieving one's desires in the proverbial wisdom is earned by "pious integration into a divine order which is imposed on man and in which alone he can find blessing" (von Rad 1972: 80). This is an essentially religious image of justice, which precedes and poetically founds the philosophical ideas of justice.

Although recent critics emphasize David's deviousness in his ascent to the kingship, they seldom advert to the double-talker being in a double bind. He is bound on the one side by his own anointing by Samuel and on the other by Saul's prior anointing. Both come from God, and so both are to be respected. It is curious that, despite near universal sympathy for Saul in current exegesis of 1 Samuel, few remark on David being the first to exhibit this trait. He does not treat Saul as an opponent, but as a threat from which to flee. David does not eschew using his popularity (1 Sam. 18:7–8) to undermine Saul's position because he feels subjective pity for Saul. His heart does not smite him on cutting Saul's royal robe because he feels that Saul has been dealt a cruel hand by God. He does not express the feeling that Saul is in an unfortunate position, as a king whose authority the Lord has withdrawn. He shows reverence for Saul's person because Saul, like Cain, bears the mysterious mark of "the LORD's" protection. The sign of anointing was holy ground for him, as coronation is sacramental for us. David does not call his opponent "Saul," that is, does not "use a simple and direct name of him, but one referring to his status, to his power." And it is in this acknowledgement of the marked man as "the Lord's anointed" (Chrysostom 2003: 23–24) that Saul's pathos appears. It is in this series of episodes, where our human sympathy for Saul has evaporated, that Saul becomes a sympathetic character. It

18. Ibid.

is here, where he is reduced to his bare, forked anointing, as the sole reason for respecting his person, that Saul comes closest to being a tragic figure. It is here that he exhibits the pathos that invites us to enter his plight. Imaginatively, it is in the strange lacuna from the revocation of his kingship until his death, in his murderous and fruitless pursuit of David, that Saul invites sympathy. The biblical stories about Saul's last, desperate pursuit of David invite us to meditate on the meaning of mercy. Because God's justice compels him to respect the Lord's anointed, David is taught that justice can consist in mercy.

For the judge-heroes, doing justice is permitting God to use their strength or their stratagems as God wills them to do. The judge has to rely on God, but the meaning of justice is fairly clear, fairly natural. When the judge-hero kills Philistines, he or she is executing God's justice on the uncircumcised: it is the same when David kills Goliath. The punishment fits the crime. Faith here is an intellectually simple matter of believing that God can make the underdog or the smaller force triumph over the more numerous "bad hats." David has to show more faith than this in his contest with Saul, because, now, observing God's justice does not mean executing a natural plan of revenge against his would-be murderer, but awaiting God's verdict. David has been anointed by God's prophet, Samuel, but he has not been advanced the right to slay King Saul: "The LORD judge between me and thee, and the LORD avenge me of thee: but my hand shall not be upon thee" (24:12). He has to cooperate with the divine providence by doing nothing: the story of David exhibits

> the paradox that all evil must be punished, but it is heroic to refrain from punishing. Critics of Hamlet's revenge . . . must remember both horns of the dilemma. Some unquestioningly accept Hamlet's desire for revenge as a conventional duty and wonder why he does not act more decisively. Others decry his bloodthirstiness and question whether he should act at all. . . . Claudius *does* need to be punished; Hamlet *is* wrong to want to murder him. Emphasizing one pole of the paradox minimizes Hamlet's, and David's tragic dilemma. For David and . . . for Hamlet, resolution of the dilemma comes in trusting a just, holy, and active God, leaving judgment and their own actions open to his will.[19]

It is just because David's faith is tested to the extent of having to cooperate with a justice that is not visible to his naked eyes that he learns to be merciful. Faced with Saul, who, though a villain, is mysteriously placed beyond reach of harm by the sign of God's anointing, David is not able to fit punishment to crime, and so discovers the quality of mercy.

If we remembered him only as the harpist or the slayer of Goliath, David would still have a touch of the romantic *Übermensch*; as it is, he is truly a *mensch*, for "David's heroism comes not from deeds of war but from his heroic mercy. Forced to choose between justice and mercy, David consistently opts for mercy. . . . David's

19. Ibid., 80, emphasis original.

heroic mercy is sustained and kept intact through his faith in a God who alone is just, whom he can trust to punish the evil he faces. Saul, Nabal, Amnon, and Absalom all receive mercy from David's hand, but the 'accidents' that befall them and their ultimate destruction are all seen as the judgment of God."[20]

David's demonstration of mercy is a variation on the wisdom tradition. Wisdom plays on analogies, but it also likes the play of opposites. The wise man and the foolish man, the wise wife and the foolish wife, are the clearest examples of proverbial appositions (Prov. 14:16; 15:21; 18:22; 19:25; 29:11; Sirach 10:2, 12; 20:7; 21:27; Abigail and Nabal in 1 Sam. 25, the wise wife and her "fool" husband). Saul and David are, respectively, the envious and the merciful man. Although envy and mercy are a more complex pairing than wisdom and folly, it is not an offbeat or tangential opposition. Whereas envy wishes ill fortune on the other and thereby makes him a rival, mercy wills good fortune and so creates friendship. Whereas Saul initiates their conflict by begrudging David his "ten thousands" (18:7–8), David brings the conflict to closure by showing mercy to the king.

Episode Five: The Fool Has Said in His Heart (1 Sam. 25)

David's flight from Saul has taken him farther and farther south, that is, out of Israel and into Judah. He now comes to the southeastern Judahite territory of Carmel. He sends a request to Nabal for a share of his ample sheep holdings, claiming he is owed a cut since he has yet to plunder Nabal's herds. When Abigail, a "woman of good understanding" (25:3), learns from a servant that her husband has sent David's messenger packing and appreciates that David's brigands will now tender violence instead of "protection," she rushes to forestall the consequences of her "evil" husband's words. Having turned David back from his intended slaughter of all the males of her household, that is, as the King James Version has it, "any that pisseth against the wall" (25:22, 34), Abigail tells a hungover Nabal of his narrow escape. Nabal's "heart died within him, and he became as a stone" (25:37); ten days after the Carmelite chieftain goes into a coma, God finishes what David and Abigail had begun: "The LORD smote Nabal, that he died" (25:38). David marries the resourceful Abigail and takes another wife too: "Ahinoam of Jezreel" (25:43). Second Sam. 12:8 may indicate that this is the same Ahinoam who had been wife to Saul (1 Sam. 14:50) (Levenson 1978: 27). David's first wife, Saul's daughter Michal, who "loved David" (18:20), has been married by her father to one Phalti (25:44; cf. 2 Sam. 3:14–16).

Augustine tells us that "the utterances of the prophets are found to have a threefold meaning, in that some have in view the earthly Jerusalem, others the heavenly, and others refer to both." The three kinds of meaning are the purely literal, the purely allegorical, and the combination of literalism and allegory that

20. Ibid.

some call symbolical. Augustine's favorite is the symbolical, containing the spiritual meaning in the literal referent: "This class of prophecy, in which there is a compounding and commingling, as it were, of both references, is of the greatest importance in the ancient canonical books, which contain historical narratives." Some think that everything in scripture is allegorical and thus that nothing in the Old Testament is just there because it happened: "On this theory," Augustine says dryly, "the utterances of the prophets will be of two types only, not three." Augustine does not accept the theory, common in his time, that the entire Old Testament is either allegorical or symbolical. He is no historical critic of scripture, but neither can he believe that everything in the Old Testament histories is allegorical or symbolical in its intent: "It is certainly a complete mistake to suppose that no narrative of events in this type of literature has any significance beyond the purely historical record; but it is equally rash to maintain that every single statement in those books is a complex of allegorical meanings. That is why I have spoken of a triple, instead of a double classification; for this is my own considered judgment. In spite of that, I do not censure those who have succeeded in carving out a spiritual meaning from each and every event in the narrative, always providing that they have maintained its original basis of historical truth" (*City of God* 17.3). Since Augustine makes this statement of his exegetical principles in the course of a cursory survey of 1–2 Samuel, one may infer that he is explaining why he feels no obligation to include the bulk of the story of the installation of Israel's monarchy in his detailed study of the installation of the city of man and the city of God in world history. Saint Augustine may have considered that tales about David's connubial enterprises are present in scripture for our historical rather than spiritual enlightenment.

The backstory to this episode may be historically interesting. In 2 Samuel, David becomes the king of a united Israel. Immediately after the deaths of Saul and Jonathan, David goes on God's injunction to the Judahite city of Hebron: "And his two wives Ahinoam the Jezreelitess and Abigail the wife of Nabal of Carmel" were with him; "and the men of Judah came and anointed David there, to be king over the house of Judah" (2 Sam. 2:1–4a, trans. Levenson). Why were the men of Judah so obeisantly eager to make "David the brigand" their king? In addition to good fortune always dropping into David's lap, one could propose, as does Levenson, that he "swaggered into Hebron with the wife of a Celibite chieftain on one arm and that of the Israelite king on the other." In his first message to Nabal, David calls himself "thy son" (1 Sam. 25:8): where one is the *subject* of a monarch, one is a *child* to a chief. With his large holdings of "three thousand sheep, and a thousand goats" (25:2), Nabal is a little big man in Judah. The advantage David has achieved by marrying Abigail, the widow of a materially "very great" (25:2) man, is a power base in the southeastern territory. Nabal is said to have "held a feast in his house, like the feast of a king" (25:36). Taking the widow of a big man to wife could have been the pivotal move in David's future acceptance as king in southern Judahite Hebron. This "lovely tale of the handsome warrior, and the beautiful, clever" Abigail "masks a political struggle with the greatest consequences": by marrying Nabal's widow, he has acquired both the chiefling's aura and his role in Carmel, which could be converted into the kingship "in Judah and eventually in all Israel" (1978: 25–28). Forced to elude Saul by traveling into the southern badlands, beyond Saul's direct control, David *seems* to be down-and-out, but in reality "he is free to demonstrate and develop his skills while creating a powerbase of his own outside the incumbent's house." By marrying again outside his own kinship group, and among the Judahites, David is extending "the network of relationships that will help him economically, socially, and politically. One wife is from Jezreel . . . , another the wife of a wealthy pastoralist, a third the daughter of the king of Geshur, and many others whose lineages are unknown (2 Sam. 3:2–5)" (Flanagan 1988: 244–45).

In this narrative, we see that David is no boy scout, but rather a vengeful figure who "girded on . . . his sword" and ordered "four hundred" of his men to saddle up (1 Sam. 25:13) when a Carmelite big man refused his demand to repay his "protection." His servant's message to Nabal in 25:7–8 indicates that he takes the chieftain to be indebted to him for the good conduct of his boys. David shows he is "not above murder and the confiscation of women married to other men": Brueggemann may mean Saul's wife Ahinoam, since Abigail is widowed before David proposes to her. Whereas Brueggemann admires the "buoyant, charismatic quality" of David that this narrative so "trustfully celebrates,"[21] and von Balthasar seems to enjoy the "burlesque interlude with Nabal (i.e., 'fool') and the sly Abigail, whom David in the end marries along with her considerable dowry" (1983–91: 6.111), Lemche takes a stern view of David's behavior, opining that "David committed a really dirty trick in this instance, frightening a man to death and stealing his wife. The offer made to Nabal for the protection of his possessions is sheer pressure, since whom did David protect Nabal against? Of course, against David himself, as is evident from David's reaction to Nabal's indignant refusal of the robber's request!" This is one of the few episodes in David's rise that Lemche takes to be historically probable (1978: 12)—before he decides that none of the Deuteronomistic History is historical.

David's request to Nabal may seem impertinent, but there is more in the message than a demand for protection money (or sheep). David conceives the good deportment of his men as a gift to the big man, and it is a rule of archaic cultures that a gift requires a return: "The act of giving . . . was always the first half of a reciprocal action, the other half of which was a counter-gift."[22] Cultural reciprocity between equals is construed by David as a law of nature, part of the way of things. We find in his words to Nabal the wisdom idea of like following like, good returning for good, and evil for evil: "I have heard that thou hast shearers: now thy shepherds

---

21. Walter Brueggemann, *David's Truth in Israel's Imagination and Memory* (Minneapolis: Fortress, 1985), 21.

22. M. I. Finley, *The World of Odysseus* (London: Chatto & Windus, 1956), 69.

which were with us, we hurt them not, neither was there aught missing unto them, all the while they were in Carmel. Ask thy young men, and they will show thee. Wherefore let the young men find favour in thy eyes (for we come in a good day): give, I pray thee, whatsoever cometh to thy hand unto thy servants, and to thy son David" (25:7–8). The Proverbs speak of a natural order within which good deeds are karmically propitious; the karmic law of analogy holds that past good behavior creates future goods in its trail. The proverbial "thought rhyme" (von Rad 1972: 27), like "a false witness will not go unpunished, and he who utters lies will not escape" (Prov. 19:5, trans. von Rad), expresses the belief that reality chimes. This story is a straightforward pantomime of the downfall of the unbeliever and the elevation of the believer. The story doesn't chime, as the author seems to have intended it to do, if we read David's offer of protection as if spoken by a Mafia boss.

This episode is a reprise of the former one, about the staying of David's hand from Saul, and extends its meaning beyond the special status of the king. Nabal is no anointed one, but a self-made big man who is described as "doglike" (Hebrew *kalibbi* means both "doglike" and "Calebite"; the KJV brings this connotation out well by calling Nabal "churlish" in 25:3). The name "Nabal" means "fool," as his wife unkindly puts it: "As his name is, so is he: Nabal is his name, and folly is with him" (25:25). The Old Testament has much to say about the figure of the fool. Isaiah describes the fool as a blasphemer and a grinder of the poor: "The fool utters foolishness [Hebrew *nebala*], and his mind plots evil to do foul things, to utter error about the LORD, to keep empty the throat of the hungry man, to deprive the thirsty of drink" (Isa. 32:6, trans. Levenson). The most important biblical allusion is the line of the psalmist made famous by Anselm: "The fool has said in his heart, 'There is no God'" (Ps. 14:1; 53:1 NKJV) (Levenson 1978: 13–15). The fool does foolishly: as is the man, so are his actions. That is Abigail's assessment of her husband.

Even before giving him a name that fits his character, the story characterizes Nabal as Mr. Money: "There was a man in Maon, whose possessions were in Carmel, and the man was very great, and he had three thousand sheep, and a thousand goats: and he was shearing his sheep in Carmel" (25:2). He does not turn down David's request for sheep on the grounds that he doesn't pay protection money to brigands, but because, he says, David is a nobody to him, a man of no fixed household loyalty, and he doesn't give away what is his own to nobodies: "Who is David? and who is the son of Jesse? There be many servants nowadays that break away every man from his master. Shall I then take my bread, and my water, and my flesh that I have killed for my shearers, and give it unto men, whom I know not whence they be?" (25:10–11). Nabal self-identifies as an owner of things ("my bread, . . . my water, . . . my flesh, . . . my shearers") and identifies David as a disobedient, escaped slave. Nabal and David are contrasted in this narrative as slave owner and slave or servant (translations of the same word), and not only by Nabal himself: David calls himself the Lord's "servant" (25:39). As an owner who can do as he wills to others, Nabal believes himself above the moral law: "Like the fool who says in his heart, 'There is no God,' " Nabal "is no one's slave" (Levenson 1978: 16). We can hear from the way his servant talks about him to his wife that Nabal is despised by those he imagines he owns.

The characterization of David's request common among exegetes—as an implicit threat, a demand for recompense as a condition of the continuation of his men's good will—is somewhat belied by the servant's on-the-spot report of their behavior: "But the men were very good unto us, and we were not hurt, neither missed we anything, as long as we were conversant with them, when we were in the fields: They were a wall unto us both by night and day, all the while we were with them keeping sheep" (25:15–16). We cannot whitewash David. His "gift" of protection is not conceived on an altruistic scheme, but along the lines of reciprocal exchange: in a tribal culture, "friends make gifts, gifts make friends" and "generosity creates leadership by creating followership." David's men are natural pirates, inured to surviving by sheep rustling, and he has got the cutthroat crew to become gift givers to Nabal's shepherds. It is not amoral of David to expect good in return for this gift from brigands, it is precisely what is expected: "Transactions express a willingness to live and let live." A gift effectively makes the recipient analogous to a "family member": Nabal scorns such a tie with "the son of Jesse" (25:10), with its corollary of being "of the same kind, kindness, kindred" (Sahlins 1968: 88, 10, 19). Gift gifting had its counterpart: among "peers, the exchange of gifts was as finely calibrated as the exchange of insults. 'It is tantamount to an affront should one refuse a present from a superior,' a diplomat explained; 'if the refusal is on the part of the superior, it is an expression of grave displeasure' " (Iliffe 2005: 62). The big man has refused David's gift of good behavior.

David's determination to avenge Nabal's disrespecting him is not in keeping with the character of a king. The king is not above God's law. "I never knew a woman more practical," says Heller's David (1985: 248). Realizing that one gift requires a return, she saddles up the asses with a gastronomic gift: reciprocity creates peace (Sahlins 1968: 10). It is Abigail's prudent action in riding out to meet David and to redress the wrong done by her husband that reminds him of who he is. She thinks to save her household by a diplomatic pretense that he has *already* been restrained by "the LORD . . . from coming to shed blood, and from avenging thyself" (25:26) and, above all, by recalling David to his role as the slinger. In his glory days, David relied upon the divine providence in confronting his enemies. So should he do now, Abigail says: "Forgive the trespass of thy handmaid: for the LORD will certainly make my lord a sure house; because my lord fighteth the battles of the LORD, and evil hath not been found in thee all thy days. Yet a man is risen to pursue thee, and to seek thy soul: but the soul of my lord shall be bound in the bundle of life with the LORD thy God; and the souls of thy enemies, them shall he sling out, as out of the middle of a sling" (25:28–29). Abigail compares David to the sling, his enemies to the rocks that are hurled away into the dust. The sling and its power are bundled together with the life-giving Lord, who empowers the weapons of humankind.

Abigail's action is analogous to David's own in his contest with Goliath. There, for David, the trusting thing to do was the smart thing, going out without cumbrous armor: but it took faith in God to see how the empirical facts stood. Since, "in old proverbial wisdom, sentences expressing secular experiences and sentences expressing religious experience are inextricably mixed" it makes little sense to see "any kind of tension within the perceptive apparatus," for "in all knowledge faith is also at work" (von Rad 1972: 62). David's faith was a way of seeing the facts. It took trust in God to see that vulnerability was strength. Likewise, Abigail rides with "five pretty damsels" (Heller 1985: 248) into the hands of four hundred armed men intent on murder: it takes faith to see that a dame is the only safe person in Carmel. Just as, in the wisdom tradition, one deed chimes with another, so Abigail's action in this episode rhymes with that in 1 Sam. 17. It took courageous trust in God's providence to appreciate that, by making *herself* the target—"upon me, my lord, upon me let this iniquity be" (25:24)—she could disarm David: "What is he to do with a beautiful woman?" Abigail plays with words, like David does, euphemistically renaming the food she has brought as a "blessing" and offering it, not directly to David but "unto the young men" (25:27): "Far be it from him to take protection money for himself!" (Levenson 1978: 19). She is a blessing to him, his female other half, and David acknowledges this (25:32–33). This proverbial woman has reminded David that he *can* show mercy, because his strength is not his own, but the Lord's. The law of recompense of evil for evil, good for good, is not abrogated, but left in the hands of God. So David can and must be merciful. Of course it is anachronistic to speak of David being merciful here: what he must rise to is the magnanimity and generosity expected of a king in a heroic culture.

Abigail asks David to "act like a king now" by telling him that he will one day be "ruler over Israel" (25:30): she is, for the author, "a woman of providence, a person who . . . from intelligence (*sekel*, v. 3) rather than from special revelation, senses the drift of history" (Levenson 1978: 20). Old Testament history writing shares many of the principles of the wisdom tradition. The moral that David draws from this episode is that justice lies with God: "When David heard that Nabal was dead, he said, 'Blessed be the LORD, that hath pleaded the cause of my reproach from the hand of Nabal, and hath kept his servant from evil: for the LORD hath returned the wickedness of Nabal upon his own head' " (25:39).

Episode Six: The Quality of Mercy (1 Sam. 26)

First Sam. 24 is similar to 1 Sam. 26 and little "excites a biblicist's historical impulses more than a series of parallel episodes . . . if in all three chapters David refrains from violence against an enemy, then . . . such repetition inclines many interpreters to fond thoughts of redaction" (Polzin 1989: 205). Lemche says that the same scene has been repeated in the cave at En-gedi and at Gibeah Hachilah: "In chs. 24 and 26 we have a genuine historical tradition in the sense that the same event has been located in different places" (1978: 10). In medieval times, it was commonly accepted that Samuel was the author of 1 Sam. 1–24 and that Nathan was the author of 1 Sam. 25–31 and 2 Samuel. A curious feature of this ancient belief is that it captures the tonality in which David is pictured in each portion. Samuel's half depicts the younger, innocent David with whom the historical prophet was acquainted, whereas Nathan, who had to rebuke the king for getting Uriah murdered, gives us the darker David.

The tale of Abigail's swift action to forestall David's wrath by reminding him that justice is in God's hands is esthetically analogous to the story of David's refusal to harm "the LORD's anointed" in 1 Sam. 24 and thus to this repetition of that event in 1 Sam. 26. The three episodes are thematically integrated. The connection with the previous story is brought out when Saul says, "I have played the fool" (26:21). But the very fact of their similarity also makes us notice differences and perhaps even a change in the presentation of David's character. Partly because 1 Sam. 24 and 1 Sam. 26 are wrapped around the Nabal story in 1 Sam. 25, David comes across rather differently. Following on 1 Sam. 25, he seems both more resolute in his restraint (no playful snipping of garments) and a harsher, more world-weary man. All three episodes are about David's *not* killing: in the first, he forestalls himself; in the second, though, it is solely Abigail's "rhetorical genius" that withholds David "from bloodying his hands." Though the idea of original sin is a Pauline, christological insight, the Old Testament characters are fallen: our historian-author does not take an optimistic view of his human characters. The Nabal story "is the first revelation of evil in David's character. He can kill." Though "he stops short," our new knowledge of him "continues to darken our perception of David's character" (Levenson 1978: 23). Because of the Nabal incident, we are much more aware now of how easy it would be for David to put an end to Saul's hunting him like "a partridge in the mountains" (26:20), by turning on his pursuer in vengeance.

David seems to be aware of this too. Instead of the intimate scene between David alone and Saul, we have a public presentation of Saul's spear to Abner and Saul's army and harsh, sarcastic words. Taking Saul's spear, "David went over to the other side, and stood on the top of a hill afar off; a great space being between them: And David cried to the people, and to Abner the son of Ner, saying, 'Answerest thou not, Abner?' Then Abner answered and said, 'Who art thou that criest to the king?' And David said to Abner, 'Art not thou a valiant man? and who is like to thee in Israel? Wherefore then hast thou not kept thy lord the king? for there came one of the people in to destroy the king thy lord. This thing is not good that thou hast done. As the LORD liveth, ye are worthy to die, because ye have not kept your master, the LORD's anointed. And now see where the king's spear is, and the cruse of water that was at his bolster'" (26:13–16). He is acting from a position of greater strength than in 1 Sam. 24. Because of the sequence in which the three episodes are arranged, what is most striking in 1 Sam. 24 is David's remorse for his near giving way to temptation, whereas what comes out

in 1 Sam. 26 is the public demonstration of the evidence. Because by the conclusion of this third incident the question of Saul's death has been raised three times
(Polzin 1989: 213), the third episode is more threatening than the first. David
exploits the opportunity to retaliate by showing Saul's army that their king was
in his power and could have been killed. He is showing them that the apparently
weaker is really the stronger.

He knows that full well himself. David has fully become David, dark and light.
He, and we, know now, after En-gedi and after his violent reaction to Nabal, that
David is a many-sided man. When the church received the scriptures that report
David's story, it was not canonizing a plaster saint. The canonization of the Davidic history was, in its way, a hostage to fortune, for it was bound to generate the
reaction of the Marcionites, Gnostics, and Manicheans, who insisted on seeing
only the dark, amoral side of David. For Manicheans like Faustus, apparently,
Christianity's admitting the bandit David to take refuge in its scriptures was an
indication of the bad judgment and irrationality of their religious teaching. The
Manicheans have their twenty-first-century heirs, who paint a subversively attractive portrait of David in order to discredit him and his history. Our unbelieving
contemporaries are imaginatively susceptible to a picture of David as a charming
power grabber, but few Christian thinkers will think it worthwhile to rebut this
characterization until Hollywood picks it up. They may find then that Augustine
got there first. For he himself had with great difficulty escaped the imprisonment
of his imagination by Manichaeism. Augustine writes that "we read of both good
and bad actions" on David's part. "But where David's strength lay, and what the
secret of his success was, is sufficiently plain, not to the blind malevolence with
which Faustus assails holy writings and holy men, but to pious discernment, which
bows to the divine authority and at the same time judges human conduct correctly.
The Manichaeanism will find, if they read the Scriptures, that God rebukes David
more than Faustus does. But they will read also of the sacrifice of his penitence,
of his unsurpassing gentleness to his merciless and bloodthirsty enemy, whom
David, pious as he was brave, dismissed unhurt when now and again he fell into
his hands" (*Against Faustus* 22.66, in Franke 2005: 317). Augustine stresses the
multifacetedness of David's character, the soldier who could be gentle. He also
claims that it takes "pious discernment" to develop the sensibility capable of making complex moral assessments of such a many-sided thing as human character or
to evaluate "human conduct correctly."

David's lair in Hachilah given away by Ziphite informers (26:1), Saul pur-
sues David in "the wilderness of Ziph" (26:2). The hunter becomes the hunted
man: David in return "sent out spies" (26:4) and stalks his pursuant down to his
camp. Rather than Saul wandering by mistake into David's pathetic hideaway,
David deliberately and boldly enters his foe's camp by night, with two lieutenants,
Abishai and Ahimelech (26:6–7). Saul is passive and slightly pathetic in both
scenes, relieving himself in the one and prone in his sleeping bag beside his spear
in the other. But in the first, David and his men, too, recoiled and hid themselves

in the dark sides of the cave at Saul's approach, whereas, now, David has taken the initiative and is the aggressor. He has turned the tables and confronted his pursuant. This is a good way to frighten him into the peace talks with which the episode concludes.

David has become David: it is not the general but his lieutenant, Abishai, who wants to do the sticky deed: "Then said Abishai to David, 'God hath delivered thy enemy into thy hand this day: now therefore let me smite him, I pray thee, with the spear even to the earth at once, and I will not smite him the second time'" (26:8). This episode does not swap the slice of the robe for a spear and water jug and leave the rest the same. Abishai thinks of murder; David does not. The single, deadly spear thrust proposed by Abishai is more redolent of death than anything that happened at En-gedi or even in the Nabal story. Somewhat as he had restrained his toughs as they mingled with Nabal's shepherds, so now David restrains Abishai. His wife Abigail has brought him to a royal recognition of the divine providence: "David said to Abishai, 'Destroy him not: for who can stretch forth his hand against the LORD's anointed, and be guiltless?' David said furthermore, 'As the LORD liveth, the LORD shall smite him, or his day shall come to die, or he shall descend into battle, and perish'" (26:9–10). Justice will come from the living Lord.

God is alive, David tells Abishai, and has given him two providential signs, the spear and the water jug, Saul's weapon and water carrier. These iron and bronze implements of life and death are a sign to David that Saul's life is spent. Saul's life is in God's hands: David will not take it. But God's providence includes David, to whom he has made the gift of the spear and water jug. David tells Abishai to respect the king's life and to take the signs in reserve: "The LORD forbid that I should stretch forth my hand against the LORD's anointed: but, I pray thee, take thou now the spear that is at his bolster, and the cruse of water, and let us go" (26:11). With David's nonpossessive possession of Saul's life in these symbols, he holds Saul in his power by theatrically deploying his nonuse of them. Right back to the Philistine guards' "come up" to Jonathan (14:10, 12), signs are treated as evidence of God's providence. They are therefore to be cooperated with. Having been given them, by dint of his boldness in seeking out Saul, David makes great use of the gifts of the sword and water jug. He was not given the slice of Saul's robe; he cut it himself, in a semisacrilegious gesture. But the sword and water jug are presented here to be appropriated: they can be appropriated either to murder Saul or to demonstrate one's power over his life by not murdering him. This is the quality of mercy. The iron spear and the water jug, symbols of Saul's life forfeited, are to David a providential indication that his strength lies in mercy. And, since providential signs are to be used, David knows he can achieve his needed peace talks by showing off his mercy. David employs the spear as a prop to dramatize Saul's escape from it. He uses the spear to vindicate his magnanimity to Saul, and thus his strength. David's vindication was given to him by God in the signs of the spear and water jug.

When Saul hears a man "on the top of a hill afar off" (26:13) shouting mockery of the king's guard (26:14–16), he "knew David's voice, and said, 'Is this thy voice, my son David?' And David said, 'It is my voice, my lord, O king'" (26:17). When Saul hears David's voice and recognizes him in it, he comes to himself: a person's word, and therefore their voice, is the person. Saul recognizes David and thus realizes the madness of his hatred for him. Saul sees that the spear stands for David's respect for his life. He has been intent on murdering David, because he believed that he wanted to kill him for his kingdom. The proffered spear makes him acknowledge that David has no design on his life, and thus the spear, as a sign of mercy, breaks the cycle of vengeance: "Then said Saul, 'I have sinned: return, my son David, for I will no more do thee harm, because my soul was precious in thy eyes this day'" (26:21). Saul need no longer hunt David, and David retaliate by stalking Saul, because of their mutual recognition that David is not a killer of God's kings. For Saul to recognize David as merciful and cease his pursuit, David had to recognize *himself* as having the magnanimity of a king. When Saul outlawed him, David simply fled, the natural leader collecting a defensive force of brigands as he went. His private expression of remorse to Saul in 1 Sam. 24 is his first effort to repay evil with good. This came about inadvertently, through Saul's happening upon his hideout. Now, in 1 Sam. 26 David's character is publicly presented to Saul, General Abner, and his assembled army. The act of mercy has become David's choice. He broadcasts it in his parting words, ironically inviting a Saulide volunteer to come and recover their master's life: "Behold the king's spear, and let one of the young men come over and fetch it" (26:22). Saul's spear has become the sign of the truce between Saul and David.

It is not surprising that the lectionary (seventh Sunday in Ordinary Time, Year C) pairs this episode with the Sermon on the Mount:

> Love your enemies, do good to those who hate you, bless those who curse you, pray for those who abuse you. To one who strikes you on the cheek, offer the other also, and from one who takes away your cloak do not withhold your tunic either. Give to everyone who begs from you, and from one who takes away your goods do not demand them back. And as you wish that others would do to you, do so to them. If you love those who love you, what benefit is that to you? For even sinners love those who love them. And if you do good to those who do good to you, what benefit is that to you? For even sinners do the same. And if you lend to those from whom you expect to receive, what credit is that to you? Even sinners lend to sinners, to get back the same amount. But love your enemies, and do good, and lend, expecting nothing in return, and your reward will be great, and you will be sons of the Most High, for he is kind to the ungrateful and the evil. Be merciful, even as your Father is merciful. Judge not, and you will not be judged; condemn not, and you will not be condemned; forgive, and you will be forgiven; give, and it will be given to you. Good measure, pressed down, shaken together, running over, will be put into your lap. For with the measure you use it will be measured back to you. (Luke 6:27–38)

What is surprising is how seldom a sermon touches on the accompanying Old Testament reading. For the real sermon on the Sermon on the Mount is the way David dramatizes the divine injunction to be merciful, given to him in the signs of spear and jug. He plays the magnanimous king by taking the "fool's" (1 Sam. 26:21) life in his hands and giving it back, because it belongs to the Lord.

David recognizes that the measurer of justice is the Lord, who will recompense his act of mercy: "The LORD render to every man his righteousness and his faithfulness: for the LORD delivered thee into my hand today, but I would not stretch forth my hand against the LORD's anointed. And behold, as thy life was much set by this day in my eyes, so let my life be much set by in the eyes of the LORD, and let him deliver me out of all tribulation" (26:23–24); "for with the measure you use it will be measured back to you" (Luke 6:38). If there is a wisdom in the way of nature and of human action, effect tracking cause, good following from good and evil from evil, that is because there is, not just a measure of good, a standard of better and worse, but a living measuring out of goods. Standards do not create betters and worses, they are just another name for the same thing. If good is returned for good in the cosmos and in human action, this way of nature or karmic law exists because God measures out goodness in creation. As the Proverb has it: "The balance and true scales are Yahweh's, all the weights in the bag are his work" (Prov. 16:11, trans. von Rad 1972: 27). If it is God who does the measuring, he and not his creatures is the judge of goodness. If we not only measure our goodness by his or take God as the standard, but recognize God as the one who is providentially measuring out goods, we will not aim to be providence to our friends and foes, but leave the measuring to God. By recognizing that God is the standard of justice and the measurer out of justice, we become agents of God's merciful providence. This is the meaning of the last words David speaks to Saul, "As thy life was much set by this day in my eyes, so let my life be much set by in the eyes of the LORD, and let him deliver me out of all tribulation" (1 Sam. 26:24).

Saul acknowledges that David has become the agent of divine providence. In his parting word, "Saul said to David, 'Blessed be thou, my son David: thou shalt both do great things, and also shalt still prevail'" (26:25). First Sam. 24–26 guides Saul in the direction of death and enables him to make a getaway from it. These episodes are repetitive because in them Saul's final downfall is deferred, by the will of God: "Even here in chapters 24–26, where a predeterminate view of David's rise and Saul's fall is most explicit, the theme of a mysterious and providential delay in the affairs of God and humanity complicates the story in ways that repeat what has already occurred and foreshadow what is to come" (Polzin 1989: 213).

Episode Seven: Achish Fooled (1 Sam. 27:1–28:2)

David and his followers become hired slingers to Achish, who is described as heir apparent to "Maoch, king of Gath" (27:2), rather than king, as in 21:10.

No shekels change hands: instead, Achish gives them the city of Ziklag. When David refused Saul's armor (1 Sam. 17), there's just a hint of diplomacy in how he sweetly denied himself this hindrance. When he protested himself unworthy of the poisoned chalice of betrothal to Michal that Saul offers him (18:18), the former shepherd just *might* conceivably be very modest. But the other shoe has to drop when he tells Achish, "Let them give me a place in some town in the country, that I may dwell there: for why should thy servant dwell in the royal city with thee?" (27:5). The upshot of David's acting the obeisant servant is that "Achish gave him Ziklag that day" (27:6)! David's modesty makes him a successful political operator. Achish must anticipate that the six hundred pirates could be useful to him in return: David and his army have become mercenaries. Like any mercenary, David is freelancing, and his assault on the Geshurites, Gezrites, and Amalekites is his own private expedition. He deceives Achish about his militia's route, pretending to have attacked the southern parts of Judah. Achish believes that David has vilified himself with his own tribes' people and that he has permanently enchained himself to the Philistines. David is thus with Achish when the Philistine cities combine forces to attack Israel.

After the last episode, which concluded with a mutual nonaggression pact, it's reasonable to ask why David still felt sufficiently unsafe in Saul's lands to emigrate from them. Did he jump or was he pushed? Von Balthasar reads the episode reverentially, speaking of David's "enforced desertion to the enemy" (1983–91: 6.111). At the opposite extreme, Lemche thinks that, although this episode "bears the stamp of the author's endeavors to acquit David of charges of treachery" and of complicity in Saul's death, still, "we have in ch. 27 a tacit criticism of David" in "that David's decision to seek refuge among the Philistines is described as David's own idea without divine approval" (1978: 13). It was only when "it was told Saul that David was fled to Gath" that "he sought no more again for him" (27:4). First Sam. 27:4 marks the end of a thread that has run since 1 Sam. 18: Saul's pursuit of David is at an end. It looks like this display of passivity, a retreat from Israelite territory, was the turning point that finally stayed Saul's wrath. David succeeded in obtaining peace with Saul by going over to the Philistines as a mercenary.

David is moving to the southeast. It is here, where the low country runs east to west, from Haifa to the Jezreel Valley to the Yarmouk River, and intersects with the southern coast that most of the remains of iron products from the Early Iron Age have been found (Flanagan 1988: 283–84). The further David moves away from Saul's court, the more he plants his flag among more technologically advanced peoples. David's year abroad among the Philistines earned one of their towns for Judah: "Wherefore Ziklag pertaineth unto the kings of Judah unto this day" (27:6).

If David in Achish's service had taken part in military campaigns against Israelite territory, it would be a serious matter. Judging him from what we read here, he put his energy to use in extirpating the ancient enemies of Israel. The phraseology is reminiscent of Saul's disastrous Amalekite campaign in 1 Sam. 15: "David and his men went up and invaded the Geshurites, and the Gezrites, and the Amalekites: for those nations were of old the inhabitants of the land, as thou goest to Shur, even unto the land of Egypt. And David smote the land, and left neither man nor woman alive, and took away the sheep, and the oxen, and the asses, and the camels, and the apparel, and returned, and came to Achish" (27:8–9).

He carries out a thorough massacre, not to fulfil any laws of holy war, but to ensure that he is not informed upon: "David saved neither man nor woman alive, to bring tidings to Gath, saying, 'Lest they should tell on us, saying, "So did David, and so will be his manner all the while he dwelleth in the country of the Philistines"'" (27:11). The Amalekites, Geshurites, and Gezrites were probably allied to the Philistines, so David has good reason not to want the news of his exploits to spread. He is in fact behaving as a thoroughly disobedient servant to his Philistine paymaster. While keeping the letter of his bargain with Achish, he has ignored the spirit of it.

David brings back the spoils for his master, but camouflages the source of the provender. When "Achish said, 'Whither have ye made a road today?' . . . David said, 'Against the south of Judah, and against the south of the Jerahmeelites, and against the south of the Kenites'" (27:10). His pretense has Achish thinking that David has trapped himself into eternal loyalty to the Philistines, sealing an exit back into Israel: "Achish believed David, saying, 'He hath made his people Israel utterly to abhor him, therefore he will be my servant for ever'" (27:12). Achish believed David, who is, we know, not to be believed. David's actions are morally questionable: "The reader's recognition of Achish's foolishness carries a . . . realization of David's growing duplicity. The story of David's rise to power is contrived as much against him as for him" (Polzin 1989: 217). But it may be that the episode is not really about David's dishonesty. It seems to be another fool story: this time, David makes a fool of Achish. David is like those servants about whom Nabal complained when he said, "There be many servants nowadays that break away every man from his master" (25:10). Since the fool believes "there is no God," he has a "lack of realism" and "miscalculates his potentiality; he lives in deception" (von Rad 1972: 65): "The folly of fools is deception" (Prov. 14:8 NIV). It is poetic justice to fool the fool. The double-talk with which the episode concludes is witty: Achish tells David, "Know thou assuredly, that thou shalt go out with me to battle, thou and thy men," to which the wise man replies ironically, "Surely thou shalt know what thy servant can do" (28:1–2). This is an Israelite in whom there is much guile.

David's lie to Achish seems to us to be in the same register within scripture as Abram's lie to the Egyptians about Sarai being his sister, not his wife (Gen. 12), or Isaac's similar pretense to the Philistine King Abimelech (Gen 26:6–11). Such episodes bother biblical exegetes more than they worry the biblical narrators. Neither the J writer in Genesis nor our author-historian seem to take the behavior of Abraham, Isaac, or David as an infringement of the ninth commandment. They recount the pretense, and the most it seems to teach us is that, if these episodes are historically based, these ancient tribes people did not put playacting to foreigners in the same category as bearing false witness. Whereas we, who rate sincerity highly, regard duplicitousness and deviousness as crimes against authenticity, neither J nor our author necessarily do so. They seem to regard guilelessness as a quality some people have, like Jonathan and Joseph, fitting them for specific purposes or roles. They do not seem to treat it as an attribute necessary to the bearing of a moral personality.

While, in the past, commentators and preachers who wanted to see David as a walking catalog of moral ideas took pains circuitously to explain why a lie in this circumstance was not really a lie, today, exegetes who delight in the clay-footed hero's roguishness go forth and multiply examples of David's deviousness. The medieval and early modern commentators respected honesty and thought David must have been so, somehow. We postmoderns are torn between the modern high evaluation of authenticity and the hypermodern (extreme subjectivist) preference for what we take to be devious characters like David over straightforward ones like Jonathan. David lives up to the hermeneutics of suspicion to which hypermoderns are attached. We therefore tend to exaggerate David's deviousness because it is what most strikes us affectively about him. That might lead us further away from the meaning of his character than the medievals or early moderns were. They took it straightforwardly, as the victorious pantomime hero, rather than as complicated and multisided. It is difficult to get either as much approbation as the old commentators needed or as much disapprobation as the new exegetes would like out of the episode, because the moral code that both apply makes David a man of another time.

Without being a lesson in situation ethics, 1 Sam. 27 does seem to be about doing one's best within tricky moral confines. David uses his enforced military service to the Philistines to despoil some of the ancient enemies of Israel, the Amalekites. He then lies about it to Achish, which creates the further deception in this foolish Philistine that David is his good servant. The narrative seems to say that the pretense was good, not overly concerning itself about the pretense, but simply saying that it was put to good ends. Though it may seem simplistic by comparison with the application of a hermeneutic of suspicion to the David stories, it may be the narrator just rates actions as good when put to Yahwistic ends. David deploys subterfuge when in enemy territory, pretending to be a honorary Philistine, and uses it not only to his own advantage, but also to the glory of God. Recent critics are right to notice David's deviousness, but wrong in their assessment of its moral tonality.

C. S. Lewis once remarked that adults always say "the one thing I cannot abide is lying" because lying is the child's only defense against the adults. David's pretense is childish, that is, a mark of his extreme vulnerability, even though, by the end of the episode, he is glorying in his deception and pushing it to the verge of sarcasm. It may be because they take such childishness as natural that the biblical narrators are neutral on deceptions that are placed in the service of the Lord. One hesitates to put it like this, because those who think of adulthood as a progress upon childhood will take it as a negative value judgment, but primitive people—the characters in this story were living around 1000 BC—do seem childish to moderns, straightforward when moderns would be tactful, devious when moderns might be authentic. Homer's heroes, supposed to have lived a couple of centuries before Saul and David, weep and embrace one another without loss of public face; Odysseus is named "many-wayed" by Homer without a trace of opprobrium: the man called "Nobody" escaped the Cyclops because he, too, knew that words mean different things at different times. Homer's Odysseus habitually "masks his identity behind lies": the king of Ithaca pretends to be a Cretan; he makes believe to the suitors that he has been stripped of his wealth by Zeus—like the "Nobody" name, not true but true.[23] Children still get this: Batman and Superman both wear disguises, and though these guys in tights and capes look ridiculous to adults, the childish mind appreciates the existential credibility of an incredible who masks his identity.

The author of this story, who thought pictorially like a graphic novelist, is fascinated by the capacity of one and the same picture to say different things. If he recurrently depicts David saying one thing and meaning another, it is not because he wants us to notice his unscrupulosity, but because he admires his inventive self-presentation. As the symbolic Israelite culture hero who initiated Israel's transition from a way of life that was primitive in relation to its Philistine neighbors to a civilized urban monarchy with a beautiful temple at Jerusalem, David is the Bible's best representative of what Origen was the first to call *spolia Egyptorum*. On the analogy of the Israelites' theft of their masters' jewelry before their departure from Egypt, "spoiling the Egyptians" means appropriating pagan letters or philosophy to the service of Christian faith. The first emigrants were not adept at this, before David. They copied pagan religious rituals, and they were unimaginative with respect to the military and artistic deployment of metallurgy. Spoiling the Egyptians is neither imitating them in their own religious order nor ignoring their achievements. It is carbonizing their achievements in the fire of Israelite faith and putting the innovation that results in the service of God. David seems to symbolize the Israelite attempt to put craft at the service of the Lord. In order to spoil the Egyptians, one has to go among them. One may have to go among Philistine or Egyptian in disguise: or as Paul observed, one can be "all things to all men" (1 Cor. 9:22). David represents the point where faith harvests what is good in the human world, because he not only makes sense to supernatural faith, but appeals to the human, religious spirit. That is because this comic-book character is the hero of a divine comedy.

---

23. Clark, *Art of the Odyssey*, 24.

SERIES SEVEN

THE DEATH OF THE BROTHER

1 Samuel 28–31

With the Philistine armies mustering against him, Saul invokes the ghost of Samuel (1 Sam. 28). Samuel's animated return from Sheol is startling because scripture conceives life as a vigorous, operative power and death as its opposite (Martin-Achard 1960: 5). The living God is the true God: the heathen are out of their depth when confronted with the ark, because they don't know what a true God is like. Coexistence with the ark showed up the Philistine cult and culture as smoke and mirrors. Acting as the agent of this invincible truth, David walks over Achish. In 1 Sam. 21–27 David saves his skin by the device that Aquinas called "figurative pretense" (*Summa theologiae* II–II Q. 3 A. 1, reply obj. 1), a superficial deception that cloaks a deeper truth. Now Saul does the opposite: the public opponent of necromancy "disguised himself, and put on other raiment" (28:8) than that fitting a king; it tells a meaningless lie, one that corresponds with no reality and is unmasked by the witch. Illuminated by the apparition of Samuel, she asks, "Why hast thou deceived me? for thou art Saul" (28:12). A pairing and a disanalogy is set up between David's figurative pretenses and Saul's making a pretended figure, a lie. Whereas David's deeper truths are never unmasked and permit him to prosper, Saul's lie is theodicially unmasked: reality and truth are gained in this ethical judgment. The spectral prophet speaks deadly words to the king: even "Saul's death" is anticlimactic, "after this journey into the abyss of divine abandonment" (Exum 1992: 22). Much of the narrative has been about truth and untruth, delusion and its overthrow in the uncovering of truth. The truthiness of this ghostly apparition recapitulates the theme that, whereas human beings see the often-deceptive externals, God knows the heart. This is the wisdom thinking of 1 Samuel. In 1 Sam. 29–30, Achish dismisses the Israelite mercenaries from his army, so David is offstage despoiling the Amalekites, when the Philistines march to Jezreel to meet Saul. The Bible has many pairs of warring brothers, like Cain and Abel, and Esau and Isaac. Do Saul and David belong among them?

Episode One: Divine Abandonment (1 Sam. 28:3–25)

Samuel's death is mentioned for the second time (28:3). This swift plot update makes Samuel appearing from the dead more concrete than if the author had left it to the reader to remember 25:1. First Sam. 28:3–25 is the only ghost story in the Hebrew scripture. The Old Testament tells of the endings of human lives using lapidary expressions such as that a character has "gone to sleep with his fathers" or has "been gathered to his fathers." These scriptures steer clear of mentioning the dead (Eichrodt 1961–67: 2.213). Because contacting departed beings was considered an evil thing, this unique occurrence of the *mysterium tremendum et fascins* is horrible: "For sheer starkness and terror, and in its gripping evocation of isolation and hopelessness, this scene stands out in biblical narrative" (Exum 1992: 22). Saul's guilty intrusion into the realm of the dead provokes its proportionate reprisal in Samuel's utter rejection of his mission.

There are similarities between the way that Bronze Age Mycenaean culture imagined the dead and their domain and how ancient Israelite culture did. Archaic cultures had similar insights: "The world of the dead, the Sheol of the Hebrews corresponds in every particular to the hades of the Greeks and the Arallu of the Assyro-Babylonians" (Martin-Achard 1960: 36–37). Just as the shade of Achilles is recognizable to Odysseus, so Samuel is still recognizable. The shades that Odysseus sees on his journey to hades are crepuscular images of their former selves (Homer, *Odyssey* 11.690; 11.233–56). These shadowy replicates of living beings are not what we would call "disembodied souls," since the idea that the soul as distinct from the body is the real human person had yet to emerge. "In Homeric language," Burkert says, "the *psyche* . . . leaves man at the moment of death and enters . . . Hades. *Psyche* means breath. . . . *Psyche* is not the soul . . . it is not the person, nor is it a kind of *Doppelgänger*. Yet from the moment it leaves man it is also termed an *eidolon*, a phantom image, like the image reflected in a mirror which can be seen . . . but cannot be grasped."[1] The phantom (*eidolon*) of Hercules in the *Odyssey* is a virtual Hercules. When Achilles meets the dead Patroclus in a dream and moves to embrace him, and when Odysseus tries to embrace his mother in hades, the *psyche* of the departed eludes the living men (Homer, *Iliad* 23.99–107; *Odyssey* 11.232–38).

1. Walter Burkert, *Greek Religion*, trans. John Raffan (Cambridge: Harvard University Press, 1985), 193.

In ancient Mycenae, the aristocratic dead were buried with the symbols that befit their status, a lord with his chariot horses.[2] For both Mycenaean culture and the Israel of the patriarchs, the settlement, and the monarchy, the dead retain the emblems that identified their earthly status, for the status *is* the human person. In the Israelite Sheol, "kings sit on their thrones" and "the prophet wears his mantle." Because its inhabitants have lost their earthly bodies, Sheol "is a place of silence and stillness where the impotence of the shadow beings makes the boisterous vigour of real life quite impossible. . . . The shades . . . bear the name *rᵉpā'îm*, the 'weak' or 'powerless' ones." It is as if there were two countries: the land of the dispirited dead and the land of the living. Homer's dead are called *eidoloi* ("copies"), "shadows" or *psychoi* ("breaths" perhaps "wraiths"), and similarly the denizens of Sheol are called, not *ruah* ("spirit"), but *"mētîm* or *rᵉpā'îm*, the 'dead' or the 'weak.' Israel fully shared the primitive belief that a shadowy image of the dead person detached itself from him and continued to eke out a bare existence. . . . Death results from God's withdrawing the breath of life, the *rūaḥ*, whereupon Man . . . once more becomes dust, that is, inanimate matter (Gen. 3.19; Job 34.14f.; Eccles. 12.7)" (Eichrodt 1961–67: 2.211, 214). The dead are earthlings still, but without the vitality or spiritedness (*ruah*) of life. They keep the status that identified them on earth. The voice is the voice of Samuel, and the prophet retains the formidable gravitas he exercised in the land of the living. Saul asks, " 'What form is he of?' And she said, 'An old man cometh up, and he is covered with a mantle. And Saul perceived that it was Samuel, and he stooped with his face to the ground, and bowed himself' " (28:14).

There is also an analogy between what Homer and the biblical authors made of death. That its heroes *really* die is a touchstone of the *Iliad*: Griffin speaks of "the significance of death" as "the central fact of the *Iliad*." He observes that a "tragic and consistent view of human life" as ineluctably facing final ending "is what makes the epic so great."[3] Tugwell thinks that the *Iliad's* "insistence" on human "mortality . . . represents a deliberate and original choice on the part of its author."[4] By the eighth century BC, Indian cultures had sophisticated ideas about souls transmigrating and returning to this world in new bodies, and Homer could have been acquainted with them. So one could "see a religious decision in the conscious renunciation by Homer of metamorphoses in the other world." Homer's heroes are real because they face a real, not an ameliorated, death: "Before the foil of Hades . . . the doomed form of the hero takes on its unprecedented sharpness of outline," a genuine finitude, which "intensifies man's relationship to the deity" (von Balthasar 1983–91: 4.47–48). Using the Greeks as an analogy through which to understand the Old Testament works better than comparisons with ancient Near Eastern cultures like Egypt and Mesopotamia because Homer

2. Ibid., 34.
3. Jasper Griffin, *Homer on Life and Death* (Oxford: Clarendon, 1980), 105, 143.
4. Simon Tugwell, *Human Immortality and the Redemption of Death* (London: Darton, Longman & Todd, 1991), 44.

(and the tragedians) share with ancient Israel the paradoxical intuition that the finitude of the human person is what gives it absolute value. For Homer, humans are not *athanatoi*, not immortals: likewise the biblical writers down to postexilic times do not use the word "immortality." There is no conception of the immortality of the human soul in any scripture written before the fourth century BC: "For the Israelites, the soul is not superior to the body . . . its destiny depends, not on its nature, but on the Living God" (Martin-Achard 1960: 17). The word "immortality" does not occur in scripture until Wisdom of Solomon and Sirach. For the authors of the Pentateuch and Regum, once a person is dead, he or she is gone from life. It is not Samuel's immortal soul that rises to unmask Saul.

These beliefs were expressed in the conviction that the dead are with their ancestors. In some ancient cultures, like the Chinese, ancestors are supplicated by their descendants; in precolonial Africa, the ancestors are the most proximate deities; and the highest god is their father.[5] But in the cultures of the ancient Near East, the dead were not worshiped, but rather consulted for their spectral wisdom. In Deuteronomic law, worshiping the dead was not specifically forbidden, and the prophets do not decry this form of idolatry, as they do Baal worship. One may infer from this that ancient Near Eastern cultures did not lay this temptation before the Israelite peoples. The dead were felt to be thrillingly creepy: their quality of belonging to a numinous, far country is expressed by the use of the same word, *rephaim*, to designate the antediluvian giants of Canaan and the dead themselves (Martin-Achard 1960: 34–36). Such uncanny zombies could easily be imagined to have superhuman knowledge. What was forbidden to Israel was using a medium to contact the dead. What the inquirer wanted from the dead and what the necromancer, wizard, or man or woman "with a familiar spirit" professed to glean from them was their wisdom. These professions were prohibited: "A man, or woman, in whom there is a pythonical or divining spirit, dying let them die: they shall stone them: their blood be upon them" (Lev. 20:27 Douay-Rheims; cf. 19:31 and Deut. 18:10–12). A "divining spirit" translates the Hebrew *yiddeoni* ("knowing ones").

When Saul is told, "there is a woman that hath a familiar spirit at En-dor," he goes to her and commands, "Divine unto me by the familiar spirit, and bring me him up, whom I shall name unto thee" (1 Sam. 28:7–8). The *yiddeoni* uses his or her "familiar" or "divining" spirit to make contact with Sheol, "causing the dead to appear and speak" (Eichrodt 1961–67: 2.215). Because Saul can get no answer from God, "neither by dreams, nor by Urim, nor by prophets" (28:6), he seeks the shade of Samuel to learn from him how to save his kingdom from the Philistines. Like Isaiah in the eighth century BC (Isa. 8:19; 19:3; 28:15, 18; 29:6; 2 Kgs. 23:24), the author is coldly contemptuous that Saul's fear drives

---

5. Temba L. J. Mafico, "The Biblical God of the Fathers and the African Ancestors," in *The Bible in Africa: Transactions, Trajectories, and Trends*, ed. Gerald O. West and Musa W. Dube (Leiden: Brill, 2000), 481.

him to necromancy. The author does not just assume that the reader knows the various Pentateuchal prohibitions of necromancy, but makes Saul first a vigorous promoter of these Deuteronomic laws and then a secret consorter of witches. Some scholars think it anachronistic to have Saul drive the witches out of Israel before the Josianic reform of the cult in 622 BC and before the Deuteronomist had written Deuteronomy down. The law states, "When you enter the land the LORD your God is giving you, do not learn to imitate the detestable ways of the nations there. Let no one be found among you who ... practices divination or sorcery, interprets omens, engages in witchcraft, or casts spells, or who is a medium or spiritist or who consults the dead" (Deut. 18:9–11 NIV). This is interwoven with both the instructions concerning the powers of the prophet (18:15–22) and the law of the king (17:14–20), texts that are basic to the motivation of events in 1 Samuel. Isaiah seems to have known of such a law. The prophet's plenipotentiary and unique status as interpreter of the divine will hangs on the expulsion of competitors: Deut. 18 makes the magical arts taboo "with the intention of creating a prophetic monopoly in the mantic market" (Halpern 1981: 233). "Saul died because he was unfaithful to the LORD; he did not keep the word of the LORD and even consulted a medium for guidance" (1 Chr. 10:13 NIV). It seems to cut against the grain of 1 Samuel as a whole to regard the ascription of a "witch hunt" to Saul as anachronistic.

The hypocrisy of Saul's capitulation, after having expelled "those that had familiar spirits, and the wizards, out of the land" (1 Sam. 28:3), is emphasized by the king's traveling in disguise, "by night" (28:8), and by the she-diviner's fear that he is an undercover agent of the king, setting a trap "for my life, to cause me to die" (28:9; cf. Lev. 20:27). That the crime against which a public figure rails loudest is that in which they are caught red-handed is so widespread that readers take it in stride, without spontaneously feeling that the author is ignobly blackening Saul's reputation. Moderns explain the tendency to be vocally condemnatory of precisely that moral turpitude to which we are tempted in terms of the psychological mechanism of projection. The Old Testament application of the principle is the use of the Lord's omniscience to ironize actions that the protagonist imagines take place by night, hidden from all eyes. Because the pattern of setting up a character occurs frequently in Old Testament narrative, we expect it and appreciate that this meeting between Saul and Samuel is predestined. It is like an inverted version of their first, divinely guided meeting. In the first encounter, Saul did not intend to meet Samuel, but does, and is involuntarily offered the kingdom; in their last meeting, he wills to meet Samuel and is told that his army will fall "into the hand of the Philistines" because the "kingdom" has been given by God "to David" (1 Sam. 28:19, 17).

In the ancient Israelite conception, "deaders" were cut off, not only from living earthlings, but from God. The *repaim* were believed to have no communication with God: "It was on this earth that God's kingdom was to be set up. The direction of all his forces to this end gave a man's life its whole content and value. Hence

Yahweh claimed the living for himself . . . ; the dead had no further relationship with him" (Eichrodt 1961–67: 2.221). There was thus no reward for the pious, as against the unrighteous, dead: Saul would eventually go to sit along Samuel himself. All in Sheol alike are doomed to everlasting separation from this world and thus from God. Yahweh was literally the "God of the living, not of the dead" (Matt. 22:32 Good News Bible). Resurrection is more than continuing to look as one did when alive; it is not just the public identifiability of the same body-person, in the Wittgensteinian sense. It is the regaining of living existence. Samuel has not resurrected from the dead. He has not returned to life. He has been invoked by the witch to visit the upper world, the land of the living, as a shade. Although it was normal ancient belief that human beings survive death, it was unknown to suggest that a real historical person, such as Samuel, had returned to life from the land of the dead. Whence Achilles' bitter complaint to Odysseus: he is doomed to remain a specter of his former self forever (Homer, *Odyssey* 10.555–59). A belief in "lifeless survival" could not evolve into belief in actual resurrection from death, because, for Homer and for Israel before the Hellenization of the Near East, deaders are "such a pale and pitiful reflexion of human existence" that they are really just "a metaphorical expression of nonbeing" (Martin-Achard 1960: 17). In 33 AD Christianity would be "born into a world where its central claim was known to be false."[6] When Justin Martyr preached the resurrection of Christ and so of the Christian believer to real, embodied life, he affirmed what he called a "new and strange hope" (*Dialogue with Trypho* 10).[7] For our author, Samuel rose from a place of hopeless duration in twilight, a place of separation from the divine light of life.

Israelite conceptions of the fate of the soul track the development of Greek thinking. When Socrates courageously told the jury at his trial that death is either "an annihilation, and the dead have no consciousness of anything, or, as we are told, it is really a change, a migration of the soul from this place to another," he was offering a new attitude to the deepest question of all. When Socrates cheerfully asked his jurors, "How much would one of you give to meet Orpheus and Musaeus, Hesiod and Homer?" (Plato, *Apology* 74–75), the philosopher was putting himself at odds with the poet whose hero lamented that he would prefer to be a landless serf than dead. With Plato, in the fifth century BC, the Greek *psyche* becomes the "soul," the authentic part of the human being that lives on after death because it is intrinsically immaterial, not dependent on the body for its survival. Some see in this not an advance, but a loss of the tragic awareness of human finitude: "Once we start calling the soul 'immortal' " with Plato, Tugwell warns, we will soon be giving it adventures in a mythological afterworld "and robbing death too cheaply of its sting."[8]

6. N. T. Wright, *The Resurrection of the Son of God* (Minneapolis: Fortress, 2003), 35.
7. Cited in ibid., 503.
8. Tugwell, *Human Immortality and the Redemption of Death*, 35.

The idea of justice plays a pivotal role in both Plato and later biblical ideas of the afterlife (Martin-Achard 1960: 137). In the Wisdom of Solomon and Sirach, perhaps contemporary with Plato, scripture inches toward conceptions of immortality: "Justice is perpetual and immortal" (Wis. 1:15); "to be allied to wisdom is immortality" (Wis. 8:17). The writer seems to mean by this, not that the soul obtains immortality by its wisdom, but that it touches the immortal by acquaintance with divine wisdom: "By the means of her I shall have immortality: and shall leave behind me an everlasting memory to them that come after me" (Wis. 8:13). The writer's claim that "to know thee [God] is perfect justice: and to know thy justice, and thy power, is the root of immortality" (Wis. 15:3) is balanced by the observation in Sirach that "the son of man is not immortal" (Sir. 17:29). For the wisdom writer, immortality is not, as for Plato, an innate property of the human soul; it is something for which the wise and the righteous live in hope: "Their hope is full of immortality" (Wis. 3:4—all Douay-Rheims).

With the Maccabean Wars in the 160s BC came the reward of that hope. The righteous Jews who died fighting the Hellenistic overlords were believed to have been rewarded by God. Daniel (ca. 165 BC) contains the first unequivocal statement of resurrection in scripture, predicated on an idea of divine just reward and punishment: "Many of those who sleep in the dust of the earth shall awake, some to everlasting life, and some to shame and everlasting contempt" (Dan. 12:2 ESV). In 2 Maccabees seven brothers are tortured to death by the Greek king for refusing to demonstrate their Hellenization by consuming pork. The fourth brother dies exclaiming, "Ours is the better choice, to meet death at men's hands, yet relying on God's promise that we shall be raised up by him; whereas for you there can be no resurrection to new life" (2 Macc. 7:14 New Jerusalem Bible). The afterlife thus becomes a place of punishment and reward. The God of Exod. 3, being/life itself, and the Creator God of Gen. 1–2 is the lord of life *and* death, being and nonbeing. Thus, "the emerging Israelite belief in resurrection . . . was a development . . . whose roots lay deep within ancient Israel itself," arising directly from faith in "YHWH as the god who both kills and makes alive." Fourth Maccabees and Philo of Alexandria teach the immortality of the soul, not God's miraculous resurrection of the body-soul person.[9]

Noncanonical intertestamental literature such as 1 Enoch testifies to the growing hope of reward in heaven for the righteous. Hellenistic in inspiration, this literature imagines heavenly netherworlds currently populated by angels and later, after the judgment, to be peopled by *psychoi* or "souls," that is, disincarnate spirits. In 1 Enoch, Enoch travels to a world in which places of punishment anticipate sinners and Elysian comforts await the blessed. Enoch sees "a tree such as I have never smelt . . . and its leaves and its flowers and its wood never wither." The angel Michael tells him that "this beautiful fragrant tree—and no creature of flesh has authority to touch it until the great judgment . . . this will be given to the

---

9. Wright, *Resurrection of the Son of God*, 125, 142–44.

righteous and humble. From its fruit life will be given to the chosen."[10] The dead whom Enoch encounters are disembodied souls, like those in Plato's *Republic*. Like Plato, the writer uses the afterlife as a theater of judgment, although, as a Jew, he gives the judgment to God rather than to the inbuilt course of cosmic justice. Such notions of the afterlife were popular in Second Temple Pharisaic Judaism. The ancient tradition no longer slaked the human thirst for poetic justice: the Homeric and older biblical belief that hero and slave, righteous and sinner, alike are finite mortals, doomed to the tragedy of death, seemed to them unjust. With the emergence of apocalyptic speculation about a final return of Yahweh to justify the Jews' religiopolitical hope, the afterlife becomes the theater of a theodicy in which the evil of death is trumped by the punishment of sinners and the rewarding of the valiant.

The thinking of Pharisaic Judaism about the afterlife is analogous to conceptions that would later appear in Islam: in both, the soul's survival of death is a given, and paradise and hell are places of reward and punishment. Neither regards human life as finite and therefore tragic. Both take the continuation of the self *as itself* for granted: human life ends not in the deprivation of existence, but in comeuppance or judgment. Neither Second Temple Judaism nor Islam include original sin in their conception of human life. Neither teaches that human beings have lost the gift of immortality because of a fall. For Christians, on the other hand, once fallen Adam has brought the tragedy of death upon humanity, it can only regain its lost immortality in Christ. Through his death and resurrection, Christ leads us, not to a paradise of future pleasures, but to the vision of God, eternal life. For Christians, immortality is not a reward or a curse for those who would in any case have survived death as a living soul and sped forth to paradise or hell: it is, rather, something newly gained on behalf of fallen humans by Christ. It is because of the unique historical act of Christ's resurrection that the gift of immortal existence lost by Adam is regained.

It was because of the belief in Jesus's bodily resurrection that the early church taught the embodied resurrection of believers. The righteous dead would rise to heaven in resurrected bodies. But that was not because the righteous were rewarded by God upon death, as Pharisaic Judaism taught. Rather, the believer's body is resurrected because Christ's body is resurrected. Participating in his death by baptism, the believer participates in his resurrection. The believer will not merely survive, as rewarded soul, but be given new life. First Tim. 6:16 is clear that God alone is immortal: "It is as a result of a change" wrought by Christ "that that which is now mortal becomes immortal" at the "last trumpet" (1 Cor 15:53–54).[11]

Both the Pharisaic/Islamic and the Christian conceptions of the afterlife are imaginative. In the Pharisaic/Islamic conceptions, the image is a very literal one:

10. 1 Enoch 24:4 and 25:4–5 in H. D. F. Sparks, ed., *The Apocryphal Old Testament* (Oxford: Clarendon, 1984), 213–14.

11. Tugwell, *Human Immortality and the Redemption of Death*, 77.

someone is transferred, as it were, teleported, from this world into another dimension, hell or paradise. Survival is a more literal image than immortality: survival is the extension of this life into the next, with due punishment or reward accruing. If we hold that all survive death in this sense, we maintain that no one really dies: the departed simply pass on. This is why the underlying anthropology is nontragic. There is no idea here that death is an end, that the soul has to fear loss of existence. The soul fears punishment, not nonexistence. It takes imagination to conceive of rewards and punishment after death, and intertestamental Jewish texts like 1 Enoch are highly imaginative, in the way that science fiction is, but the idea of survival they use is literal rather than metaphorical.

The Christian conception of immortality or new life is a complex metaphor. It equates mere survival with death, the loss of life. As Paul and the early church symbolically conceive it, death is the dominion of the devil: to be dead is to survive in the possession of the devil. Death is not just a place, but a condition, servitude to the devil. The early Christian imagination personifies death as the devil. The unrighteous, the unbaptized, and the pre-Christian are taken to live on or survive, but to belong to the devil is to have no life, to be dead in spirit. Early Christian art depicts Christ combating the devil in hell with the image of Jonah wrestling with the whale: immortality is wrested out of the hands of death. To be in the hands of death thus personified is to be spiritually nonexistent, in the grip of the "nothinger," the devil. The early Christian conception of the afterlife recaptures the archaic Israelite and Homeric sense of the finitude of human existence. The dead survive, but echoing the older intuition of the hopeless character of the underworld, these lifeless beings dwell in the domain of the devil. Dying really is an end, because it is a passage to a nothing existence, nonlife. Immortality or new life is to be freed to exist beyond death by Christ's resurrection. Immortality is not a given state that, as the essence of the soul, lends it automatic vitality. Nor is it the old life back again, for that is gone. Immortality is that energy of new life that is achieved for believers by Christ's defeat of the devil and the nothing in his resurrection. This is in keeping with the archaic biblical apprehension that Sheol is "the world of the *Nihil* that Yahweh did not create . . . but which is not merely the void or the Nothing, but a corrosive and destructive power" (Martin-Achard 1960: 44) *and* with the Old Testament conviction that the Creator has power to create existence wheresoever he wills.

So where had Samuel come from in his spectral visit to Saul in 1 Sam. 28? Early apologists like Justin Martyr turned the old Sheol or hades (as it becomes in the Septuagint) into something close to what Christians, using more terminological distinctions, would later define as hell. Justin claims that the witch of Endor invokes Samuel, not from heaven or from an outer court of hell, custom-built for righteous spirits, but from hell itself: "That the souls survive, I have proven to you from the fact that the soul of Samuel itself had been called up by the witch as Saul requested. And it also appears from that that all the souls of the righteous and of prophets, these kindred spirits, fall into the power of the same kind as that which . . . inhabited this woman. This is why God teaches us, through his Son, to fight with all our power to become righteous and, at the approach of death, to ask that our soul not fall under the hand of any power like this one: in rending his spirit on the cross, he said: 'Father, I remit my spirit into your hands' " (*Dialogue with Trypho* 105.2–5). For Justin, preaching that eternal life in God has been achieved by Christ on our behalf, the pre-Christian Samuel must have returned from the region of the evil powers. Before Christ, as he takes it, all survive death, but fall into the grip of the devil. Though they survive, they are existentially dead, under the power of Satan. The reason for Justin's stark opposition of Sheol and the Christian heaven and for his conviction that righteous Jews like the prophet Samuel were in hell, before Christ, is his faith that the resurrection of Christ is the *only* means by which human souls can return from death to life.

In the third century, Tertullian focused on the primitive Christian belief that it is the body-soul composite that will enjoy everlasting life. He also developed a geography of the afterlife that owed as much to Hellenistic literature and to the imagery of the intertestamental Jewish apocalyptic texts as it did to faith in the power of Christ's resurrection. Tertullian intended to combat the erroneous idea that the soul survives without its body, and he grasped this one horn of Christian teaching with vigor. He knew that what he was arguing for was embodied resurrection. Against those Valentinian Gnostics and gnosticizing Christians who had begun to disavow the resurrection of the body, Tertullian proclaimed "an extravagantly materialistic notion of the resurrection body."[12] Tertullian likewise faced off the Platonist idea that the soul survives by virtue of its intrinsic immateriality. He still wanted to retain the Pharisaic scheme of punishments and rewards for the dead. In order to ensure justice for the virtuous departed and eager to paint the picture of the afterlife in vivid and materialistic colors, Tertullian envisaged hades as divided into two parts, one for the wicked, the other for the righteous. The virtuous dead will go to the bosom of Abraham, the wicked to a region on the shores of Gehenna, the lake of fire. Tertullian taught that the righteous dead are not, as Justin had imagined, yet to be freed from Satan by the resurrection of Christ, but already in the safekeeping of Abraham. On this scheme, those who deserve a reward, like the prophet Samuel, are not in the power of the devil.

It follows that a woman with a "familiar spirit," or a demon, would have had no medium with which to make contact with Samuel. Out of reach of the devil, the prophet was clear of demonic divining spirits. So Tertullian taught that it was not Samuel who rose before the eyes of Saul and the witch of Endor, but rather one of those demonic powers who "transformed [himself] into an angel of light" (2 Cor. 11:14). The voice was the voice of Samuel, but the apparition that rose before Saul was a demonic impostor. The anonymous author of *De Universo*, who has been tagged "Josephus" by patristic scholars, likewise taught that Samuel did not appear to Saul, because necromancy has no power to draw up the departed from Abraham's bosom,

---

12. Wright, *Resurrection of the Son of God*, 513, citing Carolyn Walker Bynum.

that forecourt of hades in which a proleptically blessed company of patriarchs and prophets await the coming of Christ, not to redeem them from death, but to lead them to a heaven of which they are already citizens. This bipartite hades requires *De Universo* to argue that Saul was tricked, going in disguise to be confronted by a demon disguised as Samuel. By assailing Platonic notions of a spiritual afterlife by grasping the horn of resurrection embodiedness while retaining the Platonic notion of a reward of the righteous, Tertullian and *De Universo* have let go of the other horn of Christian belief: resurrection by Christ (Origen 1986: 81–82). That after Adam and before Christ *all* are in the power of death seems to have dropped out of the picture.

This is how it appeared to Origen. He wrote a sermon intended to refute Tertullian's and *De Universo*'s contention that Samuel does not really appear in 1 Sam. 28. Unlike Tertullian, Origen was not tempted to millennialism: the striking thing for him about the resurrection of the dead is not the philosophical point that it is embodied but the theological point that it is effected by Christ. The great Alexandrian theologian had the gift of mockery, one that earned him enemies. Addressing "what those who claim that this history is not true say," Origen mimics the objections and the objectors to the christological reading of the passage with a series of rhetorical questions: "Samuel in hell? Samuel called up by the witch, he the chosen prophet, dedicated to God since his birth, and of whom they say that from his birth on he lived in the temple, he who from the time that he had been weaned wore the ephod, bearing the double cloak and became the priest of the Lord, he who, even as a child the Lord spoke and met? Samuel in hell? Samuel in the underworld, he to whom fell Eli's succession . . . ? Samuel in hell, he whom God heard at the time of the wheat harvest and made rain fall from the sky [12:17–18]?" Origen is ironizing the ideas that underlie the assumption that a good soul like Samuel would have automatically gone to his just reward, like Socrates. A Christian whose idea of the afterlife comes down to just reward for a good life would naturally demand to know, as Origen mockingly puts it, "Why would Samuel be in hell? You see that it follows that Samuel is not in hell? Samuel in hell? Why not Abraham, Isaac, and Jacob in hell too? Samuel in hell? Why not Moses as well, who is connected with Samuel in the words, 'Even if Moses and Samuel appear together before me, I would not listen to this people' [Jer. 15:1]. Samuel in hell? Why not put Isaiah in hell too. . . . And have Jeremiah as well, in hell all the prophets, in hell!" (1986: 179). Origen is being brutally sarcastic: he is ascribing to his opponents so great a fixation with the survival of good folks for their just reward that they cannot conceive of the tragic consequences of fallenness as accruing to the patriarchs and the prophets.

One logical conclusion of the principle that a righteous man like Samuel could not have been in hell is that it would be inappropriate for Christ, the Son of God, to have been in the region of the damned either. A further logical implication is that, if we devise a science-fictional geography of the afterworld with a special enclosure for the righteous pre-Christian dead, these virtuous pagans did not need Christ to be redeemed. Living in their hygienic suburb of "outer Sheol," they already are redeemed and simply have to wait for proof of this to occur in Christ's resurrection. The righteous dead await, not redemption, but the demonstration of the righteousness they had before Christ. They are not imprisoned in the devil's pit: they do not need to be bought back from the devil. Against this, Origen asks, "Why are you afraid to acknowledge that every place is in need of Christ?" Every place and dimension to which the surviving remnants of dead human beings can be transported needs redemption. Every person, including Samuel and the greatest prophets, needed Christ, Origen affirms. Even Peter was flawed in begging his Lord not to go to Jerusalem and suffer (Matt. 16:22). Though Peter "knew the greatness of Christ," Origen says, "he did not want to accept that which is more humble about him [Luke 7:20]." Even the Baptist, Origen observes, needed Christ to redeem him (1986: 195, 197, 199).

The interpretation of 1 Sam. 28 cuts to the heart of the meaning of Christ's work: did he transform the state of the *repaim* in Sheol, giving new life to those who had lost it, or was his mission to the gates of hades merely to rubber-stamp what had already been established by the virtues of its inhabitants? Does every place and every person need Christ? Did Samuel need Christ to redeem him from death? The stakes are high: Origen is contending against the propensity of the human imagination to create a geography of the next world and against that innate human moralism that requires that the just have *some* reward. Such propensities enable the novel Christian teaching of immortality to dwindle into the literalism of survival.

If Samuel's dwelling in hell entails that he had entered the contagious power of the devil, what happens to his prophecy to Saul: "The LORD is departed from thee, and is become thy enemy. . . . The LORD hath rent the kingdom out of thy hand, and given it . . . even to David" (28:16–17)? How could a creature from hell prophesy, as Samuel does? In reply to this question, Origen argues that Christ, and Samuel too, entered the place of damnation, but retained their identity as Christ and as prophet of Christ: "Is Christ no longer Christ because he was once found in hell? Was he no longer Son of God because he had gone into the subterranean place, 'That all flesh should bow at the name of Jesus Christ, among the heavenly, earthly, and subterranean beings' [Phil. 2:10]? Thus Christ was Christ even when he was below." Samuel too retained the "prophetic grace" in hell, prophesying "in the direction of heaven," for "the spirits of the deceased" have, "dare I say, need of the prophetic grace." By speaking to Saul of the kingdom of David, Origen says, Samuel was prophesying Christ (1986: 199, 203).

Neither Clement of Alexandria nor Origen accepted the reversion of Christian eschatology to Jewish apocalyptic speculation about the geography of the afterlife that was implied by Tertullian's millennialism. Both held a simple bipartite eschatology, believing that, since the death and resurrection of Christ, the righteous enter heaven, and the wicked, and they alone, go to hell. Since "there is only a single hades where the devil and his angels reign," on this schema, "there is no longer any need to hypothesize two distinct underworld regions." It mattered to Origen to contest the theory that a demonic spirit and not Samuel himself appeared to Saul in Endor because "the way in which redemption is conceived" turns on this point. Origen was "empowered by the conviction that he was not just defending one exegesis against another, but the significance that the death and resurrection of Christ have had in the history of salvation: they have opened paradise to all the righteous" (1986: 82–83). Only Christ gives eternal life. Origen argues that

> before the coming of my Lord Jesus Christ it was impossible that anyone could come to where the "tree of life" is, impossible that one pass beyond the beings posted to guard "the way of the tree of life": "He has posted cherubim with a turning sword of fire to guard the way of the tree of life" [Gen. 3:24]. Who can get past someone with a "sword of fire"? . . . Samuel could not do it, Abraham could not do it. This is why Abraham is seen (in hell) by the man who is being punished: "The rich man who was in his torments turned his eyes to see Abraham"—even if he saw him "far off," at least he saw him, "and Lazarus in his bosom." The patriarchs, the prophets, and all those awaiting the coming of my Lord Jesus Christ for him to open the way: "I am the way, I am the door" [John 14:6; 10:9]. He is the "way" to the "tree of life," so that his word should come about: "If you pass through the fire, the flame will not consume you" [Isa. 43:2]. And through what "fire"? "He has posted cherubim with a turning sword of fire to guard the way of the tree of life." It is this for this that . . . the blessed wait below, because they cannot go where the tree of life is, where the paradise of God is, or where God is a gardener, there where are the blessed, elect, and saints of God. (Origen 1986: 199, 205, 207)

Using the common baptismal image of Christ the healer or doctor of the soul,[13] Origen argues that, "since it is not the well who have need of a doctor, but the sick" (Matt. 9:12, author's translation), it "is necessary that doctors go where soldiers suffer and that they enter where the vile smell of their wounds reigns: this is what inspires therapeutic philanthropy: in the same way, the Word has inspired the savior and the prophets not only to come here below, but to descend into hell." To those who ask, "How could Samuel be in hell?" Origen replies, "Christ was in hell" for "the Lord has descended to save" (1986: 201, 189, 191).

Origen knew that, for the cultured despisers of Christianity in his time, such a faith was ridiculous. To the Roman Celsus, the idea of a god returning from the dead to eat fish with his disciples was vulgar. Celsus had mocked the gospel resurrection accounts, describing them as the delusions of women who, he said, "wanted to impress the others—who had the good sense to have abandoned him—by spreading their hallucinations about as 'visions.'" Anyone who had taken on Celsus, as Origen had done, knew that belief in bodily resurrection is tenable philosophically only if we are guided to it by faith in those women's visions of Christ's physical appearance. In *On the True Doctrine*, Celsus describes Christians as people who "believe in the absurd theory that Christians will be raised and reconstituted by God, and that somehow they will actually see God with their mortal eyes and hear him with their ears and be able to touch him with

---

13. G. M. Lukken, *Original Sin in the Roman Liturgy* (Leiden: Brill, 1973), 297–322. Lukken notes that Origen in particular accentuates this theme (299).

their hands. . . . The Christians . . . think one cannot know God except through the senses of the body."[14] Origen, the so-called Platonist, tackled Celsus on just this point, insisting that Christ did walk among the deaders in Sheol, converting some, that the Johannine fish breakfast really occurred (John 21), and that, as a consequence of this incontrovertible sensible evidence, "his disciples . . . devoted themselves to the teaching of a doctrine which . . . they would not have taught with such courage had they invented the resurrection of Jesus . . . ; and who . . . not only prepared others to despise death, but were themselves the first to manifest their disregard for its terrors" (*Contra Celsus* 2.43, 56).[15]

Since he took the gospel resurrection narratives literally, it was obvious to Origen that the inspired author of 1 Samuel clearly describes a real event. The inspired author states for instance that "the woman saw Samuel" (1 Sam. 28:12), that "Saul perceived that it was Samuel" (28:14): if he really meant that the witch *pretended* to invoke Samuel, why didn't the sacred author write, "The woman saw a demon who passed himself off as Samuel"? Origen assumes that because its author is divine, the scriptural narrative is to be trusted. Origen claims a demonic apparition could not deliver true prophecy to Saul, such as "the LORD also shall deliver the host of Israel into the hand of the Philistines" (28:19). Origen finds it untoward that a "minor demon . . . could prophesy on the subject of Saul and the people of God, that he should prophesy on the kingdom of David" (1986: 201). Origen thinks it unworthy that a demon should prophesy: only God can deliver true prophecy. He uses a principle that, "although justifiable in itself, was particularly dangerous": that "everything the prophet received on order from God to say must be worthy of God." The problem is this: "How are we to judge by our human criteria what is worthy or unworthy of God?" (*Homilies on Jeremiah* 12.1, cited in Lubac 2007: 350–51). Origen is on a sticky wicket, and his argument could easily be turned against him. His later opponents, like Eustathius of Antioch, who believed that the apparition of Samuel must have been a demonic delusion, would claim that his words to Saul could not be the prophet speaking, because what he says is unworthy of a prophet who abominated idolatry. How could the real Samuel appear to Saul, Eustathius demanded, and omit to condemn his necromancy? The bishop of Antioch invented a mealymouthed sermon that, he felt, would have been appropriate for Samuel to have given, if the real McCoy had come up from the dead: "Tell me most condemnable of mankind! . . . If then God deserted thee, and did not listen to thee at all . . . shouldst thou not rather bow before God as a suppliant and wash off your accused sins from thee by giving alms to the poor, instead of resorting to a soothsayer?!" "Eustathius judges a Scriptural passage to be not prophetic, because what is said is not in conformity with his opinion as to what a prophet should say in order to be a prophet."[16]

14. Cited from Wright, *Resurrection of the Son of God*, 521–23.
15. Ibid.
16. K. A. D. Smelik, "The Witch of Endor: 1 Samuel 28 in Rabbinic and Christian Exegesis till 800 A.D.," *Vigiliae christianae* 33 (1977): 160–79 at 169.

We tend to conceive divine inspiration the other way round to Origen: many modern Christians think of just those parts of scripture that they find to be true to be inspired by God. For Origin it is the reverse: it is the divine authorship of scripture that validates their truthfulness (Lubac 2007: 340–41). Since the veracity of scripture comes back, for Origen, to its being a solely divine communication, he maintains that

> a minor demon could not know that David had been consecrated king by the Lord, "because you have not listened to the voice of the Lord and executed the ferocity of his anger against Amalek." Were these words not spoken by God? Are they not true? It is entirely true that Saul has not done the will of the Lord, but that he has embraced "King Amalek and allowed him to live," as Samuel reproached Saul with this before his death and at the very moment at which Saul is going to die . . . "And because of this the Lord has laid this sentence against you on this day and the Lord will give Israel to strangers. . . . Hasten Saul, for tomorrow you and your sons will be with me." Is this a thing that a minor demon could know . . . [15:16–23; 28:16–19]? (Origen 1986: 185–87)

Origen works from the authorship of scripture to the truthfulness of the text and therefore regards it as impossible that we could see through the author's word and grasp that he really means to tell us something contrary to what he literally tells.

A century later, Augustine grappled with the same problem. In his early *Questions to Simplicius* (396), Augustine proposes that we read 1 Sam. 28 against its literal sense: "Samuel," he thought, really meant a phantasm caused to take Samuel's shape by a demon. But later, in line with the bishop of Hippo's move toward a literal exposition of scripture, Augustine argues in his *De cura pro mortuis* that the reality of Samuel is imposed on us by an intertextual corroboration of its literal sense. Scripture itself, the ultimate authority, takes the apparition literally: in his profile of Samuel's life, Ben Sirach records that "after this he slept, and he made known to the king, and showed him the end of his life, and he lifted up his voice from the earth in prophecy to blot out the wickedness of the nation" (Sir. 46:23 Douay-Rheims). Augustine adds for good measure that, since Moses appeared at the transfiguration, there is no reason why Samuel should not present himself to Saul "at God's command." The opponents of a real apparition of Samuel, who by Augustine's time had added Eustathius, Gregory of Nyssa, and the redoubtable Jerome to their number, staked their case on the claim that power to draw a saint like Samuel from heaven could not be ascribed to a witch. Against this, Augustine claims that it was not necromancy but God's power that caused Samuel to appear.[17]

Supposing that Origen and Augustine are right to say that the text calls for a literal reading, a modern reader would probably wish to expand on this by

17. Ibid., 177–78.

connecting it to the literary texture of the episode and to the esthetic of the Old
Testament scriptures. The notion that what Saul perceives as Samuel in this episode is really a deceptive, conjuring trick is unpersuasive because of the felt truth
of the episode. Since the ending of 1 Sam. 15, Saul has known that the kingdom
has been taken from him, and, in denial of that reality, he has sought to prevent
divine providence from taking its course. Saul found a medium or vehicle for his
denial in David. He has projected the cause of his downfall onto David, since
the onset of his jealous madness in 1 Sam. 16. In 1 Sam. 16 David and the evil
spirit were present together, and Saul had to choose between the hatred inspired
in him by the evil spirit and love for the harpist, the only person who could save
him. Instead of welcoming David's help, as Chrysostom says, Saul "soon envied
his physician" (*Homilies on 2 Corinthians* 24.4, in Franke 2005: 278). Saul has
been living the lie, battling against the truth of divine providence. The apparition
of Samuel forces Saul to awake from the illusions that have driven his pursuit of
David. The esthetic effect of this is of truth regaining its ground. Why should
Saul ask the witch to call up Samuel, of all people? Because Saul knows that
Samuel can be relied upon to speak the truth to him; Samuel is the plumb line
of truthfulness, in the narrative, and Saul knows it: "With Samuel, Saul is forced
back to brutal reality, away from brutal illusion. He has been battling David all
this time, as he thought, but in reality he has been battling Yahweh" (Good 1965:
77–78). The theory that Samuel is an illusion, a demon in disguise, runs counter
to the feeling of the victory of truth over deception in the deliverance of that
"wanted-unwanted" oracle to Saul. The unswerving integrity of Samuel comes
down to his being God's spokesman. The omniscience of the always anonymous
Old Testament narrator reflects the omniscience of the Lord. Are there any other
cases in the Old Testament in which the narrator laid aside his "omniscient eye"
and described an event purely from the perspective of one character, without ever
relating the true story? If not, then the deceptive apparition of Samuel is a *hapax
legomenon*, a once-off. The omniscience of the Lord is significant in this story. Saul
is guided to the meeting with Samuel, as he had been in 1 Sam. 11. The wisdom of
the *yiddeoni* ("the knowing ones") is contrasted with the omniscience of God. The
omniscient hand of God, who delivers to Saul exactly what he wants in precisely
the way he does not want it is contrasted with the wisdom that he seeks from the
dead. The only word he can receive from the dead is the breath of death. Origen's
contention that the word of scripture always speaks truth because it is the inspired
speech of God is reflected in 1 Sam. 28's stress upon God's uniquely all-knowing
character. Origen's conception of revelation is applicable to 1 Sam. 28.

    In his fourth-century *Treatise on the Witch of Endor against Origen* 21–22, Eu-
stathius of Antioch "accuses Origen of 'allegorizing all the scriptures.'" Eustathius
charges Origen with taking literally "'this single passage' of the Bible, instead of
'explaining it figuratively' as he himself did: 'He who is in the habit of stuffing
everything with allegories has not known how to explain figuratively only the
words of the Witch!'" In fact, the real "complaint of this Antiochian against the

master of Alexander is a complaint about his narrow literalism!" (cited in Lubac 2007: 26–27). Origen affirmed that "the historical text itself and its examination are necessary to see what awaits us after death" (1986: 185). Origen's idea of the divine inspiration of scripture is what we would call propositionalist: given the authority of the inspired author, sentences or phrases like "the woman saw Samuel" or "Saul perceived that it was Samuel" are knockdown proof that it must have been Samuel who arose from Sheol. To those moderns who do not adhere to propositionalist theories of biblical inspiration, the same principle is evident from the imaginative way in which our author identifies Samuel, that is, by his mantle. Samuel's dress has been his signature since Hannah brought him a new robe each year at Shiloh (2:19):

> From the earliest days of his youth to his resurrection in chapter 28, Samuel wears a robe representing the royalty that is wrapped around Israel during the course of the story. . . . That young berobed Samuel is now an old man and dead, and the robe has become a shroud. . . . Samuel's robe was torn by Saul (15:27). . . . Jonathan's robe played a similar role when he stripped it off to hand over to David (18:4), again signifying the transfer of royal power. . . . David himself cut off the end of Saul's robe in 24:5, presenting Saul and the reader with a . . . more clearcut image of the seizing of kingship. . . . This robe of royalty appears one final time . . . wrapped around a dead person. . . . Samuel is clothed in a dead man's robe as he foretells the imminent death of Saul and his sons. The robe as shroud enfolds Saul's death as well as Samuel's. (Polzin 1989: 218–19)

The symbolic robe incarnates the kingdom. Rather than saying that a demon could not prophesy the kingdom of David and thus that of Christ, we might prefer to contend that the author's symbol system is not internally subversive of itself. A demon cannot symbolize the kingdom. The prophet's mantle can.

Serious theological matters underlie the objections to a literal reading of 1 Sam. 28. It seems to undermine the omnipotence of God if a witch can cause the shade of Samuel to leave the world of the dead once God has withdrawn the life from him. Equally important, if we take the encounter as a whole literally, we must also contend with Elohim appearing from the dead. Even before Samuel raises his mantled head, we read that "the king said unto her, 'Be not afraid: for what sawest thou?' And the woman said unto Saul, 'I saw gods [*elohim*] ascending out of the earth'" (28:13). Literally translated, *elohim* are "divine beings or gods" in the plural. Cyril of Alexandria and Gregory of Nyssa claimed that to take these verses literally is to deny monotheism. Once paraphrased reverentially into "demons" in the plural, the *elohim* are the wedge that required Saints Cyril and Gregory to take the entire episode with a grain of salt.[18] The Septuagint took the plural, and Origen sidestepped the problem of polytheism by translating the "gods" that the Septuagint supplies as "souls of the righteous." That might approximate to the

18. Ibid., 168–69.

literal intentions of the Hebrew writer. Some conjecture that the use of *elohim* here reflects a linguistic borrowing from Canaanite belief in the divinity of the dead, meaning for our author, "a being from the world of the gods," since the far country of the deaders was felt to be supernatural (Martin-Achard 1960: 93–94). Each of the patriarchs gave the God he worshiped a specific name (for instance, Abraham called on God as "benefactor of Abraham" [cf. Gen. 15:1], and Isaac prayed to the "kinsman of Isaac" [cf. Gen. 31:42]). Later, "the ancestors" god came to be known by the single generic title: Elohim, the God of the fathers. In Exod. 3:15–16, Yahweh, "he who is," identifies himself to Moses as the *same* Elohim, the God of Israel's ancestors: with that, the "gods of the fathers now come together in the one God. Yahweh now encompasses the gods of the ancestors." When our author has the witch of Endor telling Saul that she sees Elohim, she could mean that she sees "ancestral spirits," or what Origen politely called "the souls of the righteous." As one exegete notes, "What she saw were the *'elohim 'olim* ('the dead coming up'), among whom was Samuel, an old man, one of the ancestors. A painting in the Paris National museum . . . captures this image well; the painter portrays several *'elohim* (spirits) rising from their sleep and Samuel standing in front of Saul. These *'elohim* are the gods of the fathers. They are the gods whom their fathers have worshiped, and who are present with the spirits of the deceased fathers as they are with the living."[19] Just as Yahweh is the true God of the fathers, so Christ is the true ancestor, because he alone gives life to the dead.

Like Augustine, Origen thinks that some parts of the Old Testament were of more interest to the theologian than others. He says that some of this history is existential for us and some of it is not: "There are histories which don't touch us, and other ones which are necessities for our hope." Origen believed that "if the history about Saul and the witch touches us, that is because there is necessarily a truth in the letter of the text." The truth of which the text speaks is a hard word, unappealing to us: "Who, after having departed this life, would actually want to be in the power of a minor demon, so that a witch could conjure one up? . . . Is it not true that, if a personage of this importance were under the ground and the witch had called him up, a demon had power over the soul of a prophet? What can one say? Are these things written? Are they true or are they not true? If one says they are not true, one invokes a skepticism which comes back to haunt one's own position, but if they are true, it poses for us a question and a problem." The problem raised by taking 1 Sam. 28 to be literally true is that of our salvation: do we want to be in the power of the devil after death or with Christ in paradise? Something has changed, historically, since the time of Samuel and Saul: Christ has entered Sheol. "We have something more" even than Samuel had, says Origen:

> We who have "come to the end of the ages" [Heb. 9:26]. What more? If we leave
> here having become virtuous and good, not carrying the burden of sin, we too will

19. Mafico, "Biblical God of the Fathers," 483–84.

pass through the fiery sword, and we will not descend to the place where those who died before the coming of Christ waited, but we will pass without the "sword of fire" causing us any harm . . . [1 Cor. 3:13–15]. We thus pass through and we have "something more" than them; we cannot, if we have experienced good, leave as evil. Among the ancients, not even the patriarchs and the prophets said what we can say . . . "it is better to be dissolved and to be with Christ" [Phil. 1:21]. . . . Since you have come "last," you will receive the reward "first" [Matt. 20:10], from the master of the house, in Christ Jesus our Lord. (Origen 1986: 175, 177, 207, 209)

There may be those who think we have said nothing to address the desperate plight of Saul in this episode. What sight could be more pitiful than King Saul falling headlong on the ground with horror ("Saul fell straightway all along on the earth"; 1 Sam. 28:20), dragging his body "from the earth" (28:23), and being nursed with food by a witch as he stares death in the face? And not only Saul, perhaps, but the whole of Israel, with its doomed dream of an earthly Jerusalem. When Saul complains to Samuel, "God is departed from me, and answereth me no more, neither by prophets, nor by dreams" (28:15), we may hear "the voice of Israel in exile, looking across the divide that separates its life from the past and reflecting upon a centuries-old dalliance with kingship" (Polzin 1989: 220). Samuel's rejection of Saul contains in microcosm the ultimate rejection of Israel's impious kings. After that high drama, the conclusion to the episode seems incongruous. Saul falls to the ground and faints, not with horror at this numinous apparition and judgment, but because he is famished: "And there was no strength in him: for he had eaten no bread all the day, nor all the night" (28:20). The meal brought by the woman "ameliorates the despair and pathos of the episode" says Exum (1992: 24). The "woman had a fat calf in the house, . . . and killed it, and took flour, and kneaded it, and did bake unleavened bread" (28:24). A woman living alone does not kill a fatted calf for every uninvited guest. The woman feeds Saul as befits a king. In each of the three episodes in which Saul has lately appeared (1 Sam. 24; 26; 28), he has been shown mercy because he is a king. This reception of mercy and succor from the lowliest of his subjects pinpoints Saul's wretchedness.

It may seem that, instead of addressing the theodicial problems raised by the text, we have entered into a distant and convoluted theological debate. But perhaps Origen's christological reading of this episode is the only answer to those who, deeply sensing Saul's plight, have subverted the meaning of the story, making it the last act in the tragedy of Saul, cursed by a demonic God. We have as yet no way of knowing whether Saul was ultimately converted by the magnanimity of Christ.

Episode Two: Out of Line (1 Sam. 29)

It is peculiar that some commentators find it impossible to imagine God working through a witch, when, throughout 1 Samuel, God achieves providential designs by means of the enemies of his "beloved" David. The other four Philistine lords discover that David has been in Achish's employ, and they think it is Achish who is crazy! The lords prevail on Achish to discharge David, since the slayer of Goliath and doughty Yahwist would be a liability in the Philistines' proposed assault on Israelite territory. The danger of his turncoating in the heat of battle trumps any military benefit he might bring them. Overriding David's humble protestations of loyalty, Achish sends the good soldier and his followers back to Philistine territory.

The author goes to some length to show that David was not party to Saul's death and did not usurp the throne. He draws our attention to Saul's kingship not falling by the will or design of David. The author does not wish to present a head-on collision between Saul and David. Anything resembling a civil war deliberately promoted by David would have altered the theology of 1 Samuel. For God to replace Saul with David is one thing, but to use David to overthrow him is another. The author presents the relationship between Saul and David as tangential, not as one of direct conflict. It is as if the narrative wants to present David as moving past Saul without an adversarial head-to-head encounter—moving past and ahead of him, without touching him. Even at En-gedi and in Saul's encampment (1 Sam. 24; 26), there is no grappling, face to face: Saul is unconscious of David's thefts, and the incursions are followed by apparent reconciliations, of "father" to "son."

In the narrative, Saul's sinfulness is strictly related to God: it does not emerge from an adverse comparison with David; and the goodness of David is his stalwart Yahwism, not his preferability to Saul. The author does not want to say that Saul's antique, prestate kingship was an inferior development superseded by David's construction of the united monarchy. He specifically avoids creating that picture by not bringing the two into confrontation. Saul's kingship was one thing, and David's kingship is another, incommensurable with it. Saul brings the old world of the judges, settlement, and conquest to a close, and David inaugurates the new world of the monarchy. Saul has been a charismatic king. Our author does not mean to suggest that the passing of that antique world is a good thing and that the momentous emergence of the monarchy is a progressive step forward. This he would have done if he had pitted David in the ranks of the Philistines, in the battle in which Saul and his family lose their human hold on Israel's chieftainship.

Episode Three: The Cost of Freedom (1 Sam. 30)

In 27:6 Achish had given charge of the city of Ziklag to David. David had promptly gone behind his lord's back and raided the Geshurite, Gezrite, and the Amalekite villages round about, foreclosing the chance of his exploits being given away to the Philistine king by murdering all their inhabitants (27:8–9). The revenge that the Amalekites now take upon David is to raze Ziklag by "burn[ing] it with fire" and to enslave its women (30:1–2). David and his men return to find that "their wives, and their sons, and their daughters, were taken captives," including "David's two wives, . . . Ahinoam the Jezreelitess and Abigail the wife of Nabal" (30:3–5). The Amalekites have determined to despoil the Israelite of his marital successes. By punishing David through the wives and children of Ziklag, the Amalekites have cunningly stripped him of his local support. David is in danger, for it is his own raids that have brought this revenge on his people: "The people spoke of stoning him, because the soul of all the people was grieved" (30:6). David "encouraged himself in the LORD his God" and, through the oracle, asks whether to "pursue" the kidnappers (30:6–8). David has a specific question in view: if they give chase, do he and his men have a chance of catching up with the despoilers? He gets a specific answer: "Pursue: for thou shalt surely overtake them, and without fail recover all" (30:8). The pursuit is so rapid that "two hundred" of David's men collapse in exhaustion at Besor, unable to ford the stream (30:10). This enhances the realism of the piece of Davidic luck that follows: it makes sense within the story that both sides deposit stragglers in their wake (at least to those whose sense is informed by Westerns). David's men happen upon an Egyptian backslider, left behind by the Amalekite party when he fell too sick to keep up with his master; after three days in the wilderness, the man is famished. Grateful for the food and water given him by David's men, the Egyptian offers to lead them to the Amalekites, turning informer in return for safe conduct and his freedom.

The Amalekites had, the Egyptian tells David, attacked from the south, taking in the Cherethites, Philistines who hailed originally from Crete, the southern Judahite coastline, and Ziklag itself (30:14). Led down country by the Egyptian turncoat, David and his men meet the spectacle of a prone Amalekite raiding band, beside themselves with their ill-gotten gains (30:16). David attacks at evening, before the party can be slept off, and fights hard "from the twilight even unto the evening of the next day," killing every man jack of them, except "four hundred young men," who make a getaway on their long-legged camels (30:17). Having "rescued his two wives" and recovered all the spoil the Amalekites had seized, every wife and child, David "took" for himself "all the flocks and the herds," saying, "This is David's spoil" (30:18–20). David wins big: he not only makes good his losses from Ziklag, but inherits everything the Amalekites had taken from the Philistine and Judahite coastal villages.

Returning to Ziklag with their goods, the 401 victors ride back to the stream at Besor. Four hundred of them have no wish to share their booty with the two hundred who couldn't hack the pursuit: "Because they went not with us, we will not give them aught of the spoil that we have recovered, save to every man his wife and children" (30:22): the begrudging "men of Belial" have no intention of sharing the spoils of the counterattack with the men who didn't fight for it. David thinks differently, in terms of justice: "As his part is that goeth down to the battle," David rules, "so shall his part be" that covers their back and their provisions; "they shall [share] alike," for the victory and its spoils belong not to us but to God (30:24). David's generosity extends further: he sends his spoils to "the elders of Judah ... saying, 'Behold a present for you of the spoil of the enemies of the LORD,'" and gives gifts to the peoples of Bethel, the villages of south Ramoth and Jattir, the peoples of Aroer, those of Siphmoth, Eshtemoa, Rachal, and the Jerahmeelites, and the Israelites "in the cities of the Kenites," and the peoples of Hormah, Chor-ashan, Athach, and Hebron (30:26–31).

David is thanking those who helped him in his years in the southern Judahite hills: he sends his gifts to "all the places where David himself and his men were wont to haunt" (30:31). One gift requires another, and David is making good his gift debts. A big man must not only accumulate but also "distribute wealth: 'treasure' or cattle ..., food to support or feast the community" (Iliffe 2005: 111). David is generating a network of gift friendships with his generosity. He is also building up a stock of political loyalties: should Saul fall to the Philistines, these Judahite villages will rally behind their benefactor, and David will find himself king not only of Israel but of Judah too.

That David had such extensive spoils to distribute should raise eyebrows, for those he despoiled were Amalekites, Israel's hereditary enemy. The law of *herem* against the Amalekites (Exod. 17:8–16; Deut. 25:17–19) was discussed extensively in episode four scene four, for it was by violating it that Saul was stripped of his kingship (1 Sam. 15). By breaking the same Mosaic law, David has levered himself into position to win a throne. Both Saul and David took booty from the Amalekites instead of utterly eradicating all that was theirs, and that seems to raise questions about the justice of God's treatment of the pair: "Yahweh will eliminate Saul for taking Amalekite spoil (15:18–21), but will disregard David's like action" (30:19–20). It seems difficult to explain why, for David, any kind of success in battle seems acceptable and just in the Lord's eyes, whereas even "penitent Saul cannot be forgiven." For Brueggemann, since the "narrative evidences no curiosity" about the disparity of the treatment of this pair of kings, it must be telling us that Israel's God is amoral, like the mind behind the world of some Coen brothers movies. So far as Brueggemann can tell, the authors of the scriptures had figured out that the God with which they lived was just explicably weird and shrugged it off: "The lived experience of Israel has to come to terms with this inexplicable, inscrutable 'tilt' that does not act morally or reasonably or honorably or consistently, and that things work out oddly, even though Israel credits the oddity to Yahweh" (1997: 370–71).

Brueggemann effectively sets aside questions of historicity in his interpretation of the theology of the Old Testament. Without embracing historical minimalism and without abandoning the idea of source contexts like J, E, P, and D, he does little to connect more ancient and later oral and written sources to historical context and evidence. The impression is thus of a somewhat one-dimensional, time-free Old Testament. The scriptural texts are taken as they stand, in their final form, in the manner of literary exegetes. Any old-fashioned historical critic would see many layers of composition in this episode. In an interesting, early example of higher criticism, English political philosopher Thomas Hobbes notes that the books of Samuel must have been "written after" Samuel's own time since in 30:25, "after David had adjudged equall part of the spoiles, to them that guarded the Ammunition, with them that fought, the Writer saith, *He made it a Statute and an Ordinance to* Israel *to this day*."[20] After these classicist beginnings, historical critics later found, not uniformly late compositions, but writings into which editors had interwoven older sources. Scripture is thus seen as internally multidimensional, since the rough textures of older documents are espied within the language of the text itself.

The church has no dogmatic teaching as to when Regum was written or who its author was. But the tradition of the church regards these books as historical, and a reasonable heuristic measure to account for this is that their author drew on evidential sources: this episode would have made a good ballad in ancient times, as well as a good movie today. Once one starts to conceive of 1 Samuel as drawing on evidential witness with regard to historical facts, one may consequently draw from it some evidential conclusions about the God of which it speaks. Whereas for the antievidentialist, "Yahweh will be arbitrary in David's favor and need justify it to none" (Brueggemann 1997: 371), those who look to the historicity of these events find a historical elucidation of God's actions.

The historical *credibilia* to which one is required to subscribe for this elucidation to work do not require the faith of Søren Kierkegaard. It is reasonable to maintain that Saul is in the chronological and the cultural rearguard of David. The battles that he conducts at Jabesh-gilead (1 Sam. 11) and at Michmash Pass have the atmosphere of archaic holy war, fought under primitive constraints. They belong to the world of the judges. Though an anointed chieftain, Saul belongs to the charismatic heroes of a prestate society; though charismatically anointed by Samuel (1 Sam. 16), David belongs to the world of politics. Sociologists since Max Weber have found the changeover from a primitive to a relatively modern culture in many civilizations, and they have distinguished these two kinds of culture by reference to the degree of autonomy ascribed to human life or by the relatively greater sacrality of everyday life in the older culture and its relative secularity in the more modern society. The God of 1 Samuel puts Saul under "the strictest obedience" (von Balthasar 1983–91: 6.106): this is in keeping with the steeping of all human actions in divine rule and law in archaic cultures. For the God of the era of the settlement of Israel and Judah to require absolute obedience from his people was in keeping with the religious consciousness of a primitive society. In such societies, the realms of the sacred and the secular are not wholly separable, but intermingle: the Bible moralizes or personalizes this widespread perception of the religious quality of all nature, culture, and human action by linking it to obedience to God's word, through his prophet.

20. Thomas Hobbes, *Leviathan*, ed. C. B. MacPherson (London: Penguin, 1985 [orig. 1651]), 419, emphasis original.

Saul's subjection to the prophet Samuel is literal, as fits a primitive culture. This is the world that Saul represents, and, for Israel, he is its last representative. Saul "is precisely *not* launched on a wide-open field of political action" (von Balthasar 1983–91: 6.106), because politics as such has little part in an ancient, sacral universe. David represents Israel's initiation into the world of politics proper, in which human law and practice are given a scope and breathing space in which to obey the command of God in a human way. In the sacral culture, close to the world of magic, there is a literal, one-on-one correspondence between divine decree and human action; in the political culture, obedience to the law of God is still required, but that law takes human shapes and becomes analogous to the law of God, rather than its literal reflection. The Israel of the Pentateuch doesn't ponder this question, because Abraham and his descendants have no land: they are simply a people. From the period of the settlement, the issue goes live and is initially resolved in the way of a sacral culture: Yahweh selects individual leaders, charismatic heroes who literally carry out his commands. They conduct holy wars, if not holy war in the technical sense of the term. Saul becomes a king under these conditions. He is Israel's experiment in having a chief who must literally obey his prophet and promulgate the word of the Lord in a specific one-to-one way. David will be a postsacral king: under the new conditions, there are hundreds of ways in which the moral law of Israel could be put into political practice. In a political culture, the divine law can be interpreted in many different ways, by human imagination, and, because it passes through human imagination and institution, it appears as analogous, not identical, to the divine law. As the one who takes Israel into a new culture, "David is allowed the free obedience of one who is to shape the world, who is responsible to himself" (von Balthasar 1983–91: 6.106). As a new political order emerges, ethics and politics diverge, not in the sense that the leader can do as he pleases, but that politics is seen as the imaginative application of the ethical law, not as its literal enforcement.

As Hobbes notes, the establishment of a rule of law can be seen in this episode. The four hundred men who want to keep *their* well-fought loot for themselves are denizens of a prestate society, in which it is every man for himself, in the competition for prestige: "Africa's stateless societies often bore out Freud's dictum: 'A hero is a man who stands up manfully against his own father and in the end victoriously overcomes him.'" Although Marxists admire their collectivism, prestate, tribal cultures are also, and simultaneously, intensely egotistical. As we can see from their having to resolve the kidnapping of their wives and children for themselves, "lack of a state to impose law made vengeance a . . . common means of defending honor. Intense competition made stateless societies far from egalitarian and shaped their responses to innovation" (Iliffe 2005: 100–101). Secular, authentically political societies cannot emerge from collectivist individualism to personalism without faith in a transcendent God. Honor is a matter of individual achievement, coming back to what each individual can create of himself, whereas justice, that basic communal and political good, stands above individuals and unites them in a common pursuit. Justice transcends. David claims that the rewards of the day's fight are a communal treasure, belonging equally to those who fought and those who rested, because their success was not their own, but the Lord's. When his soldiers demand that the strong take for themselves alone the prestige of the victory and its spoils, "'Ye shall not do so, my brethren, with that which the LORD hath given us, who hath preserved us, and delivered the company that came against us into our hand. ... As his part is that goeth down to the battle, so shall his part be that tarrieth by the stuff: they shall part alike.' And it was so from that day forward, that he made it a statute and an ordinance for Israel unto this day" (30:23–25). David is taking Israel into the culture of a rule of law. God's forbearance toward his elected's way of going about it is his enablement of the existence of a political world. Though David is bound to the moral law, "nowhere is there exacted from him the strict obedience prophetically enjoined upon Saul" (von Balthasar 1983–91: 6.106): henceforth kings will have to figure for themselves the multiple ways in which to make their kingdoms conform to the transcendent justice of God.

The biblical text shows no curiosity about the departure of the old sacral world that Saul symbolizes because, for the author and his audience, the disappearance of this world is simply a fact, a given. The world that Saul represents with his charismatic kingship is irrecoverable, and with their realistic historical sense, they know it. This is one of the theological lessons of 1 Samuel for modern Christians. Christians are as prone as any who lack historical scriptures to unhistorical nostalgia in their political aspirations. The political kingship of Christ on earth can never be a sacral kingship. However tragic it is, and the author does see it as tragic, the sacral kingship of Saul is dead and buried, in 1 Sam. 31. It is David's kingship, in which ruler and ruled act with responsible human freedom, that is given to us to emulate.

Episode Four: Tragedy (1 Sam. 31)

First Sam. 31 records that Saul died by his own hand in a battle against the Philistines on Mount Gilboa, around 1010 BC. This time, we hear nothing of the heavy chariots of the Philistines, useless in hill country. Instead, like the English at Agincourt, the Philistines outmatch the Israelites with a legion of archers: "The battle went sore against Saul, and the archers hit him, and he was sore wounded of the archers" (31:3). Saul, a Benjamite, recognizes defeat in the deadly hail of arrows on his body.

There are those who contend that, even if this battle contains historical ironies, still, Saul's death, as recounted in scripture, is no tragedy. Saul's story occurs between Judges and the later three books of Regum; although his monarchy gets more attention than that of some other kings, the author does not make the life of Saul a story in itself. If the spotlight is anywhere, some would say, it is not on Saul but on his successor, David. We know that Regum was dispersed into four volumes only by later editors, who had to consider scroll length (Toorn 2007: 21–22). So we might think that this episode, and Saul's story as a whole, is no tragedy, but simply there in order to lead up to David. As Harold Fisch puts it, Saul "can only fully realize" the "role" of a tragic protagonist "if his story is isolated from its context, which . . . emphasizes the history of the royal house to be founded by . . . the young David. Saul's replacement by David rather than his tragic death in battle is what ultimately counts and it is on that that our attention . . . focuses. . . . Biblical stories of the 'fall' of a hero lack the closure that tragedy seems to require; instead of fable rounded in on itself, we have the undetermined movement of historical time, a witnessing to purposes still to be disclosed and by no means confined to the fate of the hero."[21]

In fact, though, the classical tragedies written in Greece in the sixth century BC were trilogies, in which the third play presented a resolution of the disastrous denouement of the first play. The Oedipus who leaves the stage self-blinded in *Oedipus Rex* gains a healing shelter for his old age in *Oedipus at Colonus*. Even Shakespearian tragedy doesn't close on the tragic death of the hero: *Hamlet* concludes with Fortinbras's army entering Denmark, and the French king is about to retake England as the curtain comes down in *King Lear*. In this way, tragedy pays its tribute to the historical character of human life, which goes on, through the generations, leaving individual tragedies, and comedies, in its wake. Tragedy would lose something of its realism if it did not indicate that the curtain never comes down absolutely in human history. Though every individual person experiences the drama of his or her own life as unique, the tragedian cannot permit a protagonist to live and die in the spotlight of his or her own drama, because the reality of it is that the impersonal forces of others surround and contain us. When it shows the drama flowing on, past the hero and down the generations, tragedy is opening its fictional spectacle to reality and letting the fictional and the real mingle, so that we know that the dramatic fiction is an analogy through which we can see truth. The world the tragedian creates is analogous to reality. Tragedy pays tribute to real life to help us acknowledge that its poetry is not mere fantasy, but poetic truth.

Our author is proceeding in the inverse direction: he is paying tribute to tragedy within history. His task as a historian is not only to make us believe in the empirical truth of his record, but also to give shape to history. He has to do the one in order to do the other. Human beings give shape to their own lives by making sense of them, because events don't just impact on us, but rather we live them. They occur in our consciousness, as interpreted events, as well as externally, as facts. What really happened is not just what happened, but what we believe happened, how we interpret it. A shapeless, one-fact-after-another history gains in science what it loses in humanity, because its way of describing events doesn't

---

21. Harold Fisch, *Poetry with a Purpose: Biblical Poetics and Interpretation* (Bloomington: Indiana University Press, 1990), 42.

connect to the way in which men and women consciously experience events. Hence, our historian-author, like all historians, *heightens* the element of form in his telling of the historical facts. Whereas the poet-tragedian (or comedian) *lessens* the element of form, in order not to give his play full closure, and thus lets it breathe the air of reality, the historian tightens every ethical and esthetic tension he can find in the historical facts, to give his story shape and make it like a play, with a beginning and an end. That is partly how we experience life, from within, although, seen from without, human lives have no absolute beginnings or endings, but always carry on from what went before and are supplemented by what comes after. When he heightens its esthetic and ethical elements, the historian is bringing out the human and thus the personal element. To give form to history is to give it personality.

And yet both Christian doctrine and human experience teach that human personality has been broken and misshapen since the fall of humankind. Ever since the fall, the human form has lost its immortal form and its inner freedom has become corrupted. We can see that just as much from the character of David as of Saul in 1 Sam. 29–31. With his deep appreciation of human wickedness, the author of Regum cannot portray the beheading and death of the old quasimonastic prepolitical culture and the lurch forward into the human freedoms of the monarchy as a straightforward progress. That is why he presents both promonarchic and antimonarchic evidence in his portrayal of Saul and why the depiction of David the Beloved contains light and dark. David will be permitted "the very free obedience of one who is to shape the world, who is responsible to himself." But this very "release . . . into the sphere of freedom proper to the 'image and likeness' of God is an event so ominous and full of dangers that scripture can portray it only in a dialectical and tragic fashion: the story of the rejection of the sacral kingdom of God of the early period," that is, the story of the rejection of Saul, which concludes here, "and its replacement with the kingdom of men in the classical period is accompanied by a great number of reasons for and against this development, and of estimates of losses and gains, and the final redactor of the text has been careful not to smooth over such circumspection" (von Balthasar 1983–91: 6.106–7). Saul's story is dramatic, not only because it is formed, but still more because it contains the texture of this tragic dialectic of human fallenness.

Real life is dramatic; real lives are like dramas. In writing a history, our author is not setting forth a drama (though the scripture as a whole may do this), but describing many little dramas, the lives of men and women. He interweaves disparate dramas, the lives of Eli, Samuel, Saul, and David. These individual dramas go to make up the personality of the historical narrative that includes them all. Within this overarching design, the little drama of Saul is a tragedy, and perhaps uniquely so in the Old Testament: Northrop Frye has a right to claim that "Saul is the one great tragic hero of the Bible."[22] This has been recognized increasingly

22. Northrop Frye, *The Great Code* (London: Routledge Kegan Paul, 1981), 181.

since the seventeenth century, when the humanism of the books of Samuel was first appreciated and as their historical character gained the attention of exegetes. Unless we think tradition ended just before the Quattrocento or that Christians have ceased to learn about the scriptures in the last five hundred years, we will see gains as well as losses in these developments. With the growing recognition of the humanity of the figures who people the books of Regum came an acknowledgment of their moral complexity. For anyone who considers that there is more than a black-and-white moralism in the characterization of Saul in 1 Samuel, it seems esthetically right to see the historical drama of his life as a tragedy. But what kind of tragic figure is Saul? Why is Saul a tragic figure? What makes him so? Here the exegetes are divided.

One proposal is that Saul is the victim of the Lord's "dark side." For Exum the deity plays an "ambivalent role" in 1 Samuel (1992: 17). Likewise for Gunn, part of the purpose of the story is to show that God can be "unpredictably terrible, jealous of his status, quick to anger and impatient of the complexities of human action and motivation" (1980: 131). This interpretation of the story has some value insofar as it is intended to distance us from the influence of unimaginative homiletics. A common reaction to the story is to ignore it, because we take a pious reading to be both required and intolerable. Putting questions to it is a better way to go. The motivation of the literary readers is to release the grip of simplistic moralism on our reading of scripture and let us experience the story without feeling that judgmentalism is a prerequisite of piety. On this literary interpretation, our author reproduced in the Saul story what Exum calls "the Aeschylean paradox of human guilt and the wicked God." Exum puts it much more strongly than an earnest Christian reader might like, but many readers do have questions about the treatment of Saul. As she sees it, Saul really is guilty, in that he has been embroiled in the peoples' sin of demanding a human king from God, who willed to be Israel's only king. "Saul is" thus, Exum claims, "a *pharmakos*, a scapegoat for the people's sin of requesting a human king" (1992: 17, 38). There is a truth in this, in that Saul is literally broken under the strain of divine commands to which he cannot rise.

One could even conjecture that Augustine, who sees in the Old Testament history the prefiguration of the coming kingdom of Christ, would not wholly demure from such a hypothesis as Exum proposes, for Augustine believes that the loss of the earthly kingdom to Israel prefigures the loss of the kingdom to the Jews and its transference to the church. The breaking of Saul could be seen by modern Christians who believe that Christianity supersedes Judaism symbolically to represent the breaking of the covenant and the rejection of Israel, for the "account of the death of Saul and his sons is also about the death of Israel and its kings." Like 1 Sam. 3, it indicates that the glory is to be taken from Israel. Hebrew *kabod* (sometimes translated "glory") literally means "heavy," and in 31:3, when "the battle weighed heavy" on Saul, the verb is *wattikbad*. Demanding a king, as the author knew from the outset, was "an act of political and communal suicide"

(Polzin 1989: 219, 47, 223). On this analysis, Saul's death symbolizes the death of Israel, rather as Augustine teaches in the *City of God*. Augustine of course draws the line at the preamble of the esthetic readings, that 1 Samuel gives us "glimpses of God in other forms" than merely "all good" (Gunn 1980: 131).

Readings such as Exum's and Gunn's are a worthwhile reminder of a skeleton in the Christian cupboard that modern nonsupersessionist Christians prefer to forget: the only major interpretation of the Saul story in Western Christian tradition, that of Augustine, makes Saul the representative of the rejection of Israel from God's grace. As supersessionism fell from favor, conservative-minded Christians still wanted Saul to be the bad guy, and the only way open to them to do so was to make him a bad person who deserved to fall from God's graces. They wanted Saul to get his just deserts, but with no hint of divine providence pursuing him to breaking point. Rightly following Augustine in maintaining that God is all good, they ceased wholeheartedly to follow Augustine in his blanket supersessionism or in his division of the human race into the saved and the damned. So they had to avert their eyes from features of the biblical story that had ceased to be explicable without the dividing hand of divine providence. But those features are there. When attention returned to those features of the story from which they recoiled, such as the "evil spirit" sent by the Lord upon Saul, divine providence returned, bearing the secular name of Fate. The esthetic readings of the Saul story are like a contemporary secular version of the narrative of the two cities in Augustine's masterpiece.

For Christians, that will be a reason to reject Exum's and Gunn's rationales for Saul's story being a tragedy. As Christians will see it, by secularizing Augustine's narrative of the two cities, modern esthetes have turned it into a melodrama, not a tragedy. Tragedy requires a transcendent God or gods because it is anchored in the assumption that human life is of absolute value. Lucy Beckett takes to task those who leave this premise out of their definitions of tragedy. In his book *Tragedy*, Adrian Poole makes an observation that "may be taken as representative of the late twentieth century's intellectual confusion: 'Tragedy embodies our most paradoxical feelings and thoughts and beliefs. It gives them flesh and blood, emotional and intellectual and spiritual substance. Through tragedy we recognize and refeel our sense of both the value and the futility of human life, of both its purposes and its emptiness.' Well, which?" Beckett asks. "That having it both ways is rationally impossible does not seem to strike such writers. Either everything means something or nothing means anything. But the first requires belief in God, while the second is perhaps too frightening to be faced by those . . . without Nietzsche's desperate courage."[23] If human life is not of absolute value, the breaking of individual human beings, like Saul, is not tragic. If there is no transcendent God or gods, such gods as we conceive of are natural or material forces. Because of the

23. Lucy Beckett, *In the Light of Christ: Writings in the Western Tradition* (San Francisco: Ignatius, 2006), 32.

inalienable moralism of human beings, we project the internal compass of the human conscience into the cosmos, and because of our ineliminable rationalism, we wish to explain evil. Therefore, a natural schema has proposed itself to many religions and cultures, in which good, natural forces compete for control of the cosmos with evil natural forces. To conceive the cosmos in this way is to see it as a perpetual melodrama. The melodramatic imagination is irrational, because it makes too much sense: there is no reason why the cosmos should contain good or evil if there is no transcendent God. And the melodramatic imagination is amoral, because it projects the motivation of our evil deeds into the dark side of the gods. Accurately perceiving that "at the core of tragedy lies the problem and mystery of evil" (Exum 1992: 10), Exum lacks the "desperate courage" to assign the mystery of evil to creaturely freedom and hence effectively trivializes Saul's tragedy by making it melodrama in which all the pieces neatly fit.

If we wish to avoid melodramatizing the story of Saul, we must permit Saul the freedom to take some moral responsibility for his predicament in 1 Sam. 31. Saul commits suicide: "Saul took a sword, and fell upon it. . . . So Saul died" (31:4, 6). Saul's illusions have been stripped from him, since the deathly encounter with Samuel at Endor, and the assertion that Saul "assumes some control over his fate by knowingly confronting it"[24] has some merit. It is true that Saul knowingly meets death, and, although suicide seems to be a relinquishment of self-possession, the suicide forestalls defeat by pulling out of the game, not abandoning control, but at least preventing the enemy from experiencing victory over him. By defeating himself, the suicide refuses to admit defeat to another, his enemy. Exum likens Saul's denouement to that of *Oedipus Rex*: "Saul's suicide," she writes, "functions as his last desperate attempt to wrest from his destiny its final meaning. . . . It can be compared to Oedipus' self-blinding" (1992: 24). Taking responsibility for the guilt in which fate has implicated him, Oedipus blinds himself in self-punishment. Saul commits suicide in order to control the status of his death, seeing self-slaughter as more honorable than the indignity of dismemberment by the Philistines: "Then said Saul unto his armour-bearer, 'Draw thy sword, and thrust me through therewith, lest these uncircumcised come and thrust me through, and abuse me'" (31:4). Good seems closer to the mark than Exum when he notes that "death at his own hand in battle reveals for the last time" Saul's "concern for his 'image.' His lack of confidence in himself and in Yahweh to make him king has led to the tragic illusion that he has lost his stature among the people. He bids the armor-bearer kill him . . . 'lest these uncircumcised ones come and make sport of me.' . . . To avoid the mockery of being captured—like Agag—he falls on his own sword, his act of suicide a final failure of nerve" (1965: 78). To be diffident is not the same as to be humble. It is the diffidence in us, not the humility, which fears and takes flight from mockery. This timidity in the face of mockery comes from

24. W. Lee Humphreys, "The Tragedy of King Saul: A Study of the Structure of 1 Samuel 9–31," *Journal for the Study of the Old Testament* 6 (1978): 24.

lack of trust in oneself. Once he has been launched into the kingship by God's providence, the only way in which Saul could have been able to trust himself, and be free, in confident possession of his actions would have been by humbly uniting his freedom to the divine freedom. Just as he gave away that freedom and just as he lost his self-identity, so now he loses his life, all at his own hand, because everything had to be at his own hand. Polzin comments on this tragic death: "Saul one last impatient time refuses to let the Lord's providence run its course and takes matters into his hands by ending his life" (1989: 224).

If we locate the why of Saul's tragedy in his arrogant determination to control his own destiny and in his thereby losing control of everything, we could ascribe his fault to hubris. Hubris is the taint of many of Herodotus's villains, such as Darius and his son Xerxes, the Persian kings who sought to conquer Greece. Aeschylus likewise convicts Xerxes of hubris in *The Persians*. Hubris is inflated human pride tempting a man or woman to go too far, rising above what is given to humans to achieve, and to trespass on the privileges of the immortal gods. In Herodotus's *History*, as in Greek tragedy, hubris is swiftly followed by nemesis, the divine punishment of human self-exaltation. Good makes a case for a hubristic Saul like this: "There is a kind of nemesis hovering above Saul, the certainty that David will succeed and Saul will not. There is what can be called *hybris* in Saul's decisive choice for what will raise him in the people's estimation rather than for what he has been divinely commanded in the Amalek incident. It might be argued that that is not *hybris*, a 'reaching out beyond himself,' an extension of greatness too far, since Saul chose the lesser authority rather than the greater. Yet it is a choice of a *different* authority from that under which Saul stands. It is a decision against the divine, and such a decision always implicitly elevates the decider above the divine" (1965: 79, emphasis original).

"And it came to pass on the morrow when the Philistines came to strip the slain, that they found Saul and his three sons fallen in mount Gilboa. And they cut off his head, and stripped off his armour, and sent into the land of the Philistines round about to publish it in the house of their idols, and among the people. And they put his armour in the house of Ashtaroth: and they fastened his body to the wall of Beth-shan" (31:8–10). This is violent desecration indeed, for an Israelite. It seems wholly to undo Saul's purpose, in slaying himself. His corpse is publicly mocked. As sharers in the same archaic conceptions of death as the Israelites, the Philistines surely despoil Saul's corpse knowing and believing that the "lot of the departed depends on what happens to his body." Within Israel, "even the enemy, even the condemned by common law are entitled to burial (Deut. xxi.22; II Kings ix.34; II Sam. xxi.14). Not to be buried is a terrible penalty. The lot of such as have made a violent death . . . is especially hard. Their condition in Sheol is worse than that of those who have died a natural death; moreover, they are unable to rest as long as they go unavenged or, failing that, as long as their blood has not been covered with earth so that it may cease from calling for help" (Martin-Achard 1960: 29, citing Gen. 37:26; Lev. 27:13; Ezek. 24:17 and Gen.

4:10; Ezek. 24:7; Isa. 26:21; Job 16:18; 1 Enoch 47:1). But something happens to mitigate the abomination.

It is ironic, because it is what Saul least expected. The final irony to befall Saul is that, while he signally failed "to wrest from his destiny its final meaning" (Exum 1992: 24), because its meaning had to be accepted, not wrested, he ultimately is given the stature and respect that he wanted, by others. The image that he had untrustingly sought to control is bestowed on him by others: there is a tragic irony in his commanding respect, unknown to the diffident Saul (Good 1965: 78). Saul's moment of glory in 1 Samuel was his raising the defense of Jabesh-gilead in 1 Sam. 11. They have not forgotten his rescue of them from the Ammonites. In a deed of great courage, they carry out a night rescue of the remains of Saul and his sons from the walls of the Philistine enclave of Beth-shan: "When the inhabitants of Jabesh-gilead heard of that which the Philistines had done to Saul: all the valiant men arose, and went all night, and took the body of Saul and the bodies of his sons from the wall of Beth-shan, and came to Jabesh, and burnt them there" (31:11–12). Saul and his sons Jonathan, Abinadab, and Malchishua are given a hero's burial: "And they took their bones, and buried them under a tree at Jabesh, and fasted seven days" (31:13). The Saulides sleep with their ancestors in their place of greatest heroism. Saul the charismatic king is given the last word.

The wake that the men of Jabesh-gilead give to Saul makes his story conclude, not in his failure, but in the living memory and the memorial of his success, when, inspired by the Spirit of the Lord, a courageous soldier and open to the implication of the divinely ordained anointing, Saul could say "the LORD hath wrought salvation in Israel" (11:13). Often enough undignified in his life, Saul is dignified in death by the remembrance of his moment of glory. As he goes to "sleep with the fathers," Saul is one of the fathers of Israel, still a member of the body of his people, not cast out beyond the pale of grace. Justice, which recalls his courage against Nahash the Ammonite, requires that Saul is remembered mercifully. And so, closure with its condemnation and judgment is not absolute within history. History, which flows on, bears in its tide the memory of Saul's gift to Jabesh-gilead.

In the next chapter (2 Sam. 1), an Amalekite brings David the news of Saul's death and claims to have discovered him bleeding to death on the battlefield and, at Saul's request, to have shortened his death throes with a spear thrust. David has the murderer of the "king's anointed" put to death. The harpist, soon to be king, gives Saul and Jonathan a memorial that lives in colloquial speech:

> Your glory, O Israel, lies slain on your heights.
> How the mighty have fallen!
>
> Tell it not in Gath,
>   proclaim it not in the streets of Ashkelon,
> lest the daughters of the Philistines be glad,
>   lest the daughters of the uncircumcised rejoice.

O mountains of Gilboa,
  may you have neither dew nor rain,
  nor fields that yield offerings of grain.
For there the shield of the mighty was defiled,
  the shield of Saul—no longer rubbed with oil.
From the blood of the slain,
  from the flesh of the mighty,
the bow of Jonathan did not turn back,
  the sword of Saul did not return unsatisfied.

Saul and Jonathan—
  in life they were loved and gracious,
  and in death they were not parted.
They were swifter than eagles,
  they were stronger than lions.

O daughters of Israel,
  weep for Saul,
who clothed you in scarlet and finery,
  who adorned your garments with ornaments of gold.

How the mighty have fallen in battle!
  Jonathan lies slain on your heights.
I grieve for you, Jonathan my brother;
  you were very dear to me.
Your love for me was wonderful,
  more wonderful than that of women.

How the mighty have fallen!
  The weapons of war have perished! (2 Sam. 1:19–27 NIV)

David calls Jonathan his "brother." He had envisaged his relation to Saul as that of son to father. One could add Saul and David to what Ratzinger calls "Barth's great antithetical pairs of salvation history": Cain and Abel, Ishmael and Isaac, Esau and Jacob. They have not struggled, but changed places, so that David is the father to Saul, the preserver of his memory. Like the men of Jabesh-gilead, David has always respected Saul's person, and it has been in the compass of David's compassion that Saul has become a sympathetic figure in his last days. Rather than rejecting or superseding him, David has embraced Saul and drawn him into his own ambiance of grace. As Ratzinger says, "The history of these pairs of brothers has only a provisional ending in the rejection of one and the election of the other. Jesus's parable of the prodigal son, which might . . . be better called his parable of the two brothers, and the doctrine of the two peoples that Paul develops in Romans 9–11 bring about the great reversal: rejection now in the last analysis leads . . . to election—the rejected man is now chosen in his very rejection." The rejected man is chosen in "his very rejection" because the chosen one had been elected for his sake, and not only for his own. David is chosen on behalf, not only of the future, but in order creatively to carry forward the memory of the past in his person and to transform it. Saul is redeemed within this memorial, in which David gathers Saul's memory into his own. Saul is not superseded as the line of providential history marches on. He is not set aside as one of the predestined failures. He was not chosen by God only to represent rejection, but also to be vicariously included in David's election. David is himself chosen in order that his line be gathered up into that of those elected in Christ. David is chosen for Saul and for the people he represents, and "the mystery of this vicariousness, given in Christ and forming the basis of all election, is carried out from Christ according to the will of God in a whole system of vicarious relationships throughout salvation history as its fundamental law. Just as Christ, the chosen one, became in a sacred exchange the one rejected for us in order to confer on us his election, this exchange relationship recurs constantly in salvation history following him. Again and again he who is chosen . . . must be ready to be vicariously rejected, so that through him another can be chosen also. One stands in the place of the other, and it is an expression of God's faith in us that he draws us into this system of vicarious election."[25] David does not supersede Saul, nor Christianity Judaism. David is elected in the service of Saul.

25. Joseph Ratzinger, *The Meaning of Christian Brotherhood*, 2nd ed. (San Francisco: Ignatius, 1993), 77–79.

BIBLIOGRAPHY

Frequently cited works are listed here. Other works are documented in the footnotes.

Alter, Robert. 1981. *The Art of Biblical Narrative*. London: George Allen & Unwin.

Augustine. 1972. *Concerning the City of God against the Pagans*. Edited by David Knowles. Translated by Henry Bettenson. London: Penguin.

————. 2001. *Expositions of the Psalms*, vol. 3: *Psalms 51–72*. Translated by Maria Boulding. Works of Saint Augustine: A Translation for the 21st Century. Rotelle, New York: New City Press.

Balthasar, Hans Urs von. 1983–91. *The Glory of the Lord: A Theological Aesthetics*. 7 vols. Translated by Erasmo Leiva-Merikakis et al. Edited by Joseph Fessio and John Riches. San Francisco: Ignatius/New York: Crossroad.

Boling, Robert G. 1975. *Judges: Introduction, Translation, and Commentary*. Anchor Bible 6A. New York: Doubleday.

Brueggemann, Walter. 1997. *Theology of the Old Testament: Testimony, Dispute, Advocacy*. Minneapolis: Fortress.

Calvin, John. 1845–46. *Commentary on the Book of Psalms*. 2 vols. Translated by James Anderson. Edinburgh: Calvin Translation Society.

Campbell, Antony F., and Mark A. O'Brien. 2000. *Unfolding the Deuteronomistic History: Origins, Upgrades, Present Text*. Minneapolis: Fortress.

Chrysostom, John. 2003. *Old Testament Homilies*, vol. 1: *Homilies on Hannah, David, and Saul*. Translated by Robert Charles Hill. Brookline, MA: Holy Cross Orthodox Press.

Dever, William G. 2002. *What Did the Biblical Writers Know and When Did They Know It? What Archaeology Can Tell Us about the Reality of Ancient Israel*. Grand Rapids: Eerdmans.

Eichrodt, Walther. 1961–67. *Theology of the Old Testament*. 2 vols. Translated by J. A. Baker. London: SCM.

Eslinger, Lyle. 1983. "Viewpoints and Point of View in 1 Samuel 8–12." *Journal for the Study of the Old Testament* 26:61–76.

Exum, J. Cheryl. 1992. *Tragedy and Biblical Narrative: Arrows of the Almighty*. Cambridge: Cambridge University Press.

Flanagan, James W. 1988. *David's Social Drama: A Hologram of Israel's Early Iron Age*. Sheffield: Almond.

Franke, John R., ed. 2005. *Joshua, Judges, Ruth, 1–2 Samuel*. Ancient Christian Commentary on Scripture: Old Testament 4. Downers Grove, IL: InterVarsity.

Good, E. M. 1965. *Irony in the Old Testament*, London: SPCK.

Gosselin, Edward A. 1976. *The King's Progress to Jerusalem: Some Interpretations of David during the Reformation Period and Their Patristic and Medieval Background*. Malibu CA: Undena.

Grégoire le Grand. See Pierre de Cava.

Gunn, David M. 1980. *The Fate of King Saul: An Interpretation of a Biblical Story*. Sheffield: JSOT Press.

Hackett, Jo Ann. 1998. "There Was No King in Israel." Pp. 177–218 in *The Oxford History of the Biblical World*. Edited by Michael D. Coogan. Oxford: Oxford University Press.

Halpern, Baruch. 1981. *The Constitution of the Monarchy in Israel*. Chico, CA: Scholars Press.

———. 1996. *The First Historians: The Hebrew Bible and History*. University Park, PA: Pennsylvania State University Press.

Heller, Joseph. 1985. *God Knows*. London: Black Swan.

Iliffe, John. 2005. *Honour in African History*. Cambridge: Cambridge University Press.

Ishida, Tomoo. 1977. *The Royal Dynasties in Ancient Israel: A Study on the Formation and Development of Royal-Dynastic Ideology*. Berlin: de Gruyter.

Lemche, Niels Peter. 1978. "David's Rise." *Journal for the Study of the Old Testament* 10:2–25.

Levenson, Jon D. 1978. "1 Samuel 25 as Literature and as History." *Catholic Biblical Quarterly* 40:11–28.

Long, V. Philips. 1989. *The Reign and Rejection of King Saul: A Case for Literary and Theological Coherence*. Society of Biblical Literature Dissertation 118. Atlanta: Scholars Press.

Lubac, Henri de. 2007. *History and Spirit: The Understanding of Scripture according to Origen*. Translated by Anne Englund Nash and Juvenal Merriell. San Francisco: Ignatius.

Martin-Achard, Robert. 1960. *From Death to Life: A Study of the Development of the Doctrine of the Resurrection in the Old Testament*. Translated by John Penney Smith. Edinburgh: Oliver & Boyd.

McNutt, Paula M. 1990. *The Forging of Israel: Iron Technology, Symbolism, and Tradition in Ancient Society*. Sheffield: Almond.

Mendenhall, George E. 1973. *The Tenth Generation: The Origins of the Biblical Tradition*. Baltimore: Johns Hopkins University Press.

Origen. 1986. *Homélies sur Samuel*. Sources chrétiennes 328. Translated and edited by Pierre Nautin and Marie-Thérèse Nautin. Paris: Cerf.

Pierre de Cava. 2004. *Commentaire sur le premier livre des Rois*, vol. 6. Sources chrétiennes 482. Edited by Adalbert de Vogüé. Paris: Cerf.

Polzin, Robert. 1989. *Samuel and the Deuteronomist: A Literary Study of the Deuteronomic History*, part 2: *1 Samuel*. San Francisco: Harper & Row.

Rad, Gerhard von. 1962. *Old Testament Theology*, vol. 1: *The Theology of Israel's Historical Traditions*. Translated by D. M. G. Stalker. London: SCM.

———. 1972. *Wisdom in Israel*. Translated by James D. Martin. London: SCM.

Sahlins, Marshall D. 1968. *Tribesmen*. Englewood Cliffs, NJ: Prentice-Hall.

Stager, Lawrence. 1998. "Forging an Identity: The Emergence of Ancient Israel." Pp. 123–75 in *The Oxford History of the Biblical World*. Edited by Michael D. Coogan. Oxford: Oxford University Press.

Toorn, Karel van der. 2007. *Scribal Culture and the Making of the Hebrew Bible*. Cambridge, MA: Harvard University Press.

Van Seters, John. 1983. *In Search of History: Historiography in the Ancient World and the Origins of Biblical History*. New Haven: Yale University Press.

———. 2006. *The Edited Bible: The Curious History of the "Editor" in Biblical Criticism*. Winona Lake, IN: Eisenbrauns.

Wevers, John William. 1971. *The First Book of Samuel*. Pp. 155–69 in *The Interpreter's One-Volume Commentary on the Bible*. Edited by Charles Laymon. London: Collins.

SUBJECT INDEX

SCRIPTURE INDEX

1 Sam 8-12 erased Nov 29/16 H
Dogearing noted